POVERTY AND THE
INDUSTRIAL REVOLUTION

By the same author

ABDICATION

Poverty and the Industrial Revolution

by

BRIAN INGLIS

It was denounced from divine authority to the inhabitants of Canaan 'that the poor should never cease from among them'; and the history of every country with which we are acquainted abundantly proves that the denunciation never has been, or will be, confined to a single nation. It is in fact a declaration of one of those difficulties which it is the lot of humanity constantly to contest, and which, as they never can be overcome without perfect virtue, seem to be destined to furnish unceasing motives to the exercise and improvement both of our intellectual energies and our moral feelings.

Thomas Malthus: *A letter to Samuel Whitbread 1807*

HODDER AND STOUGHTON

Copyright © 1971 by Brian Inglis
First printed 1971
ISBN 0 340 12884 4
All rights reserved. No part of this publication may be
reproduced or transmitted in any form or by any means,
electronic or mechanical, including photocopy, recording,
or any information storage and retrieval system, without
permission in writing from the publisher.
Printed in Great Britain for Hodder and Stoughton Limited,
St. Paul's House, Warwick Lane, London, E.C.4 by
The Camelot Press Ltd., London and Southampton

Contents

Illustrations

Key to Acknowledgments

[1] Radio Times Hulton Picture Library   [2] The Mansell Collection   [3] Goldsmiths Library

Introduction

'BY THE SWEAT of thy brow shalt thou eat bread' . . . 'the poor shall never cease out of the land' . . . 'the poor are always with us'—for centuries, the pessimism of the Testaments was taken to embody a fact of human existence. Jesus, admittedly, when he remarked that the poor are always with us, was not trying to lay down the law, natural or divine; he was merely seeking to excuse the action of the woman who had poured expensive oil over him, instead of selling it, as Judas would have preferred, so that the proceeds could have been given to the poor. Nevertheless, the words came to be taken as a confirmation of the earlier warnings from Genesis and Deuteronomy. And as long as production remained based on manual labour, there could be no reason to doubt they had been justified.

But then, towards the end of the eighteenth century, England became the scene of two economic revolutions. They were not sudden; both represented the culmination of processes which had been continuing for years; but together they were to transform the prospect for the country, and for mankind. In agriculture, the revolution took the form of extensive enclosure of land that had formerly been farmed communally by local villagers. Converted into farms and properly fenced, drained and manured, it was potentially far more productive than common land, because up-to-date methods of crop rotation could be introduced and more efficient use made of farm machinery, to provide larger yields per acre. But the changes in agriculture were modest compared to the upheaval in industry in the same period, as a result of the inventions that began to transform the industrial scene: machines which enabled one man to do the work of many, soon to be harnessed to water power, and then to steam—holding out the prospect of the day in the not too distant future when one man, tending a machine, could produce a hundred times more than he could produce by the sweat of his brow. Inevitably, speculation began over what this could mean for mankind. Might not the wealth which was being released be used to reduce poverty—perhaps even to allow the poor to cease out of the land?

Today, two centuries later, we are still wryly speculating. Even in the most advanced and richest communities, poverty remains a problem—*the* problem—as if to ratify both the biblical warnings and Malthus's belief, that it is one of those difficulties which only perfect virtue can overcome; in other words, that never can be overcome on earth. But is this so? Or is it simply that, trapped in past assumptions about the nature of man and of society, we have been going the wrong way about overcoming it?

As this book was originally conceived, the intention was to try to answer that question by examining Britain's efforts to find a solution through the Welfare State. But the Welfare State, I was compelled to realise, was itself the product of theories, attitudes and contradictions which had developed a century before. What happened then created a kind of mould, in which not only Britain but all the countries of the Western world are still encased: struggling to extricate themselves, yet worried that in the process they may destroy our society, or its values—the fate that has befallen countries which have adopted communism, or fascism.

Why did our society choose the economic and social paths it was to follow during the period of the agricultural and industrial revolutions? There were alternative courses open to it—particularly in connection with the poor. Poverty, and how it could best be dealt with, was the constant preoccupation of governments, economists, journalists, poets. My aim has been to present their attitudes, their theories and their projects, to try to show how society came to take the form it did, in England.

In 'England'—rather than in 'Britain'. This is not because the English were solely responsible for what happened. A case, after all, could be made out for attributing the main responsibility to the Scots; they were certainly the pervasive intellectual force. But there is a difficulty: the Scots had a different social and legal system; they had no poor law. Nor did the Irish—who were equally influential, though in a different way, through their immigrants. To avoid having to make constant side-references and qualifications, I have treated of the Scots and the Irish only where they affected (which they did constantly) what was happening in England—England and Wales, to be exact: the two were not as a rule separated for administrative purposes, or in discussion, and for convenience I have not attempted to separate them.

There is one other complication: the value of money. There was a time when economic historians hoped that with the help of a cost-of-living index constructed from the information available, it might be possible to provide a simple way of comparing subsistence wages at any given period with the equivalent today. For a variety of reasons, this expectation has not been fulfilled. All that is possible to do is provide some general guidance.

The cost of commodities naturally varied from time to time, and from place to place—particularly the staple, bread; it could rise and fall spectacularly according to the vagaries of harvests. But these prices will serve as a rough guide for the period 1780–1835:

bread	1d.–4d. per lb.
butter	9d.–1s. per lb.
sugar	6d. per lb.
meat	5d.–8d. per lb.
beer	1d. per pint
tea	10s.–20s. per lb.
oatmeal	2d. per lb.
potatoes	$\frac{1}{2}$d. per lb.
soap	6d. per lb.

The wages of an unskilled labourer in England, living on what was regarded as the subsistence level (though it was very much higher than the Irish subsisted on) tended throughout the period to be between a penny and twopence an hour, according to region and sometimes to parish. A weekly wage of seven and sixpence to ten shillings was common; fifteen shillings was good.

1

THE FORERUNNERS

AT THE TIME of the first signs of coming affluence, decisions how it could be exploited for the benefit of the poor (and whether it ought to be) were affected by a variety of influences, two in particular. One was the conditioning of history. Attitudes to poverty had been formed partly by tradition—the Christian ethic; partly by the institutions which had developed out of it, the poor laws, workhouses, charities. The other was the political and social structure of the time; especially the character of the ruling oligarchy, for in the last resort its members would have the power to direct the use of the country's new wealth—provided, of course, that they could cling to that power. Much would turn on how they reacted to the theories, economic, philosophical and political, put up to advise them on the ways by which the country's new wealth could most efficiently be used.

Throughout the Middle Ages the assumption had been that the relief of the poor was every Christian's duty; almost his privilege. By this emphasis on charity, the Church was repaying an old debt. The Church had owed much of its early influence, and its ultimate staying power, to the fact that it was a religion of, and for, the poor. In Rome, particularly, its survival was largely due to the hold it had gained on the masses—as Julian the Apostate realised, when he attributed the Christians' influence to 'the brotherly love which they manifest towards strangers, the sick and the poor'.

When the Church began to pick up aristocratic converts, it tried to humble them; to make them feel that they must put aside worldly wealth, as well as worldly vices. Gradually, however, it allowed itself to be infiltrated by patrons who were not sent away sorrowing when they showed reluctance to unburden themselves of their possessions. It was easy for the Church to excuse this lenience; better that a potential convert should be allowed to hold on to his wealth, use it for appropriate charitable works in his lifetime, and leave it to the Church upon his death, than that he should be frightened away by an excessively stringent interpretation of Jesus's teachings.

With the Church becoming hierarchical in structure, too, its leaders tended more and more to associate themselves with temporal power, and enjoy temporal pleasures—palaces, servants, good living; and they found it expedient to explain that Jesus's injunctions need not be taken too literally. He had said that it was easier for a camel to get through the eye of a needle than for a rich man to enter into the kingdom of heaven; but 'the eye of a needle', it could reasonably be surmised, might well have been a nickname given to some gateway in the narrow alleys of old Jerusalem, through which the passage of a camel had indeed been difficult—but not impossible. Provided the rich man would put aside a tenth of his income for distribution among the poor, that should be a sufficient passport to paradise, so long as he had committed no other grievous sins. And if he gave more, so much the better his chances even if he *had* committed them.

In time, the duties to the poor which the early Christians had insisted should be performed by individuals, in imitation of Jesus, came to be taken over by the monastic orders. The well-off provided the funds; the monks and nuns distributed them; so the Church could still claim to be performing its divinely-appointed function. It was also being useful to the State. Men who were starving, if they could not obtain charity, were likely to steal for themselves and their dependents; if desperate, they would be tempted to join the banditti. For the rich to pay their tithes to the Church was, therefore, a social insurance premium.

The system worked well enough in countries which were relatively stable. In medieval England a kind of unwritten pact existed between Church, landlords and serfs, designed to mitigate the hardships arising from what was then the commonest form of involuntary poverty, when death or disablement removed the family breadwinner. The old, too, could hope to be looked after: a serf who could no longer perform the services to his landlord which had been the condition of his tenancy was allowed to retire to a cottage, with the right to subsistence from part of his former holding, now worked by his successor.

The system, though, was dependent upon the country's stability; and this was shaken in the fourteenth century by the Black Death. The population was halved; and the resulting shortage of labour helped finally to break up the old manorial system. Serfs who had been tied to their master's land could now leave it, confident that they would find more profitable employment elsewhere; and although laws were passed to try to stop them, a farmer who saw he was going to lose his crops if he could not get labour was unlikely to be too inquisitive about its source.

In moving, though, the serf lost the measure of security he had previously enjoyed. He could not expect to be looked after if he were incapacitated by accident, illness or old age; and he could not rely on keeping his cottage when he could no longer work the land. In the early sixteenth century, too, some landlords began to exercise their property rights, enclosing land which they had previously allowed to be farmed in common by villagers; in the process, more villagers were pushed into the labour market—and into vagrancy and begging, while they looked for work. And when Henry VIII's dissolution of the monastries removed the main source of alms for the poor, destitution became a problem which could no longer be left to look after itself. In 1531 the State intervened, taking the first tentative step towards a national poor law.

The Act was mainly concerned to put down vagrancy—as was most of the legislation in connection with the poor in this period. Its significance lay in the instructions it gave for dealing with a vagrant after he had been duly apprehended, found guilty, and whipped 'till his body be bloody by reason of such whipping'; he must be sent back 'to the place where he was born, or where he last dwelled the space of three years, and there put himself to labour as a true man oweth to do'. But suppose, when he got back to his birthplace, there was no work available? That, after all, was probably why he had left it. So, five years later, another Act had to be passed, its preamble almost shamefacedly admitting that its predecessor had made provision neither for finding work for vagabonds sent back to their parishes, nor for raising funds to provide it. In future, people were to stop giving indiscriminate relief to the poor; instead, all alms were to be given through the parish poor box, and everybody must contribute in this way, in money or in kind.

The idea was to try to restore the medieval system, adapted to the changed conditions. But no provision was made for enforcement; parishioners were enjoined, not compelled, to give alms. In Elizabeth I's reign citizens were found evading their responsibilities; and a new Act had to be passed to lay down that if, after the parson and churchwardens had gently exhorted a backslider to give what they considered his due, he still refused, he could be denounced to the bishop. The threat proved ineffectual. Ecclesiatical rebukes no longer carried their former weight; besides, there were nonconformists who did not recognise episcopal authority at all. Fresh legislation had to be introduced to enable a compulsory contribution to be levied; then, provision was made for regular poor rate assessments supervised by the justices of the peace; and finally, in the Act of 'the 43rd Elizabeth'—as the law came to be known from the year of her reign, 1601, in which it was passed—these and other laws relating to the poor were consolidated in an Act which was to remain the basis of the English poor law for over three centuries.

'More fitly, a malevolence'

The 43rd Elizabeth was based on two simple fundamental principles: the right to work—or, rather, the duty of society to provide work for anybody who needed it and was capable of doing it; and the right to subsistence, for those who could not work through old age or infirmity. And these were not simply to be abstract rights; the Act laid down the duties of parish churchwardens and overseers of the poor, and fixed penalties for failure to carry them out. The Church's function was still recognised, in that the parish vestry retained its old responsibility. But it was henceforth to act in a civil, rather than a spiritual capacity. Sometimes the vestry would consist of all parishioners, sometimes only of those who owned houses; sometimes it was elected, sometimes it was a self-perpetuating oligarchy; but whatever its composition, or its members' views, it was legally bound to meet every Easter to strike a poor rate, and to appoint overseers to collect and distribute it. With the money, work was to be provided for the able-bodied; youths were to be apprenticed; the aged and infirm relieved. Those who could work, but wouldn't, were to be sent to a house of correction along with the vagrants.

The switch from almsgiving to rate-paying soon led to a change of attitude on the part of the donors. Now that their contribution was assessed by the vestry, and compulsorily levied, they could no longer hope—as they might have hoped before—that the recording angel would mark it up in their favour; and if by their outlay they were not laying up for themselves treasure is heaven, there was nothing to be gained by generosity. Inevitably, they began to look at the poor through the eyes not of Christians, but of taxpayers.

'To do good, and to distribute, forget not, for with such sacrifices God is well pleased . . .' In the past, it had been possible for anybody slipping a coin into a poor box to look upon his action in one of two ways. It could be considered disinterested, in the sense that, provided nobody saw him do it, he could expect no material benefit; in the truest sense, therefore, he was obeying Christian precepts. But it could also be considered very much in his own interest; by behaving as a Christian should, he was lessening the risk of damnation, and perhaps cutting short his stay in Purgatory. This distinction had been the subject of much theological argument; but to the layman, it made little difference which view the scholastics happened to favour. Either way—interested or disinterested—his charity must surely be counted in his favour on Judgment Day.

Now, this could no longer be assumed. Compared with a benevolent good-will offering, the future pilgrim father John Robinson complained in 1610, payment of a compulsory poor rate should 'more fitly be called a malevolence, for the ill-will it is paid with'. Parish accounts soon came to be subject to more rigorous scrutiny; and the conviction began to spread that much of the expenditure on the poor was wasteful—indeed, positively harmful, as it was encouraging people who might have found work for themselves to rely on parish relief.

At first, the ratepayers' irritation was mainly with those individuals or families who claimed relief from the parish, but who were not parishioners by birth; and early in the reign of Charles II the Act of Settlement and Removal was passed 'for the better relief of the poor of the kingdom', designed to enforce more effectively the principle already accepted in Elizabethan legislation that each parish should look after its own, and only its own. In future, everybody must have a parish in which he was deemed to be 'settled'—ordinarily, where he was born. He could qualify for settlement in another parish at any time by acquiring a dwelling with a rateable value of ten pounds a year; but nobody who was so well-off would be likely to require poor relief. He could not acquire a settlement simply by living long enough in a parish; he might live all his working life there, yet be removed to his birthplace at the end of it, when advancing age or infirmity compelled him to ask for relief.

The Act reflected a growing feeling that the indigent poor were lazy good-for-nothings enjoying themselves at the expense of their betters, and placing a financial burden on the community. 'The strange idleness and stubbornness of the poor', an anonymous pamphleteer complained towards the end of Charles II's reign, was making English goods more expensive than those produced by other nations; 'these poor are so surly that most of them will not work at all, unless they might earn as much in two days as will keep them a week'. This was also the view put forward by John Locke, in his capacity as a member of the Board of Trade. The condition of the poor, he wrote in a report on the subject which he made to the Board in 1697, could not be blamed either on shortage of

supplies or on lack of employment, as the times were relatively prosperous: the responsibility lay with 'the relaxation of discipline and
the corruption of manners', and he suggested that harsher penalties for
begging and vagrancy were the appropriate remedy. Able-bodied beggars
should be handed over to the navy; women who were found begging could
be sent to houses of correction, along with begging children, who should
also be 'soundly whipped'. The houses of correction themselves, Locke
added, were in need of corrective treatment; too often they were 'places
of ease and preferment' for the workhouse masters, rather than of
correction and reformation to the inmates. Locke's proposal was not given
legal sanction; but it was only one of many indications that indigence
was coming to be regarded as a man's fault, rather than his misfortune.

In some regions, for example, the deserving poor had been issued with
small badges which served as a kind of begging licence, the assumption
being that the more they could wheedle from the well-off on their own
account, the less dependent they would be on the rates. But now, the
principle was subtly altered. It was laid down that all recipients of poor
relief should be compelled to wear the letter 'P' on their sleeves, and
that they should be whipped if they neglected or refused to do so. The
'P' stood for a word which had already acquired its lasting stigma:
pauper. Technically, a pauper was anybody who had received assistance
from the rates. A beggar was not a pauper, so long as he earned enough
to keep himself (although he might be subject to penalties, if he broke
the vagrancy laws). The inmates of homes for the destitute, too, were not
paupers, so long as those homes were run by private charity. But anybody
who received relief from the poor rates automatically became a pauper,
even if the amount was only a few shillings, given to a family in a week
where the breadwinner was sick—or, indeed, even if it were only the
price of the bottle of medicine that was prescribed for him. The distinction between 'needy' and 'destitute' might remain for colloquial purposes:
so far as the parish authorities were concerned, it was banished.

Still, even Locke and those who thought like him had to admit that
there might be cases where a man became destitute through no fault of
his own, through accident or illness—or perhaps simply because there
was no work for him in his own parish, the law of settlement preventing
him from making his way to where work might be found. And it was
in this period that the search began in earnest for some way to fulfil the
aim of the 43rd Elizabeth, that work should be made available for those
who needed it.

An explanation why it had not been fulfilled before had been put forward by Sir Matthew Hale, a chief justice in Charles II's reign, in a tract on the poor laws, published after his death. The trouble, Hale thought, lay in an administrative defect: that the overseers of the poor, though theoretically responsible to the destitute, were in fact responsible to the ratepayers. An overseer might realise that by purchasing, say, looms, he could provide paupers with work, the proceeds from which might go some way towards reducing the rates. But the purchase would entail expenditure; and overseers were unwilling to displease their neighbours by 'charging more than they needs must'. As a result the destitute got only bare relief—and perforce remained destitute. The remedy, Hale suggested, was to arrange for a number of years' poor relief to be paid in advance, to provide the stock with which able-bodied paupers could be set to work: 'this would prevent poverty, and in a little tract of time bring up hundreds to be able to gain their livelihoods.'

Hale's idea was to attract, among others, the philosopher Bishop Berkeley; if Parliament would authorise the raising of the capital equivalent of seven years' poor rates, he calculated, work could be provided that would 'forever free the nation from the cost of providing for the poor.' It also impressed a practical man of affairs, the Bristol slave trader John Cary, who prepared a scheme for the establishment of a central poor law authority in the town, to take over the duties of the parish guardians and overseers. If this were done, he argued, it would be possible to establish workhouses, to which able-bodied paupers who applied for relief could be directed. Spinning, he thought, would provide the most suitable employment. It required neither a heavy outlay nor protracted training; and the yarn could then be sold for whatever price it would fetch on the open market. In this way the paupers would be kept from idleness; and with good management the workhouses, by becoming self-supporting, would also bring relief to the ratepayer.

The prospect aroused some enthusiasm. Individual Acts of Parliament were passed enabling Bristol and other towns to make the experiment, and a measure was introduced to help bring the system in on a national scale. But just as it seemed likely to get through Parliament, a formidable critic appeared: Daniel Defoe.

'*Eat up with their vermin*'

Defoe had just made a reputation for himself with his *The Shortest Way with Dissenters*, in which he had satirised the attitude of the Tory High-

Churchmen to Nonconformity, and for which he had been jailed, fined, and compelled to stand in the pillory. He was now preparing to embark on a new career, as undercover agent—spy was sometimes the more appropriate description—for Robert Harley, the leader of the Tory centre; and his *Giving Alms No Charity* served notice how effective his cover—journalism—would be. In attacking the bill, he flattered those contemporaries who felt that the poor were taking advantage of the generosity of the well-off; and at the same time he was able to avenge himself on one of his persecutors—the sponsor of the workhouse bill, Sir Humphrey Mackworth, who happened to be a High Church Tory.

The poor, Defoe argued, did not really *want* work. They always pretended to, but 'they can live so well with the pretence of wanting work, they would be mad to leave it, and work in earnest. And I affirm of my own knowledge, when I have wanted a man for labouring work, and offered nine shillings a week to strolling fellows at my door, they have frequently told me to my face that they could get more a-begging, and I once set a lusty fellow in the stocks for making the experiment.' Even when the poor looked for work, Defoe went on, they only did so to earn money for drink: 'I once paid six or seven men together on a Saturday night, the least ten shillings and some thirty shillings for work, and have seen them go with it directly to the alehouse, lie there till Monday, spend it every penny, and run into debt to boot.'

It was fantasy—Defoe indulging in dreams of wealth and power; but it was effective, the more so in that he lent prejudice justification by what appeared to be conclusive economic reasoning. 'Suppose, now,' he wrote, 'a workhouse for the employment of poor children sets them to spinning of worsted. For every skein of worsted these poor children spin, there must be a skein the less spun by some poor family or person that spun it before . . . it is only transposing manufacture from Colchester to London, and taking the bread out of the mouths of the poor in Essex, to put it into the mouths of the poor of Middlesex.' If the workhouse authorities were to find some entirely new source of demand, he conceded, outside the country, that would be different—'if those gentlemen could establish a trade to Muscovy for English serges, or obtain an order from the Czar, that all his subjects should wear stockings, who wore none before'—then the workhouse labour would be clear gain. It would also be gain if something was manufactured in the workhouses which had not previously been made in England. 'But to set poor people to work on the same thing that other poor people were employed on before, and at the same time not increase the consumption, is giving to one what you take from another, putting a vagabond into an honest man's employment.'

With almost uncanny prescience, Defoe was anticipating the arguments against Government interference which were to become so familiar a century later. Trade, he claimed, 'like all nature, most obsequiously obeys the great Law of Cause and Consequence'—or, as he might easily have called it, the great law of supply and demand; and there was nothing that Mackworth or his followers could do about it. When Mackworth's bill, which had got through the House of Commons, was rejected by the Lords, Defoe was able to enjoy the credit for its defeat—especially as the result of the Bristol experiment appeared to confirm the accuracy of his diagnosis. The Bristol paupers had to work twelve hours a day, six days a week, for sixpence a day, if their goods were to be sold at competitive prices on the open market; and even then, the return was insufficient to offset the cost of materials and incidental expenses involved.

The Bristol experiment, however, had an unforeseen consequence. Wherever a workhouse had been built, the natural inclination of the local poor law officers was to make use of it. Even if it could not be made self-supporting, it might still save the ratepayers some money if it were used for a deterrent effect. As a Berkshire landowner, Matthew Marriott, put it, the advantage of having a workhouse 'does not arise from what the poor people can do towards their own subsistence, but from the apprehensions the poor have of it. These prompt them to exert and do their utmost to keep themselves off the parish, and render them exceedingly averse to submit to come into the house until extreme necessity compels them.' For those compelled by extreme necessity, there was no need for expenditure on working materials; they could break stones. The idea caught on; and although establishments of the kind that Cary had introduced went out of fashion, the erection of work-houses continued—an Act of 1723, which enabled groups of parishes to get together for the purpose of building and running them, facilitating the process.

In theory, therefore, there were now to be three types of institution providing for the destitute: the workhouse, to which all able-bodied paupers who could not find work were to be consigned; the poorhouse, or almshouse, for the aged and infirm; and the house of correction, for vagabonds and vagrants. But in practice the distinction was rarely made, and still more rarely preserved. Where a workhouse existed, ratepayers naturally did not like to see it half-empty while they were also helping to maintain a poorhouse and a house of correction. It was simpler, and cheaper, to have all paupers under the same roof. And as a result the general workhouse came into being to house all who were destitute without reference to the causes of their destitution.

From this time on the general workhouse, an accident of history, was to become the dominant feature of the English poor law—as well as, in many places, of the English landscape. From the start, though, its deficiencies began to excite concern; and ironically, one of the first to grasp its fundamental weakness was Defoe. He had not prospered as a journalist and a spy. He had been continually in financial difficulties, his efforts never receiving the recognition or the remuneration he knew they deserved; he had again found himself in prison; and the coming of the Hanoverian dynasty finally destroyed his hopes of attaining real influence. Posterity was the beneficiary; *Robinson Crusoe* appeared in 1719, followed by *Moll Flanders* and the other works on which he was to found a securer reputation.

His own poverty had made Defoe less uncharitable about the poor; and the new workhouses disturbed him. Although in appearance beneficial, he wrote in 1729, 'they have in some respects an evil tendency, for they mix the good and the bad, and often make reprobates of all alike'. Nobody, he pointed out, was immune from misfortune: and if the wife of some honest trader was unlucky enough to find he had died leaving her and her children unprovided for, 'what a shocking thing it is to think they must be mixed with vagrants, beggars, thieves and night-walkers; to receive their insults, to hear their blasphemous and obscene discourse, to be suffocated with their nastiness, and eat up with their vermin'.

Parish officials soon found themselves in difficulties on this very issue. If they rigorously enforced the deterrent principle that outdoor relief should no longer be provided for the able-bodied pauper, and that he must accept it in the workhouse, some honest labourer who had lost his job through no fault of his own—perhaps because of the bankruptcy of his employer—and who could not immediately find another job, would have to enter the workhouse, with his family, and there be forced to consort with vagrants and prostitutes. Parishes consequently often weakened in their resolve and they would give outdoor relief to cases they thought deserving. But if this increased parish expenditure, ratepayers would again begin to ask why, with the workhouse half-empty, out-relief was being provided? And so, the see-saw motion developed, between strictness (or harshness) and liberality (or laxity). The Islington overseers, for example, were told in 1738 to give relief to the able-bodied only in the workhouse; two years later that rule was rescinded. It was a dilemma which was to confront administrators of the poor laws for as long as the workhouse system lasted; and it was to be satisfactorily resolved only by the abolition, two centuries later, of the workhouse itself.

'They starve, and freeze, and rot'

Among those whose concern was aroused about the way the destitute were treated was Henry Fielding. He had made his name as the author-manager of a theatre, until the authorities closed it with the help of a Licensing Act; then, as the author of *Joseph Andrews* and *Tom Jones*. But he was also a magistrate, the reward of earlier journalistic endeavours on behalf of a government of the period; and in that capacity, he found himself continually confronted by the evidence of the destructive effects of poverty, not only on the poor themselves, but on the community, through the expense of keeping the destitute in idleness, or worse. In his *Proposal for making an effectual provision for the poor*, published in 1753, he set out to show how badly administered the laws were, and how they might be improved.

His plan was much the same as Hale's, but it was based on closer observation of how the poor actually lived. They were not enjoying a life of indolence at the ratepayers' expense: on the contrary, 'if we were to make a progress through the outskirts of the metropolis, and look into the habitations of the poor, we should there behold such pictures of human misery as must move the compassion of every citizen here that deserves the name of human. What indeed must be his composition, who could see whole families in want of every necessary of life, oppressed with hunger, cold, nakedness and filth—and with diseases, the certain consequences of all these?' Yet their sufferings were less well known than their misdeeds, Fielding suggested, because, 'they starve and freeze and rot among themselves—but they beg and steal and rob among their betters'. To blame the poor for crime was futile: crime was the natural by-product of their living conditions.

It was therefore very much in society's interest, Fielding went on, that those conditions should be improved. So what was the use of squandering the ratepayers' money on poor relief, as it clearly had no beneficial effects? Instead, it should be made productive. What was needed, as Hale had argued, was a return to the principles of the 43rd Elizabeth. That Act had directed parishes to provide work for the poor, and given instructions that the necessary stock-in-trade should be provided. But it had only told the overseers what to do, rather than how to set about doing it; and 'considering what sort of men the overseers have been', it was not surprising that they had failed to carry it out. The remedy was simple. Workhouses should be made houses of, and for, work. In this way the industrious would be separated from the idle; they would begin to earn their keep, and perhaps ultimately they would regain their independence. The idle could be placed in a house of correction (or in a separate part of the workhouse, set aside for that purpose). There, they would be made to do unpleasant work, and punished if they remained obdurate—which would drive them to find work for themselves. This would leave only the impotent poor to be looked after; and they, surely, could be left to charity.

Fielding's *Proposal* was symptomatic of a new attitude that was finding expression; that 'where a great proportion of the people are permitted to languish in hopeless misery'—as Samuel Johnson put it—'that country must be ill-policed and wretchedly governed', a decent provision for the poor being the true test of civilisation. It was at this time that the first intimations of affluence were beginning to appear, as a consequence of Kay's flying shuttle, which enabled weavers greatly to increase their output, and provided more work for spinners; and also of the new system of crop rotation introduced by the inspired amateur farmer 'Turnip' Townshend, which increased the productivity of the land, wherever a go-ahead farmer adopted it. The country's growing wealth would leave less excuse for neglect of the destitute if, as more enlightened minds were coming to believe, destitution was a misfortune, rather than a fault. But when it came actually to doing anything, Parliament appeared paralysed. Fielding's hopes that M.P.s would be impressed by his diagnosis, and would accept his prescription, were not fulfilled; they paid no attention to him. The care of the poor was a parish concern: they did not want the trouble and expense of intervention. It was to take a sustained campaign by a dedicated philanthropist to shift them: to extract the first admission that Parliament had been neglecting its duties to the poor.

'For the child must die'

As a business man, Jonas Hanway had travelled extensively in his youth—his ventures including a remarkable sales tour with a caravan-load of English cloth, which took him to Teheran via St. Petersburg and the Caspian Sea. When he returned to settle down in England, his account of his travels made his reputation as an author and man of affairs; and soon, he began to win another—as a character. He was rich enough to have a carriage, but preferred to walk in front of it, protecting his wig from the vagaries of the English weather with a small umbrella— the first man, reputedly, to brave the ribaldry of bystanders in this way: umbrellas had previously been carried only by women. And before he died he wrote more than seventy tracts, ranging from a plea for the augmentation of the merchant service to a denunciation of tea-drinking. But Hanway's chief aim was to rescue the children of the poor from being deprived of the consolations of the Christian faith. The Church of England, he complained, had long since ceased to have much concern for or contact with the poor, or with the workers as a whole; not more than one in two hundred of them, he estimated, was a practising Anglican. The Methodists, who were in the process of breaking away from the Church, were attracting a far bigger following among the workers; but he disliked their exploitation of mass hysteria. He must work for the poor, he decided, on his own.

Hanway's philanthropic efforts began in 1758 when he became a governor of the Foundling Hospital, established half a century before to provide for 'such infants as the misfortunes or inhumanity of their parents should leave deficient of support'. But he was soon dissatisfied with the way it was run; and he realised that it catered only for a tiny minority of pauper children. He decided to find out what was being done for foundlings and orphans in other countries; and then to compare what he had seen with what was being done in the poorhouses and work-houses of England. 'Alone and unaided', his friend John Pugh recalled, 'he explored the then miserable and unhealthy habitations of the parish poor in these crowded cities, exposed his tender lungs to the pestilential air of the workhouse sick wards, and procured a complete account of every workhouse in and near the metropolis.' And at the end of it, he published the gruesome facts, along with the names of the authorities he considered responsible.

In the year 1765, his researches revealed, the 'nurse' in St. Clement Danes' workhouse had twenty-three children placed in her charge: by January 25 the following year two had been discharged and of the re-mainder, eighteen were dead. Of seventy-eight children taken into the Holborn workhouse in the same period, sixty-four died; of eighteen in

St. George's Middlesex workhouse, sixteen died. According to the report of a court case which he had read, there was one London parish in which not a single pauper infant had survived in fourteen years: and he himself had seen the accounts of another 'which acknowledged, that out of fifty-three, being the whole number received in five years, not one was kept alive'. In such circumstances, he protested, the attempt to bring up an infant in a workhouse 'is but a small remove from slaughter, *for the child must die'*.

In the goodness of his heart, Hanway could not understand how such a thing could be allowed to happen *in England*. In China, he had heard on his travels, the parents were permitted to get rid of a new-born child, and there was something to be said for that—if pauper babies were to be deprived of what was necessary for their survival, they might as well be thrown, like kittens, into a pond: 'the earlier the death, the less cruel'. He had assumed, though, that this was not the English way—'the natural rectitude of the heart will surely lead us to protect the innocent'. But now, he found the English way; the damning evidence which he had collected was ignored.

Another man might have despaired of trying to make people listen; but Hanway, unlike some philanthropists, had a measure of shrewdness to direct his strategy. He began to ferret out the statistics not—as he had previously been doing—for the worst parishes, but for some of the best, socially-speaking. Reports of what happened in the poorer parts of London, he realised, affected the residents of the better-class districts hardly more than the news of a famine in Ireland. But if he could confront them with evidence from the squalid areas near their own homes. . . . So, he went to work tracking down the mortality rate of pauper children in the combined parishes of St. Giles in the Fields and St. George's, Bloomsbury. In their workhouse, he was able to show, only one infant in ten survived for more than a year after admission. And to remind the parishioners of their duty, he contrived to suggest that they had not merely been un-Christian, they had been accessories to murder.

The ruse worked. Concern, and then horror, were aroused by Hanway's revelations. A committee of inquiry, set up by the House of Commons, broadly confirmed his findings: only seven infants out of every hundred brought in to workhouses under the age of twelve months survived. A bill was introduced to give greater protection to pauper children, laying down that no child must be kept in a workhouse for more than three weeks: either the mother, if she was known, must be allowed sufficient relief to enable her to look after her children at home, or they must be boarded out—preferably in the country, as it was healthier. The measure was passed in 1767, savings hundreds of children's lives each year, Hanway could boast—with justice, for when, ten years later, a report was called for to see how the Act was working, the mortality rate for the parish infant poor had fallen to one in five.

'Humanity is in fashion'

Hanway's Act did not create any striking precedent; in theory, Parliament had long stood *in loco parentis* for all destitute orphans. But at least M.P.s had been persuaded of the need to concern themselves with the condition of the poor; and from this time on they were not to be allowed to forget it. Their concern, though, was not exclusively humanitarian. What chiefly worried them, as the report of a parliamentary committee in 1775 revealed, was the gradual but persistent rise in the poor rate.

There did not seem to be any reason why the rate should be increasing. In spite of occasional disastrous harvests, in spite of wars, the country's economy was buoyant. More and more common land was being enclosed, by Acts of Parliament, to enable it to be more efficiently farmed; and the results, so far as the landowners were concerned, were proving eminently satisfactory, in the form of increased income from rents. But the new prosperity was not filtering down through the community. When in 1770 Oliver Goldsmith described the rural scene,

> Ill fares the land, to hastening ills a prey
> Where wealth accumulates, and men decay

he was not indulging himself in nostalgia for a rose-tinted past; he was reporting what he saw. And the report of the parliamentary committee provided confirmation; on the evidence of the rising rates, men *were* decaying. They should be provided with work, the report urged, as the 43rd Elizabeth had clearly enjoined. But how? Again, M.P.s were reluctant to do anything which would lead to increased taxation—particularly as the country was again at war, with the American colonists. Lord North's Government did nothing.

The humiliating course which the war took, however, culminating in 1781 with the surrender at Yorktown, was to transform the English political scene. The oligarchy's solidarity, long precarious, was undermined; the opposition Whigs found themselves joined by M.P.s who had

previously voted with North; and the following year Lord Rockingham
was able to form a government which conceded American claims, bringing
the War of Independence to an end—a government which was likely to be
better disposed to humanitarian projects at home.

It happened that this was the period when the effects of the new
inventions were just beginning to be felt—Watt's steam engine appeared
in 1782, and within three years, steam was being used to provide the
power for machines in a cotton mill. And just as, later, the implications
of the space age began to be considered before it had properly begun, so
the new prospects which growing wealth might open up were being
discussed even before the machine age began to produce them. The
1780s presented a remarkable burgeoning of theories about how society
could use its resources to better advantage, for the benefit of all its citizens
—and especially for the poor. To this period can be traced nearly all the
projects which have since become the commonplace of welfare legislation.

'We live in an age', a London magistrate remarked at the time, 'when
humanity is in fashion.' But again, it was not simply humanity that
dictated many of the proposals; they also reflected a growing realisation
of the inefficiency of the system, to which Fielding had drawn attention.
The difference was that M.P.s were now prepared to consider them; in
particular, projects for health and unemployment insurance.

There had long been 'friendly societies' into which individuals paid
small sums, week by week, which would entitle them to an allowance in
case of illness or accident, or to an annuity in old age; but they had
hardly reached the poor. Labourers were considered a bad risk; the small
sums they could afford were a nuisance to collect; and few had the means,
even if they had the inclination, to pay the premium required for an
annuity. The friendly societies, too, had an unfortunate record; many
had gone bankrupt through bad management or fraud. But this could be
remedied—or so the lawyer Francis Maseres believed. As a character,
he was to become as conspicuous as Hanway; he refused to follow changing
fashions, so that when Charles Lamb saw him in his old age in the street,
he was still dressed in the style of the reign of George II, half a century
before. His hobby was mathematics, and he worked out an actuarial
system on which the premiums for annuities could be calculated—the
system which was in fact to be adopted by life insurance companies.
Why not, he suggested, apply this to the needs of the poor by making
each parish its own insurance company? It could be empowered to grant

annuities, on the security of the poor rate, to anybody prepared to pay the required premium.

A bill was introduced along these lines in 1782; but it had one obvious weakness. A down payment of ten pounds was required from every subscriber; and the chances of a labourer being able to save that sum were small. The bill was passed by the Commons; the Lords, more realistically, rejected it. A Devonshire clergyman, John Acland, thereupon put up a still more revolutionary proposal: a national scheme to which all workers would be compelled to contribute, so that there would be automatic provision for themselves and their families in sickness and old age. The rates that workers would be called upon to pay were to be based on average earnings: an agricultural labourer, earning tenpence a day, and a manservant, one and sixpence a week and his board, would both contribute twopence a week to the national insurance fund. A woman worker earning one and threepence a week would contribute a penny-halfpenny. Parish churchwardens and overseers were to be *ex officio* employees of the National Insurance Company; they would investigate claims, and provide the twopence-a-week subscriber who fell ill with the sum of six shillings a week bed-lying pay, or three shillings a week walking pay (with small additions for the maintenance of children, if any)—the penny-halfpenny subscribers to get proportionately less.

With wages so low, even a twopence-a-week deduction would have been a severe deprivation; and the labourer would not have had the help of contributions from employers, or from the State. But obviously such a scheme had a considerable attraction for the ratepayer; it involved him in no expense, and if it worked, it would relieve him from having to pay rates in future—except for the upkeep of houses of correction. Opposition came from another quarter. The friendly societies had had little direct concern with the kind of insurance Acland envisaged: it had never been sufficiently profitable to interest them. They would consequently lose little business, if the parish became an insurance broker. But if it established itself as such, they feared, the Government might be tempted to extend its activities into their territory. They lobbied against the proposal, when it was introduced at Westminster; and it, too, was defeated.

In another campaign, however, the reformers met with more success. The general workhouse had fulfilled Defoe's worst expectations. 'One thing is too publicly known to permit of denial,' the Quaker poet, John Scott, asserted in 1773, that workhouses are scenes of filthiness and confusion; that old and young, sick and healthy, are promiscuously crowded into ill-contrived apartments, not of sufficient capacity to contain with convenience half the number of miserable beings condemned to such deplorable inhabitation; and that speedy death is almost always to the aged and infirm, and often to the useful and robust, the consequence of a removal from salubrious air to such mansions of putridity.

Well might the indigent dread confinement in the workhouse, Scott concluded: 'well may they execrate that parochial policy which, by thus propagating disease and producing mortality, accelerates the removal of a burden to which the shoulder of avarice has ever submitted with evident reluctance.'

This had also come to be Jonas Hanway's opinion. He had originally investigated the workhouse system with a view to saving the souls of pauper children; but it was not enough, he had realised, to rescue them from death in infancy if no better prospect was open to them than what amounted to a life sentence in the workhouse. His visits to work-houses had given him a realisation of what appalling places they were, and he gave vivid descriptions of what he had seen in them—and what he had smelled: the stench of unwashed garments on long unwashed bodies was something, he claimed, that few people accustomed to relatively cleanly living would be able to tolerate, and the 'putrid vapours' might also be dangerous. In some workhouses at the time, the fever—a term then loosely used to describe infectious disorders, typhus chief among them—was endemic; in the Sunderland workhouse it killed off half the inmates in a single year. How these fevers spread was not known; but there could be no security, Hanway felt, that they would stay within the walls.

In his campaign for poor law reform, Hanway had an ally in Parliament. For years, Thomas Gilbert had been arguing for a return to the principles of the 43rd Elizabeth; in particular, that work should be provided for those who lacked it; and he brought the subject up again in 1782.

Instead of finding protection or relief, he told the Commons, 'the poor in many places have been much oppressed'. Very little of the money put aside for their relief was actually spent on relieving them; too much of it was being squandered by the incapacity, negligence or misconduct of the overseers, and by the cost of litigation between parishes over disputed settlement cases. What was needed, Gilbert reiterated, was a return to the original principles of Elizabethan legislation; the Act should be ad-minstered in a way that would enable better provision of work for the poor. Workhouses should become what their name implied: places where anybody who could not find employment could get a job. The general workhouse would have to go; almshouses must be provided for the aged and infirm, and houses of correction for the vagrant and incorrigibly idle; and the destitute should have the benefit of an institution which would combine workshop, farm and mill.

To the argument that the experiment had been tried, and failed, it was by this time possible to reply that it had never been given a proper trial: Cary had not attempted to found communities of the kind Gilbert envisaged, nor would he have had the capital to provide for them. M.P.s were impressed; and Gilbert's Act, as it came to be known, was brought into law, authorising parishes to get together to form Incorporations, and to borrow whatever money was required to provide farm land, factories and equipment on the security of the rates. It was a clear indication that Members of Parliament were coming to realise both the opportunity which the country's new wealth was providing, and the responsibility which it imposed upon them to use it to better effect.

'Weep! Weep!'

Hanway's work was not quite finished. Another category of workhouse inmate had excited his compassion: pauper apprentices. Parish officials, anxious to spare the ratepayers unnecessary expense, tried to get rid of pauper children as soon as they were old enough by apprenticing them to any master who would take them. As the kind of master who would take an apprentice from the workhouse was often more interested in the apprenticeship fee which the parish would offer him than in the apprentice, the system had had some ugly results; a succession of court cases had revealed just how little protection the boys enjoyed from being starved and maltreated, deaths being not uncommon.

After reading a letter in a newspaper on the subject in 1760, Hanway had begun to investigate it; and he came to the conclusion that apprenticeship was often little more than thinly-disguised slavery. A boy might find himself bound until he was twenty-four to a callous or cruel master who taught him nothing, and left him with no skill which he could later put to use.

As workhouse children were often undersized, they did not greatly appeal to employers—except in the one trade where that happened to be an asset. Chimney sweeps had naturally found difficulty in persuading parents to allow their children to enter the trade while they were small enough to be useful. It had even been found necessary to import children from Italy, but this was expensive. Master sweeps were therefore pleased when they could find a suitable workhouse lad; and the impression which both guardians and sweeps sought to foster, for their mutual interest, was that the arrangement benefited sweep, ratepayer and child alike. This was not how it struck William Blake.

> When my mother died I was very young,
> And my father sold me while yet my tongue
> Could scarcely cry 'weep', 'weep', 'weep, 'weep',
> So your chimneys I sweep and in soot I sleep

Hanway, too, was horrified, when he investigated the 'climbing boys', as they were known; and he began to try to arouse public interest, his campaign culminating in 1785 with the publication of his *Sentimental History of Chimney Sweepers in London*. He was still obsessed with the absence of provision for suitable religious instruction, as some of his case histories revealed. One twelve-year-old he had encountered, for example, had been climbing chimneys since he was five; Hanway complained that although he knew the Lord's Prayer and the Creed, it was obvious that his religious instruction had been defective—he had only heard of the ten commandments, and was unable to recite them. But he went on to describe the boy—three foot seven inches tall; his legs twisted into the shape of a letter 'S', so that he could not walk without crutches; blind. These had not been a disadvantage in his work, as the twisted legs helped to give him purchase on the sides of a flue, and the flue was dark anyway. But now, he had served out his apprenticeship, and had been replaced. What other job could he hope to get?

Hanway's revelations were sufficiently shocking to secure the setting up of a parliamentary committee of inquiry; and in comparison with some of the evidence provided for it, his tract might indeed have been described as sentimental. James Dunn, a master chimney sweep from Knightsbridge, gave evidence that boys were customarily sent up 'without regard to the size of the chimney or the age of the boys; and if the chimneys happen to be too small, they call the boys down, strip them and beat them, and force them up again, by which means they become crippled'. The starting age was usually seven, but he had known boys taken on at the age of four. Evidence was also given of another method of persuading a boy to climb; it was often the practice to light straw underneath him, and by that means force him up. The committee reported that it had examined the allegations which had been made, and found them true; and the sponsors of the measure to give protection to the climbing boys had no difficulty in persuading the Commons to pass it.

Hanway was dead, but the bill was based on his recommendations; and although the Lords—their fears for their property aroused by the master sweeps' warnings what would happen if boys could not be used according to need—insisted upon several amendments, the measure which was eventually passed left no doubt that Parliament felt itself responsible for the protection of children even after they had ceased to be paupers, through apprenticeship. In future, no boy was to be bound to a sweep until the age of eight; and then, for no more than eight years—and only with the consent of their parents. The master sweep had to provide apprentices annually with a suit, as well as 'linen stockings, hat and shoes'; to make sure that they went to church on Sundays. And no climbing boy was to be compelled to go up a chimney which was actually on fire.

2

THE WEALTH OF NATIONS

I. RADICALISM

SO BY THE 1780s, there appeared to be a growing recognition that
society was acquiring the means to intervene to remedy the evils of
extreme poverty, and that Parliament should endeavour to do so.
The impulse had come from reformers and philanthropists; now, they
were joined by a third force: radicalism. It was in this period that the
term came to be used to signify, as its name implied, a dissatisfaction with
remedies that were designed to remove only the symptoms of social
disorders, and a determination to tackle them at their roots.

The three attitudes, reform, philanthropy and radicalism, were not
always easy to disentangle. A man might drift from one to the other—or
even hold more than one at the same time. Nevertheless, the distinction
between them was important, as it proved to be a continual source of
confusion of purpose, and often of dissension. The philanthropists
tended to be on the Hanway model: they were usually more concerned
about the evil spiritual effects of poverty than about the evils of poverty
itself. A philanthropist might accept that the poor would never cease
out of the land—he might even believe it was God's will that they
shouldn't; what was important to him was that they should nevertheless
be able to get to heaven. The reformer was also generally less concerned
with the distress of the poor than with poverty's side-effects, but his
concern was for society on earth. He wanted to reduce pauperism because
he believed this would help to eradicate crime, and disease; or because
it would reduce the amount that had to be collected from the ratepayers
for poor relief. The radical was more inclined to assert that poverty was
deplorable in itself. There must be something wrong with any society
which, having the means to get rid of it, continued to tolerate it; what
was needed, therefore, was a reorganisation of society itself. And as
wealth and power were in the hands of a small, corrupt and incompetent
oligarchy, the obvious first step would be to arrange that they were
distributed more evenly through the whole community.

B

Radicalism arose partly out of the general ferment of ideas in the period; partly from dissatisfaction with the course political events were taking, under the premiership of the young William Pitt. He had hardly entered Parliament, soon after his coming of age, when he had introduced a motion in favour of electoral reform; the following year, 1782, he had become Chancellor of the Exchequer; in 1783, Prime Minister; and one of his earliest decisions, when he had consolidated himself in power, was to set up an inquiry into the working of the poor laws.

But Parliament had rejected his electoral reform measure; the enquiry into the poor laws had come to nothing; and apart from the Act to protect the climbing boys, there was little to show for his early years in office. The oligarchy, recovering its confidence, was too strong for him; or, perhaps, he was not really the reformer he had appeared to be. And increasingly, voices began to be heard questioning whether there might be something wrong with society as it was constituted, with a landed aristocracy depriving the poor man of any say in political and economic affairs. 'By what right', Richard Woodward (a rural dean in Ireland, later to become a bishop in spite of his views) had asked,

> did they take upon themselves to enact certain laws (for the rich compose the legislative body in every civilised country) which compelled that man to become a member of their society; which precluded him from any share in the land where he was born; any use of its spontaneous fruits, or any dominion over the beasts of the field, on pain of stripes, imprisonment, or death? How can they justify their exclusive property in the *common heritage* of mankind unless they consent, in return, for the subsistence of the poor, who were excluded from those common rights by the laws of the rich, to which they were never parties?

Thomas Spence went further. In a paper read to the Newcastle Philosophical Society in 1775, he had recommended that parishes should be converted into joint stock corporations, each having vested in it the ownership of all its land. The revenue would come from rent; when all administrative expenses were paid, what was left over would be divided up among the parishioners. This system, he pointed out—as Henry George was to do, a century later—would mean that there would no longer need to be rates; applied on a national scale, it could remove the need for taxation, including the hated excise.

Spence came to London, to try to propagate his view; but it was too radical to appeal to more than a small following. Thomas Cartwright's proposals attracted wider interest. He was no revolutionary: he had been a naval officer, and a magistrate; he was still a major in his local militia. But he was also an amateur historian, and he had become interested in some of the social ideas of the Anglo-Saxons, and of the Levellers, which he felt were applicable to the society of his time. In 1786 he put forward a scheme for radical parliamentary reform, including the introduction of constituencies with equal numbers of electors, manhood suffrage, annual parliaments, and vote by ballot; providing a blueprint for electoral reform which was to serve radicals for over half a century.

'Theft is hindering one another'

At the time they appeared, Cartwright's proposals caused the oligarchy no concern. There was little sign of social or political unrest of a kind which could have been attributed to radical agitation. Even three years later, when the news of the storming of the Bastille intoxicated radicals, there seemed no reason why reformers—and Pitt himself—should not share the enthusiasm. The term revolution did not have any sinister connotation in England; the epithet 'glorious' was attached to it, when referring to the one by which the Stuart dynasty had been ejected a century before. In their own lifetime, too—as the essayist William Hazlitt was to recall—English liberals had seen the revolution in America, where 'a more free and equal government had been established without tumult, civil discord, animosity or bloodshed, except what had arisen from the interference of the mother country'. There had also been another even gentler upheaval nearer home, in Ireland, through which Henry Grattan and his followers had won a measure of legislative independence from Westminster. Why should there not be an equally peaceable English revolution? Cartwright's ideas began to be taken seriously, offering as they did a possible basis for the constitutional reform that surely now must follow. William Blake felt that his own vision of society, expressed in his aphorism 'theft is hindering one another', was about to be realised: that a new world was going to arise in which the political and social aim of society would be to liberate men from the bondage imposed by lack of means, lack of education, and whatever else prevented them from realising their full potentialities. And sharing Blake's expectations, though on a more mundane level, was his friend Tom Paine.

After a frustrating early career as stay-maker and exciseman, Paine had emigrated to America, where he had the good fortune to get himself appointed editor of the *Pennsylvania Magazine*. It was an insignificant publication, but it gave him the opportunity (as he wrote most of it himself) to develop and expound some of the humanitarian ideals to which he was to dedicate his life. The publication in 1783 of his *Common Sense*, urging the Americans to fight not simply against taxation without representation, but also for their country's independence, made his name; and when he returned to England in 1787, he found himself admired among those Whigs who had opposed the war with America, and who wanted peace with France. The leaders of the party entertained him; he made the acquaintance of Charles James Fox and Edmund Burke; and by 1790 he was enjoying—according to his close friend Clio Rick-man—'a quiet round of philosophical leisure and enjoyment', welcome to a man in his fifties who, in his youth, had suffered more than his share of stresses and humiliations, and who might reasonably look forward to a quiet old age.

He was not to get it. Burke's *Reflections on the French Revolution*, when they appeared in November, enraged Paine; he saw the *Reflections* as venality—the impecunious Burke looking for a raise in his pension. In the first part of the *Rights of Man*, published in 1791, he attempted to demolish Burke's case—not easy, as it was based on an intuitive reaction. But Paine then went on to provide, in the second part, his own ideas how society should be constituted—and on how it could use its resources to prevent, rather than simply to relieve, destitution.

When in countries that were called civilised, Paine wrote,

> we see age going to the workhouse, and youth to the gallows, something must be wrong in the system of government. It would seem by the exterior appearances of such countries, that all was happiness; but there lies hidden from the eye of common observation, a mass of wretchedness that has scarcely any other chance, than to expire in poverty or infamy. Its entrance into life is marked with the presage of its fate; and until this is remedied, it is in vain to punish.

The thesis—that poverty is a defect of society, rather than of the individual—was by this time familiar enough; but Paine went on, as no previous writer had done, to analyse the reasons. It had been surmised that indirect taxation must weigh heavily on the poor; Paine used his experience as an exciseman to work out just how heavily, coming to the conclusion that a labourer with a wife and family might have to pay between seven and eight pounds a year in duties on the necessaries of life, from bread to candles. 'He is not sensible of this, because it is disguised to him in the articles which he buys, and he thinks only of their dearness; but as the taxes take from him, at least, a fourth of his yearly earnings, he is consequently disabled from providing for a family, especially if he himself or any of them are afflicted with sickness.'

What the State was giving to the poor, then, was not charity; it had earlier been picked from their pockets—all the more unfair, because the poor were actually called upon to bear a higher incidence of this indirect taxation than the rich. Beer, for example, was a staple drink among all classes; and one of the most productive of all sources of revenue was the excise duty levied on all beer manufactured for sale. But the aristocracy, because they were rich enough to employ their butlers to brew their own beer, paid no duty.

A simple remission of all indirect taxation which weighed on the poor, Paine claimed, would lift incomes above the destitution level, so that there would no longer be a need to use the poor rate to supplement wages by out-relief. But better than that: there need be no poor rate at all. Expenditure on poor relief had mounted to two million pounds annually; that burden could be removed, and the sums required for looking after the poor obtained instead from direct taxation, without the need to impose new taxes or increase old ones—provided only that the Government abandoned military adventures, and transferred the money spent on them to eliminating destitution.

Paine went into considerable detail to prove his point. About four million pounds a year, he estimated, could be provided if his fiscal plan was adopted; and this should be devoted primarily to helping those categories of poor who were most commonly in difficulties: old people past working, and large families. If they could be looked after, such poverty as remained would cease to be serious: it could be dealt with by friendly societies.

To help large families, he proposed family allowances: four pounds a year for all children under fourteen years of age—provided that the parents undertook to send them to school: 'by adopting this method, not only the poverty of the parents will be relieved, but ignorance will be banished from the rising generation, and the number of poor will hereafter become less, because their abilities, by the aid of education, will be greater'. For the aged, he suggested a payment of six pounds a year to all between the ages of fifty and sixty, when 'the bodily powers of laborious life are on the decline'; and after the age of sixty, ten pounds a year— enough to sustain them without the need to go on working, for 'it is painful to see old age working itself to death, in what are called civilised countries, for daily bread'.

When the needs of these two categories were satisfied, Paine calculated, there would still remain a modest residue from that four million pounds disposable surplus. With this, he proposed to subsidise education; to give every couple getting married a one-pound wedding present; and to give a pound to every mother following the birth of a child. Any funds left over could be applied to the establishment of workhouses which would really provide work, 'to receive all who shall come, without enquiring who or what they are. The only condition to be, that for so much, or so many hours, work, each person shall receive so many meals of wholesome food and a warm lodging, at least as good as a barrack.'

Stripped of their engaging trimmings, Paine's proposals were a forecast of the future welfare state: family allowances, old age pensions, unemployment relief. By the operation of his plan, he claimed,

> the poor laws, those instruments of civil torture, will be superseded and the wasteful expense of litigation prevented. The hearts of the humane will not be shocked by ragged and hungry children, and persons of seventy or eighty years of age, begging for bread. The dying poor will not be dragged from place to place to breathe their last, as a reprisal of parish upon parish. Widows will have a maintenance for their children, and not be carted away, on the death of their husbands, like culprits and criminals; and children will no longer be considered as increasing the distresses of their parents. The haunts of the wretched will be known, because it will be to their advantage and the number of petty crimes, the offspring of distress and poverty will be lessened. The poor, as well as the rich, will then be interested in the support of Government, and the cause and apprehension of riots and tumults will cease.

Had the *Rights of Man* appeared before 1789 it would have created little stir; now, its impact was immediate and unprecedented. The first part of the *Rights of Man*, it was reported to the Government, had sold about 200,000 copies. Hearing this, the crown law officers were tempted to accept Burke's recommendation that Paine should be prosecuted. Certainly it would be wise, they decided, to suppress Part Two; and they scared the printer into trying to persuade Paine to sell him the copyright. When Paine refused, the printer passed the proofs to the law officers; and what they saw convinced them that Paine was indeed advocating the overthrow of the constitution. When, for example, he described how the aristocracy were evading taxation by brewing their own beer, he asked what else could be expected of a Parliament whose members, whatever their politics, were in effect a combination of landowners? And if it were illegal for workmen to form a combination to raise wages, why was it not also illegal for the landed interest to combine 'to throw taxes from itself upon another class of the community'? These were questions that ministers did not wish to see in print, at this time; and when a new printer brought out the second part of the *Rights of Man*, and it began to sell as rapidly as the first, they decided to prosecute. Paine prepared to defend himself; but before the trial came up the news arrived that he had been elected by the voters of Calais to the French National Convention. He left for France to take his seat—prompted by William Blake, who happened to be in his company at the time, and who had a premonition of Paine's impending arrest. The men who brought the warrant arrived just too late.

The *Rights of Man* was duly condemned, and Paine outlawed—later to be sentenced to death; but he was out of authority's reach. Some of his admirers were less fortunate. Working men's clubs had sprung up in towns all over the country, nourished by the French Revolution, where artisans and craftsmen met to discuss the events and ideas of the day, and to correspond with other clubs. Naturally, parliamentary reform was one of the chief topics: why not, when Pitt himself had tried to secure it? Besides, it was supported by a very aristocratic body, who styled themselves 'The Friends of the People', among them Charles Grey, the future Prime Minister; the Earl of Lauderdale, Richard Brinsley Sheridan, and Sir Philip Francis. And as part of their campaign for reform, the Friends of the People published, early in 1793, a report showing that a majority of the House of Commons was returned by about 11,000 electors; that in fifty constituencies, there were less than fifty voters apiece; and that at election time, some seats were actually advertised for sale.

Subversion, Pitt decided, must be checked. The crown law officers must make an example of somebody. It might have been unwise to move against the Friends of the People; but the members of the London Corresponding Society could expect no influential protection. Thomas Hardy, its organiser, found himself brought up for interrogation before a committee of the Privy Council, among whose members he recognised Pitt himself. Hardy was a respectable shoemaker 'on whose inoffensive upright character', Francis Place—a journeyman tailor himself in danger, as a member of the society, at the time—was to recall, 'calumny has never breathed from the mouth of anyone who ever knew him'. Ordinarily, Hardy could have expected to live out his life in estimable anonymity. Now, he found himself and some of his fellow members of the society threatened with a charge which, if they were found guilty, could lead to their being sentenced to being hanged, taken down while still alive, disembowelled and quartered.

Thanks to a resolute jury, they were acquitted; but this only led Pitt to pass measures to frighten reformers into compliance—the suspension of habeas corpus, and new treason laws, backed by an elaborate spy system financed out of secret service funds. To sell the *Rights of Man* became treasonable; even to advocate Paine's reform proposals could be hazardous. The Government's panic, Place believed, was partly due to a semantic misunderstanding. He and his fellow members of the Corresponding Society had regarded themselves as republicans only in the sense that they believed in a more representative, more democratic, form of government; the crown happened to be identified with the unrepresentative form. But the distinction between reformer and republican, democrat and Jacobin, ceased to have any meaning, so far as the authorities were concerned. The Corresponding Society had been founded to obtain a reform of the House of Commons 'by legal and constitutional means'; but for Hardy to point this out availed him little at a time when John Scott, one of the crown law officers, was asserting that it was treasonable for anybody to advocate representative government, because it was 'the direct contrary of the government which is established here'. Besides, as Pitt argued, even those 'Friends of the People' who disclaimed revolutionary sentiments could not but admit that some of the views they had put forward had been shared by men who wished to overthrow the constitution—thus giving grounds for suspicion that their interest in reform was 'nothing more than a preliminary to the overthrow of the whole system of government'. This early example of the smear technique was echoed by the young William Wilberforce, alarmed in case his known devotion to such humanitarian causes as the abolition of the slave trade should lead to his being mistaken for a Jacobin. Not merely reformers, he argued, but those who were known to have associated with them, deserved to be proceeded against; 'it ought never to be forgotten that men who expose themselves to suspicion must often incur the disadvantages of guilt'.

'From simplicity, frugality, and truth'

The course which the revolution took in France made not merely Pitt's followers, but also most of the liberals who had originally welcomed the news of the fall of the Bastille, feel that the Government's reaction was justified. But just before repression finally closed in, one work was to appear which was to make an even greater impact than the *Rights of Man*, though on a more limited circle of readers: William Godwin's *Political Justice.*

Godwin had been brought up in a strict Calvinist sect—so strict that it regarded more orthodox Calvinists as damned for being too liberal; he had himself been a minister until, under the influence of the French philosophers, he became a convert to what would now be called Humanism. Trying to make a living as a journalist, he conceived the idea of writing a book which would present the case for a different kind of society. Up to this time, the radicals who had made the most impact had accepted—as Tom Paine did—the assumption that life in a society of their making would continue on much the same lines as before: the difference would simply be that everybody would be given the chance to exercise his talents, economic or political. But there had also been a few exponents of what might be described as moral radicalism. They agreed that society as it existed was sick, and sometimes expressed their distaste very effectively; notably the theologian William Paley, in his *Principles of Moral and Political Philosophy*, published in 1785—in a passage which, a friend warned him, would cost him his chance of becoming a bishop.

> If you should see a flock of pigeons in a field of corn; and if (instead of each picking where and what it liked, taking just as much as it wanted, and no more) you should see ninety-nine of them gathering all they had got into a heap; reserving nothing for themselves, but the chaff and the refuse; keeping this heap for one, and that the weakest, perhaps, and worst pigeon of the flock; sitting round, and looking on all the winter, whilst this one was devouring, throwing about and wasting it; and, if a pigeon more hardy or hungry than the rest, touched a grain of the hoard, all the others instantly flying upon it, and tearing it to pieces; if you should see this, you would see nothing more than what is every day practised and established among men.

To Paley, and to other moral radicals of the time: Joseph Priestley the chemist, the philosopher Richard Price, and, in France, the Marquis de Condorcet, there was something fundamentally wrong with a society which, given the chance, did not use it to try to improve the condition of its least favoured members. 'The care of the poor', Paley asserted, 'ought to be the principal object of all laws; for this plain reason, that the rich are able to take care of themselves.' But to Godwin, it was useless to tell the rich how they ought to behave. They were in the grip of an acquisitiveness which they could not control, arising out of the institution of private property.

The monopoly of property, Godwin felt, was responsible for society's worst evils. It degraded the poor because, by compelling them to work for the rich in order to live, it deprived them of their independence, of their power to regulate their lives according to their abilities and desires: 'no man can be either useful to others or happy in himself who is a stranger to the grace of firmness, and who is not habituated to prefer the dictates of his own sense of rectitude to all the tyranny of command, and allurements of temptation'. It was also pernicious for the rich: 'wealth is acquired by over-reaching our neighbours, and it is spent in insulting them'. As a result, 'ninety-nine persons in a hundred are no more excited to any regular exertions of general and curious thought, than the brutes themselves'.

One by one, Godwin examined and rejected the excuses advanced on behalf of the institution of private property. It had been affirmed that 'private vices are public benefits', with the implication that the true benefactor of mankind was 'the elegant voluptuary who employs thousands in sober and healthful industry to procure dainties for his table, who unites distant nations in commerce to supply him with furniture, and who encourages the fine arts and all the sublimities of invention to furnish decorations for his residence'. But the voluptuary did not in fact fact help the poor; on the contrary, in his service he degraded them to the level of brutes. As for the accusation that egalitarianism would put an end to industry, so much the better if it did. Already, one man by his labour could produce enough to keep twenty others. Instead of continuing to make nine men slave to keep the tenth, the work should be amicably divided; then, 'it would occupy the twentieth part of every man's time'. And more of that time could be devoted to producing the simple things which people needed; man would derive 'infinitely more pleasure from simplicity, frugality and truth, than from luxury, empire and fame'. A society liberated from competitiveness, too, would have a further great advantage. People who possessed property naturally felt that it must be protected, if necessary by force; people who lacked it were naturally tempted to acquire it, if necessary by theft, or fraud. The natural companions of property, therefore, were envy, malice and revenge:

> In a state of society where men lived in the midst of plenty, where all shared alike the bounties of nature, these sentiments would inevitably expire. The narrow principle of selfishness would vanish. No man being obliged to guard his little store, or provide with anxiety or pain for his restless wants, each could lose his own individual existence in the thought of the general good.

No man would be an enemy to his neighbour; and of consequence, philanthropy would resume the empire which reason assigns her.

But Godwin was unlucky in the timing of *Political Justice*. By the time it was ready for publication, early in 1793, the guillotine had replaced the cap of liberty as the symbol of the revolution in France. Godwin tried to be reassuring: 'we must contrast a moment of terror and distress with ages of felicity'. He might have been less detached if, like Tom Paine, his own moment of terror had come with arrest and imprisonment in Paris, execution being every day a possibility; only an accident, in fact—a jailer marking the wrong side of his cell door—saved Paine from death. Godwin's attitude might also have been very different if, like Condorcet, he had been driven into hiding until, having finished his book, he went out to die. As for the English Government, its members had understandably come to fear that their own moment of terror might follow the rising of some English Jacquerie. The prospect of aeons of felicity was not going to tempt them to listen to Godwin.

He was lucky to escape prosecution. Paine had been sentenced to death *in absentia* by an English court only a month before *Political Justice*—a far more revolutionary work—appeared; and Godwin, it was known, had helped Paine to find a publisher. He had also openly criticised the judge at the trial of Thomas Hardy; the charge to the jury amounted, Godwin claimed, to a case for the prosecution. But he was lucky. Although he was kept under surveillance for a time when the cabinet discussed whether he should be prosecuted, Pitt persuaded his colleagues that as the cost of a copy of *Political Justice* was three guineas, it was unlikely to reach the kind of readers whom it would inflame.

Unlike many of his ministers, Pitt was quite cynical about the policy of repression; 'Tom Paine', he was reported to have told them, 'is quite right.' But in his estimate of *Political Justice* he was quite wrong; it did indeed fire the imagination of many of its readers. No work of the period, the essayist William Hazlitt thought, made so much impression on the philosophical mind of the country: 'Tom Paine was considered for a time as Tom Fool to him; Paley an old woman; Edmund Burke a flashy sophist.' It was also the great formative influence on the minds of the young poets: Wordsworth, Southey, Coleridge, and a little later, Shelley. Wordsworth had shared Blake's hope that the French Revolution meant the dawn of a new era, he had even contemplated seeking election to the French assembly as a follower of Brissot, and in his 'Letter to the

Bishop of Llandaff'—written, though discreetly not published, in 1793—he was still taking the line that 'the great evils which desolate states, proceed from the governors having an interest distinct from that of the governed'—not yet aware of the extent to which it was that very evil which was now desolating France. After reading Godwin, he advised his students to burn their textbooks, and turn to *Political Justice*. The impact of the book on Southey and Coleridge, who had just met at Oxford, was also striking; they almost reeled off to Kentucky to found a 'Pantisocracy', on Godwinian principles, on the banks of the Susquehanna—because the river's name sounded alluring to them—with the intention, they told their publisher, of making it a social colony in which there was to be community of property, and all that was selfish was to be proscribed, in order to present an example 'of the eminence to which men might arrive under the unrestrained influence of sound principles.' But the ascent to that eminence—or the preparations for it—proved too difficult: they got no further than Bristol.

Soon, all three were disillusioned with the French Revolution. As Hazlitt—similarly placed—recalled, difficult though it was not to resent the attitude of Burke, who had been able to see nothing but evil in the early stages of the revolution, it was even more difficult not to agree with those who reacted to what had happened later with horror. And in the reaction, the chance of further ameliorative measures being introduced was lost. There was not to be even a mild instalment of electoral reform. The oligarchy was in control again, and determined to stay that way.

2. SPEENHAMLAND

No sooner was the reform movement crushed than Pitt found himself confronted by a potentially still more serious threat to his authority. The harvest of 1794 was indifferent, and its successor promised to be even worse—the month of June was so cold that the newspapers published reports of new-born lambs found frozen to death; in August, storms flattened the corn. The price of bread and other provisions began to rise. Rumours spread that farmers, middle-men and shopkeepers were exploiting the scarcity to charge inflated prices; and in some parts of the country the farm workers proceeded to take the law into their own hands— literally; they seized cartloads of produce; took over shops; fixed what they regarded as fair prices; held sales; and handed over their takings to the owner. It was done with so notable an absence of revolutionary ardour that the charge of Jacobinism could not be made to stick.

But if the motive was not political, what had come over the poor, to rouse them to revolt? Various diagnoses were put forward at the time, and over the next few years; but on one point there was no disagreement—there were more of them. The term 'the poor' was then used, as it still is today, in a number of senses. It could be applied to the masses, to distinguish them from 'the rich'; or it could be confined to the actually destitute. But the commonest sense in which it was used was to describe anybody who had to work for his living: for if he lost his job, he would immediately become destitute. In theory, of course, this might apply to those well-off members of society who lived up to the limit of their income—or beyond it, as many did. But they ordinarily could continue to get credit, until they found another job. An unemployed agricultural labourer would have to rely on charity, or the rates.

When used in this sense—as it usually was by economists and observers of the social scene—it had not applied to the then substantial class of cottagers. There was no rigid line differentiating the cottagers from the yeoman, or smallholder, on the one side, and the agricultural labourer, on the other; but in any analysis they formed a separate group. The yeoman, or smallholder, considered himself a farmer. The cottager might have a plot of land, but it was not regarded as a farm so much as an allotment. He was also usually a craftsman, offering some specialist service which he could perform within the neighbourhood; he might be a weaver; his wife might spin yarn. He could have a strip of land on the local common field, to grow vegetables; and grazing rights on the common itself, for a cow, or a flock of geese. And he could take a labouring job when there was a demand, as at harvest time. It was a sparse existence, leaving him as a rule with little disposable income; but he had his independence. When times were bad, he could at a pinch live off his plot, and the milk from his cow, with the help of such jobs as came his way.

The agricultural labourer ordinarily expected to work all the year round for his master, taking his meals at the farm table and differing from the other servants only in that he lived out (though often in a 'tied' cottage) and worked on the land. His standing depended less on his income, generally between sixpence and a shilling a day, than on the means and generosity of his master—which could determine whether the labourers' cottages had vegetable gardens and whether they could expect other perks. Under a good master the labourer might be better off, and more secure, than the cottager. In any case, both were decidedly better off, on balance, than Irish or French peasants of the time. The peasants regarded themselves as farmers; but the Irish were so crushed by rent, and the French by taxes, that their standard of living was much lower. The English labourers and cottagers, too, if they fell into difficulties owing to illness or some other cause beyond their control, could expect help from local charity, provided they were considered deserving. And, in the last resort, the local poor law overseers might be generous with outdoor relief in time of temporary hardship—say, following a bad harvest.

But there was another category: the agricultural labourer who was unable to get a regular farm job, and who had to take what work he could find, applying to the overseers for relief for himself and his family whenever none was available. It was this class which appeared to be growing more numerous. But why—at a time when the nation had been growing ever more prosperous, when the land was being made more productive, and when rents were rising?

'That abject state into which they are sunk'

The first tentative attempt to analyse the reasons why was provided in 1795 by the rector of a Berkshire parish, David Davies, in *The care of the labourers in husbandry*. Davies presented what he regarded as a subsistence budget, based on the weekly expenditure of one of his parishioners, a labourer with a wife and family:

bread (or flour)	6s. 8d.
yeast and salt	4d.
meat	8d.
tea, sugar and butter	1s. 0d.
soap, starch	2½d.
candles	3d.
thread	3d.

But the labourer, at the current rate of wages, could only hope to earn eight shillings a week; in other words, he was being forced to spend more than his income on food alone, without making any allowance for clothes ('it is but little in the present state of things that the belly can spare for the back') or for fuel—or for rent, though in this particular case the labourer had a 'tied' cottage, rent free. As for educating his children, that was out of the question; to send them to the local school would cost twopence or threepence a week. And this budget, Davies pointed out, had been compiled before the most recent price increases.

There were a variety of reasons, Davies went on, why the labourers were in such difficulties, apart from the increase in the cost of bread. Taxes had begun to rise, to pay for the war; and the value of money had begun to depreciate. But the real trouble, he felt, lay in a change for the worse in the condition of both labourers and cottagers as a result of the enclosures of common land, and the consolidation of many plots and smallholdings into farms.

Enclosures had been justified on the ground that they would increase the productivity of the land, creating more wealth from it, and more employment. But inevitably, they also deprived cottagers of their grazing rights, and their vegetable plots; and by doing so compelled them, as soon as they had exhausted their meagre compensation, to seek work as labourers. But this meant an increased supply of labour; and it had proved greater than the new farms could absorb. Not merely had this pushed down wages; it had encouraged the farmer to give up employing labourers all the year round. As he knew there was no risk of a labour shortage, he could lay off workers during the winter, hiring them only when he needed them.

The result had been an increase in the number of labourers applying for poor relief. But at this point, Davies explained, the poor law operated most cruelly, owing to the regulation that relief should not be given to anybody who had means. It sounded reasonable, but it meant that any labourer who had done what the authorities had long exhorted him to do, and put part of his earnings into a friendly society—or who had saved the sum given to him in compensation for the loss of his rights after an enclosure of common land—was disqualified from being granted relief. Yet his feckless neighbour who had never saved, and had spent his compensation money on drink, could support himself and his family off the rates.

The final cruelty of the system, as it was operating, was that owing to the Act of Settlement the labourer could not leave his parish, when there was a labour surplus there, to look for work elsewhere (unless he chose to take his chance in the industrial north, where owing to the demand for labour, parishes were less disposed to worry).

The law of settlement had been under attack for many years by magistrates who had to administer it; notably Richard Burn, the author of a history of the poor laws published soon after his fellow magistrate Fielding's *Proposal*. When the poor rate began to rise, Burn had observed, parish officials—representing, as they did, the interest of the rate-payer—naturally began to put pressure on the overseers of the poor, who were under their orders, to enforce the Act more rigorously. As a result, the overseers came to regard it as their function

> to bind out poor children apprentices, no matter to whom or to what trade, but to take especial care that the master live in another parish; to move heaven and earth if any dispute happens about a settlement, and in that particular, to invert the general rule, and stick at no expense; to pull down cottages; to drive out as many inhabitants, and admit as few, as possibly they are – that is, to depopulate the parish in order to lessen the poor rate; to be generous indeed, sometimes, in giving a portion, with the mother of a bastard child, to the reputed father, on condition he will marry her – always provided that the husband is settled elsewhere . . . and if any of the poor has a mercantile genius, they will purchase him a box, with pins, needles, laces, buckles and such-like wares, and send him abroad in the quality of a petty chapman; with the profits whereof, and a moderate knack at stealing, he can decently support himself, and educate his children in the same industrious way.

As for seeking to ensure that the poor really were industrious; that they were provided with a decent stock of materials with which to work; that the aged and impotent were comfortably sustained, the sick healed, 'and all of them clothed with neatness and decency: these, and such like, it is to be feared, are not so generally regarded'.

That many M.P.s agreed with Burn was clear from the report of the 1775 parliamentary committee on the poor laws; but they could see no way to get rid of the Act of Settlement, except by making provision for the poor the responsibility of the national exchequer, which was the last thing they wanted. And so long as the funds for poor relief had to be raised and distributed by the parishes, the parish must have some protection from having to relieve paupers who were not its responsibility. What happened if this sanction was taken away had been made the theme of a warning tale by the choleric Scots peer Lord Kames, one of the most pungent critics of the English poor law. A rich Bedford alderman, Kames recalled, had left his fortune to the poor of the town, but without specifying that recipients should be settled there. The money had been laid out to provide charity schools, and to defray the cost of apprentice-ship—even to assist young married couples to set up house. As soon as the glad news got around, paupers from near and far had flocked to

Bedford, and in the effort to provide for them, or get rid of them, the poor rate there became one of the highest in the country.

Gilbert's Act might have provided the solution: if the workhouses which were to be set up by the new Incorporations of parishes had proved to be self-supporting, as was hoped, there would no longer be the same pressure on the rates. But Gilbert's Act had not worked. About sixty Incorporations had been formed, but none established the communities— farms, factories, shops and houses—which Gilbert had had in mind, and by the 1790s it was already clear that the system was a failure. So, the Act of Settlement had continued to deter labourers in areas where there was a labour surplus from going elsewhere to look for work.

Davies had various proposals for remedying the condition of the poor; chief among them, the need to reverse the process by which the labourer was being uprooted from the land. It was not enough, he argued, to provide compensation for smallholdings or commons' rights taken away by enclosures, or by the consolidation of small plots into farms. Whatever a labourer lost should be made good to him by purchasing uncultivated or waste land, of which there was plenty, dividing it into plots, and distributing it among all landless men. In the meantime, magistrates should be given the power to fix a minimum wage, related to the cost of bread, and sufficient to maintain a family of average size, leaving only the larger families to be provided for by a supplementary allowance out of the rates. It was not the labourers' fault, after all, that there had been unrest. There had been grumbling, he knew, about the way in which workers enjoyed a life of indolence, thanks to the poor laws.

> Of this, however, I am confident. When the case of labouring families comes to be fully known and considered, it cannot fail to awaken the general compassion in their favour; to silence the absurd complaints, so frequently made on account of the great progressive increase on the rates; and to procure for this deserving class of people able and zealous advocates, who will plead their cause with effect, and rescue them from that abject state into which they are sunk.

Whether or not Davies's tract was responsible, the magistrates of his county, Berkshire, soon showed that they agreed with him that the labourers could not be blamed if their wages had fallen below subsistence levels. At a Newbury quarter sessions in 1795 they came to the conclusion that wages locally were no longer sufficient to support 'an industrious man and his family'; and they summoned a county meeting of J.P.s and 'other discreet persons', to be held in the Pelican Inn in the Berkshire parish of Speenhamland, to work out a wages policy. There, they decided 'very earnestly to recommend to farmers and other employers throughout the country to increase the pay of their labourers in proportion to the present price of provisions.' Where a farmer failed to do so, his labourers were to be entitled to claim an allowance to the size of their families, on a sliding scale calculated with reference to the cost of bread. Where the standard 'gallon' (8 lb. 11 oz.) loaf cost a shilling every labourer was to have a guaranteed minimum of three shillings a week, plus one and six for his wife and for each additional member of his family. For every penny which the loaf rose above a shilling there was to be an additional threepence a week for the labourers, and a penny a week each for his dependents. Any labourer whose wages came to less than he and his family were entitled to, under the Speenhamland scale, could have the difference made up out of the rates.

The bread scale attracted immediate notice, and imitation, wherever labourers' wages had fallen to, or below subsistence levels. It was rarely found in regions where enclosures had been less drastic; but in many areas of the midlands and the south the allowance system came to be regarded as an integral part of the poor law.

'A matter of right, and an honour'

But family allowances, although they implied recognition by the magistrates that it was not the labourers' fault if his wages failed to provide him and his family with subsistence, did nothing to remedy the situation which had pulled his wages down. That was for Parliament; and in the winter of 1795 Samuel Whitbread introduced a bill to give magistrates the power to enforce a minimum wage, wherever they considered it desirable.

Whitbread, a son of the founder of the great London firm of brewers, was one of the few Whigs who had remained faithful to his old leader Charles James Fox; and Fox seconded his proposal, criticising the allowance system on the ground that it was not fitting, in a free country, that the poor should have to depend on the charity of the rich. If the price of provisions had risen disproportionately to the price of labour, something must be wrong: that the general price of labour ought to be adequate to support the general mass of the community was, Fox thought, 'indisputably the right principle'. Pitt agreed. But Whitbread's measure, he argued, was based on a wrong principle: it would sanction interference by the State in wage bargaining. The view of 'the most celebrated writers on political economy', Pitt explained, was that it was not merely unwise but futile for the State to attempt to interfere in the economic mechanism which automatically regulated the price of labour, according to the laws of supply and demand.

Pitt had no need to bring political economy into his argument. Two years before, he had established a Board of Agriculture—an embryonic prototype of later Corporations, financed by the Government yet not under direct ministerial control; and Arthur Young had been appointed its first Secretary. In the autumn of 1795, Young circulated a request for comments on the propriety and practicability of wage regulation, and the response had been generally unfavourable; even those who approved of the idea often did not believe it could work. Was the energetic labourer to be paid only as much as a lazy incompetent one? How could a bench of magistrates decide a man's worth to the farmer who employed him?

Pitt, however, preferred to criticise Whitbread on a point of economic principle, derived from the teachings of Adam Smith. He had come under the influence of *The Wealth of Nations* while he was a student at Cambridge, and later through his political mentor, Smith's old friend, Lord Shelburne. Two of Smith's principles, in particular, had impressed him: that the price of labour, as of goods, was regulated by the economic laws of supply and demand; and that to accept this fact need cause no concern, as, if the economy were left to regulate itself according to those laws, free from the intervention of governments or guilds, it would regulate itself much better than it had been doing in the bad old mercantilist past. Each citizen, though seeking his own advantage, would be 'led by an invisible hand to promote an end which was not part of his intention'—the prosperity of society. Governments should therefore content themselves with providing protection from enemies at home and abroad, and raising sufficient revenue to provide for essential public services; otherwise they should stay out of the ring.

Pitt was also prompted by another convert to political economy: Edmund Burke. In his *Thoughts on Scarcity*, written in the form of memorandum to Pitt and published a few days before Whitbread introduced his bill, Burke discussed the areas in which the State might legitimately intervene; he left no doubt that wage regulation was not among them.

Whether Adam Smith would have accepted the interpretation Burke and Pitt put on his doctrine could not be tested: he had died in 1790. He had in fact also insisted that the primary object of political economy was to provide adequate subsistence for the workers and their families. The workers, he had pointed out, made up the far greater part of every society; and 'no society can be flourishing and happy, of which the far greater part of the members are poor and miserable'; and it was but equity, that 'they who feed, clothe and lodge the whole body of the people should have such a share of the produce of their own labour as to be themselves tolerably well-fed, clothed and lodged.' Although he would certainly have agreed that the State could not successfully intervene to raise the wages of labourers, when there was a labour surplus, Smith might have been expected to ask why that surplus had come about; was it, perhaps, the consequence of the aristocracy's monopoly of the available land?

The way Pitt presented the law of supply and demand, though, in his criticism of Whitbread's proposal, was calculated to make it appear as if Whitbread was ignorant of the first principles of economics. They should look to the instances where interferences had shackled industry, Pitt argued: 'trade, industry and barter would always find their own level, and be impeded by regulations which violated their natural operation, and deranged their proper effect'. Whitbread, abashed, could only reply that although the laws of supply and demand might in theory operate in connection with the price of labour, in practice, 'the deductions of reason' were apt to be 'confuted by experience'. And when Sheridan— another of the tiny group of Whigs loyal to Fox—criticised Pitt for dismissing Whitbread's proposal in so cavalier a fashion, Pitt blandly replied that no discourtesy had been intended; it was simply that he himself was planning a measure which would be more comprehensive than Whitbread's—nothing less than a major reform of the poor laws.

It was Pitt's last chance to justify the reputation he had won as a reformer; and he set about it with a determination that revealed how anxious he was that he should succeed. He even had copies made of a draft of his proposals, and privately circulated among those whose opinions he respected, with specially wide margins so that there would be plenty of space for them to write in their comments. And his speech introducing the bill confirmed that it was indeed, as he had claimed, intended to be a plan for a general overhaul, not just for repairs.

A minimum wage, Pitt reiterated, such as Whitbread suggested, was not merely futile, in that it was an attempt to interfere with the natural processes by which the wages of labour found their level; it would also be unfair even if it worked, because it would mean that a single man would earn more, and a man with a family less, than he needed. Family allowances on the Speenhamland principle solved this difficulty, without interfering in wage bargaining. Nor should the fact that the money was to come from the rates mean that it was tainted with the stigma of pauperism; on the contrary, the family allowance should be regarded as 'a matter of right and an honour'.

Obviously Pitt had sensed a weakness in his case. For a century, pauperism had carried a stigma; and however unjust it might be in individual cases, the feeling had continued that this was desirable, in order to deter men from seeking relief unecessarily. But with England at war, Pitt could not afford the risk of disaffection, and perhaps insurrection, at home; and he also felt, as did most of his contemporaries, that she must build up her manpower, if she was to survive in a hostile world. If he had to reject wage regulation, he had no alternative but to accept wage subsidies and family allowances paid for out of the rates; and he had to justify them as best he could.

He would do more: he would justify himself. Pitt did not share the distinctly contemptuous attitude to the poor, with 'their miserable understandings', which Burke had displayed in his *Thoughts on Scarcity*. The text of his bill showed that he was more inclined to accept the views Davies had put forward—apart from the minimum wage. Pitt also realised that, much as he would have liked to get rid of the Act of Settlement, he could not hope to persuade Parliament to abolish it if this meant, as it would, that poor relief would in future have to come from taxes, rather than from rates. He was determined, though, to make the Act more humane. In future, he proposed, nobody was to be removed to his place of settlement unless he had actually become a charge on the rates of the parish in which he was living and working; and if he became a charge owing to accident, or sickness, the removal order was not to be carried out until the magistrates were satisfied that it could be executed without danger.

The regulation that relief should not be granted to anybody with savings or possessions must also disappear; it was degrading, Pitt felt— 'no temporary occasion should force a British subject to be parted from the last shilling of his little capital, and compelled to descend to a state of wretchedness from which he could never recover'. A fund should be set up to provide landless agricultural labourers with loans to enable them to buy a plot large enough to graze a cow, and grow vegetables. Pitt also proposed that training schools should be established—as Locke had recommended a century before—to teach young paupers a trade, and help to keep them off the rates.

But to Pitt's chagrin, these proposals were coolly received. Members of Parliament were prepared to accept family allowances, for want of an alternative: and they raised no serious objection to the attempt to humanise the law of settlement. But the other clauses had a hostile, almost derisory reception—Sheridan went so far as to say the bill was the most absurd piece of legislation he had ever seen. Pitt was not yet in a position—as he was to be a few years later, when the war with France was going badly, and he seemed to be the only possible leader—to threaten resignation in order to get his way. He was heavily in debt; if he tried to resign on a point of principle to which his political backers were unsympathetic, they could unleash his creditors. In an embarrassed speech, he confessed that he was 'inexperienced in country affairs, and in the condition of the poor'; and as this made him diffident in imposing his opinions, he would withdraw the bill.

3. SURVIVAL OF THE FITTEST

It was to be Pitt's last appearance as a reformer. Coleridge, musing over his ineffectiveness in that capacity, attributed it to the fact that 'he was cast, rather than grew'—fortuitously, his initial political contacts happened to have been with reformers, and they had moulded him. It was not that he was insincere; on the contrary, 'he was probably as sincere as a being who had derived so little knowledge from actual impressions could be'. But the French Revolution, and the war, had shown that his beliefs were abstractions. 'Once indeed, in an evil hour, intriguing for popularity he suffered himself to be persuaded to evince a talent for the Real, the Individual; and he brought in his POOR BILL! When we hear the minister's talent so loudly trumpeted, we turn involuntarily to his POOR BILL—that acknowledged abortion—that unanswerable evidence of his ignorance respecting all the fundamental relations and actions of property, and of the social union!'

Coleridge was being unjust: Pitt might be ignorant of rural matters, but the bill was far from irrelevant to the needs of the poor. But Pitt was up against a combination of forces which were too powerful for him. There was the reluctance of Parliament to regard the executive as any-

BUILDING AND FURNITURE

FOR AN

INDUSTRY-HOUSE

ESTABLISHMENT,

For 2000 Perfons, of all Ages,

ON THE

PANOPTICON OR CENTRAL-INSPECTION PRINCIPLE.

☞ For the Explanation of the feveral Figures of this PLATE, fee " Outline of a Work, intitled PAUPER MANAGEMENT " IMPROVED ;" by *Jeremy Bentham*, Efq. as printed in ANNALS OF AGRICULTURE, Vol. XXX.

The Ranges of Bed-Stages and Cribs are refpectively fuppofed to run from End to End of the *radial* Walls, as exhibited in the GROUND PLAN: they are here reprefented as cut through by a Line parallel to the Side of the Polygon: in the Bed-Stages, what is reprefented as *one* in the Draught, is propofed to be in *two* in the Defcription.

FIG. I.—ELEVATION.

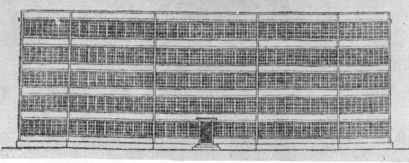

Figs. I–VI. 'Pauper management improved, particularly by means of an application of the Panopticon principle of construction'; Bentham's idea for workhouses.

Fig. II.—Section.

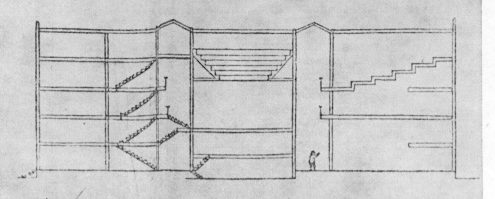

Fig. III.—Ground Plan.

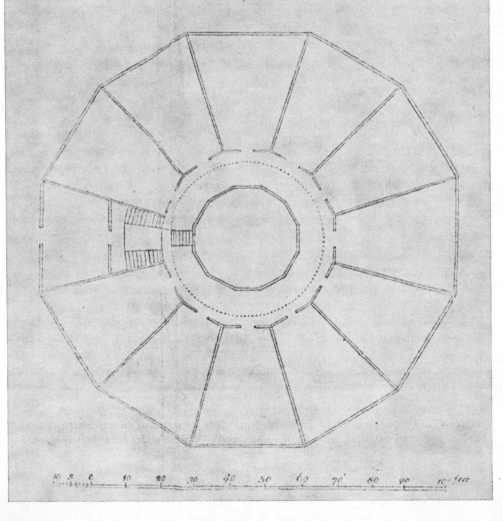

10 5 0   10   20   30   40   50   60   70   80   90   100 feet

Fig. IV.—Bed-Stages for Single Persons.

Fig. V.—Bed-Stages for Married Couples; alternating with sets of Cribs for Children, four in a set.

Fig. VI.—Cribs for Infants.

thing but an executive—M.P.s wanted the Prime Minister to carry out their wishes, not his own. There was the feeling that any such projects would prove expensive, which could certainly be unpopular, and might lead to demands from tenants for reduced rents. And there was a growing impression, which Pitt unwittingly had strengthened, that on the best principles of political economy any legislative interference was only going to make things worse.

'The very attempt, mischievous'

This was the feeling expressed in Jeremy Bentham's evisceration of Pitt's measure in his *Observations on the Poor Bill*, written in 1797. Bentham, too, considered himself a disciple of Adam Smith; he believed that there was a close affinity between the hypothesis of 'the hidden hand' and his own utilitarian goal of the greatest good of the greatest number. He had derived the idea from Priestley, who had argued that governments should concentrate on providing for 'the good and the happiness of the members—that is, the majority of the members—of any state'; and in his *Manual of Political Economy*, which he wrote in 1793, Bentham claimed that this doctrine and Adam Smith's largely coincided. He made a distinction, though, between the science of political economy, with which Smith had been mainly concerned—the elucidation of economic laws and principles; and the art—which mainly concerned Bentham—the great object of which was to decide 'what ought, and what ought not, to be done by government'. What governments must learn to realise, he insisted, was that there was no way in which they could help the poor, or anybody else, except by increasing the nation's capital. In theory, it might be possible to direct the capital already available into more profitable channels; but in practice individuals were more likely to do this than any government—for how could ministers hope to understand, say, the distilling industry as well as a distiller? So ministers should restrain themselves from intervention.

Applying this gauge to Pitt's proposals, Bentham set out to show in his *Observations on the Poor Bill* that the intervention therein contemplated would be disastrous. What would happen if the poor were allowed to keep their savings, yet still qualify for relief? The results would be pernicious: 'to guarantee to every man the perpetuity of his status in the scale of opulence would be altogether impracticable; the very attempt, mischievous'.

But bad though the principle was of 'opulence relief' as he derisively called it, Bentham felt that 'cow money' would be even worse. What would happen to the labourer if, having obtained his State loan, acquired his plot, and bought his cow, the cow died? Or if (as was only too probable) it was stolen? And what was the guarantee that the loan would be expended on a cow, in the first place? Apparently the recipient of this 'extraordinary bounty' was to be left 'perfectly at liberty to use it to buy either *milk,* or *gin,* according to his taste!' The whole idea, Bentham argued, was retrograde. It was going back on enclosures; and enclosures, as a host of authorities had testified, were of benefit to rich and poor alike. As for the provision of training schools, they would mean that a man who had saved up for the benefit of his sons, to give them a trade, would find them no better off than the sons of workhouse paupers—trained partly at his expense, as a ratepayer.

Bentham's *Observations* were not published until over forty years later; and although he did not keep the arguments to himself—he was a prolific letter writer, and he had an extensive and influential circle of correspondents—they were unlikely to make as much impression at the time as those of another critic of the bill: his 'disciple' (or so Bentham claimed) and 'highly valued friend', Sir Frederick Eden, whose monumental *State of the Poor* was published in 1797. Pitt ought to have made some preliminary enquiries, Eden thought, before producing his measure— not realising that Pitt *had* made them; he also felt that the proposals broke the very economic principles which Pitt was claiming to defend.

Eden, too, thought of himself as a political economist—a verdict which was to be echoed by Karl Marx, who went so far as to describe him as the only eighteenth-century follower of Adam Smith to produce any work of importance. And its importance indeed lay less in the detailed account of the condition of the poor in England, than in the way Eden used political economy to explain what was happening, and to justify his recommendations—regardless of whether the facts, as observed, fitted the theory, as presented.

The market price of any commodity, Eden asserted, 'whether it be labour or its substantial produce, does not depend on the avarice, whim or caprice of any individual, but on the general demand and supply, neither of which can be affected by him to any sensible degree'. It followed that (as Bentham had insisted) the only way in which the condition of the poor could be improved was by increasing the nation's capital, so that there would be an increased quantity of wealth, in which the labourers would share. This, in turn, could only be achieved by increasing the productivity of the land; and *that* could only be achieved through enclosures.

But Eden went further. A landowner who did *not* enclose common land, when he had the legal right to do so, could reasonably be criticised for prolonging the suffering of those who used it—quite apart from neglecting his own best economic interests. Where the common was enclosed, cottagers no longer had to waste their lives, 'picking up a few dry sticks, or grubbing up, on some bleak moor, a little furze, or heath'; they could turn to more profitable, regular labour, to earn a decent wage. As for their animals, 'their starved pig or two, together with a few wandering goslings, besides involving them in perpetual altercations with their neighbours, and almost driving them and compelling them to become trespassers, are dearly paid for, by the care and time, and bought food, which are necessary to rear them'. Why, then, should good landlords be expected to leave the commons 'to maintain the poor in a way most costly to themselves, and least beneficial to the poor?' Why should they continue to tolerate the continued existence of thousands and thousands of wretched acres,

> the sorry pastures of geese, hogs, asses, half-grown horses and half-starved cattle, which want but to be enclosed and taken care of, to be as rich, and as valuable, as any lands now in tillage? In whatever way, then, it may seem fit to the legislature, to make those cottagers some amends for the loss, or supposed loss, they may sustain, by the reclaiming of wastes, it must necessarily be better for them than their previous precarious, disputable, and expensive advantages obtained, if at all, by an ill-judged connivance, or indulgence, by the owners of the land; and by a needless sacrifice of property of which no one takes any account; and for which, of course, no one thanks them.

Eden's thesis offered an additional advantage to the landowner. If cottagers would ultimately be beneficiaries from the change, they should not in justice claim much by way of compensation for being deprived of their rights. It could even have been argued that the landlord ought to be compensated for the trouble and expense he had to go to, in order to release the cottagers from their old bondage. The poor, Eden advised, must learn to accept that all the arguments of the philanthropists were unlikely to have any effect in raising wages; 'for it is by imperious circumstances alone, which neither master nor workman can control, that the demands of the one, and the concessions of the other, are regulated'. All the labourer could do was 'by judicious contrivance' to alter his habits, and particularly his diet: he will 'thereby secure himself a fund for future independence, and increasing gratification'.

The idea that the poor could improve their condition by changing their diet was very popular at the time. Among its most ardent supporters had been Jonas Hanway; cheaper fare, he insisted, would do the poor good—a nourishing soup, in particular, might sustain them better than the meals they actually consumed. He had offered his own recipe: an oxhead, along with peas, oatmeal, and any available vegetables, boiled together for three and a half hours. The comments made upon his soup, when it was tried as a workhouse experiment, led him to lament the arrogance, as well as the ignorance, of the poor.

Undeterred, Arthur Young had taken up the idea as a way to reduce expenditure on poor relief. If overseers stopped providing the poor with bread, he told a parliamentary committee, or the money to buy it with, and instead substituted rice, flour and potatoes, the change of diet 'would have a very great effect indeed in remedying all the evils of the present situation'. He, too, had a soup recipe—and his soup, he boasted, was 'relished exceedingly' by the poor who had tasted it. A project for a network of soup kitchens was put forward by an old friend of Adam Smith's, a former provost of Glasgow, Patrick Colquhoun, who had come south—like so many of his distinguished countrymen in this period—to make a career in London; in the course of it he was to write a number of tracts on poverty and crime. It would help, he thought, if the poor could be persuaded to give up eating bacon, which was really beyond their means, and which whetted rather than allayed their appetites. It also made them thirsty, which meant that they drank beer. If they took soup instead, it would satisfy their appetite for nourishment, and relieve them of their thirst. The final seal of approval came from the American-born Benjamin Thompson, Count Rumford, whose system of poor relief, established in Bavaria at the request of the Elector, had won him an international reputation. Soup, Rumford urged, should be the pauper's staple; and he gave his recipe:

> 5 lb. barley meal
> 5 lb. Indian corn
> 4 red herrings
> vinegar, salt, pepper and sweet herbs

This, he claimed, would feed sixty-four people, at a cost of a farthing a meal.

It had been left to Davies to present an objection. Why should the poor lower their traditional living standards, simply to salve the conscience of the rich, whose standards of living had so greatly improved? Why should the rich not sacrifice something? Instead of grudging the poor the few small enjoyments they still had, like a morsel of good white bread with their miserable tea, Davies suggested,

> instead of attempting to show them how it may yet be possible for them to live *worse* than they do – it well becomes the wisdom and humanity of the present age to devise means how they may be better accommodated. Give to some the ability to keep a cow and they will all have milk. Give to all the ability to drink small beer, and then few will frequent alehouses. He that can procure for them these two benefits, nay, he that can produce for them *one* of these two, will receive the blessing of the grateful poor, and deserve the applause of all good men.

But such arguments meant nothing to Eden, who believed in frugality for its own sake. When he presented budgets to show how some families contrived to go without meat, cheese and even milk, in the effort to live within their means, Eden's reaction was not of compassion, or anger that working men and their families should be thus deprived of what they had regarded as necessities, but admiration. One old woman he had come across, for example, managed to live on 'hasty pudding' (a drab kind of porridge), milk, butter and potatoes; nothing else. 'She never had a teapot in her house in her life', Eden admiringly commented. Here, to him, was a woman who did not waste her slender means on luxuries.

Up to that time, the term 'countryman' in England had conjured up a picture of a John Bull; a yeoman, burly, robust, bucolic—obviously a good trencherman, who enjoyed his glass of beer. Eden set up an alternative: James Strudwick, who had worked for sixty years on the same farm, married a servant girl, and raised seven children, all on a wage of a shilling a day, until 'at the age of four score, in 1787, he closed in peace, a not inglorious life; for to the day of his death, he never received a farthing in the way of parochial aid'. The poor-but-honest, forelock-touching farm worker became the model, and remains so, for some people, to this day.

Inevitably, Eden did not care for the poor laws. Like Pitt, he felt that they could be justified in the national interest; he believed that England needed more and better manpower, which meant that provision should be made for the children of the poor, for the sick, and for the starving. But poor relief, he insisted, could not be justified on economic grounds. If it should be demonstrated that a larger population was *not* in the national interest, in other words, the final justification for the poor law would be removed. And in 1798, Thomas Malthus set about removing it, in his *Essay on the Principle of Population*.

'The prodigals must first be fed'

The book's antecedents were curious. For many years there had been a controversy on population, sparked off by Benjamin Franklin's *Observations concerning the increase of mankind*, published in 1751, and David Hume's essay on the subject the following year. The main issue—in the absence of national censuses—had been whether population was growing or declining—the general assumption being that, as David Hume had put it, 'wherever there is most happiness and virtue and the wisest institutions, there will be most people'. The only worry, as expressed by the Edinburgh divine Robert Wallace, was that under a perfect government, 'mankind would increase so prodigiously, that the earth would at last be overstocked, and become unable to support its numerous inhabitants'; but as governments were so very far from perfect, this had not been taken seriously.

The controversy was maintained mainly in tracts published—if necessary at their own expense—by members of the clergy. By this time, the country parson was a religious anachronism; his 'living', as it was appropriately described, was usually in the gift of the local landowner; and as such it was generally used to provide for younger sons, relations and friends. The work was often left to a miserably-paid curate, while the parson lived where he liked, and occupied himself according to his inclinations; where his income was insufficient to gratify more expensive tastes or hobbies, he might turn to writing as a pastime. Just occasionally, as in Acland's case, and in Davies's, the proposals put forward would attract attention. But most of the tracts were read only by the closed circle involved in the controversy; they were soon forgotten, unless they sparked off some new controversy.

This was what happened to *A Dissertation on the Poor Laws*, brought out in 1786 by 'A Well-wisher to Mankind'—later identified as Joseph Townsend, the rector of a Wiltshire parish. 'There never was greater distress among the poor,' Townsend asserted; 'there never was more money collected for their relief'; surely there must be something wrong that this could have come about? Not that the existence of poverty disturbed him. On the contrary, it was a law of nature that there must be poor, 'so that there may always be some to fulfil the most servile, the most sordid, and the most ignoble offices in the community'. And it was as well for society that this should be the case: 'the stock of human happiness is thereby much increased, while the more delicate are not only relieved from drudgery, and freed from those occasional employments which would make them miserable, but are left at liberty, without interruption, to pursue those callings which are suited to their various dispositions, and most useful to the state'. But there was no point, Townsend went on, in having any more poor than were absolutely necessary for that function. What had gone wrong in England, he surmised, was that the population had grown too fast for the country's resources, resulting in an unemployable surplus. The abstract issue whether or not an increase of population was, or was not, a benefit was really irrelevant. What mattered was that the relationship of population to resources should be preserved.

For a country to encourage an increase of population unless its resources were sufficient to absorb it, Townsend argued, was simply to promote destitution. But this was precisely what the English poor laws were doing. They were in any case unjust, because they compelled the ordinary citizen to set aside part of his earnings to provide for others before he had provided for his own. The small farmer, for example, 'works hard and farms hard, yet with all his labour and care he can scarcely provide subsistence for his numerous family. He would feed them better, but the prodigals must *first* be fed; he would purchase warmer clothing, but the children of the prostitute must *first* be clothed.' But even more unfortunate, for society, was that the poor laws increased the number of the destitute. And to explain why, he provided a striking analogy:

In the South Seas there is an island, which from the first discoverer is called Juan Fernandez. In this sequested spot, Juan Fernando placed a colony of goats, consisting of one male attended by his female. This happy couple, finding pasture in abundance, could readily obey the first commandment, to increase and multiply, till in the process of time they had replenished their little island. In advancing to this period they were strangers to misery and want, and seemed to glory in their numbers; but from this unhappy moment they began to suffer hunger, yet continuing for a time to increase their numbers. Had they been endowed with reason, they must have apprehended the extremity of famine. In this situation, the weakest first gave way, and plenty was again restored. Thus they fluctuated between happiness and

(*Top*) Child labour, eighteenth century: pinmaking.
(*Below*) Child labour, nineteenth century: a textile mill, 1820.

Poor BULL & his BURDEN — or the Political MURRAION !!! —
"And the land stank — so num'rous was the fry."
— What will become of these Vermin, if the Bull should Rise —? !!!!!!!!!!

John Bull crushed by taxation. Cruickshank, 1819.

misery, and either suffered want or rejoiced in abundance, according as their numbers were diminished or increased.

The Spaniards, however, found that English pirates were using the island to stock up with goat's meat. They decided to put ashore a greyhound dog and bitch.

These in their turn increased and multiplied, in proportion to the quantity of food they met with; but in consequence, as the Spaniards had foreseen, the breed of goats diminished. Had they been totally destroyed, the dogs likewise must have perished. But, as many of the goats retired to the craggy rocks, where the dogs could never follow them, descending only for short intervals to feed with fear and circumspection in the valleys, few of these, besides the careless and the rash, became a prey; and none but the most watchful, strong and active of the dogs could get a sufficiency of food. Thus a new kind of balance was established. The weakest of both species were among the first to pay the debt of nature: the most active and vigorous preserved their lives.

This law of nature, Townsend insisted, applied to man, as well as to goats and greyhounds. Population was regulated by the quantity of food. If a man did not restrain his appetites, the human species would multiply in the same way. 'Some check, some balance, is therefore absolutely needful, and hunger is the proper balance.' Of motives such as pride, honour, ambition, the poor knew little. Only hunger they understood. 'Yet our laws have said they shall never hunger.'

It was this passage, and the conclusions Townsend drew from it, which presented Malthus with the text for his *Essay*. Following an argument with his father—a friend of Jean-Jacques Rousseau, and of Godwin— Malthus had returned to his country parish determined to write a refutation of the theory of the perfectibility of man; and the *Dissertation* provided him with precisely the argument he needed—particularly as Townsend had gone on to describe the impossibility, under any circumstances, of avoiding the effects of the remorseless law of nature. If the strong tried to help the weak (as humans might do, even if goats did not) it would be futile; 'should they introduce a community of goods, and at the same time leave every man at liberty to marry, they would at first increase their numbers, but not the sum total of their happiness, till by degrees, all being equally reduced to want and misery, the weakly would be the first to perish.'

c

'The periodical or constant action of vice and misery'

Malthus restated Townsend's thesis, but added his own embellishment: the law of population:

> The power of population is infinitely greater than the power of the earth to produce subsistence for man. Population, when unchecked, increases in a geometrical ratio. Subsistence increases only in an arithmetical ratio. A slight acquaintance with numbers will show the immensity of the first power in comparison with the second. By that law of our nature which makes food necessary for the life of man, the effects of these two unequal powers must be kept equal. This implies a strong and constantly operating check on population from the difficulty of subsistence.

Ordinarily, Malthus claimed, a built-in check operated. Suppose, in England's case, the population increased from eleven to eleven and a half millions. At first, as no more food would be available, its price would rise; but, as the supply of labour would be increased, wages would fall. Inevitably, many of the poor would suffer severe distress; and as a result of their miserable condition, and the vices arising out of it, their numbers would again be reduced. By this time, though, more land would have been brought under cultivation to meet the growing demand for food; there would be a greater demand for labour; and a time would come when the poor would regain their former subsistence level, in a population greater than before.

But they could not hope to improve their situation; because any attempt to improve it by redistribution of wealth on egalitarian principles would simply start up the over-population cycle again. Even if the whole earth were to become like a beautiful garden, 'the distress for want of food would be constantly pressing on all mankind, if they were all equal. Though the produce of the earth might be increasing every year, population would be increasing much faster; and the redundancy must necessarily be repressed by the periodical or constant action of vice and misery.' And it was not as if the land brought into cultivaton could be expected to be as productive as that which was already in use; ordinarily it would be marginal land, from which diminishing returns could be expected. It followed that there was no point in seeking to better the condition of the poor by changing society; 'the great error under which Mr. Godwin labours throughout his whole work is the attributing of almost all the vices and misery that are seen in civil society to human institutions'.

When the *Essay on the Principles of Population* was published in 1798, its author, like Townsend, elected to remain anonymous; and there was no reason to believe that it would cause any more stir than Townsend's *Dissertation*. But it began to be talked about, and apparently even purchased, by people who had not concerned themselves with the subject before. To Southey, the most likely explanation for the *Essay*'s success was the nature of his target: 'Mr. Malthus could not have obtained more credit in the eighth century for laying the devil, than he has in the eighteenth for laying Mr. Godwin.' But by 1798 Godwin was no longer taken seriously, even by Southey. True, his novel *Caleb Williams*, published in the year after *Political Justice,* had had some success; and in it Godwin was still putting across his message that property and social status are themselves productive of misery and evil. The landowner, Falkland, is admired and revered by everybody who comes into contact with him, including his secretary, Caleb; even the discovery that he has committed a brutal murder, and allowed two innocent men to be hanged for the crime, fails to alter this good opinion—charging him with the murder, Caleb nevertheless proclaims 'to all the world that Mr. Falkland is a man worthy of affection and kindness.' Freed from the cruel compulsions of society, Godwin's implication was, Falkland would not have been forced into crime—nor, for that matter, would the gang who befriend Caleb when he is on the run. Yet it can be doubted whether many readers took Godwin's point. The book was described as 'the adventures of Caleb Williams'; it was indeed an adventure story, and easily read as such. And although *Political Justice* continued to attract readers—it went into three editions in the 1790s—the course the French Revolution took meant that it came to be looked on as a vision of, rather than as a manifesto for, a new society; as Southey put it, in 1795, Godwin 'theorises for another state, not for the rule of the present'.

A more probable explanation of the interest in Malthus's *Essay on Population* was its timing; it provided an argument against the poor laws, at a time when they were attracting criticism because of the rising rates. Malthus himself had not felt strongly on the subject; as he was to admit, he had actually supported Pitt's bill, and he had regarded family allowances as 'highly beneficial'. But when he came to write his refutation of Godwin, he realised how well Townsend's argument against the poor laws fitted in with his own against human perfectibility. Even then, he did not pursue the logic of his argument to its eventual conclusion: he was prepared to suggest, for example, that in place of parish rates, there should be country workhouses paid for by the Exchequer, which hardly accorded with his design to show that any attempt artificially to relieve poverty were futile. But he made it clear he had changed his mind about Pitt's measure: 'it has no tendency that I can discover to increase the produce of the country; and if it tend to increase population, without increasing the produce, the necessary and inevitable consequences would appear to be, that the same produce must be divided among a greater number, and consequently that a day's labour will purchase a smaller quantity of provisions, and that the poor in general must be more distressed'.

By this time, such criticism was becoming familiar. When in 1793 the Royal Irish Academy offered a prize for the best original essay on the poor law, the award had been given to Samuel Crumpe, who described it as an institution 'which holds out, as it were, a premium to idleness; which supplies, with food, clothing and medicine, the indolent wretch who does not work at all; and which levies such supplies on the industry of his laborious neighbours'. And Lord Kames used to point out that the poor laws were not only absurd (imagine a traveller returning from a distant land, he argued, and reporting that the burden of maintaining the idle and profligate there was laid on the frugal and industrious: 'What would we think of such a nation?'); they were also unnecessary—the deserving poor in Scotland were sufficiently well looked after by the Kirk, he claimed, out of alms voluntarily given by its members; charity should suffice.

But though criticism of the poor laws had been growing in England, uncertainty had remained whether they could be got rid of quite so easily as Kames suggested. By English law, for over two centuries—and by English custom, long before that—the poor had been entitled as of right to subsistence. Of course, if Kames was correct, the deserving poor would still get subsistence from charity; but, as Eden pointed out, the situation in Scotland was not really comparable. The Scots citizen might not have to pay rates, but he had to subscribe to the Kirk, according to his means, and that came to much the same thing; his alms were voluntary only in theory. Besides, there was no equivalent to the Kirk in England; the Anglican clergy would have been utterly incapable of exercising the same control over their flock, let alone over Methodists and dissenters. If the poor were left to voluntary charity in England, Eden warned, it would 'necessarily take the burden off the shoulders of the hard-hearted and unfeeling (who are now, so far as the regulations of human wisdom can oblige them, compelled to contribute in proportion to their abilities) and throw it entirely on the considerate and the benevolent'.

But this was to accept that the considerate and benevolent were under an obligation to continue to provide for the destitute. The appeal of Malthus's *Essay* was that it challenged this assumption. He not only reiterated Townsend's argument, that it was pointless to continue to provide relief for the poor, because this was a futile exercise, calculated simply to perpetuate their misery. He went further, denying that the poor had any *right* to relief. A man who is born into an already full world, Malthus argued, 'if he cannot get subsistence from his parents, on whom he has a just demand, and if society does not want his labour, has no claim of *right* to the smallest portion of food and, in fact, has no business to be where he is. At nature's mighty feast there is no vacant cover for him. She tells him to be gone, and will quickly execute her own orders, if he do not work upon the compassion of some of her guests.' And if those guests *were* compassionate, all that happened was that other intruders would appear, demanding the same favour; plenty would be changed into scarcity; and the guests would learn, too late, how they have erred 'in counteracting those strict orders to all intruders, issued by the great mistress of the feast who, wishing that all her guests should have plenty, and knowing that she could not provide for unlimited numbers, refused to admit fresh comers when her table was already full'. And this was naturally a comforting theory for anybody who might otherwise feel guilty about enjoying the bounty at nature's table, while others starved.

Yet the main reason for the initial impact of Malthus's *Essay* may have been simpler still; that he presented his basic proposition in such easily assimilable form:

Population growth:	1	2	4	8	16	32	64	128	256
Food growth:	1	2	3	4	5	6	7	8	9

'The ratios' were simple; they were striking; and they sounded scientific. Perhaps still more important, like Adam Smith's law of supply and demand, they were something that the casual reader, or even the man who picked them up in conversation, could grasp, and remember.

'The poor are always inconsiderate'

If only the first edition of the *Essay* had been published, it might have remained a collector's item. Malthus, though, was stung by the reaction of the man whom he had hoped to refute. Godwin did not choose to do battle with the son of his old friend. Instead, in his *Dr. Parr's Spital Sermon,* he attacked other critics of his own theories, but singled out Malthus for praise for his contribution—contenting himself with denying that it was relevant to the issue of the perfectibility of man in society. In a letter to Malthus, he explained why. The action of vice and misery, he pointed out, was not the only influence holding down population. Malthus had neglected moral restraint.

To Malthus, this was an unwelcome reminder; as a clergyman, he could hardly deny that man was capable of morally restraining himself from adding to the population. But a request from his publisher that he should provide a second edition gave him his opportunity. When it appeared in 1803, it was virtually a new work, in two volumes; and he was able to provide a mass of additional evidence which not only appeared conclusively to prove that his theory of population had been correct, but also to refute the criticisms—including Godwin's—that had been made of his theory. Godwin, he recalled, had claimed there were checks on population other than misery and vice: 'I cannot agree with him.' And as if justifying this forthright reply, he went on to say he would thank Mr. Godwin 'to name to me any check that in past ages has contributed to keep down the population to the level of the means of subsistence, that does not fairly come under some form of vice or misery, except indeed the check of moral restraint, which I have mentioned in the course of this work'.

What Malthus did not mention was that the addition of 'the check of moral restraint' at this point was an afterthought, prompted by Godwin himself. The ruse, though, was detected by William Hazlitt, who wrote a series of articles on the *Essay,* later to be published as a book. 'What are we to think of a man', Hazlitt asked, 'who writes a book to prove that vice and misery are the only security for the happiness of the human race, and then writes another to say that vice and folly are not the only security, but that our only resource must be either in vice and folly, or in wisdom and virtue? This is like making a white skin part of the definition of a man, and defending it by saying that they are all white, except those who are black or tawny!' But to ordinary readers, unaware of the verbal sleight of hand, the wording of the second edition appeared to provide a crushing rejoinder to Godwin.

The desire to cover himself on the issue also induced Malthus to lay even more emphasis on the iniquity of the poor law. Moral restraint, he argued, could operate among the poor only with very inconsiderable force, because the poor law removed the need for it, by offering allowances for children. Abolish the allowances, and the poor who exercised moral restraint would then be rewarded if they had no more children than they could afford—or, better, no children at all.

Thus, haphazardly, the notion was confirmed that the poor laws *caused* the population increase; and the impression created that any relief for the destitute, whatever form it took, must help to put up the population still further, causing further pressure on the means of subsistence, and therefore causing more destitution. At the time, the proposition seemed only common sense. It had long been accepted that men and women decided to get married and have children on the basis of their prospects; as Arthur Young wrote, 'it is employment that creates population; marriages are early and numerous in proportion to the amount of employment'. Conversely, those who could not get jobs did not get married; and the only reason why many of them did get married, and have children, was that they knew that poor relief, and particularly family allowances, would suffice them if work was not available. It followed that if they were deprived of this security, moral restraint could begin to operate. Townsend was right; hunger was the deterrent—hunger, 'not as directly felt, or feared by the individual for himself, but as fore-seen and feared for his immediate offspring'.

Malthus, however, was aware that if he were taken as recommending the immediate repeal of the poor laws, his critics would be able to denounce him as un-Christian; and he hit upon an ingenious compromise. Every child born into the world under the old law, he conceded, could reasonably claim relief as of right—not in the moral but in the legal sense, because that had been the law. This had to be admitted. But an Act should be passed declaring that no child born of any marriage which took place after the expiration of one year from the date it came into force, and no illegitimate child born two years after that date, should in future be entitled to parish assistance; this would serve notice on the parents that they would enjoy their old legal right no longer. Nor could they expect any alternative form of relief, through public works schemes. Malthus quietly dropped his former plan for workhouses—by providing subsistence, they would help to put up the population.

This was a hypothesis, not a proven theory; and doubt was promptly cast upon it in a published reply to Malthus by Thomas Jarrold. As a doctor, Jarrold had worked among the poor; and he was impatient with such theorising. 'Do the poor calculate with nicety?' he asked; 'is the period of love with them the period of calculation?' Clearly, no: 'it would increase their happiness were it so; but the poor are always inconsiderate.' And the reason, Jarrold pointed out, was obvious; 'the fear of poverty is never felt by a poor man, it is the rich who are in bondage to it. A year of bad trade, or a reduction in wages from any cause, may for a time suspend a marriage; but habitual poverty, however great, has not this effect. No person who has never been richer thinks himself too poor to marry.' It followed, Jarrold concluded, that if Malthus's population theory were correct, governments should not, as Malthus was suggesting, leave vice and misery to take their toll; they should rather try to raise the standard of living of the people, so that the poor would come to share the natural restraints accepted by the better-off section of the community. If the living standards of the poor were raised, in fact, it might even become necessary to guard against a *falling* population.

Another doctor, also writing from his experience of the poor, criticised Malthus's theory from a different angle. Charles Hall took up his point that the poor man had no right to subsistence, 'if society does not want his labour'. But who was 'society' to lay down this law to the labourer?

> I say he produces six or eight times as much as his family consumes or requires, but which is taken from him by those who produce nothing. What he is entitled to is all that his hands have made or produced, the whole fruits of his labour, not that pittance his wages enable him to purchase . . . It is not true that he has doomed himself, or that nature has doomed him, and his family, to starve; that cruel doom is brought on him by the rich.

What was wrong, in other words, was society itself. The rich were not merely taking everything from the poor, but, at the same time, were claiming that the poor owed everything to them. The effect of the system was 'to enable a few of mankind to obtain all possible enjoyments, both of mind and body, that their nature is suceptible of; but at the expense of depriving the bulk of mankind of the necessaries and comforts of life.' To suggest that the workers necessarily benefited from increased production, Hall pointed out, was about the same as saying, at the sight of a great store of honey, that the bees from whom it had been taken must be rich. And now, here was Malthus claiming that because invention was enabling the rich to live in greater luxury from less labour, they had the right to reduce mankind's numbers. What sort of Christian morality was that?

There were other critics: even Southey and Coleridge came to Godwin's defence, though they no longer shared his egalitarian views. Bonaparte had given them the excuse they needed to break finally with their past. 'Damn the French!' Southey wrote on New Year's Day, 1800, adding, 'that came heartily from the depths of a Jacobin heart.' They were moving, with Wordsworth, to High Church, high Torysim; but of a kind far removed from the Toryism of ministers. Coleridge, his reputation by this time secure after *Kubla Khan* and *The Ancient Mariner*, expressed their new inegalitarian view when he claimed that the best government was that in which the power of the political influence of the individual was in proportion to his property, provided that the tendency of wealth to accumulate into a few hands was not unduly encouraged, and that private property did not come to be considered an arbitrary right, unconnected with duty. He annotated Malthus's *Essay*, and Southey wove his comments into a criticism, based on this assumption: that the rich, although they had a right to their wealth, could earn that right only by performing their duty to the poor.

But Malthus's critics were few, and of less immediate consequence than those readers who were impressed by his theory; among them, significantly, James Mill. Coming down to London from Scotland in 1800 Mill was soon to establish himself as a leading authority on political economy; and only a year after the appearance of the second edition of the *Essay*, he could write, 'no proposition is better established than this, that the multiplication of the human species is always in proportion to the means of subsistence. No proposition, too, is more incontrovertible than this, that the tendency of the human species to multiply is much greater than the rapidity with which it seems possible to increase the produce of the earth for their maintenance.' And if anybody wanted a fuller elucidation of this proposition—'if anyone is capable of doubting it'—Mill suggested they should refer to Mr Malthus's ingenious book.

Ingenious was an appropriate description, though perhaps not quite in the sense Mill used it. Malthus had shown himself masterly at masking inconsistencies; and the second edition, Hazlitt had to admit, impressed an even wider range of readers, delighted to find somebody who could salve their consciences 'by relieving them from the troublesome feelings so frequently occasioned by the remains of certain silly prejudices, and by enabling them to set so completely at defiance the claims of "worthless importunity in rags"'. And Malthus's popularity, he forecast, could prove fatal to the poor of the country.

His name hangs suspended over their heads, *in terrorem*, like some baleful meteor. It is the shield behind which the archers may take their stand, and gall them at their leisure. He has set them up as a defenceless mark, on which both friends and foes may exercise their malice, or their wantonness, as they think proper . . . The poor labour under a natural stigma; they are *naturally* despised. Their interests are at best but coldly and remotely felt by the other classes of society. Mr. Malthus's book has done all that was wanting to increase this indifference and apathy.

4. FACTORIES

The poor law, Pitt's proposals for its reform, and Malthus's recommendation that it should be abolished were all based on the assumption, hardly as yet challenged, that England's wealth lay in her land. And in terms of the number of workers employed, agriculture still commanded easily the largest proportion of the labour force. But with the introduction of the new machinery, and then of steam power, the cotton industry had been transformed. By the turn of the century it was expanding very rapidly. Adam Smith had scarcely even mentioned it in *The Wealth of Nations*; but the rapidity of its growth could be regarded as a testimonial to his theory, because the State had not intervened to regulate it—except to extract some customs revenue.

There were few complaints, because few people were deprived of a living by the rise of the industry—except housewives, who lost some needed pin money as a result of the new spinning machines. The agricultural worker who braved the law of settlement to look for a job in the north found, if he got it, that he was better paid than he had been before. And the expansion was not only in the cotton industry. Miners, in particular, benefited from the growing demand for coal. Their earnings varied, Thomas Gisborne noted in a survey published in 1798, but they were 'on an average great; and in many instances very far exceed all prospect of gain, which a labourer in husbandry can propose to himself'. Describing what life had been like in the Potteries when he was a child, Josiah Wedgwood recalled how the labourers eked out a bare subsistence from wretched plots of land, and lived in huts: 'compare this picture, which I know to be a true one, with the present state of the same country; the workers earning nearly double their former wages, their houses mainly new and comfortable, and the lands, roads and every other circumstance bearing evident marks of the most pleasing and rapid improvements'. Most fortunate of all were the handloom weavers. The great increase in the quantity of yarn spun by machinery produced towards the end of the century, and the expanding market for cloth, particularly cotton, had led to a keen demand for their services; they could earn twenty-five shillings a week, or more.

'The unvarying regularity of the complex automaton'

Already, though, there were signs that industrialisation was going to create its own problems for society; the most pressing of them being the demands that the new machines were making on those who had to tend them.

As soon as ways had been found to apply water power to drive the new spinning machines, the geography of the cotton industry had begun to alter. Employers, realising that the best place for a mill was by some fast-flowing stream, went to the Pennines, or to Scotland, to set up their establishments. But labour was scarce in such districts; nor was it easy to recruit workers willing to accept factory life. As Richard Arkwright—one of the original inventors, and the first large-scale entrepreneur in the cotton industry—complained, it was difficult to train human beings 'to renounce their desultory habits of work, and identify themselves with the unvarying regularity of the complex automaton'. To be efficiently used, the complex automaton required to be constantly watched; and few countrymen or women relished the idea of spending ten or more hours a day shut up in a factory watching a machine. High wages would have been an inducement; but to offer high wages would have been to lose the very advantage—low production costs—which machinery offered. Besides, it seemed ridiculous to offer high wages for unskilled work, which a child could do.

Which a child could do . . . well, and why not? The effects of Hanway's intervention on behalf of workhouse children were beginning to be felt. Hundreds more of them were surviving infancy every year. Here, then, was a ready source of labour—and a very welcome one. The children, provided with employment, would be rescued from pauperism; and the ratepayers would be relieved of their part of the burden. So mill-owners began to appear in London, visiting parish officers, and making the necessary arrangements. The children were formally indentured as apprentices, and transferred to their new homes. What happened to them then was nobody's concern. A parish in London, having got rid of a batch of unwanted pauper children, was unlikely to interest itself in their subsequent fate; the ratepayers would not be pleased if it did. No provision was made for inspection of the mills; and whereas it had been possible for a London apprentice who considered himself ill-used to appeal, as a last resort, to the courts, in Lancashire he stood little chance of escaping, for that purpose, from the mill. Nearly half a century later, the miserable existence a child could lead in the mills was to be recalled by one of them, Robert Blincoe; but at the time, there was no suspicion of what was happening.

There were, however, a number of mills near Manchester. Although the town was growing rapidly, it had no corporation to manage its affairs; but it had a bench of magistrates, who occasionally could act on its citizens' behalf. When infectious fever broke out in 1784, at one of the nearby cotton mills, it was the magistrates who were approached, by nervous citizens, to do something. Not knowing what to do, they asked some of the town's doctors to conduct an investigation; among them, Thomas Percival.

Percival was both knowledgeable—the youngest man, it was claimed, ever to be elected a Fellow of the Royal Society—and enlightened; he was the founder of the Manchester Literary and Philosophical Society. What he found in the mill appalled him. Although he and his colleagues were unable to trace the source of the fever, they were in no doubt that it had been 'supported, diffused and aggravated by the ready communication of contagion to numbers crowded together; by the accession to its virulence from putrid effluvia; and by the injury done to young persons through confinement and too long continued labour; to which several evils the cotton mills have given occasion'; and they recommended 'a long recess from labour at noon, and a more early dismission from it in the evening' for all who worked in cotton mills—but particularly to those under the age of fourteen. The magistrates who had called for the enquiry expressed their thanks, and passed a resolution that in future they would not allow any children to be apprenticed to a factory where they would be compelled to work at night, or for more than ten hours in the day—an opinion which they transmitted to the magistrates in adjoining counties.

But there were ways by which an employer could get around this ban, if it were enforced; the easiest being to have his apprentices indentured somewhere else, where the magistrates were less fussy. Ten years later John Aikin, preparing a book on Manchester and its environs, found the factory scene unchanged.

Children of very tender age are employed; many of them collected from the workhouses in London and Westminster, and transported in crowds as apprentices to masters resident many hundred miles distant, where they serve unknown, unprotected and forgotten by those to whose care nature or the laws had consigned them. These children are usually too long confined to work in close rooms, often during the whole night; the air they breathe from the oil, etc., employed in the machinery, and other circumstances, is injurious; little regard is paid to their cleanliness; and frequent changes from a warm and dense to a cold and thin atmosphere are predisposing causes to sickness and disability, and particularly to the epidemic fever which is so generally to be met with in these factories.

In 1795—the year Aikin's book was published—Percival took up the subject again, with the help of the Manchester Board of Health, which he and some friends were instrumental in founding. In its first report, brought out the following year, the Board claimed that its design was 'to prevent the generation of diseases; to obviate the spreading of them by contagion; and to shorten the duration of those which exist'. Their enquiries had revealed that workers in the large cotton factories were particularly susceptible to contagious fever; that factory life was injurious to the workers' health, 'from the debilitating effects of hot or impure air, and from want of the active exercises which nature points out as essential in childhood and youth, to invigorate the system, and to fit our species for the employments and for the duties of manhood'; that night labour, and long hours of work during the day, tended to diminish life expectation, 'impairing the strength and destroying the vital stamina of the rising generation'; and that factory children were generally debarred from all opportunities of education. To remedy these evils—some well-run mills had already proved that they could be remedied—the Board recommended that Parliament should intervene 'to establish a general system of laws for the wise, humane and equal government of all such works'.

That the northern magistrates continued to feel strongly on this issue was shown in 1800, when nearly forty of them from the West Riding of Yorkshire echoed the resolutions made earlier by the Lancashire magistrates. In future, they too would not allow any poor child to be apprenticed to a mill where the hours of work were excessive, or where he might be compelled to do night work. They went further; save in special circumstances, they would no longer allow parish apprentices to be bound to any master resident in another parish; and the condition of all pauper children in their areas was in future to be more carefully scrutinised, 'in order that the justices, who are the legal guardians of such poor children, may the better do their duty, and render the situation of a parish apprentice more comfortably, and less dreaded, than at present'.

But the powers of the magistracy were limited; and Robert Peel, M.P. for Tamworth, and father of the future Prime Minister, decided to introduce a measure to provide more effective protection for pauper apprentices working in cotton mills. Peel was himself a prosperous and humane mill-owner; Aikin had singled out his establishment for 'the particular healthiness of the people employed' which, he thought, could be attributed to 'the judicious and humane regulations put in practice by Mr. Peel'. But this was a consequence of an earlier criticism, which had led Peel to inspect one of his mills. He had been shocked by 'the uniform appearance of bad health, and in many cases the stunted growth, of the children.' An overseer he had left in charge, he found, had introduced payment by amount of work done, thereby forcing the children to work excessive hours. Peel decided to make honorable amends by seeking to prevent such exploitation in future; and in 1802 he introduced his Health and Morals of Apprentices Bill. To enlist clerical support it emphasised the moral danger that lurked in such establishments. Sleeping accommodation for apprentices of different sexes, the bill laid down, must be kept separate; not more than two apprentices were to share the same bed. Apprentices, too, were to be instructed in the Christian faith, and prepared for confirmation between the ages of fourteen and eighteen. Clauses of this kind, even if they were never enforced, would help to ease its passage through Parliament—as would the clause laying down standards of hygiene to be observed in the factory, to ensure cleanliness and airiness, and reduce the risk to the community of outbreaks of infectious disease.

The real test, though, was whether the clause limiting hours would get through—'that no apprentice . . . shall be employed or compelled to work for more than twelve hours in any one day (reckoning from six in the morning to nine at night) exclusive of the time they might be occupied in eating the necessary meals'—and that apprentices should no longer be compelled to do night work. Such interference in the rights of employers was unusual. But it was not unprecedented; the Act giving protection to the climbing boys had demonstrated that Parliament regarded itself as responsible for the protection of all children who were not in their parents' immediate care. The clause was accepted, and the bill passed.

There had been no concerted campaign by the mill-owners against the bill. They were not established men, like the master clothiers; they had no lobby; and the fact that Peel was himself a mill-owner made it difficult for them to claim that they were being ill-used. But individual employers were alarmed—particularly those who had grown accustomed to running their machinery around the clock on a double shift basis; and one of them arranged for a medical report on the health of the children in his mills at Burley, with a view to opening a campaign to have the Act repealed. He asked a well-known Leeds surgeon, William Hey, to visit the mills; and Hey, describing what he saw, expressed himself satisfied that the children's health was not adversely affected by night work. On the strength of his verdict, the manufacturer contended, 'a repeal of the late Act, or a considerable modification of its obnoxious clauses, will appear indispensably necessary to the future success of a great number of persons embarked in the spinning and manufacturing of cotton; who have not only contributed largely to the public revenue but, after having rescued a great number of children from vice and misery, have, at a heavy expense, trained them up in the habits of industry and religion, and rendered them (before, a load upon society) now some of its most useful members'.

The report sounded convincing; but it happened to fall into the hands of a member of the Society for Bettering the Condition and Increasing the Comforts of the Poor. The Society had been founded in 1796 by a group of Evangelicals, following a meeting in Wilberforce's house. Its patron was King George III; its chairman, the Bishop of Durham; among its members were Count Rumford, Patrick Colquhoun, the Earl of Winchilsea, and Henry Addington—soon to succeed Pitt (himself a modest subscriber to the society) as Prime Minister. Such high-powered bodies are not necessarily efficient, but in this case the Secretary was Sir Thomas Bernard, a man on the Hanway model, with a shrewd critical eye, and a capacity for getting other people involved in the Society actually to work for it. A committee of enquiry was set up to investigate Surgeon Hey's investigation, and it reported a few weeks later. The members of the committee, its report claimed, were aware of the importance of the cotton industry, and realised that 'a body of men so respectable as those manufacturers who, at the same time that they have made princely fortunes for themselves, have added fresh resources to the strength and prosperity of their country, must always be entitled to respect and attention'. Nevertheless, the committee could not help feeling that some of the arguments which the manufacturer had used were destructive of his own case. For example, he maintained that apprentices must be used at night, because 'free labourers cannot be obtained to perform night work, except on very disadvantageous terms to the manufacturers'. Whatever the disadvantage to the manufacturers, the committee felt, 'it is evidently cruel and unjust that the poor orphan, or the deserted child, should be *compelled* to do that night work which the free labourer cannot, on any practicable or moderate terms, be *induced* to undertake'.

It was also unwise of the manufacturer, the report went on, to suggest that if the magistrates used the very limited powers given them under Peel's Act, 'all subordination will be at an end; let the visitors conduct themselves as with what discretion they may, the mills and factories will become a scene either of idleness and disorder, or of open rebellion'. This came oddly, the Committee thought from a manufacturer who had based his own case on the report of an investigator—the surgeon Hey. Surely the subordination of the apprentices could only be *preserved* by the watchfulness of the magistrates, under whose control they had been placed?

In any case, the committee observed, Hey's report, though favourable, made some disquieting admissions. The apprentices who were on night shift might stay on it for as long as four or five years, without a break. Their hours were from seven in the evening until six in the morning; and although they were provided with dinner at midnight, the machinery did not stop; and they had to take their food as best they could, in period of inactivity. 'Now, if', the committee concluded,

we were to read in the history of some part of Asia or Africa an account of children who, from seven to twelve years, or from eight to thirteen years of age, were doomed to *unceasing labour every night*, without the glad and natural return of day – without a few minutes of respite for their meals – and (in the winter half year at least), without even an half hour for relaxation, which is the comfort of mature age, but the essential possession of the young – should we not *shudder* at the perusal? Should we give very willing credit to any detail that was subjoined, of the *health* and *happiness* of these children? And if (to pursue the consideration) the government of the country should have prepared for the progressive emancipation of these children, at the end of two years, what language should we hold as to those, who would unite to prevent their receiving the benefit of so just and politic a law?

Thereafter members of the society periodically visited and inspected mills, reporting back on them to its headquarters. From their reports, three main points emerged. Contrary to the assertion of some manufacturers, it was not essential to have apprentices; some of the most efficient factories did not employ them. The term 'apprenticeship' was in any case a misnomer; as one of the reports put it, 'we cannot consider cotton spinning as a *trade*; at best, not such a trade, the learning of which can secure an independent provision when the apprentice is out of his time'. And although some mill-owners observed the provisions of the Act, millowners who chose to ignore it could do so with impunity. 'No attention whatever is paid to the Act of Parliament', a member of the society complained, perhaps because provision had not been made for their mills to be inspected.

'In the employment of a vast capital'

Peel's Act, in other words, although it had confirmed that the State could intervene to protect apprentices working in factories, did not provide them with effective protection; and it gave no protection to child workers who were not apprentices, let alone to adults. And the way things were going, the chances that Parliament could be persuaded to give such protection were dwindling with every year that passed.

Long before the appearance of *The Wealth of Nations*, the old rules and customs which had regulated wages and conditions in the mercantilist era had begun to disintegrate. The magistracy had some powers to fix wages and conditions, but they were ill-defined; and wage bargaining was generally left, as Adam Smith insisted it ought to be, to the higgling of the market place. There were, however, associations of employers trying to keep down wages, and combinations of workmen, trying to push them up—and he disapproved of both.

The combinations, embryo trade unions, were mostly of skilled and semi-skilled workers, artisans and craftsmen; and unluckily for their prospects, they had become identified in the mind of Pitt and his ministers, through their links with the corresponding societies, with Jacobinism. When in the late 1790s they began to use their strength to try to secure wage increases to offset the rising cost of living, their employers had no difficulty in persuading Pitt that combinations represented a threat to the national security; his fears being reflected in (and also aroused by) the *Anti-Jacobin*, which began to appear in 1797 with

George Canning as its chief contributor, and Gillray as cartoonist. Canning's *The Needy Knife-Grinder* was to remain familiar through many a collection of humorous or satirical verse; appearing, to the casual eye, no more than engaging mockery of the woolly philanthropist. But it was less amiable than it now looks. The 'Friend of Humanity' who tries to put ideas into the knife-grinder's head,

> Did some great man tyrannically use you?
> Was it the squire, or parson of the parish?
> Or the attorney?

goes on to ask the knife-grinder if he has read Paine's *Rights of Man*—a question which takes on a different meaning when it is recalled that Paine had been outlawed for writing it only five years before, and that anybody caught selling it could be held guilty of sedition. In Canning's postscript, too, when the Friend of Humanity has kicked the knife-grinder and overturned his wheel, he leaves 'in a transport of Republican enthusiasm and universal philanthropy'—a linkage which the *Anti-Jacobin* propagated as sedulously as, in the 1960s, the John Birch Society was to equate liberalism with communism.

In the prevailing political atmosphere, Pitt was able to push through Acts designed to put a summary end to the combinations—which Wilberforce claimed were a disease of society. When Pitt proposed not merely to make it illegal for workers to join a combination to try to increase wages or to shorten hours of work, but also to make it a crime even to attend a meeting for that purpose, Wilberforce's comment was that he had not gone far enough. In the commons, only Sheridan protested at the removal of the workers' right to ask for trial by jury; instead, they were to be automatically liable to summary proceedings in a magistrate's court. Pitt replied that summary trial was in the workers' interest: 'it would save them time, trouble and expense'.

Once again, Pitt used the principles of political economy to justify himself; combinations of workmen were an attempt to upset the natural workings of the labour market. For form's sake, employers' combinations were banned, too. But Adam Smith had been careful to emphasise that formally banning combinations of employers was not enough: it was too easy for them to reach wage or price agreements among themselves in secret. The warning was not heeded in Pitt's measure; the Combination Acts of 1798 and 1799 were, in fact, the first indication of how easily Adam Smith's principles could be bent by a government for the benefit of employers. And ministers and employers were assured of the co-operation of the courts. 'Justice was entirely out of the question', Francis Place was to recall; workers accused of combining 'could seldom obtain a hearing, before a magistrate; never without impatience or insult'. Had a record been kept of the trials, at all levels, 'the gross injustice, the foul invective, and terrible punishments inflicted would not, after a few years had passed away, be credited'; and as a result, workers in many industries, particularly in cotton manufacture, 'were reduced to, and kept in, the most wretched state'. Soon, there were few prosecutions of workers for combining. If they combined at all, they were careful to keep their organisation underground.

But Parliament was still confronted with the need to make some decisions about the future of wage-bargaining in industry. Granted that there was to be no State interference; ought there nevertheless to be some assistance to the two sides to reach wage agreements, and ensure they were kept? Ought the traditional regulations and customs designed to preserve the quality of products to be preserved, or, if necessary, revived? And was the apprenticeship system really necessary when, as in the cotton industry, the apprentice was in fact being exploited simply as cheap labour, learning no useful trade?

For a time, the Government made an effort to assist employers and journeymen to reach wage agreements, and to keep them, in the hope that this would improve industrial relations—and encourage trade. An Act of 1800 laid down that in any dispute over wage rates in the cotton industry, the employer and the journeyman were each entitled to appoint an arbitrator; and if the arbitrators failed to reach agreement, the case could be referred to a magistrate. It very soon became clear, though, that the Act was not going to be a success. Workers would try to bully an employer by each bringing forward separate arbitration actions; to which the employers had found an ingenious way of retaliating, by nominating as their arbitrators men who lived a hundred miles away or more—knowing that the workers were unlikely to be able to travel that distance; knowing, too, that the magistracy could not be invoked, because a magistrate was only to be called upon if arbitration had failed, and it could not be said to have failed if it had not even begun.

If the arbitration scheme failed, ministers did not have to worry, so long as the journeymen did not take it into their heads to resort to conspiracy, and violence, to get their higher wages. But the question whether the State ought, or ought not, to intervene to protect standards proved more difficult to settle. When in 1802 rioting broke out in the west country over the use of machines to raise the 'nap' on woollen cloth, it was found that there were old statutes, not repealed, forbidding the practice; and Parliament, at the request of the master clothiers, had to pass a measure suspending the old laws, until it could decide how best to replace them.

The issue seemed simple enough. The journeymen claimed that they did not object to the introduction of machinery as such—it had vastly improved the standards of the weavers in the cotton industry, and might do the same in wool. Their objection was to the use of machinery, minded by 'apprentices', to make spurious imitations of their products; for this reduced their earnings to below the subsistence level. It was difficult for M.P.s to ignore this complaint; on the other hand, they had no desire to set up the kind of civil service organisation that would be required to maintain standards by inspection—the nearest equivalent, the excisemen, were expensive and detested. So recourse was had to delaying tactics; a committee of inquiry was set up in 1804, but too late in the session for there to be any chance for a bill to be introduced and passed on the basis of whatever recommendations it might make.

The same thing happened in 1805, and might have happened again in 1806, if the suspicions of the journeymen had not been aroused. Early in the session they petitioned Parliament, pointing out that as the 'temporary' suspension of all the old regulations was very much in the employers' interest, they were deliberately stalling; 'during each succeeding session, they waited until near its close, and then urged the want of time for investigation as a ground for their soliciting a further bill of suspension'. Would M.P.s kindly make up their mind what they wanted to be done?

As it was no longer wise to prevaricate, the committee was reconstituted in time to produce a report; and it laid down the guidelines of future parliamentary policy not merely for wool, but for industry in general. The journeymen, the report claimed, might pretend that they were worried about the way machinery was being used to make cheap and shoddy imitations of their handiwork; but this was not the real reason for their concern. What was alarming them was that machinery, fairly used, would put them out of work. On the evidence, though, this fear had been shown to be baseless. The rapid expansion of industry meant that labour was easily absorbed; and this expansion was 'principally to be ascribed to the general spirit of enterprise among a free and enlightened people, left to the unrestrained exercise of their talents in the employment of a vast capital, pushing to the utmost the principle of the division of labour'. Only by leaving these forces free to do what the market demanded could the country's prosperity be ensured; because if the State intervened, Britain was surrounded by powerful nations 'who are the more eager to become our competitors in trade from having witnessed the astonishing effects of our commercial prosperity'. Should any regulation be made restricting the use of machines in Britain, 'they would infallibly find their way into foreign nations'. The committee accordingly recommended that all restrictive legislation should be repealed.

On the subject of apprentices, though, the report was more sympathetic to the journeymen—at first sight. If apprenticeship simply meant the employment of children in jobs, rather than training them for a trade when they grew up, it was obviously outmoded. It should no longer be compulsory. But it need not be abolished. In other words—as Peter Moore, the nearest the House of Commons had at the time to a radical M.P., complained—where it was a nuisance to an employer to have apprentices, he could refuse to accept them; but where he needed cheap labour, he could continue to employ them. As Moore explained when he secured a debate on the subject in 1807, employers were realising that in industries where machinery had promoted the division of labour, there were many jobs which a boy could be quickly taught to do as well as a journeyman; and as an apprentice cost between four and seven shillings a week, compared to the twenty-five shillings that had been the journey-man's wage, there was a standing temptation to employ as many appren-tices as possible. Far from learning a trade, though, the apprentice actually deprived himself of an adult livelihood; 'as soon as a boy was out of his apprenticeship, he also found himself out of bread'—unless he undertook to continue to accept an apprentice's wage. Supporting Moore, Sheridan claimed that he knew of one master who employed fifty apprentices in this way, and only two journeymen; and he turned on the parliamentary lawyers who were opposing the motion on the ground that legislation was unnecessary—if 'by some chemical or philosophical process' little boys and girls were able to practice at the Bar, he was sure that there would be 'more clamour from the gentlemen of the long robe in Westminster Hall, than from all the combining manufacturers of Lancashire put together'.

But the Commons declined to listen. When, in 1809, the Acts controlling the woollen trade, annually suspended since 1803, were finally repealed, no regulations were put in their place. A clause was added, though, that nothing in the Act should annul any contract 'whereby any person shall have bound, or shall bind to himself, an apprentice in any branch of the woollen trade'. Apprenticeship in its original purpose of improving craftsmanship, and affording the workers in an industry some protection, was abandoned. But apprenticeship of a kind which would make it easier for an employer to exploit child labour— that was to be permitted to continue.

As for wage regulation, by this time it had become apparent that the Commons were no longer prepared even to consider it. In 1807, admittedly, a committee was set up to investigate a handloom weavers' petition for a minimum wage, following a trade recession which had greatly reduced their earnings. But this was for show. It met only six times, before reporting that a minimum wage was 'wholly inadmissible in principle; incapable of being introduced in practice by any means which can possibly be devised; and, if practicable, would be productive of the most fatal consequences'; and the debate on a later motion in favour of a minimum wage was used mainly by members to explain, on economic principles, why it would be both impracticable and fatal.

The Commons, in fact, had moved far from Adam Smith. He had warned Parliament against heeding employers, when they begged it to leave them to run industry their way, if they could combine, openly or secretly, to run it for their own profit. Now, it was doing just this. They could fix wages; they could scrap old standards of quality and workmanship; and they could exploit child labour, on the ground that it was necessary to reduce costs in order to increase exports—another excuse that Smith had specifically warned Parliament to reject. But Parliament was ignoring his warnings. The last of the effective controls which it had retained were being dismantled.

5. LUDDISM

It was easy to understand why Parliament was renouncing authority over industry. Few M.P.s had any first-hand, or even second-hand, knowledge of industrial problems; they were either themselves members of a landowning aristocracy, or its nominees. If, as they were now continually being assured on apparently the best economic authority, it was wise to leave industry to run itself, so much the better—so long as the system led to no obvious ill effects. But agriculture was a different matter. The acceptance of allowances from the rates in aid of wages was—or so it had been assumed—a temporary expedient, to tide the labourers over an unprecedentedly difficult period. The beneficial effects of enclosures and consolidation of farms should surely, on Eden's evidence, begin to make itself felt, providing more employment, and reducing the rates. But although there was a temporary improvement, it did not last. At the turn of the century the price of bread rose again; and the labourers' condition again began to appear desperate.

Arthur Young had been one of the most ardent supporters of the enclosure system. In the days when he had been making his reputation, though not his fortune, as a commentator on the agricultural scene, he had taken a hard-headed line on the subject, even to the point of arguing that it did not matter whether the poor benefited or not; everybody but an idiot, he had asserted, knew that the poor must be kept poor, or they would cease to be industrious. He had also been one of the most vehement of the anti-Jacobins—his appointment as Secretary to the Board of Agriculture, in fact, was commonly attributed to the event which, he was to claim, created a greater impression than anything else he did in his life; his proposal that property owners ought to form themselves into a militia, for their mutual protection, and for the protection of their country. But in his capacity as Secretary to the Board he began to realise that enclosures were simply not giving the results he had expected. His conversion was gradual, but it seems to have been precipitated by the death of a much loved daughter in 1797. The experience softened Young, and made him look at the lives led by poor families with a more compassionate eye. What he saw on a tour he made of East Anglia in 1800 shocked him. Asked to visit a poor woman in a cottage, he found her condition

> poor indeed! the cottage almost tumbling down, the wind blowing through it on every side. On a bed which was hardly good enough for a hog, was the woman very ill and moaning; she had been lately brought to bed, and her infant was dead in a cradle by the bedside . . . my heart sank within me at the sight of so much misery, and so dark, cold, tattered and wretched a room.

What impressed Arthur Young was not just the misery, but that it was unnecessary. There was waste land—or simply unused land—available, which if cultivated would have produced enough food to keep the poor from starvation, or from the workhouse. But so little did the landowners care that often the poor did not even know who the land belonged to.

These poor people know not by what tenure they hold their lands; they say they once belonged to the duke, but that the duke has swopped them away to Lord Ossory. How little do the great know what they swop, and what they receive . . . what a field is here! How very trifling the repairs to render those poor families warm and comfortable! Above their gardens on one side there is a waste fern tract now enclosed, from which small additions might be given them, yet would enable them to live from their ground at least much better than at present. What have not great and rich people to answer, for not examining into the situation of their poor neighbours?

After his tour, Young wrote *An Inquiry into the propriety of applying wastes to the maintenance and support of the poor,* which made it clear why he had shifted his ground. Wherever he had gone, he had asked what the effect of enclosures had been on the poor; and in the great majority of parishes he had heard 'highly injurious', or some such reply. It was not enclosures that were at fault, he emphasised; it was the fact that the compensation for them had been inadequate, and of the wrong kind—money, rather than land.

The whole enclosure system, Young had come to realise, was rigged by the landowners for their own benefit. Before an enclosure could be made, a board of commissioners was appointed to decide whether the land should be enclosed, and how much compensation should be paid to the cottagers affected. But the cottager usually had no representatives to put his case, either to the commission or in Parliament, when the enclosure bill was presented. He had little or no weight, Young pointed out, 'in regulating the clauses of the Act of Parliament; has seldom if ever the opportunity of putting a single one in the Bill favourable to his rights; and has as little influence in the choice of commissioners; of consequence, they have seldom any great inducement to be attentive to his interest'. As those commissioners were appointed by the landowners themselves 'every passion of resentment and prejudice may be gratified without control, for they are vested with a despotic power known to no other branch of business in this free country'. There was an appeal to the courts—but as the court in question was Chancery, the remedy, Young felt, was as bad as the disease. In any case, the costs would be taken out of the fund available for compensation: so the villagers might end up worse off even if they won.

It was really in everybody's interest—including the landowner's—Young concluded, that the labourers should be given back some land. They could only be expected to be frugal and industrious if they had the prospect of acquiring it, and the hope of preserving it—for what other motive had they to save? For the ratepayers, the advantage was obvious; parishes were 'at as great an expense to keep them in a state of distress as would fix them in a comfortable situation'. And experience showed that where the labourers were provided with land, the results were strikingly beneficial.

'Let us investigate practically'

That this was not just wishful thinking on Young's part was confirmed by the parallel investigations of the Society for Bettering the Condition of the Poor. Under Sir Thomas Bernard's shrewd guidance, it was concentrating its attention and resources not on charitable activities, but on tying to find out why the poor were in such a condition of distress (the term almost invariably employed at the time, in a wider sense than it is now, to convey the state in which the poor were living, as well as how they felt about it); and what, if anything, could be done for them. 'Let us investigate *practically*', Bernard urged, 'and upon *system*'. He took pains to find out what methods were used in foreign countries—enlisting the help of Count Rumford, who had set up his own system in Bavaria, by which, he claimed, 'mendicity was completely abolished', and for which he had been made a Papal Count. But Bernard's chief concern was to attempt to test out the hypotheses of the time. His invariable question was, 'Does it *work?*'; and, wherever possible, he tried to establish the answer by experiment.

One of the Society's investigations compared the condition of labourers who had land, and those who did not. This was not as difficult as it might appear, as the experiment had, in a sense, already been set up for them; for in a few cases, Enclosure Acts had contained clauses providing cottagers with gardens or plots of land in compensation. The Dilhorn Enclosure Act of 1781 had made this provision; and when Bernard visited the estate sixteen years later he was told by the landowner that he could hardly recall any cottager who had afterwards been compelled to apply for poor relief.

Whenever Bernard or other members of the society investigated estates of this kind, they heard the same story. One of the papers read to the society, for example, was from Lord Winchilsea 'On the advantage of cottagers renting land', in which he described how on his estate in Rutland there were from seventy to eighty labourers, each of whom kept from one to four cows. They managed their land well, and paid their rents regularly: 'from what I have seen of them, I am more and more confirmed in the opinion I have long had, that nothing is so beneficial both to them and to the landowners as their having land to be occupied either for the keeping of cows, or as gardens, according to circumstances... By means of these advantages the labourers and their families live better, and are consequently more fit to endure labour; they are more contented and more attached to their situation, and acquire a sort of independence which makes them set a higher value upon their character.' And in the parishes where the labourers had plots, Lord Winchilsea added, the poor rates were only sixpence in the pound, or less.

By contrast, Bernard observed, anybody travelling through the midlands and making enquiries, as he had done, would hear of a great many cottagers who had formerly kept cows, but whose land had been thrown to the farmers; 'and if he enquires still further he will find that, in those parishes, the poor rates have increased in an amazing degree'. The reason, Bernard explained, why the possession of even a small plot could make so great a difference was that land cultivated as a garden could produce a greater quantity of food than any other method; and, as much of the work could be done by the farmer's wife and by his children, there need be no fear that the labourer would spend too much of his time on it, and too little on his employer's farm.

As Secretary to the Board of Agriculture, and with such high-powered support, Arthur Young had high hopes that he would be able to convince the Government of the desirability of his scheme—a simple one, originally presented in 1800 in his *The Question of Scarcity plainly stated*, in which he suggested that 'the means which would of all others perhaps tend most surely to prevent future scarcities, and oppression of the poor as at present, would be to secure to every country labourer in the kingdom that has three children and upward, half an acre of land for potatoes and grass enough to feed one or two cows'—the potatoes being a safeguard against a poor harvest of corn. To his chagrin, he found that his scheme aroused little interest; and among landowners, antipathy. 'Everybody', he complained in his journal, 'is against it.'

Young was in no doubt where the responsibility lay. Practical experience might show that the condition of labourers would be improved if they were provided with plots of land to grow potatoes, and grass on which to graze a cow; 'but Adam Smith prevailed; political principles were thought more nourishing'. This was unfair to Adam Smith, who had not had occasion to pronounce on the subject. And although landowners and M.P.s were indeed citing political economy, they were relying increasingly for their authority not on Smith, but on Malthus.

'How flat the subject is'

The most striking testimony to Malthus's rapidly-growing influence was presented during the brief life of the coalition ministry which took office in 1806, following the death of Pitt: 'All the Talents' with Lord Grenville as Prime Minister and Fox as Foreign Secretary.

As a loyal follower of Fox, Samuel Whitbread thought he deserved a ministerial post more elevated than any he was offered; and he elected to stay on the back benches. But he had influence with ministers; and it occurred to him that he might use it to revive his plan for poor law reform.

He had already made one attempt to revive the Commons' interest in the subject in 1800. His earlier bill, he reminded members, had not been defeated; it had been set aside because Pitt had promised a more systematic revision of the poor laws. But Pitt's measure had been rejected; so he felt he must bring up his own again. All he wanted was that magistrates should be allowed to set a minimum wage. It would not ordinarily be necessary for them to do so; but in bad times, it could be invoked to compel the farmers to do their duty. But Pitt, though saying that he would not oppose, again criticised the project on the grounds that it was contrary to the principles of political economy; 'it went to introduce legislative interference into that which ought to be allowed invariably to take its natural course'—the greater the freedom allowed to every kind of mercantile transaction, the more all parties would benefit. Whitbread's bill attracted no support, and was dropped.

Since 1800, though, there had been Arthur Young's change of heart, and the investigations of the Society for Bettering the Condition of the Poor; and also, perhaps even more significant, George Rose's pamphlet *Observations on the Poor Laws*, which appeared in 1805. Rose had been Pitt's closest political associate, the go-between whom Pitt used to manage his supporters; he was also a friend of, and occasional host to, King George III. His influence was much greater than his comparatively minor Government post at the Board of Trade suggested. He was also genuinely concerned about the condition of the poor: he had, in fact, been responsible for one of the very few remedial measures to reach the Statute book—an Act to encourage labourers to join friendly societies, by laying down that labourers who were members would not be removable from the parish in which they were living, until they actually became a charge on the rates.

From his *Observations*, it was clear that Rose was aware of the gravity of the situation, both for the labourers and the ratepayers. In 1803, he pointed out, the rates were twice as high as they had been in 1783; more than three times higher than in 1776. Yet at the same time the value of land, as measured in rent, had greatly increased. Rose did not present any solution, but he insisted that one must be found: relief of the poor was required by religion and humanity, but 'no less obviously required by the plainest dictates of good policy'.

Rose, in other words, was rejecting the Malthusian theory. And he was so well dug in politically (he had amassed a remarkable collection of sinecures; when he died in 1817 the *Black Dwarf* listed them, ranging from Treasurer of the Navy to Verderer of the New Forest) that even after Pitt's death, his help—which he had promised—would have been invaluable to Whitbread in getting through some compact, simple reform. But Whitbread had more ample ideas. He wanted an Act by which he would be remembered; and he wanted to make sure that it would be remembered as his. He did not even seek the Government's help in drafting his measure, excusing himself to Charles Grey, who had been given office, on the ground that 'knowing how flat the subject is' he had not wished to bother ministers; all he wanted from them was 'a patient and candid hearing'. So he could take full responsibility when he introduced what he described as 'one of the most interesting propositions which ever occupied the attention of any deliberate assembly upon earth'— nothing less than an attempt to solve that most difficult of political problems, 'how to reduce the sum of vice and misery, and how to augment that of human happiness and virtue amongst the subjects of this realm'.

The sum of vice and misery . . . the words already had a familiar ring. Why, Whitbread asked, had the condition of the poor declined, and the rates risen? Fortunately they now knew why: 'one philosopher in particular has arisen among us, who has gone deeply into the causes of our present situation. I mean Mr. Malthus'. By elucidating the principles of population—principles which, Whitbread believed, were incontrovertible —Malthus had explained why it was that the poor laws had been productive of more wretchedness than they relieved.

Whitbread's bill showed how complete his conversion had been; he had even abandoned his earlier proposal for a minimum wage. And he admitted that many people shared Malthus's view that the poor laws ought to go—this, in fact, seemed to him to be now the prevailing sentiment. The trouble was that their repeal would create a formidable risk of convulsion. Even Malthus's proposal for the tapering off of relief, Whitbread felt, was unacceptable; to create two classes of poor, one entitled to relief, the other not, would be 'pregnant with cruelty'. No, the poor laws could not simply be repealed; it was necessary, he had decided, to look for ways to render them obsolete, by elevating the character of the working classes, so that they would become aware of the necessity of exercising moral restraint.

The proposals which Whitbread presented for this purpose revealed his confusion of mind. Some of them were based on Pitt's, of ten years before; plots of land for labourers; encouragement for savings societies; training schools for the children of the poor; reform of the Act of Settlement. Some were administrative; votes at vestry meetings should be weighted, Whitbread proposed, according to the value of the ratepayer's property. Some were simply naïve: merit awards for labourers who exercised due moral restraint; and for the undeserving labourer, 'a badge denoting his crime, with the name of the parish, in large letters, on his outer garment'.

Rose could not support such a bill—nor, it soon became clear, could it expect any support, as it stood; Whitbread realised he would have to withdraw it, and try to get through some of the individual proposals piecemeal. But his testimonial gave Malthus just the opportunity he was waiting for: in his *Letter to Samuel Whitbread* he presented what was ostensibly a commentary on the bill, but in reality provided an appendix to the second edition of the *Essay on Population;* covering tracks which, in the light of criticisms, Malthus had begun to regret having left. His earlier stark warning to the pauper, for example—'at nature's mighty feast there is no vacant cover for him'—Malthus explained, had been misunderstood. What he had intended to convey was merely (as Eden put it) 'it may be doubted whether any right, the gratification of which seems to be impractable, can be said to exist'. Were it possible to avoid the depression of the independent labourers, Malthus insisted, he would be the first to ask that those who were actually in want, should be most liberally relieved.

He also made what amounted to an even more striking climb-down—though again, few readers would have realised its significance. If his theory was correct, a rising birth rate could have been expected in those areas where family allowances were being provided. But investigation had shown that this was not necessarily the case. As the law of population could not be wrong, 'the difficulty of procuring habitations' must be the reason. It was hard on the poor to be deprived of cottages, but the question had to be faced whether it was not better for them in the long run that this scarcity existed. As things were, only one eighth, or one seventh, of the population were paupers; whereas if adequate accommodation were available, one third or one half might be reduced to that undesirable condition. Give the labourer a cottage, and he would be tempted to marry; better, therefore, that he should be left to live in squalor.

This represented a break from the earlier attitude of political economists. Even Eden approved of labourers having some land—a plot, or at least a garden. But on the Malthusian interpretation, it must in the long term have unfortunate results. It might improve their immediate prospects; it might keep them from having to apply for relief, and so temporarily reduce the rates. But as it would encourage them to breed, the population pressure on resources would soon again be felt. And so it came about that the law of population began to be used against any kind of measure, except education, to improve the condition of the poor— not because it had been Malthus's original thesis, but because, backed into a corner by his critics, he had been compelled to find a way round them.

'Commerce has been tripled; and so have the parish paupers'

The return of the old Whigs to office in the ministry of All the Talents, Grey among them, had encouraged the hope that there might be a revival of the parliamentary reform movement, cleansed of its Jacobin taint; and during the year it was in office, greater freedom of expression was permitted in the newspapers, and on the hustings. In 1807 two radicals, Sir Francis Burdett and Admiral Cochrane, were returned to Parliament for the constituency of Westminster, following a campaign shrewdly stage-managed by Francis Place.

In his youth, Place had known what it was like to try to live in London after losing his job, following an abortive journeyman's strike against the master tailors. While he was out of work, a son had died of smallpox, and the workhouse had never been more than a few days ahead. 'Persons who have never been in such circumstances', he was mildly to recall, 'can form but faint ideas of the misery even the best and most frugal workmen sometimes endure'. As a former member of Hardy's

Corresponding Society, too, Place had lived for a time under the threat of a charge of sedition, with transportation or execution the likely consequence of an adverse verdict. But it was not the ministers, he had decided, who were to blame; it was the system, political and economic, in which they operated. And before the system could be changed, it would be necessary to secure a reformed House of Commons, more representative of the people—to get rid of the rotten boroughs, where a handful of voters could sell the seat to the highest bidder.

In this view, Place found allies in the disciples of Adam Smith; particularly Bentham and James Mill. Mill regarded it as intolerable that Parliament and the Government should be dominated by landowners and their nominees, unable to appreciate political economy and determined to cling to their rights and their privileges; and Bentham's views on electoral reform were those of Cartwright—still on the scene, though he was coming to be regarded as an old fogey by the younger radicals: among them Henry Hunt, a farmer who appealed to his country constituency to do what Westminster had done, and return radicals to Parliament. Spence, too, was still propounding his thesis that land should be communalised. In his *Restorer of Society to its Natural State,* published in 1800, he had insisted that there was no chance of seeing 'anything else than the utmost screwing and grinding of the poor' until the system of landed proprietors had been got rid of. 'Anything short of total destruction of the power of these Samsons', he urged, 'will not do'—a view that was attracting a small but dedicated group of disciples.

But the radical who was rapidly acquiring the biggest following around the country was William Cobbett. His credentials were unusual. His father had been a smallholder, and kept a wayside inn; his mother could neither read nor write; but their son, by his own account, began to acquire literary tastes at the age of eleven, through reading Swift's *Tale of a Tub.* He was to make effective use of them. Service in the army took him to North America, and later he returned there for a while to emulate Paine as a polemicist. His views, though, were diametrically opposed to Paine's (or so he believed). As 'Peter Porcupine' he was the scourge of democrats and Jacobins. When he returned to England in 1800 he found his fame had preceded him. William Windham, the friend of Johnson and of Burke, had him to dinner to meet Pitt, Canning, and other members of the Government; at long last, the Tories thought, they had a journalist who would be able to give them effective support.

For a while, he did. His *Political Register,* when it appeared in 1802, was an immediate success. But very soon, Cobbett became disillusioned with the England that he found on his return. From one end of the country to the other, he complained, he found the houses in which families like his own had dwelt falling into ruin. Most of their windows had been blocked up (to save payment of window tax) 'leaving just light enough for some labourer—whose father was, perhaps, a small farmer—to look upon his half-naked and half-famished children while, from his door, he surveys all around him, land teeming with the means of luxury to his opulent and overgrown master'.

Such opinions naturally dissatisfied his own patrons; and they afforded amusement to those who remembered Cobbett in his 'Peter Porcupine' phase. Cobbett refused to be disconcerted: 'You may cry Jacobin and Leveller so long as you please', he replied; 'I wish to see the poor men of England what the poor men of England were when I was born, and from endeavouring to accomplish this wish, nothing but the want of the means shall make me desist.'

The cause of the decay of the countryside, he decided, was to be found in the economic system introduced by Pitt to find the money to pay for the war. The financiers who could afford to lend it, and the employers who enriched themselves at the taxpayer's expense by providing the materials of war, were using some of their new wealth to buy land—not for its own sake, but simply as a speculation. For the fate of the men who had made their living off the land, either as smallholders or as labourers, the speculator had no concern. As a result the workers on the land, so far from benefiting from its increasing value, actually suffered from it. England, he feared, was moving rapidly towards a state when there would only be two classes of men: masters, and slaves.

By 1806, Cobbett's last connection with ministers had been severed; he had linked up with Place (though their relationship was never to be very cordial) and he presented himself, without success, as a candidate for Parliament in the radical interest. When the Tories returned to office after the interlude of All the Talents, they found that their former supporter had become their most trenchant and influential critic. The *Register* acquired the largest circulation of any newspaper in the country, and it was read by thousands who could not afford to become subscribers, copies being passed from neighbour to neighbour, or studied in coffee houses. Cobbett propounded two main themes: that the oligarchy which ruled the country was trading on its aristocratic background, but was in practice not fulfilling the traditional functions of an aristocracy; and

(*Top*) Child labour, eighteenth century: ropemaking.
(*Below*) Interior of the general mixed workhouse, Clerkenwell, 1809.

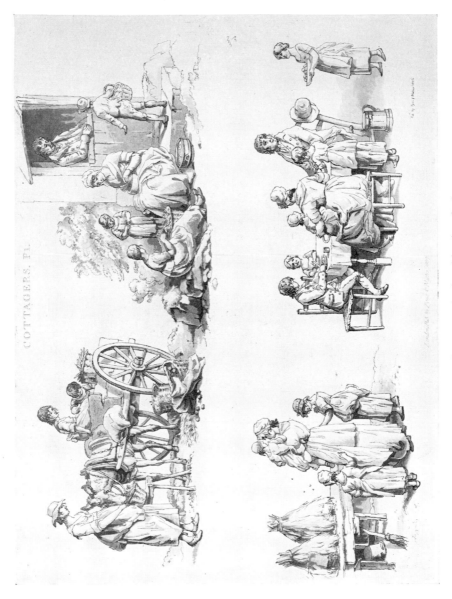

Cottagers, from Pyne's sketchbook, 1806.

that the new wealth provided by machinery, in the factory or on the farm, ought not to be considered wealth from the point of view of the workers, as they got no benefit from it; they could not afford the goods which the machines produced. Those goods were exported, in trade; and trade was considered so important that wars were fought to preserve it. But of what use was it to clothe foreigners, while English children went inadequately clad? And why, if trade was so valuable, did it bring so little back to the people? 'You have seen commerce tripled since the fatal day when Pitt became minister; and have you found your taxes have not been increased? Commerce has been tripled; and so have the parish paupers.'

Cobbett's pugnacious style put off some radicals who shared his opinions; but Mill had to admit that his arguments were frequently shrewd, in spite of the fact that they were based on intuition rather than on reason. In particular, Mill thought, Cobbett had 'assumed the patronage of the poor, at a time when they are depressed below the place which they have fortunately held in this country for a century, and when the current of our policy runs to depress them still further'. Tory ministers were less disposed to be tolerant. They loathed journalists—and with some reason, as their correspondence revealed; journalists were the most persistent and obnoxious of the whole swarming venal tribe of would-be placemen and pensioners, forever pointing out how they and their newspapers could help the Government, if only it would help them and their newspapers. In the past ministers had found it possible to control them with the help of financial inducements; but Cobbett was now doing too well with his *Register* for there to be any hope of winning him over. The alternative was prosecution. In 1809 Cobbett, in what he regarded as justifiable patriotic anger, denounced the use of a guard of Hessian mercenaries during the flogging of English soldiers. He was indicted for sedition, heavily fined, and sentenced to two years in jail.

'Subjected to the most unexampled privations'

But there was a potentially more serious threat to the Government than Cobbett: industrial action. By appointing a committee to investigate the handloom weavers' petition for a minimum wage, and then by debating the subject, the Government had hoped to show its concern; all that it had managed to show was that it was determined not to intervene. The weavers decided to take action themselves; a week after the bill was rejected, they went on strike. They turned out to be unexpectedly

D

well-disciplined. Where a weaver preferred to continue to work, he would be 'visited' and advised to desist; if he was recalcitrant, the shuttle would be removed from his loom. The strike was for an increase of one third in their earnings—not so grasping as it sounds, as the intention was to restore their former wage level. A few weavers were proceeded against under the Combination Acts, but the strike was generally successful, their wages, it was estimated, rising by around twenty per cent.

What was not realised at the time was that the increase had been granted mainly because trade was beginning to pick up; clothing manufacturers and merchants needed the weavers, and could afford to pay them more. The boom did not last. In an effort to blockade Napoleon, the Government introduced its Orders in Council. In 1809 the United States, irritated by the blockade, closed its ports to British ships, and the following year imposed a ban on trade, which soon began to have a destructive effect on the cotton industry.

In 1811, petitions began to pour in from constituencies in Lancashire, describing the distress which had arisen 'from the extreme depression of the various manufacturers occasioning a deficiency of employment', and from the great reduction of wages which, added to the high prices of provisions, had 'subjected them to the most unexampled privations'. From being among the most prosperous classes of workers in the country, the handloom weavers—500,000 of them, an M.P. estimated—had quite suddenly found themselves faced with destitution.

That they were not exaggerating was testified to by the M.P.s presenting the petitions, among them Colonel Stanley and Robert Peel. Nicholas Vansittart, the Chancellor of the Exchequer, made it clear that he had every sympathy with them, and that it was the Government's desire to afford every practicable relief. But he felt it necessary 'to guard against encouraging any hope which was not likely to be realised'; and when, early in June, Stanley moved for a committee of enquiry, it became clear what was meant by this warning. An enquiry, Vansittart complained, would 'merely cherish a fallacious expectation in the minds of those who were concerned'. Although a committee was appointed, it took its duties no more seriously than its predecessor of three years earlier. It met only four times, before reporting that 'no interference of the legislature with the freedom of trade, or with the perfect liberty of every individual to dispose of his time and his labour in the way and on the terms which he may judge most conducive to his own interests, can take place without violating general principles of the first importance to the prosperity and happiness of the community; without establishing the most pernicious precedent; or without aggravating, after a very short time, the general distress'. There was, however, some uneasiness about the possible effects of the admission that Parliament, faced with such distress as undoubtedly existed in the north, proposed on the recommendations of a committee to do nothing. Could the report be quietly disposed of, the Chancellor of the Exchequer wondered? In such cases, the Speaker suggested, the usual course was for some M.P. to move that the report should receive further consideration at a date 'beyond the probable duration of the session'. This was agreed.

The circumstances, though, were clearly different. The slump of 1811 was the direct consequence of a Government decision—the Orders in Council. For the Government to repudiate all responsibility for the consequences could be regarded as a blunt intimation to the workers that, if their situation became intolerable, they could rely only on their own resources. In the winter of 1811, their situation began to become intolerable. A bad harvest sent the price of wheat over a hundred shillings a quarter; by the following summer, it was over a hundred and fifty shillings—higher than it had ever been. Denied hope of help from Westminster, the weavers were naturally tempted to join in the Luddite movement.

In its initial stage, Luddism was the product of much the same causes as the rioting in the West Country, ten years earlier. Different categories of workers had different grievances, but the one which provoked the most serious outbreak in Nottinghamshire was characteristic. Stocking-making had been a skilled craft, and still was—if the stockinger could find a market for his wares. But increasingly, manufacturers were making stockings with the help of new machinery. The stockings were cheaper, because the machines could be minded by apprentices; and they were also inferior, because the machines which were being used were not capable of producing anything better than a spurious imitation of the stockinger's product. And the stockingers did not see why they should starve, while employers were allowed to make fortunes producing imitation stockings with the help of child labour. They began smashing the machines.

Locally, the Luddites had many sympathisers—as the agricultural labourers had had in 1795. Employers who valued the reputation of their goods were not sorry to see rivals who had been undercutting them with inferior products forced out of business. In general, too, the weavers had a good reputation, as respectable citizens; and there could be no question that the combination of the trade slump and the bad harvest had plunged them into unprecedented distress. But the Government, noting the almost military precision with which the Luddites were conducting their campaign, and fearing that if it spread, it would fuse with radicalism into a revived Jacobin movement, decided that the only remedy lay in a reintroduction of Pitt's repressive measures. An Act was passed making machine-breaking punishable by death; the spy system was reintroduced; care was taken to see that the trials of suspected Luddites were held before judges who could be relied upon to be firm; and with the help of executions, and sentences of transportation to the prison colonies in the Antipodes, Luddism was soon broken.

The Orders in Council were repealed—but mainly owing to the outcry from the manufacturers, shrewdly exploited by the young Henry Brougham. Brougham had been one of the founders of the *Edinburgh Review* in 1802, and was its most prolific writer, among his favourite topics being political economy. In 1812 he secured the appointment of a select committee into the state of trade, and with its help cajoled and bullied the Liverpool government into withdrawing the Orders—leaving Castlereagh to reflect that this was the first occasion in which the new industrial element had successfully opposed the Government. What did this portend, he wondered, for the landed aristocracy?

In the short term, though, the landowning aristocracy could thank Brougham for having helped to ease the political situation. As commerce began to flow again, there were indeed more orders, more jobs, and less discontent. But Luddism was to retain the stigma of having been a futile effort to halt the beneficent march of progress.

Byron—whose *Childe Harold* appeared in 1812—was one of the few members of either house to speak up for the Luddites, 'Meagre with famine, sullen with despair', they were now faced with capital punishment if they broke the machines which had taken away their livelihood; but even that penalty might be ineffective, if it made them careless of the lives which Parliament had now valued at 'less than the price of a stocking frame'. But he won no support in the Lords; and the Commons lacked an effective liberal voice. Fox had died before the fall of All the Talents; Sheridan lost his seat, and was too encumbered with debt to have much prospect of finding another; and Whitbread's conversion to Malthusianism was even leading him to denounce high wages. They led, he told the

Commons in 1815, to 'idleness, extravagance and dissipation'; men might plough, sow, reap and generally work their hearts out, but 'there would always be some little brat or other to consume the superabundant corn which this activity might produce'. Later in the year he committed suicide. And the new M.P.s provided no compensation. Lord Cochrane was expelled from Parliament, following a financial scandal; and Sir Francis Burdett's cantankerousness only weakened the Radical movement, so that by the end of the war it could hardly be said to be represented at Westminster.

For a time, the condition of the labouring poor ceased to be a matter for concern there. Occasionally an M.P. would draw attention to the maladministration and the cost of the poor laws; but ministers were determined not to allow themselves to be entangled in any reform project until the war ended, and they were encouraged by better harvests, which reduced distress and discontent. Arthur Young was not deceived. He was by this time an old man, almost blind; but his faculties were unimpaired, and his information network still operated. 'Country labourers throughout the kingdom are in the greatest distress, as I know from many of my correspondents', he noted in his journal in 1815; but the extent of the distress might not be realised; 'these poor families never petition, even when starving'.

6. 1815

But how could the agricultural labourers, who still provided the bulk of the country's working population, be worse off, if the country had been growing rapidly wealthier—as all the evidence showed that it had? By 1815 it was no longer possible to doubt that in spite of the wars and other setbacks, England's material wealth had been increasing at a rate unprecedented in history. The cotton industry showed the most striking development. In the early part of the eighteenth century the amount of raw cotton imported into England to be manufactured into cloth totalled little more than a million pounds in weight; and by 1780 the amount had risen only to seven million pounds. But then the figures began to increase very rapidly:

1790	30m. lb. per annum
1800	60m. lb. per annum
1810	130m. lb. per annum

No other industry had a comparable record, but some had benefited indirectly—coal and iron—and others, like wool, had begun to expand with the help of new machinery and steam power. Commerce in general had been increasing; both the volume and the value of Britain's trade with foreign countries had trebled between 1780 and 1800. Thousands of new jobs were being created every year. Common sense, as well as economic theory, suggested that a new demand must have been created for farm produce of all kinds, which the agricultural revolution, by rationalising production, should have helped to satisfy—with the farm workers as grateful beneficiaries.

But they had not benefited—except in and around industrial areas, where the demand both for food and for labour kept wages relatively high. Elsewhere, over most of the traditional farming country, wages were depressed; and it was no longer possible to disguise the fact that the labourers' condition was worst where the agricultural revolution had swept away the old common fields and commons.

There was still no satisfactory statistical apparatus, but a reasonably clear picture of what had been happening had begun to emerge from the surveys of commentators like David Davies and John Howlett, presenting the evidence from their parishes. In his 1796 pamphlet on Pitt's measure to reform the poor laws, Howlett had been able to show from account books kept in Dunmow for half a century that a labourer who had maintained himself and his family on the then regular wage of fifteen pounds a year—and even saved a little—could no longer, fifty years later, hope to keep them at the same standard on a wage of twenty pounds a year, which he would be lucky to get. Then, labourers families had been decently clothed and comfortably fed: 'now, on the contrary, the father and mother are covered with rags; their children are running about like little savages, without shoes or stockings to their feet; and by day and night, they are forced to break down the hedges and the trees and pilfer their fuel, or perish with the cold'.

No serious attempt was made at the time to deny the facts that Howlett, Davies and others presented. The introduction of family allowances was in fact an admission, if not of guilt, at least of responsibility. But although the allowances were a humane, and in some ways an enlightened expedient, they had the fatal defect of further depressing wages. When labourers' pay was going to be made up to subsistence level out of the rates, the farmer had no inducement to raise that pay; why should he take from his own pocket what would otherwise be taken from the pockets of the ratepayers? So, as the allowance system operated, it was a subsidy less to the labourers than to the farmer—and indirectly to the landowner, as he could keep up his rents.

For a time the supporters of enclosures and consolidations could continue to believe that the system they had advocated must eventually produce the results they had promised. Even the shock of 1795 could be explained away as arising from an unlucky combination of the war and a disastrous harvest. But by the turn of the century, it was no longer possible for anybody who, like Arthur Young, or Sir Thomas Bernard, kept his eyes open, to ignore what was happening. And by then it was too late. To begin to restore land to the labourers would require legislation— unwelcome in itself, but even more disturbing in that it might mean interfering with the landowner's right to do what he liked with his own. It would also require funds; and the exchequer was in difficulties enough, finding sufficient revenue to prosecute the war. So ministers had looked around for an excuse not to intervene along the lines Young was advocating; and they had found it in the doctrines of political economy.

Pitt was the first to exploit them, with his rejection of a minimum wage; and soon, they were being invoked against any proposal to provide help for the poor. But simply to claim that the State could not intervene was hardly convincing. The State had, after all, intervened to procure enclosures; it could presumably intervene to reverse or modify that process. Another argument was needed; and Malthus had provided it. If the labourers were given land, they would be encouraged to marry, and breed; any relief to the ratepayer would be short-lived; soon, both labourers and ratepayers, and the community as a whole, would be worse off.

'Take the children'

The doctrines of political economy would have carried little weight if they had been opposed to the landowner's interest; but because he could cite them in self-justification, they were invaluable. And they were also useful to him, though for a less immediate purpose, in connection with industry. Few landowners stood to benefit directly from the development of, say, the cotton industry. But the landowning class, as represented at Westminster, had a powerful indirect interest in the expansion of commerce, from which much of the nation's revenue was extracted in the form of levies and duties. Increased trade reduced the need for unpopular taxes.

There was one other valuable service industry could perform; running itself. Ministers did not want to have to exercise control: all past experience had shown what a thankless and expensive task it would be. The old regulatory system had fallen into disuse; and they were not anxious to incur the expense of restoring it. So when the industrialists cited political economy to justify being allowed to run industry their way, ministers were disposed to listen.

As a result, the new factory-based industry which had begun to emerge in the north of England was permitted to develop on the principle that labour should be hired in the cheapest possible market, even if this meant hiring children. Adult males working in factories might receive good wages, relative to the agricultural labourer; but employers employed few adult males. From two-thirds to three-quarters of the workers in the early factories were under the age of eighteen; and they were lucky if they earned a halfpenny an hour. For this, they were made to work as children had never been made to work before; rarely less than eleven hours a day.

In some factories the conditions were reasonable; in some, dreadful. Some managements were responsible; some vile. But the essential feature of factory life, as it developed in England, was that the children were enslaved. Before, apprentices had often been made to work long hours under appalling conditions, as court cases had often shown; but they had worked for a master who, at least in theory, was teaching them a trade. In the factories they were employed in their own right, as machine-minders, learning no trade—being effectively prevented from learning one, as well as from getting any education, apart from Sunday School. If they proved themselves obedient and reliable, they might be promoted to an adult job when they grew older; but their promotion would be on the strength of those qualities, rather than of skills they had acquired.

That children should be exploited in this way was not accepted unquestioningly. The revulsion expressed in Percival's report to the Manchester magistrates, and by the Society for Bettering the Condition of the Poor, revealed that there were strong feelings against uncontrolled child employment, and the favourable reaction at Westminster to Peel's bill showed that M.P.s shared them. But although the desire was there to protect the children, it was less powerful than the fear of State interference. Regulations were introduced, but not the means to ensure that they were enforced.

The French historian Michelet suspected that this was actually part of a bargain struck between Pitt, on the one hand, anxious to get on with the war; and the employers, on the other, anxious to be allowed to run industry their way. Levies and duties, they naturally reminded him, were contrary to the best economic principles, as they interfered with the free workings of commerce. So did factory regulations. Pitt could not afford to give up the revenue, so he had conceded the other request: he had said, 'Take the children!' And that was, in effect, what had happened. The factory children had been the victims not so much of Pitt, as of a social system poorly designed to give them adequate protection, and a war which removed the incentive to provide it.

Again, the principles of political economy had provided the excuse— though hardly of the kind that Adam Smith could have been expected to approve. He had no experience of factories; but there was certainly nothing in *The Wealth of Nations* to suggest he would have approved the uses to which child labour was being put. As for allowing the employers to run industry, he had specifically warned against it. But ministers were their own interpreters of his doctrine; and more and more they were equating political economy with *laissez-faire*. 'It has been well said in a foreign country,' Lord Liverpool, the new Prime Minister, said in 1812, 'when it was asked what should be done to make commerce prosper, the answer was *laissez-faire*; and it was undoubtedly true that the less commerce and manufactures were meddled with, the more they were likely to prosper.' By agreeing to dismantle what remained of the old mercantilist structure, Parliament had shown that it accepted this view.

'To live without idleness, without poverty . . .'

Yet it was still possible to accept *laissez-faire*, as a general economic principle, without accepting that an employer had the right to run his factories, and to treat his employees, exactly how he liked. Peel's Factory Act was still on the statute book, testifying to Parliament's belief that it had a duty to rescue pauper apprentices from exploitation. Suppose that some way could be found to regulate working conditions for children, and provide them with amenities and education, without extending the influence of the State—and without requiring additional taxation? It could be just what was wanted . . . And shortly before the defeat of Bonaparte, Robert Owen presented such a prospect in his *New View of Society*.

Owen had been a draper's assistant, until good fortune put him in the way of becoming a mill manager. He prospered; and when in 1800 he took charge of the mills in New Lanark, near Glasgow, he was able to persuade his partners to let him run them his way. At the time he took over, about three hundred pauper children were employed. They had been well looked after by the standards of the time, 'yet their limbs were very generally deformed, their growth stunted'. In future, he decided, he would employ no child under the age of ten, and the working hours would also be reduced to ten and a half a day—an hour and a half less than most of his competitors. The wages, admittedly, were to remain a little lower than the average: adults received only ten shillings a week (women six shillings) youths under eighteen four and threepence a week (girls three and fivepence). But any adult who cared to go on piecework could earn a third to a half as much again; and in addition, fringe benefits were offered of a kind that few workers elsewhere enjoyed; good houses at cheap rents, a contributory sickness and superannuation fund, free medical services, and schooling for children at a charge of threepence a month. There were also facilities for recreation, gardens, and allotments.

The results fulfilled Owen's hopes; within a few years, more workers were employed in New Lanark than in any other factory in the country, and it still made substantial profits. When in 1813 the owners began to wonder whether those profits might not be made still greater, by cutting down on some of the welfare expenditure, Owen felt sufficiently sure of himself to go to London to look for other backers; and he had no difficulty in raising the capital to set up a new partnership, one of the partners being Jeremy Bentham.

By this time, New Lanark was becoming a showplace, attracting visitors from all over the world. But its success only stimulated Owen's imagination. He was no longer satisfied with it simply as an example of how a business could and should be run: he had begun to see it as a microcosm of a new society. The differences between men were the consequence not of innate characteristics, he had decided, but of their environment. Not that he would have denied that there were differences of ability, or character, as between individuals; but he refused to accept that there were differences of class, or any inherent traits like criminality. 'Any general character,' he wrote in 1812, 'from the best to the worst, from the most ignorant to the most enlightened, may be given to any community, even to the world at large, by the application of proper means; which means are to a great extent at the command and under the control of those who have influence in the affairs of men'.

It followed that education had a vital part in this process; and from the start, Owen's greatest concern in New Lanark had been for its schools.

Children, he claimed, 'are without exception passive and wonderfully contrived compounds'; they could be moulded into whatever form society desired. But he diverged from those who, like the Jesuits, had traditionally held a similar view. There was no need for society to make its own mould; the children should simply be placed in an agreeable and harmonious environment, and encouraged to pursue their own interest. Young children were 'not to be annoyed with books': they were to be helped to satisfy their own natural curiousity, but not compelled to learn anything. And, as children could not be held responsible for their behaviour, there was to be neither punishment for idleness or disobedience, nor rewards for meritorious effort or conduct.

The essays which comprised the first part of *A New View of Society*, published in 1813, presented these views, pointing out what a difference it would make if his system was adopted. Employers would see the profitability of their firms greatly increasing; but the chief beneficiary would be the Government, which would find that the members of the community could by degrees 'be trained to live *without idleness, without poverty, without crime and without punishment*'. Owen took care that the *New View* should be laid before influential ministers, some of whom he had met in his capacity as spokesman for the cotton industry; and they were impressed. Luddism had alarmed them: here was Owen offering a way to improve both the condition and the conduct of workers, and one which would require no increase of State expenditure, provided that employers could be persuaded it was in their own self-interest to improve the living and working standards of their workers. And if they could be persuaded to offer education, as Owen had done, ministers might be helped to escape from the constant attentions of a group of their faithful but nagging supporters: the Evangelicals.

Towards the end of eighteenth century a variety of experimental educational systems had emerged in England: Robert Raikes' Sunday Schools, Hannah More's schools for the children of the poor in the West Country, and the establishments of Joseph Lancaster and Andrew Bell, where much of the teaching was done by older children, acting as monitors. Ministers continually found themselves urged to make provision for schools, and for teachers, so that all poor children could receive an education; but they were reluctant to incur the expense and, as Commons' debates on the subject revealed, they would in any case have had difficulty in securing agreement on what kind of education should be provided. To the Evangelicals, who were the most fervent supporters of free schools, 'education' meant only instruction in the scriptures and (as Hannah More put it) 'such books as are preparatory to, and connected with, them'. Ministers had no desire to offend the Evangelicals; but to accept their proposals would have incurred the wrath of other members of the Established Church, not to mention of dissenters.

Owen's New Lanark schools appeared to offer renewed hope. Not that ministers cared for Owen's educational theories; what was important was that he had been able to run the schools out of the profits of his factories. If all mill-owners would do the same, the problem of how to educate children in industrial areas would solve itself. And if all mill-owners would do as Owen had done, supporting his workers through the worst of the depression of 1812, there would be less to fear in future from Luddism or Jacobinism.

Owen, too, had a way with him. He managed to convince everybody he met that he was a true philanthropist, devoid of personal or political ambition. Although his views might be Godwinian, nobody thought him dangerous on that account. So impressed was Lord Sidmouth, the Home Secretary, that he was to promise to circulate the second collection of essays in the *New View*, when it appeared in 1816, in a privately printed edition, destined for embassies and learned societies abroad (one copy even found its way to Bonaparte, in exile on St. Helena). Sidmouth was not a man of any obvious sensibility. Before his elevation to the peerage, when for a time he replaced Pitt as Prime Minister, he had been impaled on Canning's quip

> Pitt is to Addington
> As London is to Paddington

and his subsequent record as Home Secretary did nothing to suggest that he can have had any sympathy with Owen's social theories. If he was impressed, it was simply because Owen was offering a possible way out of the Government's domestic difficulties; one which, with the war over, Parliament might be encouraged to examine.

3

PEACE AND WANT

1. POLITICAL ECONOMY

WITH NAPOLEON SAFELY on St. Helena, and his conquerors getting together to try to find a lasting peace settlement, the mood in Britain could reasonably be self-congratulatory. Peace, it was hoped, would solve most of the problems left by war. But one of them, it had come to be realised, could not be left to the amelioration of economic conditions which peace would surely eventually bring. The condition of the rural poor constituted too immediate a threat to the country's stability. Writers of all shades of political opinion were agreed that the agricultural labourers had suffered severely, were suffering, and would continue to suffer until something drastic was done; and this turned out to be the feeling at Westminster, too. The need to provide them with employment was in fact one of the chief arguments used by supporters of the first important peace-time bill to be brought before Parliament: the measure which, with various amendments and accretions, came to be known and execrated as 'the Corn Laws'.

The war had kept up the price of home-grown corn; in peace-time when cheaper corn could more easily be imported from abroad, it might be expected to fall to pre-war levels. The Government therefore proposed to prohibit importation except when the price of home-grown corn went above eighty shillings a quarter—about double the pre-war average. To Alexander Baring—a member of the banking family, and therefore rich enough to, in effect, hire a seat for the duration of that parliament—this simply reflected the determination of the landed aristocracy to cling to the tribute that the war had enabled them to levy from the rest of the community. Their aim, he told the Commons, was 'to enhance the price of bread, to procure a bounty for the growers of corn'. They might not be aware that this was their motive; but surely, in their capacity as Members of Parliament, they should realise that they ought not to set themselves up as impartial arbiters of the national need, in a matter where their self-interest was so deeply involved.

A flood of petitions arrived at Westminster in Baring's support, including one from the Lord Mayor of London. They were ignored. One speaker, Lord Proby, admitted that he had been influenced by his own—landed—interest; but what, he asked, was wrong with that? Baring himself, after all, was a striking example of the advantages which merchants' sons enjoyed; he should realise that there was no reason why 'the sons and daughters of farmers should not share them'. Such frankness was unusual. Most speakers argued that import regulations were necessary to provide the farmer with a fair price for his corn, because only then could he afford to pay good wages to his labourers—or even to employ them. One M.P. claimed that on a recent visit to a village near Hull, he had been begged by the locals to support legislation to increase the price of home-grown corn; they realised that this might mean an increase in the price of bread, but what use was cheap bread to them—they had told him—if it meant that the farmer could not sell his corn at a profit, and therefore could not employ them? In the Lords, the Earl of Lauderdale announced that he would support the proposed corn laws, not from concern for his own interest, but because 'they would be most beneficial to the labouring agricultural classes, the most valuable part of the superior orders of the community, and likewise to the people of the country at large'. The Prime Minister, Lord Liverpool, gratefully accepted this thesis, and the measure passed rapidly through both Houses with massive majorities; just in time to mitigate what, for the landowners, might otherwise have been the unfortunate effects of the bountiful 1815 harvest, which resulted in the price of wheat falling to fifty-five shillings a quarter—almost back to pre-war levels.

Less was heard about the needs of the labourer, however, when a second measure was put before Parliament; to abolish the property tax which Pitt had imposed to pay for the war. Petitions came flowing in against it on the ground that it was an infringement of the rights of the property-owner which, though permissible in a national emergency, could not be tolerated in peace-time, particularly as it would require the services of an inquisition to help collect it. So to meet the country's expenditure—by this time considerably inflated by the need to pay interest to the fund-holders, as they were generally described, who had subscribed to the national loans to finance the war—the Government was compelled to fall back on an excise duty on soap, the change of tax relieving the propertied classes of approximately the same amount as was paid out in poor rates.

Then, Parliament could turn its attention to the condition of the poor. Three projects had been waiting in the wings for the war to end—arising out of the failure of earlier legislation. The Act to give protection to the climbing boys had proved to be unenforceable; Peel's Factory Act, though it had had some effect, was ceasing to be relevant to conditions in the cotton industry; and the various Acts which together constituted the poor laws were proving both expensive to run, and unfortunate in their consequences.

'To the neglect and ruin of the land'

Characteristically, it was the expense of the poor laws that Parliament got round to debating first. Certainly the figures gave cause for alarm. From a total of about one million pounds a year in the middle of the eighteenth century, the poor rates had risen to two million pounds shortly before the beginning of the war; to four million in 1803; and to seven million in 1813. After that there had been better harvests, a fall in the cost of bread, and a slight fall in the rates. But should there be another bad harvest . . .

The issue of reform of the poor laws was raised in 1816 by an old friend of Burke's, John Christian Curwen. It was absurd, Curwen suggested, that a country whose total revenue from taxation ordinarily came to little more than fifty million pounds a year, should be spending close to one sixth of that sum in relieving the poor. Surely this could only mean that something was seriously wrong with the laws? On behalf of the Government, the leader of the House of Commons, Lord Castlereagh, agreed—making it clear that he thought poor relief in aid of wages was the real cause of the trouble. It was not simply, he insisted, that they were so costly to the ratepayer; they also tended to destroy the true wealth of the poor man—'the capability of making exertions for his own livelihood'. If relief was to be granted with the laxity which now prevailed, and if 'all the cunning of uncultivated minds was to be directed to the means of escaping from labour, and enjoying the fruits of the labour of others', then a national calamity 'might be said to be overtaking us by a double operation—in the increased burdens imposed upon the country, and the diminution of the industry from which its resources were derived'.

This was an ingenious line of argument. It conceded the wretched condition of the labourers; but by putting the blame on family allowances—conveniently forgetting that they had been designed and introduced by magistrates who were landowners—it shifted the responsibility off the landowning class. And although the poor could hardly be held responsible for the consequences, the implication was that they were fast learning to exploit them. Castlereagh provided examples which, he claimed, he had acquired at first hand from his own home parish, giving the impression that the allowance system was being systematically exploited by indolent labourers to avoid doing a proper day's work. An enquiry was needed into the whole subject of the poor laws, Castlereagh suggested. It should be treated as a matter of urgency, 'as no other question went so deeply to affect the happiness of the whole community'.

The enquiry was undertaken by a parliamentary committee under the chairmanship of Sturges Bourne—an old schoolfellow and lifelong friend of Canning's, and a disciple of Pitt. He was also a student of political economy; and, just as the committees on the state of the cotton and the woollen industries had worked on the principle that the State ought not to intervene in commerce, or to try to relieve distress arising from redundancy, so his committee, in its report, denied that there might be any way for the State to help the agricultural labourers.

The committee even went so far as to refuse to hear a witness who wanted to present a scheme which might involve State expenditure. Interested by the success of Robert Owen's New Lanark experiment, the Society for Bettering the Condition of the Poor had asked him whether he could suggest any scheme based on it which might provide employment in country districts. This was just the kind of challenge that appealed to him; he had worked out a plan for communities on the lines of his own, though predominantly agricultural, in which paupers could be helped to become self-supporting. The first duty of these new communities, Owen insisted, must be to the impotent poor: 'the first business of society is to provide for these sufferers'. Pauper children must also be provided with education and training, and jobs when they grew up. But the general purpose of the communities was very much what Gilbert's had been, to provide work for the able-bodied unemployed—except that in Owen's project, homes were to be provided for the workers. He even provided a sketch plan of the way the buildings might be laid out.

This proved a mistake; the sketch looked forbiddingly like a jail, and although Owen insisted that nobody should be compelled to enter any of the communities, it could be argued that if paupers were to be denied any other kind of assistance, they would be compelled to. As a result, radicals were hostile; Cobbett ridiculed what he called Owen's 'parallelo-

grams of paupers'. The Society were impressed; but, as they lacked the
necessary funds, they suggested to Owen that he should submit his
project to the Sturges Bourne committee, then hearing evidence. Owen
arrived with his plan, intending to expound it. He was kept hanging
around in an ante-room while the committee discussed not the merits of
his scheme, but whether it should be admitted as evidence. Eventually
they decided it should not.

When the report of the committee appeared in 1817, it was obvious
why. No attempt was made to minimise the suffering of the agricultural
labourers; but the responsibility for it was placed on the poor laws, and
in particular the allowance system in those districts where relief was paid
in aid of wages. The point that Patrick Colquhoun had made in his
Treatise on indigence—published in 1806, but making little impact at
the time—had obviously impressed the committee: that there ought to be
a rigid distinction between poverty—'the state of everyone who must
labour for his subsistence'— and indigence—the state of everyone whose
labour failed to supply that subsistence. The weakness of the poor laws,
the committee decided, lay in their failure to make that distinction. The
system, too,

> is perpetually encouraging and increasing the amount of misery it was designed
> to alleviate, creating at the same time an unlimited demand on funds which it
> cannot augment; and as every system of reliefs must be divested of the character
> of benevolence, so it is without its beneficial effects. As it proceeds from no
> impulse of charity, it creates no feelings of gratitude, and not infrequently
> engenders dispositions and habits calculated to separate rather than unite the
> interests of the higher and lower orders of the community. Even the obligations
> of natural affection are no longer left to their own impulse, but the mutual
> support of the nearest relations has been actually enjoined by a positive law,
> which the authority of the magistrates is continually required to enforce . . .
> The result appears to have been highly prejudicial to the moral habits, and
> consequent happiness, of a great body of the people, who have been reduced
> to the degradation of a dependence upon parish support.

Some of the proposals which Pitt had presented in his bill were again
recommended: the Act of Settlement should be drastically reformed, and
consideration given to the establishment of industrial training schools.
But the essential step, the committee urged, was to separate poverty
from destitution. Allowances in aid of wages must go; partly because
they had familiarised the labourer with a dependence upon the parish

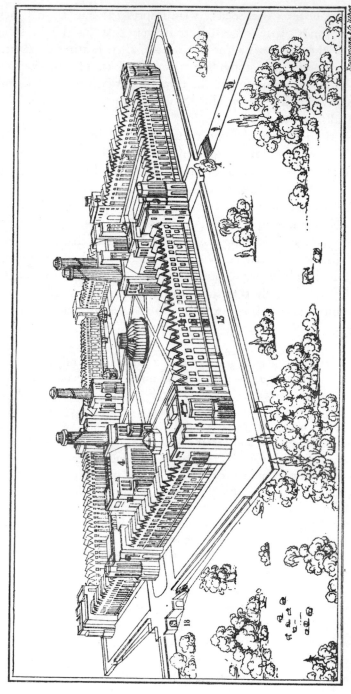

DESIGN

for a Community of 2,000 Persons founded upon a principle
Commended by Plato Lord Bacon and Sir Thomas More

and combined with all the advantages of scientific discoveries down to the present

EXPLANATION OF THE PARTS NUMBERED ON THE PLATE.

1 Gymnasiums or Covered Places for Exercise, attached to the Schools and Infirmary.
2 Conservatory, in the midst of Gardens botanically arranged.
3 Baths, warm and cold, of which there are four for the Males, and four for the Females.
4 Dining Halls, with Kitchens, &c. beneath them.
5 Angle Buildings, occupied by the Schools for Infants, Children, and Youths, and the Infirmary ; on the ground floors are Conversation-rooms for Adults.
6 Library, Detached Reading Rooms, Bookbindery, Printing Office, &c.
7 Ball room and Music rooms.
8 Theatre for Lectures, Exhibitions, Discussions, &c. with Laboratory, Small Library, &c.
9 Museum, with Library of Description and Reference, Rooms for preparing Specimens, &c.
10 The Brew-houses, Bake-houses, Wash-houses, Laundries, &c. arranged round the Bases of the Towers.
11 The Refectories for the infants and children are on each side of the Vestibules of the Dining halls
12 The Illuminators of the Establishment, Clock-towers, and Observatories, and from the elevated summits of which all the smoke and vitiated air of the buildings is discharged into the atmosphere.
13 Suites of adult sitting rooms and chambers.
14 Suites of Chambers, which may be easily and quickly made of any dimensions required ; Dormitories for the Unmarried and Children.
15 Esplanade one hundred feet wide, about twelve feet above the natural surface.
16 Paved Footpath.
17 The Arcade and its Terrace, giving both a covered and an open communication with every part of the building.
18 Sub-way leading to the Kitchens, &c. and along which meat, vegetables, coals, &c. are conveyed to the Stores, and dust and refuse brought out.

Robert Owen's community principle illustrated in a design by Stedman Whitwell, 1830.

which he would formerly have considered a degradation, but essentially because unless they were terminated, the poor rates would continue to rise until they absorbed the entire profits of the property on which it was assessed, 'to the neglect and ruin of the land, the waste or removal of other property, and the utter subversion of that happy order of society so long upheld in these kingdoms'.

This was just what Castlereagh had wanted. But, in the meantime, the political situation had changed. The harvest had been poor; the price of wheat had risen to over a hundred shillings a quarter. Agricultural workers suspected that any benefits that might have been expected to seep down to them from the higher price the farmer got for his corn were offset by the increasing use, to harvest it, of threshing machines. And in the towns, labourers found themselves doubly hit—by a post-war slump, leading to a falling-off in trade, and unemployment; and by the rising cost of bread. Luddism reappeared, among craftsmen as well as labourers, as the relative prosperity the war had given them vanished. The outbreak was even more violent than its predecessors; it also appeared to be better organised, and it was better served by the radical press. The Government had increased the stamp duty from twopence to fourpence— ostensibly for revenue, but really to restrict circulation: the *Morning Post*, *The Times* and other newspapers had to charge their subscribers sevenpence. All that the duty did, though, was drive the radical press underground. As the owners had little to lose but their liberty, they became even more virulent, led by Hone, with his parodies of passages from the Bible. Among his Ten Commandmends, as rephrased by ministers for their own convenience, was

VIII. Thou shalt not call starving to death murder.

'By the sweat of thy brow thou shalt eat bread' had once been considered doom-laden enough in itself; but now, Hone remarked, ministers laughed at people who were praying to be allowed to earn money, by the sweat of their brows, so that they might be able to buy bread. Hone was prosecuted on three different charges, on three successive days; he defended himself skilfully; the juries found him not guilty. And to their alarm, ministers had heard that tricolours and caps of liberty were being seen around the country; and that clubs modelled on the old corresponding societies were springing up again in the towns.

They did not ask themselves whether the discontent might arise simply from workers' dissatisfaction at finding themselves worse off,

now that the war was over, than they had been while it continued.
M.P.s had little contact with the workers; and the Home Office's information was unreliable. Some of it came from quite well-informed sources,
such as the magistracy; but even there, the kind of magistrate who sent
in reports to the Home Office was apt to be an alarmist. Much of the
information came from Government spies, who earned a precarious
living from the secret service funds. As their renumeration tended to be
directly proportionate to the alarm which their efforts caused, they were
naturally tempted to uncover Jacobin plots; and now, they found it easy
to persuade the Government of the existence of a sanguinary conspiracy
to overthrow the constitution, and set up a new one in its place, modelled
on the teachings of Thomas Spence.

To his acquaintances, Spence was an endearing crank; Francis Place
described him as 'a very simple, very honest, single-minded man,
querulous in his disposition and odd in his manners . . . he firmly
loved mankind, and firmly believed that the time would come when they
would be wise, virtuous and happy.' He had been in jail on more than
one occasion for airing his view that the land belonged to the people,
and that each parish should administer it for the benefit of the parishioners;
but when he died, in 1814, he had attracted only a tiny following. After
his death, however, a few of his disciples had formed small Spencean
clubs; and here, ministers let themselves be persuaded, was the hard
revolutionary core of the new Jacobinism. In case they should have been
in any doubt, their informants—John Castle, 'Oliver the Spy', and
others—had taken the precaution of obtaining the necessary evidence by
acting as *agents provocateurs*. When, for example, the Spenceans persuaded
the radical Henry Hunt to speak at a demonstration in London in
November, 1816, and to have dinner with them after it to celebrate its
success, it was Castle who proposed the toast 'May the last of the kings
be strangled with the guts of the last priest.'

Most of the leading radicals, including Hunt and Cobbett, hoped to
win reform by constitutional means. But ministers reacted as Pitt had
done, preferring to believe that revolution was imminent. Their measures
took the traditional form of 'Gagging Acts', as Cobbett called them,
designed to make it even more hazardous to express opinions which could
be interpreted as seditious; and the suspension, in March, 1817, of
habeas corpus, releasing the Government from the necessity of bringing
its critics to trial, after they had been arrested. There was embarassingly
little evidence at that time of any serious revolutionary movement, but

it was provided three months afterwards when a few hundred clothing workers near Nottingham staged an abortive insurrection; and although a few weeks later the *Leeds Mercury* was able to show that their rising had been fomented by Oliver the Spy, ministers were not disturbed by the exposure. If there were workers who were ready to embark on an insurrection, then the country was in danger, even if it were the Government's own agents who were responsible for precipitating it.

But faced with the threat—as they believed it—of revolution, ministers also remembered that family allowances had been introduced to allay revolutionary discontent among the agricultural labourers; and that their necessity had been accepted by Pitt. It now seemed wise, twenty years later, not to disturb that beneficent arrangement. A committee of the House of Lords, which had also been investigating the poor laws, pronounced itself as 'decidedly of the opinion that the general system of these laws, interwoven as it is with the habits of the people, ought, in the consideration of any measures to be adopted for their amelioration and improvement, to be essentially maintained'. And conveniently for the Government, the Sturges Bourne report was presented to the House too late in the session of 1817 for legislative action to be taken.

At the time, ministers contrived to give the impression that this did not matter, as they would expedite legislation in the following session. But when the 1818 session opened, the members of the committee found they had been deceived. The speech from the throne, in which the Government spelled out its legislative intentions, contained no reference to reform of the poor laws. Curwen was not going to let ministers get away with it. Why—he wanted to know—after all the the keen interest the Government had expressed, were they now backing down? Castlereagh, who had not been so naïve as to imagine that the absence of proposals for reform would pass unnoticed, had his answer ready. The Government, he said, had intended to bring in a measure of its own. But, gratified by the widespread interest which M.P.s had shown in the subject, ministers had come to the conclusion it would not be proper for them to pre-empt decisions which ought to be taken by Parliament as a whole, free from their direction.

In this Castlereagh was telling the truth; ministers had indeed decided that if the poor laws were to be altered, Parliament as a whole, rather than the Government, ought to take the responsibility. He was not, however, telling the whole truth. They had hoped to be able to bask in the credit for bringing the war to a successful conclusion, and to enjoy the fruits of the commercial prosperity which, it had been assumed, would follow. Now, they found themselves so generally execrated that to meddle with the poor law might provoke a revolution. Castlereagh invited Sturges Bourne to reconstitute his committee, and present a bill based on its findings; but it was obvious to Sturges Bourne, and everybody else, that this could only mean that a bill based on the earlier committee's findings would stand no chance of getting through. The fact that the committee was sitting again, too, could be used as an excuse to delay any full-scale debate on the condition of the poor. Sturges Bourne did his best by beginning to introduce individual minor reforms which his committee recommended, piecemeal; but on the main issue, family allowances, he could get no farther. That summer William Huskisson admitted that the members of the committee 'had not yet seen their way on this most delicate subject'. Before they had seen their way, Parliament was dissolved, and they were facing a general election.

'Terrible almost beyond belief'

The committee on the poor laws had largely confined its enquiries to their effects in country districts. Although the Lords' committee had noted that in the towns, too, 'the population has of late greatly exceeded the demand for labour', it had not gone on to investigate why. Family allowances could not be blamed, because it was unusual for them to be provided in the new industrial areas of the north; there were other causes—the appearance on the labour market of tens of thousands of ex-servicemen, after demobilisation, along with civilians who had been engaged in the manufacture of war materials; the competition of immigrants; and the fact that so many of the jobs available were being offered to children.

The immigrants were from Ireland. Following the rebellion of 1798, Pitt had decided that Ireland must lose her parliament: and in 1800 the Act of Union restored her to the United Kingdom. Some of her industries, deprived of protection, were collapsing; and men who were thrown out of work, along with agricultural workers squeezed off the land by the mounting pressure of an expanding population, came to England to look for jobs. Their standard of living was much lower than that of the ordinary English worker. He might have been able to afford only small amounts of meat, butter, cheese or beer, but he still regarded them as staples; to the Irish, accustomed to a diet of potatoes and very little else, they were luxuries. The Irish were also prepared to accept accommodation of a kind that the English worker would not have considered habitable; it could hardly be worse than the mud cabins many of them had left. They were consequently able to offer their services as labourers for less than the English worker; an offer which employers were delighted to accept.

The Irish at first took only unskilled jobs; but their presence helped to pull down wages throughout industry. It was natural for any English labourer who wished to preserve his former living standards to decide to become a handloom weaver—an occupation which during the war had remained better paid than labouring, in spite of occasional trade recessions. Little capital was required to become a weaver, and little skill. At first, this lifted the weavers out of immediate competition with the Irish for jobs. But the industry began to become overstocked with labour. The weavers' earnings, which had amounted to twenty-five shillings a week and even more, at the turn of the century, had fallen by half at the end of the war. They were also threatened by the invention of the power loom. Until 1815, and for a few years to come, there were not many power looms; but where an employer had installed them, he naturally tended to fall back on them when demand fell. It was handloom weavers who suffered first in a recession.

But the main cause of unemployment was that so many of the jobs which were available in the new factories were being taken by children. In cotton mills, the employers had found that children were just as good as adults at minding the machines; and they were much cheaper to hire. In the new woollen mills of the West Riding of Yorkshire, too, and in factories utilising machinery for the making of other kinds of clothing material, it was children that the employers wanted.

Adult workers who could not obtain employment were naturally disposed to ask why, if the landowners had justified the corn laws by emphasising the need to provide employment for the agricultural labourer, similar concern should not also be shown for the men who (it was generally conceded) had fought for their country, or delivered the goods which had given Britain her commercial ascendancy, enabling her to survive the wars? At first, their requests were moderate in tone as well as in content. They did not ask to be rescued from the effects of the competition of the new machinery; they merely wanted Parliament to ensure that it was fair competition, by laying down that the machines should be worked and watched by adults. Child labour, it was argued in one petition:

by depriving parents of sufficient employ, makes them dependent on their
children for support; which as experience too tragically proves, deprives them
of the authority over youth which is necessary to retard the progress of vice
and promote virtue. The evils of a factory life are incalculable.

There, uninformed, unrestrained youth of both sexes mingle, absent from
parental vigilance, from reproof and instruction, confined in an artificial
heat to the injury of health, the mind exposed to corruption, and life and
limbs exposed to machinery, spending a youth where the 40th year of the
age is the sixtieth of the constitution, till they let themselves become dependent
on their offspring, or the parish.

The fact that there was a precedent for factory legislation, in the Act
of 1802, was a further encouragement. The Act, admittedly, had not been
very effective. A parliamentary committee had been set up at the end of
the war to investigate the condition of pauper children sent out as
'apprentices'. It found that they were still being sent in wagon-loads
from workhouses in London to mills in the north of England, and the
evils of the system, the committee reported,

at all times severe, and aggravating the miseries of poverty, are yet felt more
acutely and with a greater degree of aggravation, in the case of children of six
or seven years of age, who are removed from the care of their parents and
relations at that tender time of life; and are in many cases prematurely subjected to a laborious employment, frequently very injurious to their health,
and generally highly so to their morals, and from which they cannot hope to
be set free under a period of fourteen or fifteen years, as with the exception
of two parishes only in the metropolis they invariably are bound to the age of
twenty-two years.

Each pauper child indentured, in other words, was serving the equivalent of a sentence of fourteen years hard labour, from which he could not
legally escape, except in the unlikely event of his master being convicted
of misuse of his powers; and an Act passed based on the report's
findings endeavoured to tighten up some of the safeguards, and banned
the apprenticeship of pauper children under the age of nine. By 1816,
however, the fate of pauper children was no longer the main cause for
concern. Robert Peel—by this time a baronet—believed that his 1802
Act, although it had not accomplished all he wanted, had done some
good, bringing about a reduction of the hours worked by children in
cotton mills, and a general improvement in their health. But—as he
wrote in a memorandum on the subject—for the great majority of
children who worked in the mills, the Act's provisions had ceased to be

relevant. 'Instead of parish apprentices being sought after, the children of the poor are preferred, whose masters being free from the operation of the former Act of Parliament are subjected to no limitation of time in the prosecution of their business; children are frequently admitted there to work thirteen to fourteen hours per day, at the tender age of seven years, and even in some cases still younger.' Although reluctant to demand fresh legislation, he had been forced to the conclusion it was necessary; and he had accordingly agreed to bring in a bill to regulate child employment in the mills, to prevent it from becoming, instead of a benefit, the nation's 'bitterest curse'.

Peel had no reason to suppose that his proposals would be unacceptable. As the new industrial towns of the north still had no representation at Westminster, M.P.s were unlikely to have had any idea of what was happening in them; they would be shocked by what they heard, when he laid the facts before them; and they would have no more inhibitions about intervening than they had had earlier. To campaign on behalf of children was respectable; even Wilberforce was prepared to bestir himself, though not so energetically as he did for slaves. The fact that the bill was being presented not by a radical, but by a successful Tory mill-owner, too, was calculated to disarm suspicion—especially as it had been drafted by Robert Owen. For Owen was not, at this stage, regarded with suspicion by his fellow mill-owners. He had done his best to prove to them that his New Lanark mills were not to be regarded as some Utopian experiment, but as a sound and profitable business enterprise, based on the reasonable commercial proposition that if it were important to take care of inanimate machinery, 'what may not be expected if you devote equal attention to your vital machines, which are much more wonderfully constructed'.

This might not be a common attitude, among employers; but they did not think any the worse of Owen for holding it. They had confidence in him, as one of the group who represented them in negotiations with the Government over the reduction of import duty on raw cotton—duties which were a gift, as he argued in a memorandum on the subject, to their foreign competitors, who were not required to pay it, but who could, and did, persuade their governments to put import duties on cotton goods manufactured in Britain. Neither the Godwinian opinions expressed in Owen's *New View of Society*, nor his assertion, in a speech he made the following year to his fellow mill-owners, that cotton manufacture as it was then carried on was 'destructive of the health, wealth, and social

comforts of the mass of the people engaged in it', lost him that confidence;
for had he not also insisted in the same speech that the industry was vital
to the country's economy and, indeed, to her existence? Still more
important, Owen had the ear of ministers, as no other mill-owner had,
not even Peel. He had reasoned so effectively with Nicholas Vansittart,
the Chancellor of the Exchequer, that the mill-owners had at last been
granted a fifty per cent reduction in the duty.

There was no overt hostility at first to the measure Owen had prepared,
and which Peel introduced. It proposed to prohibit the employment in
mills of children under ten years of age, and to limit the working day of
children under the age of eighteen to twelve and a half hours, inclusive
of two hours for lessons and meals. But it also—and this was where the
mill-owners began to have doubts—provided for the appointment of
factory inspectors by the local magistrates, to ensure that the Act's
provisions were enforced. Even those mill-owners who agreed with Peel
about the desirability of limiting the working hours of children were
uneasy at the thought of inspection. What else, they began to wonder,
might be in store for them, if the measure went through? Could they
have time, they asked, to give it further thought? Peel, who had no
desire to anatagonise them, agreed to hold over until the following
session.

By the time he was ready to reintroduce it, the mill-owners had grown
alarmed about its possible consequences. The post-war boom had gone;
they were faced by the prospect of sharper competition not only from
each other but from mills in countries where there would be no legislative
restrictions. To meet their worries, Peel agreed to modifications. The
age at which children would be allowed to work in factories would be
nine, rather than ten; and their maximum hours, thirteen instead of
twelve and a half. He also agreed to a proposal which would inevitably
further delay the bill's passage: that a select committee of the House of
Commons should be set up to examine the whole question of the state
of children employed 'in the manufactories of the United Kingdom'.
Understandably, the cotton mill owners had protested about being
singled out for attention, while other manufacturers were not to be
affected. This deficiency might now be remedied, by a general survey.

As things turned out, the delay was utilised more effectively by Owen
than by the bill's critics. It gave him the chance to complete an extended
tour of the principal mills in the north, collecting evidence from manufacturers and from workers. He was accompanied by his son, Robert

Dale Owen, who in his memoirs was to recall the impression that had been made on him:

> The facts we collected seemed to me terrible almost beyond belief. Not in exceptional cases, but as a rule, we found children of ten years worked regularly fourteen hours a day, with but half an hour's interval for the midday meal, which was eaten in the factory. In the fine yarn cotton mills they were subjected to this labour in a temperature usually exceeding seventy-five degrees; and in all the cotton factories they breathed an atmosphere more or less injurious to the lungs, because of the dust and minute cotton fibres that pervaded it. In some cases we found that greed of gain had impelled the mill-owners to still greater extremes of inhumanity utterly disgraceful, indeed, to a civilised nation. The mills were run fifteen, and, in exceptional cases, *sixteen* hours a day, with a single set of hands; and they did not scruple to employ children of both sexes from the age of eight. We actually found a considerable number below that age.

The account that the Owens rendered of what they had seen was to be challenged in a few particulars; but its general accuracy was not disputed. About five thousand children under the age of seven, it was estimated, were employed in the mills; and from the mill-owners' own figures, it appeared that about half the total of their employees were under the age of eighteen. In the great majority of mills, children—whatever their age—had a working day of at least fourteen hours, out of which they might, if they were lucky, get a half-hour off for breakfast, and an hour for lunch. If demand was heavy, the hours could be increased to fifteen, and even sixteen. No legal protection for the children existed unless they were 'apprentices', and as the time when mill-owners had had to rely on apprenticed children was now past, the 1802 Act was rarely invoked. The magistrate employed to superintend the Manchester police force actually admitted that he had only read the Act the day before he gave evidence to the committee. In conversation with his fellow magistrates, he had come to the conclusion it was ineffective, 'and why should any of us look into it when not called upon to do so from any business coming before us?'

A succession of eminent doctors of the day, including Astley Cooper and Sir Gilbert Blane, were called by the committee to give their views about the likely effect on the health of young children of working in the mills; and they were in agreement that such long hours could be expected to be harmful to them not only at the time, but in later life, especially as they might suffer from postural defects—and from the lack of fresh

air. A Warwickshire magistrate who had visited a mill in summer had
found that the windows could not be opened even on the hottest day,
because fluff was blown around, and if it got into the noses and throats
of the children, they had to stop work for the length of time it took to
give them an emetic, and await its results.

Even some of the political economists, whom the mill-owners were
just beginning to regard as allies, came out against them. Every friend
of humanity, Malthus wrote, would wish Owen success in his efforts
to secure legislation to limit the hours that children had to work, and
to prevent them from being made to work at too early an age. The
owners had to fall back on the argument that the hours worked were
dictated by commercial considerations; that if shorter hours were worked,
there would be no jobs at all, as the employers would be forced out of
business; and that in any case, the children's health did not suffer. The
director of a number of mills, Archibald Buchanan, said that although
he preferred not to employ children under ten, and had only a few eight
and nine-year-olds in his mills, he had seen many children who had been
taken in at the age of six 'whose health did not appear at all to suffer;
on the contrary, when they grew to greater maturity, they appeared as
healthy, stout people as any in the country'; tradesmen, too, had found it
advantageous to employ them, after they left the mills, because of the
regular habits they had learned. A few industrialists went further,
arguing that the long hours were essential for the well-being of the
children. The fact that the select committee's terms of reference embraced
all factory employment induced Josiah Wedgwood—son of the founder
of the firm—to come to London to give evidence; if the hours the
children worked were reduced, he told the committee, they would earn
less, their parents would not be able to keep them so well fed and clothed,
and their health would be affected.

But this argument became less telling when related to the figures for
the wages of young children in cotton mills; they were getting a couple
of shillings a week—about a farthing an hour. The employers, alarmed,
resorted to smear tactics, to try to discredit witnesses who had given
evidence which could be used in favour of the bill. Owen himself was not
spared; a rival mill-owner from Glasgow offered to find what damaging
material he could about New Lanark. He was not very successful—the
best he could do was present a complaint from a woman who claimed she
had left because Owen had instituted dancing lessons, until 'they were
more fatigued than if they were working'. George Philips, an M.P. and

a cotton mill-owner, undertook to cross-examine Owen when he gave evidence to the committee; but he overreached himself, becoming so offensive that the other members of the committee decided to expunge his remarks from the record. An attempt privately to influence Sidmouth, the Home Secretary, was also rebuffed.

The smear technique, could, however, be used against witnesses less well-protected by their reputation. John Moss, the governor of the Preston workhouse, had given evidence to the committee about the time when he had been in charge of mill apprentices. Officially they worked a fourteen-hour day, but as they had to continue work at the end of it, to make up for any breakages or stoppages, they might have to work up to sixteen hours. During this time they were not allowed to sit; and so tired were they at the end of the day that he would sometimes find them asleep on the factory floor, not even having had the energy to go for a meal. Although some became deformed, he did not think the children were particularly unhealthy; but the system of appointing older apprentices as overseers, allowing them to beat their juniors, had finally so disgusted him that he had preferred to move to his lower paid workhouse job.

The injured mill-owners went to work, and a few days later William Travers, who had worked at the mill as an assistant to Moss, arrived to give evidence before the committee. Although he had found Moss a very decent man, Travers said, he was too free with the children: 'he would take a stick and put it to a girl's petticoats, and heave them up a little, and say "Let us see what sort of legs you have got."' The impact of this revelation, however, was lessened by Travers' admission that the owners of the mill, when it had been compelled temporarily to suspend production, had simply turned the children loose into the countryside, to fend for themselves. It was from the owners, too—Travers admitted— that he expected to receive the expenses of his visit to London.

But even if the mill-owners were justified in their assumption that some of the evidence given against them was untrustworthy, they could not deny that children of nine and younger were being compelled to work from twelve to fourteen hours a day. And what this meant to a child was perhaps most graphically shown by a man who, paradoxically, knew nothing about mills, and had never been inside one. Thomas Richardson lived in Manchester; and he had acquired his knowledge of the kind of life mill children had to lead solely from the sound of nearby factory bells. They were rung at four-thirty in the morning, to wake the children; and half an hour later, for the start of work. They were rung again at nine in the evening, to mark the end of the working day. He had never seen the children, either going to the mill, or returning from it; but the bells had told their story. Six days a week, fifty-two weeks in the year, with but rarely a holiday, those mill children began their working day before it was light, except in midsummer; and ended it, except in midsummer, after it was dark. In some mills the work might not be too exacting, the discipline not too harsh. In a few, the hours were shorter. But even in the most humane of them, the children would enjoy the daylight, in the open, only on Sundays. The measure of their depriva-tion rang on, in the echo of those Manchester bells.

The evidence left a profound impression on many M.P.s, and even on ministers. Owen received assurances that the Government was willing to facilitate the passage of Peel's bill; he was always to maintain that if Peel had brought it in, it would have passed in that session with no difficulty. But Peel was disturbed by the hostility it had aroused among his manufacturing colleagues. He pleaded indisposition; and, to Owen's annoyance, he did not offer the bill to some other M.P., to put through. He simply let it be known that he would bring it up again the following year.

The delay gave the mill-owners their opportunity. They prepared to present their case in a more favourable light with the help of a pamphlet, *An Enquiry into the Principle and Tendency of the Bill for Imposing Certain Restrictions on the·Cotton Factories.* It reiterated all the arguments which had been used against Peel's measure, and added some new ones: for example, that it would be dangerous to the children to allow any interval between the end of their work and sleep: 'all experience proves that in the lower orders the deterioration of morals increases with the quantity of unemployed time of which they have the command. Thus the bill actually encourages vice—it establishes idleness by Act of Parliament; it creates and encourages those practices which it pretends to discourage.' And that the mill-owners' campaign was not without effect become clear in 1818, when Peel at last brought in his bill to provide better protection for children working in factories. Although it had been substantially modified, to placate his fellow mill-owners—so altered, in fact, that Owen repudiated it—Peel found the spokesmen for the mill-owners more hostile, and much better briefed, than they had been before.

The most effective speech against the bill in the Commons came from Lord Stanley, heir to the earldom of Derby, and father of the future Prime Minister. As a member of the aristocracy and a landowner,

Stanley might ordinarily have been expected to share the uneasy distaste that so many of his class felt for the *nouveaux riches* industrialists; but political and financial expediency had some years before linked the fortunes of his family with theirs. In the eighteenth century the Derby family had controlled the two parliamentary seats for Preston; but with the coming of the mills, their ascendancy had been challenged, and in the 1790s the family decided that it would be wise to come to terms, rather than risk humiliating defeat. It was settled that one member of the family and one representative of industry should jointly share the representation for Preston; canvassing together, if necessary, in order to deter intruders. The arrangement had proved satisfactory, but it could hardly have survived if Stanley had shown himself insensitive to the mill-owners' desires.

In his speech, Stanley made shrewd use of a point that had been brought up against Peel when he had given evidence to the select committee. 'From your long acquaintance with mankind', Peel had been asked, 'do you believe there is such a want of tenderness and humanity in the lower orders, as would induce them, knowingly, to injure the health of their children?' The question was so oddly put, he had replied, that he found difficulty in answering it; he did not think parents would knowingly do such a thing, 'but if from necessity they are obliged to send their children to a factory, where they can earn some money, they do not enquire into the treatment of the children, nor the hours of their work, but they must conform to the rules of the factory while they continue there'.

Ignoring the reply, Stanley now proceeded to exploit the question. Whether or not it was right that children should be compelled to work long hours, he said, it was certainly not right that parents should be denied control over their children. Peel, after all, had claimed that the 1802 Act needed to be brought up to date because it had dealt only with apprentices, almost all of them pauper children from workhouses; and surely, Stanley argued, it was precisely *because* they had been pauper children, in the care of the State, that they required legislative protection. The new bill was introducing a new principle; if M.P.s gave it their blessing, they would in effect be agreeing to allow the removal of children from their parents by the State. What a deplorable effect this must have on the child—'to perceive that those to whom his interests ought to be most dear were not considered by the legislature as fit to be trusted with the regulation of his conduct!' The measure could only sow dissension in families. No! The parents were, and should remain, the natural guardians of the child.

Stanley reiterated the arguments put forward by the mill-owners at the select committee; that limiting hours of work would tend 'not to regulate, but to destroy the cotton trade altogether'; and that it would not improve morals—'on the contrary, it would only give more opportunities for idleness and all the bad consequences arising from it'. Other speakers also defended the mill-owners—sometimes with the backhanded argument that conditions had indeed been bad, but had recently been improved. A few denied that there was anything for Parliament to worry about. George Philips insisted that mill children were healthy and well looked after; the work required of them was as nothing compared to that demanded by other employers—including Parliament: 'the Speaker himself, sitting in that chair, goes through more labour in a single session, calculated to impair his health, than the people in a well-regulated factory endure for a whole year'. State interference, too, would encourage the re-emergence of combinations of workmen. The petitions received against the exploitation of child labour from working men, Philips assured the house, were not from disinterested workers anxious for their children's welfare; 'the house ought to know that these petitions were obtained by disorderly workmen meeting at public houses, and forming themselves into central committees'. If they wanted the spectre of Jacobinism to be seen again in the land, M.P.s would go the right way about it by passing Peel's bill into law.

Peel had earlier appeared to have lost heart for the struggle; but now, the criticisms of his adversaries roused him. The medical evidence, he felt—thirty Manchester doctors had signed a petition in support of the bill—was more likely to be impartial than that of the mill-owners: if factory life really were as healthy as some of them had made out, then 'applications ought to be made to the legislature for the erection of cotton mills, for the purpose of furthering and more effectively providing for the health of His Majesty's liege subjects'. The poet Warton had asked

> Within what mountain's craggy cell
> Delights the Goddess Health to dwell?

The answer, Peel surmised, seemed to be that the Goddess's current address was 'the cotton mill of Messrs. Finlay and Co., at Glasgow', whose salubrity 'appeared to be six times as great as that of the most healthy part of the kingdom'.

E

The inescapable fact, Peel insisted, was that the hours which young children had to work (and very young children had to work the same hours as older ones) were too long; and privately, he knew, many mill-owners admitted as much. But unless there was legislation, any mill-owner who tried to reduce them might find himself driven from business by his less scrupulous competitors. And it was no use opponents of the bill saying there was no precedent for intervention, in such circumstances. There was—the Act regulating the conditions under which the climbing boys could be employed. Its provisions had not applied only to pauper children. Nor was it reasonable to argue that there was no longer any need for legislation, as things had improved since the bill had first been introduced. If they had, was this not because of the bill? And, if so, was it not a good bill? And, 'what security was there that if Parliament withdrew its interference, the arrangements of those establishments would not again fall into that wrong and oppressive distribution of labour which previously characterised them?'

It was a spirited speech, and an effective one; it looked as if the Commons would be prepared to pass a bill to regulate the employment of children in factories, with a substantial majority. But again, Peel found himself beset by industrialists whose good will he had no desire to lose. His original measure had concerned itself only with cotton mills: would it not be wise to restrict the new bill's provisions to them? Peel wavered, and then agreed; and in this restricted, much-amended form, it was passed.

Peel hoped that by this concession, he would assuage the bill's opponents in the Lords. Again, he was quickly undeceived. It was promptly denounced there on the ground that it unfairly singled out the cotton industry for legislative attention, although conditions in wool and flax mills were just as bad, or worse. Surely, if regulations were considered necessary to protect children in one industry, that protection should extend to all?

In the Lords, too, the bill encountered an antagonist as determined as Stanley. As a young man, the Earl of Lauderdale had been one of the 'Friends of the People': legend had it that he had once appeared at Westminster wearing Jacobin-style dress. But even before holding minor office in 'All the Talents' he was moving away from traditional radicalism. When the bill was about to come up in the Lords in May, Lauderdale warned the House against it: 'were their lordships prepared to encroach upon that great principle of political economy, that labour ought to be left free, without taking upon themselves the trouble of investigating the subject?' But their lordships, he found, were unimpressed by his reasoning; Liverpool flatly stated that he did not regard children as free agents. So, when the bill came up for debate, Lauderdale subtly altered his tactics. Lord Kenyon, sponsoring it, claimed that there was no need for further investigation, as the Commons committee had provided the necessary evidence. But if the Commons had been satisfied with their enquiry, Lauderdale asked, why had they not legislated on it when the report appeared? He had heard, indeed, 'that Sir Robert Peel had been indisposed; but notwithstanding all the respect which he entertained for the hon. baronet, he could not consider that a sufficient reason for the delay, if the measure was as necessary as its supporters considered it to be'. Surely, if there was any doubt, their lordships ought to hold their own enquiry? Their lordships allowed themselves to be persuaded.

This time the mill-owners had a much better idea of what evidence was likely to be presented in favour of the bill. Their main weakness before the Commons committee, they realised, had been on the medical issue; doctor after doctor had pronounced against them. They now brought down their own doctors, from the North, to provide first-hand testimony about the health of the mill children. The evidence their doctors gave showed that they realised they were in an invidious position. For professional reasons, they did not care to say that the evidence given earlier by so many distinguished colleagues was rubbish. But if they wanted to keep their jobs, they had to give evidence the mill-owners wanted to hear. The contortions this required of them were illustrated in the evidence given by the Manchester physician, Edward Holme. He refused to be drawn into estimating how long children could be expected to stand, at their work, without danger to their health. So long as he found mill children healthy, he explained, that was a fact; and, so far as he was concerned, it was only the facts that mattered. Cross-examination failed to move him:

Q. Should you not think a child of the age of eight years being kept standing twelve hours in the day injurious to its health?

A. I should be able to form no opinion whatever on the subject, except I knew how it turned out in practice.

Q. Suppose I were to ask you, whether you thought it injurious to a child to be kept standing three-and-twenty hours out of the four-and-twenty, should you not think it must necessarily be injurious to the health, without any fact to rest upon, as a simple proposition put to a gentleman in the medical profession?

A. Before I answered that question I should wish to have an examination to see how the case stood. If there were such an extravagant thing to take place, and it should appear that the person was not injured by having stood three-and-twenty hours, I should then say it was not inconsistent with the health of the person so employed.

Although Holme was called as an expert witness, he had to admit that he knew so little of what went on in the mills that he could not even say whether the children worked sitting down, or standing up; and in general, the medical evidence called was so self-consciously defensive that it had the opposite effect to what the mill-owners had hoped. So far as Lauderdale was concerned, however, this mattered little. By the time the committee had finished, it was too late in the session for the measure to have any chance of passing. It had to be withdrawn—to await its chance in the new Parliament following the general election.

'I would God Almighty him . . .'

Of the three measures directly concerning the poor awaiting Parliament's review after the end of the war, the one that seemed least likely to create controversy was the amendment of the Act regulating the employment of chimney sweep's apprentices: the climbing boys.

It had very soon become obvious that the Act was being evaded. Its essential purpose had been to ensure that no boy should be apprenticed to a sweep before the age of eight, and that apprentices should be given protection by the law until they were out of their indentures. But the law had proved unenforceable, because the Lords had rejected the clause which would have compelled every chimney sweep to take out a licence to practise his trade. Had he known that he would lose his licence if he was detected in any breach of the law, a master sweep would have had a powerful inducement to obey it. But in the absence of a licensing system, anybody could set up as a sweep; and there was no effective police force, as it had proved impossible to keep a check that the law was being obeyed.

The Society for Bettering the Condition of the Poor had tried to arouse public concern over the treatment of the climbing boys, but without success; and in 1803 a separate body was formed for that purpose, the Society for Superseding the Necessity of Climbing Boys— its main aim being, as its name implied, to see whether some mechanical device could be found which would sweep chimneys. A reward was offered for the inventor who could produce the best contraption; and the winner came up with a brush attached to a flexibly-jointed hollow tube, constructed on the principle that was eventually to provide the sweep's standard equipment. But, to the society's annoyance, few sweeps seemed interested. They continued to employ climbing boys.

In 1817 Lord Milton brought the matter up in the Commons, suggesting that there should be an enquiry; and he was supported by the radical Henry Bennet, son of the Earl of Tankerville, a humanitarian and a member of the Society. The committee appointed to make the enquiry took evidence from several master sweeps, the main aim being to try to find why the 'machines', as the new brooms were described, were not in more general use. The trouble, the sweeps explained, was that the machines could not clean every 'flue'—the narrow and often twisting passage which connected the fireplace, or boiler, or stove, to the chimney. In any case, if machines were used, it would be very hard on the climbing boys, who would be out of their jobs, and would have to go back to the workhouse. As it was, not only were the boys employed; they were well looked after. 'I have had them very sickly when they came to me,' a master sweep claimed, 'and they have got as healthy as possible in a short time, which is astonishing.'

It was indeed astonishing, in view of the evidence which the Society was able to put before the committee. The sweeps had found a new source of recruits; they were purchasing the boys from their parents at the age of five, or even four, part of the bargain being that the parents should testify, if the need arose, that the child was over eight, at the time he was apprenticed. The reason for getting them so young was that flues were often impassable for older children; all too often, older boys got stuck. In one case which was described to the committee, a master sweep, trying to extinguish a fire in a flue, had ordered an eight-year-old boy to climb down through the chimney to put it out 'and the consequence, as might be expected, was his almost immediate death in a state, no doubt, of inexpressible agony'. When his body was eventually extricated, his elbows and knees were found to have been burned to the bone, revealing how he had struggled unavailingly to extricate himself.

Normally, though, boys were sent up the flue; which was safer. Even so, the older boys frequently got stuck—not so often on the climb itself, when they could lever themselves up with their feet, or pull themselves up (as their hands were above their heads) by their fingertips; but on the descent. As one witness described it, giving evidence, 'the boy's shirt is often very bad; the boy coming down, if the chimney be very narrow, and numbers of them are only nine inches, gets his shirt rumpled underneath him, and he has no power after he is fixed in that way'. In such circumstances, a rope had to be put round his ankles, so that he could be hauled down. One such episode, which had ended in the courts, was described to the Commons' committee:

> When Reid was pulling the rope, Panel (the accused master sweep) said 'You have not the strength of a cat'; he took the rope into his own hands, pulling as strongly as he could. Having pulled about a quarter of an hour, Panel and Reid fastened the rope around a crowbar, which they applied to the wall as a lever, and both pulled with all their strength for about a quarter of an hour longer, when it broke. During this time witness heard the boy cry, and say 'My God Almighty'. Panel said, 'If I had you here, I would God Almighty you'. Witness thought the cries were in agony.

Apparently they were. By the time they had decided to break down the wall, the boy was dead.

The evidence which had been laid before them, the committee reported, showed that children were

> stolen from their parents, and inveigled out of workhouses; that in order to conquer the natural repugnance of the infants to ascend the narrow and dangerous chimneys, to clean which their labour is required, blows are used; that pins are forced into their feet by the boy that follows them up the chimney, in order to compel them to ascend it; and that lighted straw has been applied for that purpose; that the children are subject to sores and bruises, and wounds and burns on their thighs, knees and elbows; and that it will require many months before the extremities of the elbows and knees become sufficiently hard to resist the excoriations to which they are at first subject; and that one of the masters, being asked if those boys are employed in sweeping chimneys during the soreness of those parts, he answered, 'It depends upon the sort of master they have got. Some are obliged to put them to work sooner than others; you must keep them a little at it even during their sores, or they will never learn their business.'

The medical evidence had been particularly gruesome. Climbing boys, it was found, suffered extensively from deformities because they were forced to work in chimneys while they were still growing, and their bones were soft; carrying on their heads bags of soot weighing twenty pounds even when empty. The deformities were caused mainly by the position in which the boys had to work, supporting themselves by their feet and knees while scraping off the soot, the report drew attention to the observation of everyone as to the stunted growth, the deformed state of body, the look of wretchedness and disease which characterises this unfortunate class; but it is in evidence before them that there is a formidable complaint which chimney sweepers in particular are liable to; from which circumstances, by way of distinction, it is called the Chimney Sweeper's Cancer. Mr. Wright, a surgeon, informed your committee that whilst he was attending Guy's and St. Bartholomew's Hospitals, he had several cases under his care, some of which were operated on; but in general they are apt to let them go too far before they apply for relief.

Reputable master sweeps tried to observe the law, the report conceded; but this only encouraged competitors who were less reputable to enter the market—many of them former craftsmen, put out of work by machinery. They picked up boys wherever they could, keeping them in huts, sheds and cellars, to evade the attentions of the law, so that 'the youngest and most delicate children are in the service of the worst class of masters, and employed exclusively to clean flues which, from their peculiar construction, cannot be swept without great personal hazard'. Yet expert witnesses in evidence had shown that between seventy-five and ninety-five per cent of chimneys could be satisfactorily swept by the new machines; that most of the remainder could be easily and cheaply converted; and that where flues could not be converted, because they were too narrow, it was in any case arguable that they ought not to be swept by a climbing boy, because of the risk involved. The committee, therefore, agreed that a new Act was required, to stop climbing boys from being used.

M.P.s' horrified reaction to the evidence encouraged Bennet to bring in a bill, early in 1818; the essential clause laying down that no child under fourteen years of age should be apprenticed to a sweep—thereby virtually preventing the use of climbing boys at all, as children over that age would be too big. The master sweeps, alarmed, realised that they would have to cast around for influential support; and they were in luck. Even if it were true—which they did not accept—that the new brooms could clean most town chimneys, what about country houses? There, chimneys were apt to meander—sometimes rising vertically, sometimes having horizontal stretches: sometimes broad; sometimes narrow. Mechanical sweeping devices of any kind would be useless; and without climbing boys to remove the accumulation of soot, there would be serious risk of fire.

Most Members of Parliament had country houses; and their uneasiness was sufficient, when Bennet brought in his bill, to make it clear to him that he would have to modify it, to relieve his colleague's fears. He was prepared to concede property owners more time to have their chimneys altered—provided they would accept the bill. With this concession incorporated, it was carried in the Commons with acclamation.

But when the subject of the climbing boys was put to the Lords, Lauderdale was there to insist, as with Peel's factory bill, that their Lordships must hold their own enquiry; and this was agreed. A select committee began to take evidence; and it was clear that the master sweeps, like the mill-owners, had profited from their experience with the Commons. Again, they emphasised how well they looked after the boys, and how desirable it was for the boys to have such a fine employment opportunity; but they concentrated more on the risks to property which would be incurred if the boys could not be used. A number of society houses, they pointed out—notably Lord Lascelles's in Hanover Square— had been saved from destruction only because a climbing boy had found a fault which would have led to a fire. The Secretary to the Phoenix Fire Office was brought in to advise that it would be dangerous to prohibit the use of climbing boys entirely; and representatives of other insurance companies echoed his warning.

Yet in some respects the evidence put before the Lords committee was even more terrible than that heard in the Commons. It revealed, among other things, that flues had been getting smaller. Boys were sometimes asked to clean flues eight inches by nine; 'these they are always obliged to climb in this posture', a witness explained—illustrating it—'keeping the arms up straight; they slip their arms down, they get jammed in; unless they get their arms close over their head they cannot climb'. The committee also heard why it was that there were so many cases of distorted limbs; a former climbing boy explained that it was the result of the process of parging, or relining, flues: 'We used to go and sit all a-twist to parge them, according to the floors, to keep the smoke from coming out; then, I could not straighten my legs; and that is the reason why there are many cripples.'

Among the stories given of fatal accidents there was one presented by the clerk to the coroner of Middlesex; an eyewitness account by a servant of the death of a twelve-year-old boy who had been sent to clean a chimney in Somers Town, where the job needed to be done in a hurry. The boy went up the flue, but quickly came down again saying it was too hot:

The master told him to make as much haste as he could. He was a long time
going up. Heard him come down as low as the shop; heard him cry out he
was hung to a nail; heard him crying and sobbing, very much; very near
nine o'clock, having been up about twenty minutes; never heard any more . . .
Upon asking the boy's master, he said there was no danger in the least. Heard
the boy cry out a great many times, and sent another boy up after him; he
went as far as he could reach his toes; the child said he could not pull him
down, 'He won't come down, master', who said, 'Damn him, let him stop.'
He was twenty-five minutes in the chimney before witness went to bed.
In about a quarter of an hour his mistress came, and called him up. When
he got up they were taking down the flue in the shop, in which witness
assisted . . . imagines there might be about a bushel and a half of soot all
round the boy, who was not quite dead.

The builder who extricated the boy said it was very difficult, as he
was so wedged in, and the flue was so exceedingly hot. The flue was
fourteen inches by twelve, but there was 'a pinch near the turn of the
chimney'. That, and the soot, and the heat, the builder testified, must
have caused the boy's death by suffocation.

In their report, the Lords committee admitted that the evidence they
had heard was contradictory. But although some masters were careful and
humane, it was obvious that the intentions of 1788 were not being heeded.
For example, it was still a common practice in the trade to send boys
up chimneys actually on fire, for the purpose of drawing down the lighted
soot; and this, the report urged, ought to be forbidden. The evidence had
also shown that the sweeping machine could be used satisfactorily for
almost all purposes; and where it could not be used, flues could be
adapted for a trifling expense. For the time being, climbing boys would
have to continue to be employed; but they should be sent up flues for
purposes of inspection only. And as this principle was already incorporated
in Bennet's bill, the committee recommended it should be accepted
without further amendment.

But such was the impact of the evidence on Lord Auckland, who had
been in the chair for much of the enquiry, that he wanted the bill to be
delayed. As he explained to the House, he had become dissatisfied with
the bill not, as some of its critics were, because it went too far, but
because it did not go far enough. It had shown that although there were
humane master sweeps, there were others who were guilty of the grossest
inhumanity; and this left Parliament with no alternative, he thought,
but to ban the use of climbing boys altogether—'what he conceived

ought to be the principle which should guide their lordships in a case of this kind was that no persons should be permitted to impose on others, and especially on children, any labour calculated to injure their health or impair their bodily strength'. All that remained in doubt was whether the new machines would enable all chimneys to be swept without the use of climbing boys. In the experiments which had begun, at the request of the Lord's committee, sixty of the most difficult chimneys had been swept without a single failure. He therefore suggested that Parliament should await the final outcome of the experiment, before proceeding with the bill; and, as this meant it could not be proceeded with in that session, it would have to be brought in again in the next. Their lordships concurred.

2. LAISSEZ-FAIRE

Parliament, then, had had the opportunity to realise the miserable condition of the agricultural labourers, children in factories, and climbing boys: it had been able to investigate, and to debate, what could be done. In each case, investigation had revealed the existence of grave defects in the law, or in its enforcement; and the debates had shown that there was a general desire in both Houses (though more extensive in the Commons) to remedy the evils that had arisen as a result. Yet nothing had been accomplished. In the case of the climbing boys, admittedly, the final delay had been at the request of one of the sponsors of the bill; but in any case it was far from certain that it would have got through before the end of the session.

There were a number of reasons why Parliament had been unable to take decisive action, the most important being ministers' unwillingness to give a decisive lead. This was not unusual; until the younger Pitt had come into office, governments had not considered themselves as initiators of legislation. Parliament was the legislature; the executive was there to carry out its instructions; and as Parliament was well-packed with the nominees of the aristocracy, the risk that its instructions would be radical was small. Acts of Parliament were mainly designed to put patches in the constitution, where necessary, rather than to change it. Even Pitt had found, when he wanted more drastic changes, that he could not get them.

But this system had been based on the assumption that the country's economy could be left under the general supervision of the magistracy.

With the growth of industry, it was ceasing to be effective. In the past, it had been relatively simple for the magistrates to step in. If, say, the silk weavers of Spitalfields failed to reach an agreement with their masters the magistrates could impose one. But the Spitalfields weavers could not expect that the same agreement would be reached in Yorkshire; and if the London magistrates awarded them higher wages than the Yorkshire weavers were getting, there was a natural tendency for orders, and jobs, to go where the product was cheaper.

If there were to be such agreements, then, they would need to be laid down on a national scale. But the necessary machinery for regulation on such a scale—a civil service—hardly existed; and after the war the Tory Government, bitterly assailed as it was for not reducing its expenditure more rapidly, was in no mood to incur more criticism by employing more functionaries—especially as the opposition would certainly complain that ministers were merely creating places to distribute among their friends. The Government was therefore reluctant to accept any measure which would require administration, or even supervision, except such as the magistrates could continue to provide.

Another reason why reformers found their task difficult was that the great majority of ministers were members of the aristocracy. All of them were landowners, or would be when some near relation died. The war had brought them the gratifying increase in their revenue for which Byron had pilloried them:

Safe in their homes, these Sabine tillers sent
Their brethren out to battle. Why? For rent!
Year after year they voted cent for cent
Blood, sweat and tear-wrung millions – why? For rent!
They roared, they dined, they drank, they swore they meant
To die for England – why then live? For rent!

Having become accustomed to a higher standard of living, they were anxious not to let it go; they could easily find rationalisations to justify the corn laws, the abolition of the income tax, and the decision to retain family allowances. Only over industry were ministers reasonably detached; but even here, there were a growing number of landowners with a financial stake whose influence would be thrown on the side of non-intervention.

Apart from self-interest, ministers tended to allow themselves to be guided by the assumption that a government should not act, except to enforce law and order, if it could possibly help it. 'The legislature ought not to interfere,' Liverpool would argue, 'but should leave everything to find its own level.' So the chances of getting any reform through were small, unless a really decisive case could be made out for it; and as the reformers were often divided, the chances of their being able to make out a decisive case were also small. Not merely were they divided; many of them were also suspect. Their reforming zeal, it was feared, might be a cloak for Jacobinism.

'Their condition is absolutely worse'

Some of the ideas of the Tory reformers, for example—who might have been expected to have the greatest chance of influencing the Government—derived from what ministers regarded as a tainted source: Godwin. Still, they were expounded by Southey in the impeccably Tory *Quarterly Review*, founded in 1809 as a counterbalance to the *Edinburgh*. Southey had acquired respectability; he had actually been appointed Poet Laureate in 1813, to the irritated amusement of those who remembered him in his Jacobin period. He was High Church, and high Tory. So was Coleridge; and although their relations with each other were sometimes strained, their attitudes on social issues remained similar. Southey was the more prominent in this period—it was he who radicals tended to name, when they were denouncing the *Quarterly*'s Tory attitudes; but Coleridge was in the long run the more influential. John Stuart Mill was to link him with Bentham as the two great seminal influences of the time.

Southey put forward what he felt ought to be the Tory view on poverty in a *Quarterly* article, 'The condition of the poor considered', in 1816. The wealth and power of Britain, he admitted, was 'a phenomenon to which no parallel can be found in the history of the world'. But the wealth of a country could not be measured by its revenue alone; he felt bound to point out that all was not as it should be. In the course of the war, the middle classes had considerably improved their condition. Their comforts, their luxuries—he estimated—had augmented two-fold. But the poor had not benefited. If their living standard had been maintained, they would still have been relatively worse off, by contrast with the rest of the community; but it had not been maintained: 'their condition is absolutely worse; the same quantity of labour will no longer procure the same quantity of the necessities of life'.

The reason, Southey thought, was paradoxically to be looked for in the great improvement in agricultural techniques. As a consequence land

had been enclosed, and farms had been extended and consolidated, to
exploit the resources more effectively. But the benefit went to landlord
and tenant. Countless smallholders and cottagers had been deprived of
their main source of livelihood, at a time when their village crafts were
less in demand, owing to the competition of manufacturers in towns. And,
of course, they no longer had access to the common, to keep their cows
or their ducks. Why, they were even deprived of fuel! They had formerly
been able to pick up as they needed it: now they had to buy it.

Not only was this hard on the families concerned, it was unfortunate,
and even dangerous, for the country as a whole—particularly the dis-
appearance of the yeomen, 'the right English trees in which our heart
of oak was matured'. In the old days the yeoman had more than earned his
keep, in his working years; 'when he grew old, he had his place in the
chimney corner, or the beehive chair; and it was the light of his own fire
which shone upon his grey hairs. Compare this with the old age of the day
labourer, with parish allowances for a time, and the parish workhouse at
last!' By destroying this independent breed of men, Southey feared,
society was stirring up trouble for itself—and expense; for where there
was neither hope nor pride to sustain him, why should the young labourer
deny himself indulgence? 'If the landowners were to count up what they
have gained by throwing their estates into large farms, and what they have
lost by the increase of the poor rates, they would have little to congratulate
themselves on the result.'

What, then, could be done? Southey referred his readers to the reports
of the Society for Bettering the Condition of the Poor, which had
afforded convincing proof that the labourer who had a plot of land was
decidedly better off; that the provision of land for this purpose was also
in the ratepayer's interest, because a labourer who had land was less
likely to become a pauper; and that the landowner benefited, because
labourers with land were more regular and punctual with their cottage
rents. Here, then—Southey urged—was an expedient which could easily
be adopted, at relatively little expense.

There was nothing new in his argument; its importance lay in the
fact that it repudiated from a Tory standpoint the assumption, coming
to be accepted, that the distress of the agricultural workers was due to the
operation of the poor laws. Southey did not dispute that the poor laws
might contribute; but the real responsibility, he was claiming, lay with
the landowners, who had uprooted the yeoman, the cottager and the
labourer from the land. And the following year the point was taken up

and embroidered by Coleridge, in a criticism of the Sturges Bourne report. The report, he felt, had effectively demonstrated the existence of 'a peasantry sinking into pauperism, step by step with the rise of the farmer's profits'; but it had concentrated too much on the pauperising of the labourers, and too little on the landowners' and farmers' growing wealth. It was not the poor laws that were at fault; it was the new commercialism of the rich, leading them to regard the land as something to be exploited. High rents had given the landowners a relish for accumulation comparable to that of the trader; and they were 'joining in the general competition, under the same trading spirit'. Parliament, which ought to be restraining them, was in their control. They could do what they liked; and what they now chiefly liked to do was increase their incomes from their property, regardless of the effect on others. The farmers, catching the infection, had also begun to think of their farms as business concerns, out of which must be extracted every possible penny—a view which suited the landowners very well. But the agricultural labourer was the loser, as his wages were cut to improve profits. The bigger and more profitable the farms, the worse his condition tended to be; it would be found that in districts where the average acreage ran into four figures, the poor rates were highest, 'the distresses of the poor most grievous, and the prevalence of revolutionary principles most alarming'.

The mistake which had been made, Coleridge argued, was to equate fixed with movable property, and persons with things. The owner should not regard his estate as a merchant regarded his cargo; the cargo was not affected by the merchant's commercial dealings, but the land could be. And whereas it was reasonable to use things as mere means to an end, people should not be exploited for that purpose 'without directly or indirectly sharing in that end'. The system might appear of direct benefit to the farmer, who could get his work done for less money; and of indirect benefit to the landowners, who could expect higher rents. But in practice, it ensured a widely diffused lack of spending power; and this had given rise to the singular state of affairs 'in which without absurdity, a superabundant harvest can be complained of as an evil, and the recurrence of the same as a national calamity'.

This commercialising process, Coleridge concluded, was both uneconomic and demoralising, and ought to be reversed. In the first place, it should be re-established that the land belonged not to man, but to nature: as the source of subsistence for all, it should no longer be equated with other forms of private property, in which nobody but the owner had any rights. This notion, he pointed out, was of quite recent growth: 'private property' had formerly been confined to movables. Estates, though privately owned, should be treated as a trust; and one of the trust's aims should be to ensure the prosperity of the people who lived and worked on them. The Government was in a position to make a positive contribution. Its duty should be to try not merely to ensure the means of subsistence to every individual, but also to provide him with the prospect of bettering his own condition, or that of his children; and to give him the opportunity to develop 'those faculties which are essential to his humanity—that is, to his rational and moral being'.

Wordsworth shared these views. 'Everything has been put up to market', he complained in a letter written in 1817, 'and sold for the highest price it would fetch.' Farmers had formerly been attached to their labourers, and labourers to the farmers who employed them; all that kind of feeling has vanished. But the former Godwinians found it difficult to attract support outside their circle for the new—or, as they would have claimed, old—Tory philosophy. The only man of influence that they could claim as an adherent was also a literary figure: Walter Scott, then engaged on his Waverley novels.

'I am glad you are turning your mind to the state of the poor,' he wrote to tell Southey in the spring of 1817: 'should you enter into details on the subject of the best mode of assisting them, I would be happy to tell you the few observations I have made.' The observations showed that Scott, too, was disturbed by the growing tendency of landowners to think of their property only in terms of rents, and of the workers on the property only in terms of labour. He had therefore, he explained, decided to keep about thirty labourers fully employed on his own land, through the winter.

> This I do not call charity, because they executed some extensive plantations which I could never have got so cheaply, and which I always intended one day to do. But neither was it altogether selfish on my part, because I was putting myself to inconvenience and incurring the expense of several years at once, and I certainly would not have done so, but to serve mine honest neighbours, who were likely to want work but for such exertion.

But what little chance there was of the *Quarterly* philosophers impressing Tory politicians of the need to adopt different social policies was set back by a trivial but humiliating episode; the publication in 1817 of a hitherto unpublished play Southey had written in his Jacobin period—*Wat Tyler*, an enthusiastic dramatisation of the peasant revolt four centuries before. Southey had been urging that the journalists of the underground press should be prosecuted for 'sowing the seeds of rebellion, insulting the government, and defying the laws of the country'. The publication of *Wat Tyler* by a journalist who had been doing just that—the freethinking Richard Carlile—gave the other radicals the opportunity facetiously to urge the crown law officers to accept the good advice of Southey (the writer of the article), and to prosecute Southey (the writer of the play) for sedition—an embarrassing situation for him, and one which his protestations of consistency did little to improve.

'All these spring from labour'

The social philosophy which Southey and Coleridge were putting forward differed surprisingly little from that which William Cobbett was now preaching to a far wider and more enthusiastic following in his *Register*. Cobbett's imprisonment had not resulted in the collapse of his newspaper, as the Government had hoped it would. Jails at the time had not been 'reformed'; and with the help of a friendly sheriff, who admired his brand of radicalism, Cobbett was able to live in the Newgate in much the same style as he could have lived at an inn, with almost every freedom except of movement. Friends could come to visit him; even old Maseres, to show his independence of his brother judges, came to call. Imprisonment was actually an assistance, in easing Cobbett's chronic financial difficulties; with the help of his children, the *Register* appeared regularly, and its circulation—already an unprecedented six thousand when he went to the Newgate—continued to rise. Cobbett, though, was not happy even when the circulation began to approach five figures. Selling as it did at a shilling, the *Register* was out of the reach of the readers he most wanted to appeal to—the small farmers, and the farm labourers—who would be lucky if they earned that much for a day's work, and who could not ordinarily get time off to go to a reading room to see it.

When the 1816 government raised the stamp duty to fourpence, Cobbett had an inspiration. He added only a halfpenny to the price of the *Register*; and he published one of his lay sermons, an *Address to the Journeymen and Labourers*, not only in the *Register*'s ordinary contents, but also separately as a special edition. As it contained no news, he could claim it was a pamphlet, not subject to the stamp duty. So great was the response that he made the 'pamphlet' a regular weekly feature; and his

'Twopenny Trash'—an abusive comment which he gratefully appropriated—began to sell up to fifty thousand copies a week, a circulation
hitherto unparalleled.

The aim of the *Address* was to arouse the journeymen, small farmers and
labourers to a realisation not so much of their political rights, as of their
social importance. 'The real strength and all the resources of a country
ever have sprung, and ever must spring, from the *labour* of its people,'
he reminded them, 'elegant dresses, superb furniture, stately buildings,
fine roads and canals, fleet horses and carriages, numerous stout ships,
warehouses teeming with goods; all these, and many other objects that
fall under our view, are so many marks of national wealth and resources.
But all these spring from *labour*. Without the journeyman and the
labourer, none of these could exist.' But he was careful to insist that this
was not an excuse for violence against their employers or the Government,
in pursuit of abstract justice. That was when the French had been misled.
The English would not be so foolish—'we want great alteration, but we
want nothing new'.

Southey would not have put it very differently; and they were also in
agreement about what they believed to be the main cause of the countryman's decline—enclosures. Cobbett conceded that enclosures could be,
and sometimes were, used to improve the land and the condition of the
people who lived on it. But he insisted that they could only be justified
if the condition of the people *was* improved; and too often, it was not.
Nor should a common necessarily be described as unproductive because
it was not cultivated: 'it helps to rear, in health and vigour, numerous
families of the children of labourers, which children, were it not for these
wastes, must be crammed into the stinking suburbs of towns'. To the
arguments that any landowner who enclosed what had been unproductive
common land would, in his own interest, surely only do so for productive
purposes, Cobbett was able to show that this was not necessarily true;
land could also be bought as a speculation, because the rise in its value
could produce a capital gain even if it were left unused. The result was
that yeomen and smallholders were being deprived of their living and
driven to look for work as labourers; and jobs were hard to find.

For Cobbett, too, as for Southey and Coleridge—and Arthur Young—
the urgent need was a restoration of the system by which the majority
of those who lived on the land had a stake in it, even if it were no more
than a small plot, so long as it were enough to grow vegetables on, and
keep a pig, or a cow. Where Cobbett parted company from the Tory

reformers was over how these aims could be achieved. They looked for a change of heart among the landowning aristocracy; recalled to its former sense of duty, that class would use its power to undertake the necessary reforms, and in so doing both restore and preserve the constitution. Cobbett could no longer share this hope; he had observed how land-owners and aristocrats operated when corrupted by power. Nobody had been more violent than Cobbett, a few years before, in denouncing democrats; now he was insisting that the social system could be changed only by electoral reform.

But what kind of reform? And how to obtain it? On these issues, radicalism was hopelessly split. Cartwright's proposals still provided the reformers with a political aim, and Cartwright himself was still there to take the chair at campaign meetings; but there were serious differences on strategy—whether reform could be obtained by constitutional means, or would have to be won by force, or the threat of force; and also on tactics—whether small instalments of reform should be accepted, if they could be obtained.

The panic reaction of the Government to the reports of its spies, showed that the existence of these different degrees of radicalism was no more likely to be recognised by the crown law officers than it had been in the early 1790s; and Cobbett felt that not even his public repudiation of Luddism was going to help him. When the Government brought out a regulation requiring that reading rooms should be licensed—the licence to be withdrawn if papers of a seditious or immoral tendency were found on the premises—he believed that it must be directed at his Twopenny Trash—and at him. After so recently leaving the Newgate, he was in no mood to return. Three weeks after the suspension of habeas corpus, in 1817, he sailed into voluntary exile in the United States.

'Calculated to make the rich poor'

But there was one branch of the opposition which ministers would have found it difficult to proceed against, because its attacks on Government policy were conducted on a more academic plane: the political economists; James Mill, Jeremy Bentham, and their protégé David Ricardo.

Although political economy had made an impact from time to time in reports of committees of enquiry, it had as yet hardly emerged as a political philosophy; only the simplest of its principles had achieved public recognition. In 1816, however, Mrs. Jane Marcet's *Conversations on Political Economy* appeared, and they were an instant success. The conversations were between a 'Mrs. B' and 'Caroline'—Caroline, impulsive, tender-hearted and naïve; Mrs. B, worldly-wise and shrewd; and between them, they discussed the political and social problems of the time. On a few issues, where the political economists themselves had not reached agreement, Caroline and Mrs. B were prepared to advance remedies which were not, strictly-speaking, orthodox; when Caroline spoke highly of the value of a kitchen garden, for example, Mrs. B agreed, on the ground it was better for the labourer to spend his leisure there than in an alehouse. But in general Mrs. Marcet stuck closely to her brief; and, unlike some later amateurs in the field, she attracted not only readers—a new edition of the *Conversations* was required within a year— but also critical approval. The young Macaulay said that every girl who had read it would be able to teach Robert Walpole—the Prime Minister who, up to that time, had the greatest reputation as a financier—lessons in finance: the French economist Jean-Baptiste Say praised it; a quarter of a century later, McCulloch still rated it the best introduction to the science.

From Mrs. Marcet, it was therefore possible for the interested but uninstructed to find what political economists were thinking about the poor laws—something that had not been clarified by Adam Smith. The sentimental Caroline was sure that the destitute should not be allowed to starve; and Mrs. B agreed. But she insisted, and Caroline had to concede, that poor relief should no longer come from the rates, not only because it encouraged the idle and the profligate to live at the industrious ratepayer's expense, but because 'by encroaching on the funds destined for the maintenance of labourers, it diminishes the demand for labourers, and consequently lowers wages'. This was a different approach to the subject from that of either the Tory reformers or the radicals; yet it could be put forward as a radical solution, and one which was much more likely to impress M.P.s, as it promised not merely to help the poor, but in the process to reduce the burden of taxation. And the following year, it was given formal recognition in David Ricardo's *Principles of Political Economy*, which immediately became the gospel of the new radicalism, relegating *The Wealth of Nations* to the comparative standing of an Old Testament.

The price of labour, Ricardo argued—as of other commodities—was in the short term regulated by the laws of supply and demand. If too many labourers were looking for too few jobs, wages must fall. The assumption upon which the poor laws had been based, and on which they were still maintained, was that funds could be transferred from the pockets of the well-off to provide work—or failing that, relief—for those whose wages fell below subsistence level, or who could not find work at all. But this was a mistake. The money distributed as poor relief was not conjured from the air. It was taken from the individual citizen in taxes. If it had not been taken from him, he would clearly have put it to some other use; he would have spent it, or invested it. Either way, it would have helped to provide employment; and—this being to Ricardo the essential point—the funds available would have been used more effectively, more productively than they could be by the State; not necessarily because the State would spend them unwisely (though it probably would) but because it would have to waste part of them on the maintenance of the bureaucratic machine.

It was consequently futile, Ricardo thought, to imagine that public works schemes could be substituted for straightforward relief, to make the poor earn their livelihood; 'that part of the capital which employs the poor upon the roads, for example, cannot fail to employ men elsewhere'—an opinion echoed, the same year, in the Sturges Bourne report. The number of people in employment at any given time, it asserted, must depend on the amount of money available at that time to be laid out in wages. 'Whoever, therefore, is maintained by the law as a labouring pauper, is maintained only instead of some other individual, who would otherwise have earned, by his own industry, the money bestowed on the pauper.' Providing employment out of the rates did not and could not make any improvement in the condition of the workers as a whole, because compulsory application of funds 'tends (as it must always tend) to employ the portion it distributes less profitably than it would have been if left to the interested superintendence of its owners'.

Any form of poor relief, therefore, would do more harm than good. 'The clear and direct tendency of the poor laws', Ricardo asserted

> is not, as the legislature benevolently intended, to amend the condition of the poor, but to deteriorate the condition of both poor and rich; instead of making the poor rich, they are calculated to make the rich poor; and whilst the present laws are in force, it is quite in the natural order of things that the fund for the maintenance of the poor should progressively increase, till it has absorbed all the net revenue of the country, or at least so much of it as the state shall leave to us, after satisfying its own never-failing demands for the public expenditure.

The nature of the evil pointed inexorably to the remedy—the abolition of the poor laws: 'he is the best friend to the poor, and to the cause of humanity, who can point out how this end can be attained with the most security, and at the same time with the least violence'.

But that was still the trouble; how could the poor laws be abolished without disturbance? If they were simply repealed, nobody could be certain that there would overnight be released such a surge of productive energy that all the able-bodied would forthwith find employment. Suppose there still turned out to be a population surplus, so that there were not enough jobs to go round, however satisfactorily the economy was working: what was going to happen to the surplus? Were the unemployed to be left to starve?

By the time Ricardo's *Principles* appeared, however, a way out of the dilemma had presented itself. In it, he had accepted an argument in favour of the abolition of the poor laws, which was not directly derived from political economy, but could be grafted on. Apart from their inherent economic weakness, he explained, the poor laws could be shown to encourage another pernicious tendency whose influence had been hidden, but fortunately was no longer a mystery, 'since it has been fully developed by the able hand of Mr. Malthus'.

By 1817, the correctness of the Malthusian theory seemed to have been amply confirmed. The first complete census of England had been taken in 1800, and published the following year, and with the publication of the results of the second, ten years later, the long-standing argument whether the population was increasing or decreasing was finally settled. It was increasing. And there was no longer, as there had been while the war lasted, a fear that a decrease of population would endanger the national safety. Napoleon was on St. Helena; no other foreign foe had appeared. As for internal enemies, it could be argued that they were largely the product of the processes that Malthus was describing, which were creating a surplus labour force, jobless and feckless, an easy prey for the demagogue.

The growth of population, leading to a surplus of labour—Ricardo wrote to his friend, the magistrate Hutches Trower—could only be checked by the repeal of the poor laws:

> The population can only be repressed by diminishing the encouragement to its *excessive* increase – by leaving contracts between the poor and their employers perfectly free, which would limit the quantity of labour in the market to the effective demand for it. By engaging to feed all who may require food you in some measure create an unlimited demand for human beings, and if it were not for the bad administration of the poor laws, for the occasional hard-heartedness of overseers and the avarice of parishes, which in a degree checks

their evil effects, the population and the rates would go on increasing in a regular progression till the rich were reduced to poverty, and till there would no longer be any distinction of ranks.

But suppose family allowances were abolished: would this not mean that married men with families would suffer by comparison with those who remained single? It would, Ricardo admitted:

> and I can see no reason to regret it. When the wages of a married man with a family are barely adequate to his own and his family's maintenance, the wages of the single man may be ample. All this I admit, but if it is a necessary consequence of the abolition of the poor laws it must be acquiesced in under the circumstances of an abolition. Even if it were an evil, which I think it is not, it must be endured for the sake of the good which would accompany it.

The usefulness of Malthus's theory to Ricardo was not simply that it lent justification to the arguments of the political economists against the poor law. If they should be charged with inhumanity, Malthus had also provided him with the perfect answer. By providing relief, and thereby encouraging the poor to procreate, humanitarians might be sparing the living poor some suffering; but it was at the cost of more prolonged suffering to generations yet unborn, until the country became so over-crowded that it could no longer support the population, or until the rates exceeded the ratepayers' capacity to pay. Either way, the end would be catastrophic. Abolition of the poor laws, therefore, cruel though the remedy might appear, would in the long run be the most humane cure.

Because Malthus's theory of population dovetailed in so satisfactorily with the principles of political economy, Ricardo and his followers began to take for granted that his criticism of the poor law was based on the same reasoning—though in fact it was based on a hypothesis, the truth of which Malthus had assumed, rather than proved: that population growth was encouraged by the provision of outdoor relief and family allowances. The hold which this assumption was taking was illustrated in a memorandum which Robert Torrens laid before the Sturges Bourne committee. Colonel Torrens had won a reputation for valour in the unfortunate Walcheren expedition; he was now winning another as the most forthright exponent of the principles of political economy. The system of supplementing wages by allowances from the rates, he suggested, was self-evidently bound to be destructive. If the ratepayers had to give,

say, one tenth of their incomes, this would simply mean that the recipients
would breed up to the limit, until the increase in population forced them
back into misery and want.

If, on witnessing this renewal of distress, the landed proprietors and capitalists
should consent to give twenty, instead of ten per cent, upon their incomes, in
aid of wages, the same progress would be repeated – temporary relief would
be again administered, and permanent misery would again return. If thirty,
forty, fifty, say, if one hundred per cent were yielded by the landed proprietors
and capitalists, and the whole both of rent and of profit were given in aid of
wages, the process and the result would, with respect to the labouring classes,
be precisely as before.

Worse—Torrens went on—the money thus squandered would have
been taken from industry, so that there would be no surplus to provide
capital to make goods for export: 'the universal poverty of the people
must render the purchase of foreign corn impracticable, and deficient
crops must inevitably lead to famine'.

But it was Ricardo's sanction that mattered. The publication of his
Principles invested him with almost oracular authority. The book seemed
to complete the process, begun by Adam Smith, of establishing political
economy as a science—at least in the minds of believers. And although
it was not easy reading, it was capable of affecting some people with
much the same amazed delight as *Political Justice* had done—even when
they least expected it. Thomas de Quincey had held political economists
in low esteem: 'the very dregs and rinsings of the human intellect',
he had called them; but after his protracted opium bout of 1817–18,
when he had been unable to think, let alone read, his intellectual
interests were revived largely through reading Ricardo. 'Wonder and
curiosity were emotions that had long been dead in me. Yet I wondered
at once—wondered at myself that I could once again be stimulated to the
effort of reading; and much more, I wondered at the book . . . Previous
writers had been crushed and overlaid by the enormous weights of facts,
details and exceptions; Mr. Ricardo had deduced, *a priori*, from the
understanding itself, laws which first shot arrowy light into the dark
chaos of materials, and had thus constructed what hitherto was but a
collection of tentative discussions into a science of regular proportions,
now first standing upon an eternal basis.'

'By telling them disagreeable truths'

Much though ministers would have liked to accept Ricardo's simple solution to the problems of the poor laws, 1817 was not the time, they felt, to make such experiments—as their reluctance to implement the findings of the Sturges Bourne committee showed; and even when a better harvest and improved trade reduced the tension, they were in no mood to risk renewing discontent. There was consequently still a chance that they might be sympathetic to other proposals to redress the grievances of the labouring poor; and Robert Owen provided them.

Owen in this period became so prolific a speaker and writer, throwing off such an abundance of ideas, that it was difficult to keep track of his central beliefs; but they were changing. In the later essays of his *New View of Society*, published in 1816, his horizon was already broadening; he urged the introduction of labour exchanges, to help the unemployed find jobs; and the provision of work for the poor. But he was still generally regarded as a member of the employer class, and as an autocrat, though a benevolent one (the term 'benevolent' was almost invariably attached to his name, even by his most hostile critics). To radicals, his pauper communities were authoritarian; it was even suggested, in the underground press, that he was on the Government's payroll. And certainly he was still hoping to achieve the reforms he desired with Government help. Lady Liverpool, the wife of the Prime Minister, persuaded her husband to grant Owen an interview, as she wanted to meet the man who had written the essays; and having acquired such influence, Owen was naturally reluctant to lose it. But it did not deter him from putting forward his unorthodox opinions—the first philosopher ever heard of, Hazlitt commented, 'who recommended himself to the great by telling them disagreeable truths'.

Hazlitt added, however, that only when the great felt threatened, would he feel that Owen was really getting somewhere: 'only when we see Mr. Owen brought up for judgment before Lord Ellenborough, will we begin to think there is something in this New Lanark scheme of his'. And in the summer of 1817, at a public meeting in connection with the controversy over his scheme for pauper communities, Owen appeared ready to face that prospect. He had been criticised by Southey, among others, on the ground that his educational system was not founded on the eternal verities of the Christian faith, as exemplified in the teachings of the Church of England. For some time, he had been coming to suspect that religious prejudice and apathy was the reason why it was so difficult to secure acceptance of his ideas; and now he proceeded to tell his audience that they had been prevented from knowing what happiness really was 'solely in consequence of the errors—gross errors—that have been combined with the fundamental notions of every religion that has hitherto been taught to men. By the errors of religion, man had been made a weak, imbecile animal; a furious bigot and fanatic; or a miserable hypocrite. And should these qualities be carried, not only into the projected villages, but into Paradise itself, a Paradise would be no longer found.'

Owen's irritation was understandable. He had seen how the squabbles between the Church of England and the dissenters were making it impossible to provide poor children with any national education system; and he also knew, through his friend Brougham, something of the way in which the Church of England had been misapplying charitable bequests originally given to provide education for the poor. Brougham at this time was engaged on an enquiry into the charitable trusts run by the Church; he had managed to persuade M.P.s that, as trusts, Parliament had a responsibility for them. Collecting the evidence proved a laborious business, as the administrators of the charities presented every known form of obstruction; but Brougham was able to show that endowments provided for the education of the children of the poor had been extensively and often systematically put to uses far from anything the donors could conceivably have wished. They had been plundered to pay off personal debts; to increase the stipends of clergy; even to provide loans for commercial ventures. In some cases the schools had not been built, the 'teacher' living as an absentee on the proceeds of the endowment; in others, after the building had been erected, the funds had been diverted to other purposes, and the buildings allowed to fall into ruin.

But Brougham's report had not yet been published; and Owen did not attempt to account for his onslaught on religions. Yet nothing happened. Brougham was staggered; any other man, he told Owen, could have expected to be burned at the stake for such an outburst. But Owen insisted it had been made deliberately; and afterwards he was to call the speech the turning point in his life. It served notice that he was no longer to be the benevolent Mr. Owen, with his interesting ideas about how to get the best out of factory workers, and how to teach their children. Henceforth he was to be Owen the evangelist, striving to convert society from its traditional belief in a glorious life in the world to come, to the realisation that a prosperous, healthy and happy life was available in this world, if only people would follow his prescription.

Often his preaching was cloudy, confused; but occasionally, as in his *Observations on the Effect of the Manufacturing System*, published in 1818, Owen restrained his fervour sufficiently to produce a reasoned summary of what he was trying to say. In the past, he explained, manufactures had been thought of simply as a source of national wealth. But this was when manufacture was on a relatively small scale; as soon as it was diffused throughout the country, it had begun to change the character of the inhabitants. Unfortunately, the change was for the worse. The acquisition of wealth, and the desire which it naturally created for more wealth, had introduced a fondness among the well-off for luxuries; and the industry of the working classes, from whose labour the wealth was drawn, had been carried by competition 'to a point of real oppression, reducing them by successive changes, as the spirit of competition increased, and the ease of acquiring wealth diminished, to a state more wretched than can be imagined by those who have not attentively observed the changes as they have gradually occurred. In consequence, they are at present in a situation infinitely more degraded and miserable than they were before the introduction of these manufactories, upon the success of which their bare subsistence now depends.'

Owen, in other words, was no longer speaking as an employer, telling other employers that if only they adopted the methods he had introduced at New Lanark, they and their workers would benefit. He had come to the conclusion that the whole industrial system, based on competition, was faulty, because competition was creating an environment in which his plans for education—on which his new society was to be based—could not be introduced. For how could children be educated, if the new manufacturing system, relying on their labour, was allowed to continue? 'Not more than thirty years ago, the poorest parents thought the age of fourteen sufficiently early for their children to commence regular labour; and they judged well.' But now, children at nine years old, or even younger, were finding that they must labour incessantly for a bare subsistence, and were forbidden innocent, healthy and rational amusements—'they are not permitted the requisite time, if they had been previously accustomed to enjoy them. They know not what relaxation means, except by the actual cessation from labour.'

Yet it was now being argued, Owen went on—turning on the political economists—that the State must not interfere. Shall we, then, he asked,

make laws to imprison, transport, or condemn to death, those who purloin a few shillings of our property, injure any of our domestic animals, or even a growing twig? Shall we not make laws to restrain those who otherwise will not be restrained in their desire for gain, from robbing, in the pursuit of it, millions of our fellow-creatures of their health, their time for acquiring knowledge, and future improvement – of their social comfort – and of their rational enjoyment?

But what laws could be made to restrain those who otherwise could not be restrained? For Owen, this was a period of transition from acceptance of the economy as he had found it, and exploited it, to his later total rejection of it; and on his way, groping for arguments against the system, he presented one which was prescient, though it made little impression at the time.

The economy, Owen pointed out, was working so inefficiently that in 1817, although there was enormous productive capacity lying idle, there were also great numbers of men, women and children in want. Why? The reason, he suggested, was that labour had come to be considered as a commodity, subject to the same laws as other commodities. If this principle was accepted, it was reasonable, and indeed inevitable, that labour should be purchased at the lowest possible price; and with the help of machinery, worked by child labour, it had been possible to push wages down to subsistence levels. But what employers forgot was that unlike inanimate commodities, labour had another vital function—the creation of demand. If the earnings of, say, a handloom weaver were halved, his purchasing power was halved, too; and goods that he would otherwise have bought would remain unsold. Effective demand continued to come from the rich, and producers could adjust themselves to catering for their needs; but this left a great reservoir of ineffective demand from other classes, which existed, but which could not be satisfied. As Owen summed it up, 'the distress to which the people of this country are exposed arises from the scientific mechanical power producing more than the existing regulations of society permit to be consumed'.

It was natural enough for the individual industrialist, thinking in terms of his firm's profits, to feel that his interests were best served by keeping wages as low as possible. If he did not do so, in fact, he might be in trouble, because competitors would be able to undercut his prices. But for industry as a whole, the effects were unfortunate The working classes, Owen reminded his fellow employers,

in consequence of their numbers, are the greatest consumers of all articles; and it will always be found that when wages are high the country prospers;

when they are low, all classes suffer, from the highest to the lowest, but more particularly the manufacturing interest; for food must be first purchased, and the remainder only of the labourer's wages can be expended in manufactures. It is therefore essentially the interest of the master manufacturers that the wages should be high, and that he should be allowed the necessary time and instruction to enable him to spend them judiciously.

'Perish the riches'

Owen was not the only commentator to suggest that what was at fault with the economy was that labour, and in particular child labour, was being treated as a commodity, to be bought and sold at the lowest possible price; and that to put it right, some system of raising wage levels would have to be introduced. So far as Ricardo was concerned, an even more formidable antagonist had emerged on the Continent: the Swiss economist Jean de Sismondi. Sismondi had been in England as a boy, when his family had been forced into exile; he returned from time to time, and what he saw began to shake his earlier faith in the teachings of Adam Smith. He was the first to denounce *laissez-faire*: '*laissez faire la misère, laissez passer la mort!*' And in 1818, in an article in the *Edinburgh Encyclopedia*, he explained why theories could no longer satisfy him; they must be judged on their results—'the evils of competition, that war of the years of peace; the excess of production, which ceases to be wealth from the moment when it no longer finds consumers'. He went on to develop the thesis that if the true object of political economy was, as he believed, to augment the happiness of all men, rich and poor, some way must be found to spread wealth more evenly: *laissez-faire* had failed because it made for greater inequality.

In a lay sermon, published in 1817, Coleridge also blamed political economy for the condition of the poor. Under its guidance, he admitted, the power and circumstantial prosperity of the nation had greatly increased. 'We shall, perhaps, be told too that the very evils of the system, even the periodical crash itself, are to be regarded but as so much superfluous steam ejected by the escape pipes and safety valves of a self-regulating machine; and, lastly, that in a free and trading country all things find their level . . .' But what was this 'level' that they found? It might be taken as an ironical definition of what happened following a storm. In any case,

persons are not things – man does not find his level. Neither in body nor in soul does the man find his level! After a hard and calamitous season, during which the thousand wheels of some vast manufactory had remained silent as a frozen waterfall, be it that plenty has returned and that trade has once more become brisk and stirring: go, ask the overseer, and question the parish doctor, whether the workman's health and temperance, with the staid and respectful manners best taught by inward dignity of conscious self-support, have found their level again? Alas! I have more than once seen a group of children in Dorsetshire, during the heat of the dog days, each with its little shoulders up to its ears, and its chest pinched inward – the very habit and fixtures, as it were, that had been impressed on their frames by the former ill-fed, ill-clothed, and unfuelled winters.

Nor, Coleridge added, were the ill-effects confined to the labouring classes 'whom, by an ominous but too appropriate change in our phraseology, we are now accustomed to call the labouring poor'. The cycle, with its booms and its bankruptcies, could only have a deleterious effect on the speculators, too. 'Fluctuation in the wages of labour, alternate privations and excess, consequent improvidence, and over all, discontent and a system of factious confederacy: these form the history of the mechanics and lower ranks of our cities and towns.'

Walter Scott put forward a very similar diagnosis of the nation's economic disorder. In a letter he wrote in the summer of 1817, he suggested that the cause of the trouble could be traced to the way in which employers felt compelled constantly to open up new markets. In the process, they were sometimes able to make a handsome profit. But inevitably this attracted competitors: too much was produced; and a glut followed. The employer could live off the profits he had made; it was the workers, thrown out of employment, who suffered. The manufacturers, in other words, were actually creating pauperism. But the country was paying for it. The remedy, Walter Scott suggested, was a pay-roll tax. 'If it is objected that this would injure the manufacturers, I would boldly reply, "And why not injure, or rather limit, speculations, the excessive stretch of which has been productive of so much damage to the principles of the country, and to the population, whom it has, in so many respects, degraded and demoralised?"'

How widespread the idea of a re-orientated economy was at the time can be gauged from a resolution taken by some clothing workers in Leicester. It was surely obvious, they claimed,

THAT in proportion as the reduction of wages makes the great body of the people poor and wretched, in the same proportion must the consumption of our manufactures be lessened.

THAT if liberal wages were given to the mechanics throughout the country, the home consumption of our manufactures would be immediately more than doubled, and consequently every hand would soon find full employment.

Full employment was later to be presented as a socialist vision; but here, in 1817, it was being put forward as an alternative form of capitalism, in which competition would continue to be applied in the marketings of goods, but not of people. The employers' stock answer was that low wages were essential in order to enable home industries to compete abroad. But this, the framework-knitters pointed out, was incorrect, because every reduction in the prices of goods exported from England was being met by increases in protective tariffs. If the children in the mills worked for nothing, the industrialist would not be better off—he would in fact be worse off, because home demand for his products would diminish still further.

There was nothing subversive about the project of trying to reorganise the economy in this way; it even attracted some M.P.s. Why, Robert Preston, the member for Ashburton, asked, were labourers well fed and well looked after at harvest time? 'The reason is obvious; it is to enable them to perform labour corresponding with the advance of the prices they obtain at this season, when labour is in full demand.' But what happened in districts where the labourers were badly paid? 'The use of manufacturers and of taxable articles is diminished; even the price of corn and of other farm produce is reduced below its real value . . . and in the end, the farmers and the landlords become the victim of their own system. By reducing the value of labour, they reduce the price of their own commodities.'

It all sounded so simple. Raise the basic wages of the worker, and all would be well! But there was a catch: it would be contrary to the principles of political economy. Not that the economists had any objection in theory to high wages. 'If a country can only be rich by running a successful race for low wages,' Malthus had claimed in his *Essay on Population*, 'I should be disposed to say at once, perish the riches!' And the geologist G. B. Greenhough, who moved on the perimeter of Ricardo's circle, suggested in 1816 that the poor rates would fall if workers' wages were increased, which 'would not be so incompatible with the interest of their employers as at first sight would appear'. But those who accepted political economy were agreed that wages could not be *artificially* raised, by State intervention. Owen might disagree; to him, what Ricardo described as a science was 'a mere phantasm of the imagination, calculated solely to keep the world in unnecessary ignorance, vice and crime'. But it was Ricardo, rather than Owen, who came increasingly to be relied upon by men of influence at Westminster—Canning among them. Though claiming to be impartial on the factory issue, Canning admitted a prejudice in an 1817 debate: 'the conviction, resulting from all speculations on political economy, in favour of non-interference in contracts between man and man.'

3. LAISSEZ-PASSER

Although the general election of 1818 made no significant change in the balance of political power in the House of Commons, it brought in new members who had not been present for the debates on the reform of the poor laws, on Peel's Factory bill, and on Bennet's bill to regulate the use of climbing boys. The debates would have to begin all over again.

'Much better not to try'

The improved harvest of 1818, and a trade recovery, helped to dampen down discontent among the workers, and to deprive the radicals of some of their support. This was the time, Sturges Bourne thought, to re-open his campaign for the reform of the poor laws. Ministers, recovered from their fright, would be sympathetic. But there was one difficulty; the select committee investigating the poor laws had not been able to agree on recommendations. Early in February, 1819 Sturges Bourne proposed that it should be reconstituted.

Curwen could not conceal his impatience. Why were they hesitating? Everybody knew where the trouble lay. Family allowances were a disaster; a bounty on improvident marriages which unfairly shifted the tax burden onto 'the middling classes' in order to relieve the farmer of the necessity of paying a fair wage. If there had to be State intervention, it would be better to adopt Whitbread's proposal, and let the magistrates fix wages; at least this would do something to reduce the rates. But here they were, still in the enquiry stage. Why did ministers not *do* something? Why were they still so supine?

They were not being supine, Castlereagh blandly protested. They had merely been doing what ministers ought to do, seeking the will of Parliament. Of course, if Curwen 'had discovered any happy expedient, by which the burden could be removed from that part of the community they most wanted to relieve, and thrown upon another portion by which it would not be felt', then it should be communicated to the Government. But no such scheme had yet been brought to the Government's attention. The issue, he thought, should be 'handled in such a way as would identify it with every part of the house'. The committee, in other words, should get on with it; and the Government would await its recommendations sympathetically.

But in the meantime there was nothing to stop Sturges Bourne from presenting his plan to set up industrial schools. He hoped it would give ministers just the reassurance they needed—providing, as it would, an alternative to family allowances. The money distributed in allowances, he told the Commons in March, 'was often squandered, and not applied to the benefit of the children'. If it were spent on giving the children education and training, it would benefit not only the children, but the ratepayers and the country as a whole.

Up to this point, Sturges Bourne had been regarded as one of the spokesmen for political economy; but now, a new Member of Parliament arose to query his credentials. Ricardo had retired from the Stock Exchange; and he had decided to use some of the fortune he had made on it to rent a parliamentary seat. Brougham acted as the go-between; and Lord Portarlington, in exchange for a loan of £25,000 on a mortgage of his estates, and a lump sum of £4,000, agreed to nominate Ricardo for the Irish borough whose name he bore. The sitting member, who had been elected only six months before, applied for the Chiltern Hundreds; and the Portarlington electors (there were reported to be twelve, in all) duly returned Ricardo. He took his seat at the end of February, and used his brief maiden speech to criticise Sturges Bourne's bill. 'Mr. Ricardo', Hansard reported,

> thought that the two great evils for which it was desirable to provide a remedy were the tendency towards a redundant population, and the inadequacy of the wages to the support of the labouring classes; and he apprehended that the measure now proposed would not provide any security against the continuance of these evils. On the contrary, he thought that, if a provision were made for all the children of the poor, it would only increase the evil; for if parents felt assured that an asylum would be provided for their children, in which they would be treated with humanity and tenderness, there would be no check to that increase of population which was so apt to take place among the labouring classes.

Ricardo, in short, was objecting to the idea of industrial schools on Malthusian grounds. It would not have been sufficient for him to argue

How the poor lived — two Malthusian views.

Philoprogenitiveness —

Sketches by Seymour
N° 30 Pl. 4.

'Bob ar'nt you glad you ain't a black emor.'
I should think so they're such ugly warmints. Master's
daughter wots come from boarding school, says the sight
of 'em is enough to frighten one into convulsions !!

Published by C.S Thomar. 96 Gracpuate London

(Left) Climbing boys on the colour question.
(Right) Children often had to work in worse conditions, factory owners argued, than they did in cotton mills.

from political economy that State expenditure for the purpose was futile, because most political economists—including, ironically, Malthus—believed that education was an exception to this rule. Give the pauper child a proper training, they argued, and he would be able to earn a good living when he grew up, relieving the ratepayer in the process. But this, Ricardo went on, was also an illusion.

> With regard to the other evil, the inadequacy of the wages, it ought to be remembered, that if the measure should have the effect of raising them, they would still be no more than the wages of a single man, and would never rise so high as to afford provision for a man with a family.

Ricardo was moving towards rejecting any attempt by Parliament to legislate for the poor. How far he had gone was shown in his correspondence with Trower, who as a country magistrate had his feet more firmly on the ground than the better-known economists of the circle. There was surely a fallacy, Trower had suggested, in their accepted view that poor relief should be denied to anybody who had means—the regulation which Pitt had tried to get rid of, only to be ridiculed by Bentham. The fallacy, Trower thought, lay in the fact that it clashed with the principle that the labourer should be encouraged to save, so that he would escape the need to apply for poor relief, if he fell ill or lost his job. This was all very well in theory; but in practice, what happened? The outcome of the poor man's prudence was that he disqualified himself from receiving poor relief, until his savings were exhausted. While he was exhausting them, his next door neighbour, who had not bothered to save, was living comfortably off the rates. Surely, Trower argued, this was calculated to discourage the poor from saving?

'I on the contrary maintain', Ricardo replied, 'that after expending on their own wants the property they had acquired, they would be in no worse a situation for having acquired it.' In any case, he felt sure that the fear of falling into poverty could have 'very little influence on the mind of any man whose wages are such as to enable him to save a part of his earnings'. This was a psychological, not an economic, judgment; Ricardo, who had always been comfortably-off—and who by his skill at playing the stock market, had made himself rich—could hardly claim to know the poor well enough to make any such confident assertion. But once it was made, it tended, because it emanated from him, to be accepted by his followers.

Curwen realised what was happening. When Sturges Bourne's bill to provide training schools for the poor was again debated in May, he complained that the writers on political economy did not understand the condition into which the people of the country were being reduced. If capital and labour bore a fair proportion to each other, he agreed, there would be no necessity for legislative interference; as they clearly did not, he was strongly inclined towards making the experiment, 'to destroy that cruel and impolitic system of making wages that will barely support the single man the standard of labour.' Ricardo, however, spoke against the measure, as 'only the plan of Mr. Owen, in a worse shape, and carried to a greater extent'; and he was joined in his opposition by George Philips, who was obviously aware of the precedent that might be created for industry if the bill passed; children, he insisted, must not be compelled by the State to go to school.

Taken alone, the argument Ricardo and Philips advanced against the Sturges Bourne proposal might not have carried weight enough to prevent its adoption. A majority of the House felt that something needed to be done for the poor; and here at least was a scheme with impressive historical credentials. But in 1819, the pattern of 1817 was beginning to be repeated. The cost of bread was rising; in industry, there was another trade recession. In the circumstances, Lord Liverpool was grateful to the bill's critics. Some doubt had been expressed, he said, whether the measure would do any good; and if there was any doubt, it was 'much better not to try the experiment'. In every project of the kind that had been presented to him, he went on, 'it had always been stated, that though a considerable expense would at first be incurred, yet economy would be the result'; but 'the continual repetition of similar promises had rendered him very suspicious of any measure where such a promise was held out'. If the economies were to come first, he would be more disposed to listen. On his recommendation, further consideration of the bill was postponed; and it was eventually abandoned.

'And the world called it mercy'

It had not escaped Coleridge's attention that Peel's factory bill had been deliberately delayed in the Lords; and in a tract which he circulated on the subject, he did his best to forestall the arguments which he knew would be used against it when it came up again. He would not even deign to reply, he wrote, to the claim that factory children, in spite of having to work for thirteen to fifteen hours a day, were healthier and happier than those who remained at home, or who worked in the fields;

'it appears superfluous to confute a statement, the truth of which would imply one or other of two things. Either all the opinions concerning the laws of animal life, which have been hitherto received by mankind as undoubted truths, must be false; or else there is a continued interference of a miraculous power suspending or counteracting those laws, in mark of God's especial favour towards the cotton factories.' To Coleridge, there could be no question that children were being cruelly exploited. If so, there could be no possible justification on economic grounds; better that markets acquired by such means should be lost.

At this point, Liverpool did something to redeem his Government's earlier promises to Peel and Owen. When early in February 1819 Kenyon moved that the Lords' enquiry into the condition of factory children should be resumed, Lauderdale objected; he had abundant evidence, he claimed, to prove that recent disturbances in Manchester had arisen because distorted versions of the evidence given to the earlier Lords' committee had been circulated there. For a time it seemed as if his delaying tactics might continue to succeed. But when the subject was raised again, later in the month, Liverpool rejected the idea that the Government should not intervene. It was preposterous, he replied, to regard children as free agents in wage bargaining. The enquiry was re-opened.

The evidence given to the Lords' committee turned out to be more damning than any which had yet been heard. Among those who provided it was Thomas Jarrold, Malthus's old antagonist, who had worked as a doctor among mill workers for fifteen years, in and around Manchester. The health of mill children when he had first seen them, he claimed, had been generally good; their hours of work were not so long; they were allowed to go home for meals, and in the afternoon; and often they worked only a five-day week. But since that time, factory life had become systematised. As a result the children worked longer hours—thirteen, as a rule, but sometimes more—for less wages. And they were generally less healthy than other children.

Witness after witness confirmed Jarrold's evidence. The hours of work in mills for all workers were frequently from six in the morning until half-past eight at night, except after breakdowns, when they would be extended. During that period the doors were locked; children— and most of the mill workers were still children—were allowed out only 'to go to the Necessary'. They got three-quarters of an hour for their dinner, but during that time they might have to continue to tend the machines—or, if the machines were stopped, to clean them. Some-times they had to clean them while they were still running; accidents were common. In some factories it was forbidden to open any of the windows; cotton fluff was everywhere, including on the children's food, but often, as they had to stand all day, they were too fatigued to have any appetite. A six-day-week was worked, ending at six o'clock on Saturday evenings—but not for the children. They had to stay behind to give a final cleaning to the machines. The evidence, Kenyon could assert, presenting it to the Lords in June, 'imperiously called for legisla-tive interference to prevent the waste of life which such a system pro-duced'. And this time, Lauderdale did not raise objections.

Yet Philips and Lauderdale might reasonably have claimed that they had emerged the victors. The 1819 Act laid down that no child was to be employed in a cotton mill under the age of nine; and that no child under the age of sixteen was to work in a cotton mill for longer than twelve hours a day. But the twelve hours were to be exclusive of meal-times—which in effect meant a thirteen and a half hour day in the mills. 'The bill was passed', the *Quarterly* was to recall, a few years later, 'and the world called it mercy; and mercy it was by comparison with the recogni-tion of unlimited power over the labour of children; but it was still a most inadequate measure. The law still *allowed* seventy-two hours of weekly toil, amid all the grease, and gas, and noise, and filthy atmosphere; and we may be sure that what the law allowed, the masters took.' In the form the Act eventually passed, too, it was not even necessary for a master to worry about what the law allowed. If he broke it, he had little fear of being caught. The provisions made in the original draft of the bill for inspection of factories, to verify the age of children employed and to see that the regulations were being observed, had been removed.

'We come now to burning little chimney sweepers'

At the same time as he was manœuvring to delay the passing of Peel's bill, Lauderdale was also active in impeding Bennet's measure for the regulation of chimney sweepers. Bennet had hoped that the fresh series of tests undertaken by the Surveyor-General, which had shown that only one chimney in a hundred could not be cleaned by the new mechanical broom, would reassure the bill's opponents—particularly as the exceptions were usually located in the establishments of men who could well afford to pay for conversion. Instead, when he brought the bill in again in 1819, he found the opposition stronger than it had been before.

To its earlier critics were joined some new members, notably Francis Ommaney, newly elected for Barnstaple. Ommaney argued that so far as he was concerned, the results of the tests were irrelevant, because the bill must be opposed on an issue of principle; it sought to interfere with free labour. He actually boasted that he had not read the report of the 1817 committee; being concerned only with the principle, he claimed, he did not need to. In any case, he had the evidence of his own eyes to tell him how false the allegations were that climbing boys were maltreated; he 'had never seen the symptoms of misery in their countenances; on the contrary, they were generally possessed of good animal spirits and were cheerful, gay and contented'. Any boy, Bennet tartly replied, who had been tortured for hours in a chimney might be expected to look cheerful on getting out of it. Ommaney was not impressed. Even if climbing boys did suffer, he went on, this was because the sins of their fathers were being visited on them—were they not often 'the children of rich men, begotten in an improper manner'?

As if heartened by the realisation that the bill could be attacked on the grounds of economic principle, lawyers began to criticise some of its legal aspects, too. The Chief Justice, Lord Ellenborough, had long opposed any measures of this kind; citizens who were badly treated, he claimed, had a remedy in common law, so there should be no need for legislation. Now, Thomas Denman—another new M.P., himself destined later to become Chief Justice—added a more ingenious objection. If, as had been so ably demonstrated, climbing boys were unnecessary, so was the bill! Parliament could safely leave the job to be done by 'the good sense of the public'. One M.P. even criticised the bill for its humanitarian content: would its sponsors also propose, Admiral Sir Joseph Yorke asked, that boys in the navy should no longer be ordered to the masthead? When boys were ordered to the masthead, Bennet said, they did not ordinarily have matches lit under the soles of their feet to make them climb; to which the Admiral jocularly replied that he 'had often seen boys forced to ascend to the masthead by a captain who followed then with the cat-o'-nine-tails—a tolerably convincing argument.'

The Commons, though, were not prepared to turn down the bill which they had so recently passed with acclamation; and the fears which Lauderdale had aroused to persuade the Lords not to pass it had been allayed by the Surveyor-General's new report. To give additional reassurance, Lord Kenyon told the House that the bill's sponsors had agreed to allow a two-year interval to elapse before it was brought into effect; and even after that, although boys would not be allowed to clean chimneys, they could still be used, where any risk remained, for purposes of inspection. Lauderdale was not satisfied. When the bill came up in March, he condemned it on the ground that it constituted what he described as 'prophetic' legislation, because it 'presupposed that our successors would be neither so enlightened or benevolent as ourselves'. Reforms of this nature, he felt, could safely be left 'to the moral feelings of, perhaps, the most moral people on the face of the earth'. A week later, he moved that the debate on the bill should be postponed. And at the end of May, when it came up once more, he produced his clinching criticism: 'if the legislature attempted to lay down a moral code for the people, there was always a danger that every feeling of benevolence would be extirpated'. He and his followers mustered thirty-two votes against the bill; only twelve peers could be found to vote for it.

The climbing boys' bill could easily have passed on its first appearance in Parliament, Coleridge thought, 'had it not afforded that Scotch coxcomb, the plebeian Earl of Lauderdale, too tempting an occasion for displaying his muddy 3-inch depths in the gutter of his political economy'; and there could be little doubt that Lauderdale's intervention had been decisive. His political economy might be as shallow as Coleridge alleged; certainly his view that children should be considered free agents for wage bargaining purposes was not generally accepted. But neither was it publicly repudiated by Ricardo. Ricardo was assiduous in his attendance at Westminster, and it was rare for a debate on any subject related to the economy to go by without a speech from him; but he had not intervened in the debate on the factory bill, or in the debate on the climbing boys. And although he did not explain why, the reason can be inferred from the premise that was constantly appearing in his writings at the time: that the legislature must not be allowed to infringe the rights of the owners of property.

How far this view had won acceptance, even when it conflicted with the dictates of common humanity, was to be shown in an *Edinburgh Review* article that autumn, by one of the *Edinburgh*'s founders, Sydney Smith.

Smith had made his name as a preacher, and as a wit; he was also a humanitarian, determined that the horrifying evidence given before the Commons and Lords committees on the subject should not remain for ever entombed in dusty volumes in library cellars. Bringing it out into daylight in an article would not, he realised, make him popular in some

quarters—'among profligate persons who are always ready to fling an
air of ridicule upon the labours of humanity, because they are desirous
that what they have no virtue to do themselves, should appear to be
foolish and romantic when done by others', and also among 'that set
of marvellously weak gentlemen who discover democracy and revolution
in every effort to improve the condition of the lower orders'. In this case,
it was the higher orders of society who, by their selfishness, were largely
responsible for what was happening.

> We come now to burning little chimney sweepers. A large party is invited to
> dinner – a great display is to be made; and about an hour before dinner,
> there is an alarm that the kitchen chimney is on fire! It is impossible to put
> off the distinguished personages who are expected. It gets very late for the
> soup and fish – the cook is frantic – all eyes are turned upon the sable consola-
> tion of the chimney sweep – and up into the midst of the burning chimney
> is sent one of the miserable infants of the brush! There is a positive prohibition
> of this practice and an enactment of penalties in one of the Acts of Parliament
> with respect to chimney sweepers. But what matter Acts of Parliament,
> when the pleasures of genteel people are concerned? Or what is a toasted
> child, compared to the agonies of the mistress of the house with a deranged
> dinner?

But having laid the blame for the tortures of the climbing boys so
squarely where he felt it belonged, Sydney Smith did not go on to urge
that the law should be strengthened, and enforced. He concluded lamely
that there was little which could be done, without infringing the principles of political economy. He would be in favour of legislation to
regulate the construction of chimneys, so that boys would no longer be
needed to sweep them; and he wanted their careers to be 'watched over
with the most severe jealousy of the law'. But he felt that actually to
prohibit their use could not be accomplished without an increased risk
of fire and, therefore, 'without great injury to property'. For this reason,
he could not bring himself to support Bennet's bill.

The bill was abandoned, making it possible for Charles Lamb to
continue to enjoy the spectacle which gave him so much pleasure: 'those
tender novices, blooming through their first negritude . . . those young
Africans of our own growth—these almost clergy imps, who sport their
cloths without assumption; and from their little pulpits (the tops of
chimneys) in the nipping air of a December morning, preach a lesson of
patience to mankind.'

'These evils are daily increasing'

The crucial contest, though, in 1819 was fought out almost as a duel between Ricardo and Owen. Realising that he was failing to convince either Parliament or public that his ideas were sound, Owen now had an inspiration; he must demonstrate that they could work in practice. With this in view, he took up again the community project in which he had tried to interest the Sturges Bourne committee; altered, though, in that the communities were no longer to be a refuge for paupers, but models for the new society, where anybody who wanted to could come to live, and work; where there would be farms, mills, workshops, schools— everything that they would need to be self-supporting, and if necessary self-sufficient. Their aim would not be profit for the stockholder (though Owen hoped they would make a profit) but the provision of a higher standard of living for all the inhabitants, to show it could be achieved.

Ricardo was disturbed to find that this idea, which seemed to him just another of Owen's visionary notions, was attracting favourable attention, and winning influential supporters—among them the Duke of Kent, the father of the future Queen Victoria; a pompous martinet on the parade ground, but an energetic advocate of liberal causes in private life. With his active support, it was arranged that a meeting should be held in London, in June, 1819, to discuss how the necessary funds could be secured to set up a community, along the lines Owen was proposing.

It opened with an introductory speech from the duke. It was evident, he said, that 'all parties, from the highest to the lowest, now feel the evils of pauperism in one shape or another, and know that these evils are daily increasing'; it was also evident that 'the real cause of pauperism is the want of sufficient *productive* employment for those who without it must become poor, and soon, of necessity, a burden to their parish'. The fault lay, the duke suggested, in over-production. Machines were making more, but the workers were too badly paid to have the means to buy the goods that they turned out. What was needed were 'decisive measures to enable the labourer by his own exertions to create the whole of his own subsistence'; and as Owen had a plan to this end, the duke was sure that the audience would give it their best attention.

They did: and after Owen had outlined his proposals, a committee was appointed consisting of, among others, four dukes, two of them royal; the Archbishop of Canterbury and four bishops; a number of peers; Wilberforce—and Ricardo. He had come to the meeting with Torrens, out of curiosity; in an entertaining letter to Trower, he was to

describe his embarrassment when he found himself agreeing, in deference
to the wishes of the duke, to serve on the committee. But at least it gave
him the chance to put his point of view; and with him on the committee,
to lend support, would be Torrens.

As things turned out, their position on the committee was made all
the stronger because when it met, most of the big names were found to be
absent. Apparently Owen's views on the subject of religion, so forcibly
expressed two years before, were now being used against him; the bishops,
and Wilberforce, decided to stay away. The weight Ricardo's advice
carried could be observed in the committee's progress report, published
two months later. The community idea still found favour, but in a
modified form. The communities would *not* involve 'a community of
goods'—that had been either a mistake or a misrepresentation; there
would be no deviation from the established laws of property. There was
not even to be any levelling intention: Owen's plan had 'no other tendency
to equalisation but that which all such plans have, which have for their
object the extension of the comforts, the intelligence, and the virtues of
the poorer classes of society'; and he pledged himself that the aim would be
to ensure that the capital provided would return an adequate profit.
Most important of all, the communities were not to be financed by the
State. On the contrary, 'the Committee beg leave most forcibly to deny
any such intention, and to express their opinion that it would be mischievous, if it were feasible, to support the plan artificially or by any
law'. The communities were to be established on the same basis as any
other commercial concern; they would have to attract investors.

Ricardo was quite satisfied with the appeal as it stood. He had not
believed that the plan as Owen had originally presented it was feasible;
'could any reasonable person', he asked Trower, share Owen's belief

> that such a society as he projects will flourish and produce more than has ever
> yet been produced by an equal number of men, if they are to be stimulated
> to exertion by a regard to the community, instead of by a regard to their
> private interest? Is not the experience of ages against him? He can bring
> nothing to oppose to this experience but one or two ill-authenticated cases
> of societies which prospered on a principle of a community of goods, but where
> the people were under the powerful influence of religious fanaticism.

But provided the new community was set up with borrowed capital,
just like any other commercial venture, Ricardo had no objection.
A hundred thousand pounds, it had been decided, would be required to

give the project a fair start; and it was agreed to appeal for contributions to raise that sum.

By the time the appeal was made, the need for some action had become urgent. In his essay on the manufacturing system, Owen had warned that if the rich continued to regard financial gain as the only measure of wealth, they would be in for trouble.

> The poor man sees all around him hurrying forward, at mailcoach speed, to acquire individual wealth, regardless of him, his comforts, his wants, or even his sufferings, except by way of a degrading parish charity, fitted only to steel the heart of man against his fellows, or to form the tyrant and the slave . . . the employer regards the employed as mere instruments of gain, while they acquire a ferocity of character which, if legislative measures shall not be judiciously devised to prevent its increase, and ameliorate the condition of this class, will sooner or later plunge the country into a formidable and perhaps inextricable state of danger.

Now, that formidable and perhaps inextricable state of danger was at hand. Another poor harvest, pushing up the price of bread; and another recession, leading to wage reductions and unemployment, meant that in 1819 the workers—particularly the handloom weavers—became worse off even than they had been two years before. The Government took the opportunity to restore the pound sterling to its pre-war gold value, greatly enriching those fund-holders who had lent it money while its value had been depreciated; but they were not the kind of men who were likely to invest in Owen's communities. Capital for such an enterprise would inevitably be hard to come by.

True, there was a great deal of sympathy for the unemployed— particularly the handloom weavers—and a desire to help them. 'On the very mention of the distress of the poor', John Barton wrote in a pamphlet on the subject, 'our thoughts involuntarily recur to Manchester and Glasgow; we have hardly patience to discuss the causes which depressed the condition of the peasantry, when the necessities of the artisan appear so much more urgent.' Curwen, presenting a petition from the cotton weavers of Carlisle, thought it one of the most painful he had seen in all his long parliamentary career: the weavers there were being compelled to work from fourteen to seventeen hours a day, six days a week, to earn a bare subsistence, five to seven shillings; some could find no work at all. Peter Moore had the same story to tell from his Coventry constituency. The weavers there were working a sixteen hour day; some were earning as little as five shillings a week, in a few cases, even less. Could Parliament not do something for them? But Parliament did nothing for them; and again, tension began to mount.

The appeal for funds by the Duke of Kent's committee was made on August 11; five days later, the crowd which had gathered to hear Henry 'Orator' Hunt in St. Peter's Fields, Manchester, was charged by the local yeomanry—spare-time cavalrymen, drawn from the middle classes. Eleven people were sabred or trampled to death, and hundreds injured.

The Government reacted as before, only more violently. With the Six Acts, they restricted freedom of opinion even more comprehensively than Pitt had tried to do; 'Orator' Hunt, Richard Carlile and other radicals were jailed, and heavily fined. In the circumstances, it was not surprising that the Duke of Kent's appeal was a failure: the total subscribed came to less than £10,000. Even the proposal that a single small community should be set up as a pilot experiment failed to secure the necessary support; and at the beginning of December, the committee wound itself up—lamenting, in its final report, that an opportunity had thus 'at the present interesting crisis, been lost, of bringing a great question to the test of experience; when little risk, and no injury, could have accrued from the completion of the experiment.' Even should it have proved ultimately unsuccessful in its objective, it 'could not have failed to elicit much good . . . by the diffusion of knowledge, and the improvement ever to be derived from experience.'

The uncertain financial climate of the time was not the only reason for the rejection of the experiment. That autumn a scathing attack on Owen and his ideas appeared in the *Edinburgh Review*—anonymous, but according to Ricardo, written by Torrens. Its publication was significant, as by this time the political economists did not care to draw attention to the views of anybody who was not one of their number. Ricardo went so far as to object even to the dissemination of unorthodox opinions; when he was told in 1818 that the *Quarterly* was moving away from its Tory attitude, it encouraged him to hope that 'the reveries of Southey' would no longer be printed 'in any respectable journal'. Southey, he thought, mistook his own talents; he was 'really no more deserving of attention than Mr. Owen, or any other visionary writer'. But when the Duke of Kent and other notables could be persuaded that there was something in Owen's theories, then clearly it was time formally to demolish them.

Torrens began with the then mandatory brief exposition of what political economy was all about. To expose the weakness of Owen's pretensions to be an economist, he cited—as if it were the height of absurdity—Owen's claim that society had not benefited from the invention of machinery. Had not the machines created new wealth? Very well, then: for Owen to deny that they had also created benefit was tantamount to claiming 'that wealth is poverty, and that the necessities of life are unobtainable because they exist in excess'.

Although by similar reasoning, Torrens might have jeered at Tantalus for complaining of thirst when there was plenty of water available, the argument seemed to make Owen look foolish. But Owen might reply that even if society were better off as a whole, destitution remained among certain classes of the community; should they not therefore be helped along the lines he had suggested? To explain why this was impossible, Torrens had to fall back on Malthus. The labouring poor could not be helped by any means such as Owen proposed, because 'when a larger quantity of the products of labour fall to the share of labourers, their numbers are always found to increase; and hence, as the supply of labour augments with the demand, wages scarcely ever retain an elevation sufficient to depress the rate of profit in any material degree'. Conversely, 'when the labouring classes do not obtain that quantity of the necessaries of life which climate and custom have rendered essential to their healthful existence, distress diminishes their numbers, until the failing supply of labour restores its value to the market'. This was the position as stated by Malthus; and 'in the minds of all reasonable men', Torrens claimed, 'the principle for which Mr. Malthus contends is fully established'.

That Torrens was not airing some idiosyncratic opinion of his own, as he was sometimes to be accused of doing, was testified to by Ricardo himself; in his correspondence, he expressed his lively satisfaction with the review. And after the winding-up of the Duke of Kent's committee, Ricardo took the opportunity publicly to endorse the opinion Torrens had put forward. That December, two motions were put to the House of Commons relating to the distress of the labouring poor. Asking for an enquiry, Bennet described the appalling conditions in which working-class families were living in Lancashire—even those where the father had a job. The level of wages had fallen below ten shillings a week; many had been compelled to sell their clothes; 'their beddings were sacks stuffed with chips; they had no blankets; in fact the situation of themselves and their children was one of hopeless misery'. Surely, the least that Parliament could do was investigate their condition? As State intervention would be a remedy worse than the disease, Castlereagh replied, such an

investigation 'would only be calculated to increase the evil of the times';
and Wilberforce added that in his view, 'only by a strict attention to the
education of the poor in morality and religion, could there be hope for
future tranquillity and prosperity'. Because it was only an enquiry,
rather than action, that was being asked for, Ricardo did not intervene;
he approved of enquiries. But the following week, he spoke against a
motion in favour of some action being taken to establish, as an experiment,
a community along Owen's lines. Some local authorities had been showing
an interest in the idea; the Leeds guardians had that year sent Robert
Oastler, father of the future leader of the factory movement, and Edward
Baines, owner of the influential *Leeds Mercury*, to New Lanark to investigate; and they had reported very favourably. Obviously, though, there
would have to be initial outlay of capital. Why not, then, give parishes
authority to borrow it, on the security of the rates? Ricardo objected.
He would not oppose a committee of enquiry into the subject, he said;
but he was against the use of public money for public works, because
'the capital employed must be drawn from some other quarter'; and
already, the burden of taxation was far too heavy. He was already beginning to wonder, in fact, 'whether it was worth a capitalist's while' to
continue in a country where profits were so small; 'every pecuniary
motive compelled him to quit, rather than to remain'. The motion for
an enquiry was lost, by a big majority.

4

THE TRANQUIL TWENTIES

1. BOOM

GEORGE III HAD been treated as of unsound mind for years; there was no reason to suppose, when he died in 1820, that the enthronement of the Prince Regent would make any difference to the political scene; but it did. While he was Regent, his wife had lived separated from him, on the Continent. Now, Caroline arrived in England to claim her rights—recognition as queen, with her place at the coronation ceremony and her name in the prayer book. The Government demurred; and, when she refused any compromise, introduced a bill to dissolve the marriage. The opposition—Whigs, radicals and malcontents—joined in a campaign on her behalf of unparalleled vehemence and scurrility. The Government dared not prosecute: the weight of public opinion was too heavily against them. They could not even carry the divorce bill through Parliament. All that they were able to do was forcibly prevent Caroline from attending the coronation ceremony, and vote her an annuity, in the hope of keeping her quiet. Conveniently for them, she died a few days later; and to their relief, they found that her death seemed to have taken off the revolutionary pressure.

They were also helped by the unmasking of the Cato Street conspiracy. Its leader, Arthur Thistlewood, was a follower of Spence, who had grown dissatisfied with persuasion as a means of changing society. With the encouragement of one of the Government's *agents provocateurs*, he began to meditate a coup; but before he could stage it, he and his fellow conspirators were arrested. The memorials they left behind suggest that they were simple-minded social reformers who had been duped into desperate courses. While awaiting execution, one of them wrote

> . . . Ye fill the poor with dread
> And take away his right
> And raise the price of meat and bread
> And thus his labour blight.

> You never labour, never toil
> But you can eat and drink;
> You never cultivate the soil,
> Nor of the poor man think.

In Ireland, such a conspiracy might have been remembered with pride—as Emmet's hardly less futile venture in 1803 was to be; in England, the men of Cato Street were thought of as cranks, rather than martyrs. The proof of the strength of the Government's spy system was also calculated to damp down revolutionary ardour. The tension was further eased in 1821, with the suicide of Castlereagh. As leader of the House of Commons, he had come to be the minister most closely identified with the policy of repression; and from Shelley's

> I met murder on the way
> He had a mask like Castlereagh

on into the 1850s, when the trade union leader in Dickens' *Hard Times* linked his name with that of Judas Iscariot, Castlereagh was regarded as the man responsible for the spy system, the Six Acts and Peterloo. His death opened the way for Canning to take on the leadership of the Government in the Commons. For all his anti-Jacobin past, Canning was more flexible, and his followers were closer in their sympathies to the Whig opposition, now reviving, than to the old Tory 'ultras'. In the early 1820s, too, good harvests led to a fall in the price of corn. In 1817 it had stood at over a hundred shillings a quarter; by 1822 it was down to forty shillings—below the pre-war average. With trade recovering, unrest died away, and the early 1820s proved to be a period of relative political and social tranquillity.

But dissatisfaction remained with the growing inequality; with the way that, as Shelley complained in his *Defence of Poetry*, written in 1821, the rich were growing richer, and the poor, poorer. And it was in this period that the first attempt at an analysis was made to show how the aristocracy, though willing to accept the Malthusian arguments against the provision by the ratepayers of relief for the poor, were themselves engaged in milking the taxpayer for the relief of their relations and friends.

The subject was brought up in 1820 by John Maxwell, the M.P. for Renfrew, in one of the periodic attempts he made to persuade Parliament to do something for the unfortunate handloom weavers. Many, he said, insisted that it was useless for the State to interfere; 'things must find their level . . . all should be left to chance'. But in fact all was not being left to chance. How could ministers argue that it was impossible for them to intervene to provide relief for the handloom weavers, when they had just provided 'extended relief to particular individuals, and even to the throne itself?'

Maxwell was referring to the paying off of the massive debts which George IV had incurred as Prince Regent—and also, perhaps, to John Wade's *Black Book*, which came out in 1820. The most blatant of the traditional sinecures had been abolished before the end of the century, but there were still hundreds of offices which ministers could use to reward followers, or help impoverished relations and friends. Their pestering was often a source of irritation; but it provided a way by which ministers could meet political and social obligations, by shifting the expense on to the taxpayer. Charles Dickens, for example, was the grandson of the housekeeper at Crewe Hall; the Crewes were friends of Canning; and Canning had been able to secure a clerkship for Dickens' father in the Navy Pay Office, thus providing the Crewes with an agreeably simple and inexpensive way of rewarding their faithful retainer (and also, as things turned out, providing the material for the portrait of Mr. Micawber).

The *Black Book* gave the names of the placeholders of the time, along with their family connections and that part of their incomes which was paid by the taxpayer. They were listed in alphabetical order, from Abbot, Sir Charles, the Lord Chief Justice, to Zeerogel, Mr., storekeeper at the Cape of Good Hope. Supplementary details were also provided. Wade showed that the £4,000 a year which Abbot received as Lord Chief Justice was only the beginning of his emoluments. As his two marshals, he employed his sons; and what with other jobs in his gift, and various perquisites—traditional presents, for example, of cloth and sugar at Christmas—the total sum involved could not come to less than £25,000 a year.

The list, admittedly, could not give the whole story. It was impossible to tell from it whether Mr. Zeerogel was a hard-working honest functionary, who earned his income, or a sinecure holder. There was consequently no way of estimating how much of the taxpayers' money was being used to provide essential services, and how much simply to provide rich relief. But Wade's list showed the extent to which places in the gift of ministers were being given to their relations and friends; and also, how inflated salaries attached to the places were. English Secretaries of State received six times as much as their equivalents in the United States; in

England there were two Postmasters General receiving £10,000 between them; in Washington, one, whose salary was £600.

Wade also added a quantity of miscellaneous information about what he called the 'splendid paupers'. He showed that nearly 450 M.P.s, over two-thirds of the House of Commons, were relations of peers; that the Church of England was riddled with absenteeism and pluralism, some clergy holding five or six benefices; and that many charitable foundations founded for the benefit of the poor—including the public schools—were being used to educate the sons of the rich.

In his speech, Maxwell made no direct reference to these revelations. But his clear implication was that if Parliament could pay several million pounds a year to relieve the rich, it could hardly sustain the claim that it could do nothing to help the poor. Nor in honesty should ministers pretend that the Government could not interfere. It *was* interfering, all the time—by taxation, for example, which discriminated against the hand-loom weaver, in favour of the machine-made products. The handloom weaver paid taxes on many of the necessaries of life; the machine paid no tax. Why should it be considered justifiable to tax one form of production, and not the other?

When people put questions of this kind—Maxwell lamented—'they were laughed at, and treated as people not of feeling hearts, but of feeble understanding'. This was precisely how his proposal was treated by Ricardo. If the Government interfered, Ricardo replied, they could only do mischief—as they had already interfered, and done mischief, with the poor laws. And Maxwell's principles, if accepted, would likewise violate the sacredness of property, 'which constituted the great security of society'. For the Government, William Huskisson agreed, adding that it was the first time he had heard of a government being asked for a committee of enquiry into an abstract idea—how to help the poor. Maxwell's motion was not proceeded with. A similar motion, the following year—when he again suggested a commission, and recommended that it should look at the way Owen's New Lanark establishment was run—met with an even more derisive reception. Castlereagh's half-brother, Lord Londonderry, poured ridicule on the idea that the country 'should be carved into parallelo-grams in order to put the poor under the management of the Exchequer'; for the Government Canning, though paying tribute to 'the great talents and benevolent disposition of Mr. Owen', recalled, with a cynicism worthy of Pitt, Owen's attitude to religion. Again, the motion was dropped.

'And this is "prosperity", is it?'

The condition of the handloom weavers gradually improved, with the price of bread falling and trade picking up; but at the same time, the condition of the agricultural labourers, in many country districts, was actually deteriorating. Cobbett, back from America, was horrified at the state in which he found them. For a time, Cobbett had enjoyed his exile. 'To see a free country, for once', he had written to Henry Hunt:

> to see every labourer with plenty to eat and drink. Think of *that*! . . . And never to see the hangdog face of a tax-gatherer. Think of *that*! . . . No judges escorted from town to town, and sitting under a guard of dragoons. No packed juries of tenants . . . No Castleses and Olivers . . . No Cannings, Liverpools, Castle-reaghs, Eldons, Ellenboroughs, or Sidmouths. No bankers . . . No Wilber-forces. Think of *that*! . . . No Wilberforces!

But America did not stretch his talents, as England did. The news of Peterloo, and of the Six Acts, served to make him feel that he had been wise to leave, but that he was missing something. In November, 1819, he had returned to England—bringing with him, as an act of reparation, the bones of Tom Paine; and the campaign on behalf of Queen Caroline gave him the opportunity to slip back into the radical cause as if he had never been away. Throughout the 1820s he was to be the most trenchant and—at least in the opinion of the Tories—the most dangerous of the Government's critics; the more influential because instead of sitting in his editorial chair, as most journalists of his reputation would have been content to do, he took to his horse, in his sixtieth year, and began the tours of the countryside which were written partly as reports, partly as editorials, but which were to survive in a way such journalism rarely does, in *Rural Rides*.

When the rides began in 1821, Cobbett could still be regarded as temperamentally a Tory; but he was closer to the people than a Southey, or a Coleridge. He could talk to farmers as a farmer; to labourers, as one who had himself worked on his father's farm. And he was a born reporter, with the lucid integrity not of the writer who is striving to be fair, but of the man who has ceased to try to disguise his pleasure or his annoyance at what confronts him, so that he must stand enraptured in front of a field of good wheat, even if it happens to be growing on land which he knows has been ruthlessly enclosed by some minister or jobber he detests.

It was not that the labourers were poor that disturbed him. He took the existence of poverty for granted; without it, he claimed, 'there would be no industry, no enterprise'. But every labourer, he argued, should be able to secure a living wage for himself and his family: 'no human being should perish for want in a land of plenty; no one should be deficient of a sufficiency of food and raiment not only to sustain life, but also to sustain health'. And in many parts of the country, he found, labourers were not obtaining this sufficiency. Near Cirencester—he recorded in 1821—

> The labourers seem miserably poor. Their dwellings are little better than pig beds, and their looks indicate that their food is not nearly equal to that of a pig. Their wretched hovels are stuck upon little bits of ground on the road side; it seems as if they had been swept off the fields by a hurricane . . . In my whole life I never saw human wretchedness equal to this, no, not even amongst the free negroes of America who, on the average, do not work one day out of four . . . And this is 'prosperity', is it? These, O Pitt, are the fruits of thy hellish system!

Ministers feared that Cobbett might stir up unrest again; but any attempt to silence him with another prosecution might have caused even more trouble, because his catalogue of the grievances of the labouring poor was so well documented. And to suggest that he was exaggerating would have been difficult, in view of the fact that during the early 1820s Parliament was being inundated with agonised petitions from all over the country, and particularly from those regions which Cobbett was noting with dismay on his rides. So long as the price of corn had remained high, farming had been very profitable; now that it had fallen, farmers found their incomes reduced—catastrophically, in some cases, where they had borrowed on the expectation of continuing high prices, only to find that with good harvests, prices plummeted. Counties like Norfolk, with a tradition of efficient farming, were the worst hit: conditions there were 'of the most heart-breaking description', an M.P. claimed; the distress pervading every part of the county was 'dreadful to behold'. During 1822 no less than five hundred such petitions were received—mostly concerned with the plight of the farmers, though some consolation was offered to farm labourers by Lord Londonderry, who claimed that if their wages fell, this need cause no concern, as high wages 'too frequently led to extravagance and idleness'.

'If a country has a succession of good harvests', Ricardo had warned in 1820, 'she will have agricultural distress.' In England's case, Ricardo felt, the blame should be put on the landowners for their misguided attempts to subvert political economy with the corn laws. They had been able to secure an artificially high price for their corn for a time; but by doing so, they had naturally attracted competition: more farmers grew corn, and in particular, more Irish farmers. Before the war, it had been easy to put tariffs on Irish imports, or even to exclude them altogether. Now that Ireland was in the United Kingdom, this was no longer possible, and great quantities of corn were being grown there. It happened that in 1821, the potato crop failed over a widespread area in Ireland, leaving the population —as Ricardo's protégé John Ramsay McCulloch noted—'with nothing but a miserable mixture, consisting of a little oatmeal, nettles and water cresses, to subsist upon'; and the price of potatoes trebled, putting them out of the reach of the starving peasantry. But as corn was even more expensive, its price 'sustained no material elevation—none, at least, to prevent its being sent to the then overloaded markets of England'. Sympathetic though he felt to the wretched Irish, McCulloch could not repress his satisfaction that the English landowners had got their comeuppance.

Another commentator of the period agreed with the diagnosis, though he approached the subject from a very different point of view, as the full title of his book—*A few doubts as to the correctness of some opinions generally entertained on the subject of population and political economy*—indicated. The author, 'Piercy Ravenstone' (the name was taken to be a pseudonym for some retired gentleman of leisure) was dissatisfied with the new orthodoxies; but he was also dissatisfied with the landowners. Great Britain, he observed, was 'oppressed with capital even to plethory, and the labourers are starving; America complains of the deficiency of her capital, but her people are rich and happy'. The reason, Ravenstone suggested, was a mistaken view of the right to private property. That right was, or ought to be, to the fruits of one's own work; very different from 'the artificial right by which a man is entitled to appropriate to himself the ownership of land which he does not occupy, and on which he does not execute any industry'. As things were, the owners of land were appropriating the wealth derived from it for their own selfish purposes. He was not against the principle of rent; but as it was being exploited, it could be defined as 'the idle man's share of the industrious man's earnings'.

As a result, the labouring poor were suffering. 'That the condition of the labouring classes in England has, of late years, become much worse; that their earnings no longer admit of the enjoyment of the many comforts to which they were formerly accustomed, is on all sides admitted; on this point there is no dispute.' Yet instead of putting the blame where it lay, on the landowners, 'it has been the fashion of late years in this country to reprobate the laws for the relief of the poor, and to ascribe to them the increase of that wretchedness which they are indeed helpless to relieve. The misconduct of the poor will always be a favourite theme of the rich; it costs less to abuse them than to relieve their wants; it is easier to limit the amount of our benevolence, than to set bounds to the increase of their misery.' It was not the poor laws which were to blame because it was not the poor laws which had 'overloaded the country with rich, and which have starved the industrious for the maintenance of the idle'.

This was not a thesis which was likely to appeal to Members of Parliament; and when the subject of the condition of the labouring poor was brought up in 1821, it was through a motion which, in effect, proposed the Malthusian remedy. It was introduced by James Scarlett, a lawyer, one of the new Whigs—though soon destined, like so many of them, to become a Tory. The poor law, he told the House, was to blame for what was happening. By saving the labouring poor from the natural consequences of improvidence, it was putting a premium on indolence; in some parts of the country, they had reached the conclusion that there was no point in working, as they would be supported out of the rates. No wonder, then, that in some districts, farmers had actually ceased to cultivate their land, because the rates absorbed too much of the income from it. If this process was allowed to continue, he warned—echoing the Sturges Browne report— the rates 'must at some distant period absorb all the land in the kingdom, and thus consume that on which the poor had altogether to rely'.

Scarlett's proposal was welcomed by Ricardo in a brief but adulatory speech. It did not, however, find favour with the House, or with the Government. For some months, the country had been unusually free from the by this time familiar symptoms of disaffection. Ministers and M.P.s might sympathise with Scarlett's proposed measures, but they realised it would be rash to introduce them; 'from the generally distressed state of the country', Curwen warned, it was 'obvious that they could not safely be put into effect'. The bill was not proceeded with.

'Pauperism . . . is now a general system'
The farmers gradually came to terms with their changed market, switching from corn to other forms of tillage, or to grazing; the flow of petitions on their behalf to Westminster slowly died away. But this did not help the labourers; more of them were put out of work. And in those areas where there were family allowances, the fact that bread was cheaper was of

no assistance, it simply meant a reduction in their allowances from the rates. The fact that the national expenditure on the rates fell only slightly was an indication that the condition of the poor was not improving; and by 1824, their distress had become so notorious, and so widespread, that the Government at last agreed to do what it had earlier resisted doing; it allowed the setting up of a parliamentary committee to examine wage levels in agriculture, and 'the condition and morals of labourers in that employment'.

The evidence revealed that their condition, if not their morality, was deplorable. In a few areas, admittedly, agricultural labourers were earning up to fifteen shillings a week; notably in the north. The new towns created some demand for labour, so that any farm worker who could not find a job did not have far to go—or much to risk from the Act of Settlement—if he went to look for work in them; but, still more important, they created a demand for food—meat, milk, eggs, vegetables. Until the railway system came into general operation, this could only be met by local supplies; and local farmers and labourers were the beneficiaries.

Over most of the rest of the country, though, the picture presented by the 1824 evidence was of a very different kind. A shilling a day was regarded as a good wage; in some southern districts, labourers earned only three shillings a week. The ratepayers had to make up the difference, raising the wages to what was generally regarded as the subsistence level—seven and sixpence. What these wages meant in terms of living standards could be gauged by reference to the 1824 edition of the equivalent, in those days, of 'Mrs. Beeton'; Mrs. Rundell's *System of Practical Domestic Economy* which, among other instruction, provided specimen household budgets to show how different levels of income could most efficiently be expended. The lowest were for incomes of one pound thirteen shillings a week, and twenty-one shillings a week; in each case, for a family of five, two parents and three children—the expense of each child being estimated at one and ninepence a week.

From Mrs. Rundell's budgets, it was clear that even the best paid agricultural labourer must be hard put to it to keep a family housed, clothed and fed; and it was a mystery how the worst-paid survived at all, even with the subsidisation of wages from the rates, on the Speenhamland scale.

The committee also reported that the system was responsible for another unfortunate development: the 'roundsmen'. Most ratepayers naturally felt that able-bodied labourers should be made to work for their

	Earnings 33s. per week			Earnings 21s. per week	
	s.	d.		s.	d.
Bread and flour for 5 persons, 24 lb.	3	9		3	6
Butter, 2 lb. at 9d.	1	6 ⎫			
Cheese, ½ lb. at 10d.		5 ⎬		1	9
Milk		8 ⎭			
Tea, ¼ lb. at 5s. 4d.	1	4			—
Sugar, 2¾ lb. at 6d.	1	4½			9
Grocery		9½			9
Meat, 7 lb. at 6d.	3	6	(6 lb. at 4½d.)	2	3
Vegetables (including 35 lb. potatoes)	1	4	(including 28 lb. pots.)	1	2
Beer, or table ale	2	3		1	2
Coals (1½ bushels at 1s. 4d. per bushel)	2	1	(1¼ bushels)	1	9
Candles		4½			3½
Soap, etc., for washing		4½			3½
Sundries for cleaning, etc.		3			1
	£1 0s.	0d.		13s.	6d.
Clothes, haberdashery etc.	5	6		3	6
Rent	3	6		2	3
Incidents	1	3		nil	
Total expenses	£1 10s.	3d.		19s.	3d.
Saving 1/12	2s.	9d.	Saving 1/12	1s.	9d.

living. Where farming was in a depressed state owing to falling prices, leaving too few jobs, some parishes had begun to draw up a roster of farmers, sending paupers on the rounds of them—so many days work a year for each pauper, part of the wages being paid for out of the rates. On this system, the paupers would get work, the farmer would get labour for less than the market rate, and the ratepayer would not have to pay as much as he would to keep the paupers in idleness; so everybody, it was hoped, would be satisfied.

But a farmer who could get cheap labour, even if it were inefficient labour, was naturally tempted to sack his own farm workers; and in some parishes, the independent labourer had begun to disappear, to be replaced by a small army of paupers, hired out as roundsmen by the guardians. And as the system's critics were quick to point out, what this amounted to was another concealed subsidy for the farmer, and indirectly for the land-owner; cheaper labour meant, at least in theory, greater profitability and higher rents. The Commons committee expressed their disapproval; but they could not bring themselves to recommend that the roundsmen system should actually be abolished. The magistracy, they suggested, needed to be firm in their use of their powers to prevent abuses of the poor laws. But if the magistrates, as landowners, were the beneficiaries of this particular abuse, they were unlikely to be firm.

The roundsman system represented the ultimate degradation of the old poor law. It created a form of slavery in some ways more debased than the real thing, which Wilberforce and his followers were trying to abolish; and that they should be seeking to improve the conditions of the slaves in the Caribbean, ignoring the plight of the labourer at home, infuriated Cobbett. All his loathing spilled out in an 'Open Letter to Wilberforce', published in 1823. The abolitionists, he observed, were sending out their appeals on behalf of the negro slaves from an address in Piccadilly, 'amongst those who are wallowing in luxuries, proceeding from the labour of the people'. Why did Wilberforce not appeal on behalf of the English paupers, working in gravel pits, with sacking as their only protection against the weather; or breaking stones by the roadside?

> What an insult it is, and what an unfeeling, what a cold-blooded hypocrite must be he that can send it forth; what an insult to call upon people under the name of free British labourers; to appeal to them on behalf of black slaves, when these free British labourers, these poor mocked, degraded wretches, would be happy to lick the dishes and bowls, out of which the black slaves have breakfasted, dined or supped . . . will not the care, will not the anxiety of a really humane Englishman be directed towards the Whites, instead of towards the Blacks, until, at any rate, the situation of the former be made as good as that of the latter?

'Talk of serfs'

For the worker in industry, unlike the agricultural labourer, the early 1820s were a time of gradually improving living standards. The demand for cotton and other manufactured goods continued to grow, providing more jobs, and allowing even the handloom weaver to find a market for his cloth. The improvement, though, was relative only to the years of post-war depression, as the report in 1824 of a committee of enquiry emphas-ised. It was set up by an artisans' society to investigate the causes 'which have led to the extensive depreciation or reduction in the remuneration for labour in Great Britain, and the extreme privation and calamitous distress consequent thereon'; and it came to the conclusion that although the condition of the handloom weavers—there were still half a million of them, it estimated—had been improving, this had not been because of any restoration of their wartime earnings: it had been the consequences of cheaper provisions, purchased at the expense of 'the ruin of half the agriculturalists of the kingdom'.

Something must be very wrong, the report suggested, with a system where the improvement of the condition of one section of the workers could only be obtained by the distress of another; and certainly it was absurd, in the circumstances, to claim that the country was more prosper-ous, merely on the evidence from commerce. 'That trade is expanding, and that capital, so-called, is actually floating about, seeking for employ-ment', was a contention that the committee were prepared to accept: 'but so far from these facts being proof of national prosperity, however para-doxical the declaration may first appear, it will be seen, on a fair and full examination of all their bearings, that the privation and distress of the bulk of the people has increased, and must of necessity continue to increase, as long as trade is suffered to expand, and capital is suffered to continue to stalk about, on the principles now pursuing'.

The committee did not concern itself with the condition of factory workers; nor did Cobbett, whose rides in the early 1820s continued to be mainly rural—though occasionally, when he was on his favourite slavery theme, he would hurl derision on their way of life: 'Talk of vassals! Talk of villeins! Talk of serfs! Are there any of these, or did feudal times ever see any of them, so debased, so absolutely slaves, as the poor creatures who, in the "enlightened" north, are compelled to work fourteen hours a day, in a heat of eighty-four degrees; and who are liable to punishment for looking out of a window of the factory?' But so long as plenty of jobs were avail-able, the factory system was remarkably self-contained: men and women working fourteen hours, or even twelve hours, a day, six days a week, in a mill, were hardly in a position to impose effective social or political pressures. When it was found that Peel's emasculated bill was proving unenforceable, and that fresh legislation was required, the impetus for it came not from the workers, but from some of the employers; those who were anxious to keep the law, and annoyed at the way it was freely broken by competitors.

In the five years after it had come into force, only two convictions were recorded for breaches of the Act; and that this was not because it was being obeyed was made clear in an anonymous pamphlet published in 1825, *Hours of Labour, mealtimes, etc., in Manchester and its neighbourhood.* The author, who had undertaken quite an extensive enquiry, had found that the Act's provisions were being either evaded, or ignored. A fourteen-hour day was still commonly worked; and although meal-break times might be technically observed, they were used by the management to give the children a chance to clean the machinery, so that they got 'no exercise nor change of air, and what is more, are driven to the necessity of snatching by mouthfuls their food during the act of cleaning, whilst dust and cotton are flying thick around them'.

Peel had retired from active politics; but reports of what was going on in the cotton industry led the radical John Cam Hobhouse—Byron's friend—to propose amendments to the Act, incidentally revealing some of the ruses which had been adopted to circumvent it. One clause sought to tighten up the regulation on a minimum age: mill-owners had apparently been able to comply with the letter of the law so long as they asked parents the age of children looking for work; if the parents lied, it was not the mill-owner who was culpable. And one reason why there had been so few successful prosecutions under the old Act was broadly hinted at in another clause: that in future, no magistrate was to sit on the Bench to try cases under the Act if he were the owner of a mill, or if he were either the father or the son of an owner.

There was general sympathy with the bill's objects, as George Philips, leading the opposition to it, was shrewd enough to realise. He decided to vary his earlier strategy. The agitators who were campaigning for fresh legislation, he claimed, had been able to impress humanitarians with tales of injustice or hardship to children. But the campaign, though ostensibly to secure a reduction in the hours worked by children, was really to secure a reduction in the hours worked by adults. The hours of work in cotton mills had to be the same for all workers: if the children stopped, the machinery had to stop, too. And, anxious though he was—like everybody else—to see that children were given proper protection, he could not believe that M.P.s would wish to countenance legislation which would give the Government control over the hours worked by adults. If they did, it could only mean the destruction of the British manufacturing industry—with all the distress that that would entail for the workers, young and old alike.

The argument proved effective, not least in that it won the support of the Home Secretary—Robert Peel, the younger, already more advanced in the Tory hierarchy than his father had ever been. Hobhouse had to submit to his bill being amended, like its predecessor, almost out of recognition. His plea for shorter hours for mill children was rejected; they were to work the same hours as the men—twelve. And although the new Act appeared to make good some of its predecessor's deficiencies, no adequate provision for its enforcement was included, rendering it unlikely that it would be any more successful.

'Penury and ignorance . . . create a material plague'

Working conditions in factories had periodically aroused public uneasiness ever since they had first been investigated by Percival. The factory was still something new, and strange. But the living condition of workers —though that, too, had been periodically ventilated, by Fielding and others—had not been considered as being of any public concern. The poor lived in squalor, it was assumed, because they knew no better, or even because they preferred it that way; as there was nothing to stop them improving their homes if they wanted to, there was no need to worry about them.

The first stirrings of public conscience about how the poor fared were felt in 1820, following the publication of Frederick Accum's *Treatise of Adulterations of Food and Culinary Poisons*. Accum was not concerned with the poor as such; but his researches showed how much of the food and drink they consumed was deliberately contaminated with a variety of substances designed to simulate or mask flavour. Wheat flour, for example, went to the confectioners who served the rich; the bread of the poor was made with inferior grain and ground-up beans; it had to be whitened with alum. At that time the beer most popular with the working class was porter. Originally it had been heavy, black and bitter; it still was, but brewers and publicans had weakened it, keeping it looking and tasting like porter by adding ginger, copperas, quassia, and a variety of exotic—and sometimes poisonous—but inexpensive substances to make it look darker and taste more pungent, sulphuric acid even being used for this purpose. Any comestible that could be adulterated, Accum showed in this, the first great exposé of its kind, almost certainly was; and with *caveat emptor* as their justification, the suppliers were forever on the lookout for more effective frauds. The rich were protected because so much of what they ate, including their bread and their beer, was made in their homes. The poor had little protection, and little hope of redress if fraud was detected.

Accum, however, was erratic in his personal affairs; the powerful enemies he made by his book were able to strike back at him, forcing him to leave the country. The demand for reform that followed the book's publication soon died away. And another revelation about slum dwellers, in connection with their housing, attracted even less notice. It did, however, serve to introduce a man who was to play an increasingly important social role in the years to come: Southwood Smith.

Like so many of the crusaders of the period, Southwood Smith owed his zeal to a nagging but unsatisfied religious vocation. He had grown up in a strict Baptist family, and was destined for the ministry; but when he began to doubt some of the narrower sectarian aspects of his faith, he had felt compelled to renounce his Baptist College scholarship. This had led to a breach with his family; and soon after, the death of his young wife precipitated a further crisis in his career. He turned to the study of medicine, hoping to find in it the proofs he still craved of the reality of God's infinite goodness. As he described in his *Illustrations of Divine Government*, the study of physiology helped to convince him that in spite of the existence of so much pain, misery and injustice, his trust in God had not been misplaced; 'this beautiful world, into whose workings my eye now searched, presented itself to my view as a demonstration that the Creative Power is infinite in goodness, and seemed to afford, as if from the essential elements and profoundest depths of nature, a proof of His Love'.

When he came to London, however, and began to practise in the East End, Southwood Smith began to find it hard to reconcile the infinite goodness of the Creator with what he saw, and smelled. Whole families were afflicted with the disorders arising from malnutrition; 'the fever' was endemic. Southwood Smith refused to be disheartened. He felt that he must try to understand why the fever singled out the poor for its attention —it might occasionally break out and afflict well-to-do communities, but in general it was socially selective.

The theory which he evolved was that a distinction must be made between contagious disorders, like venereal disease and smallpox, which were transmitted by contact, and fevers—or, as he called them, epidemic disorders—which, he insisted, were not contagious. They would often break out simultaneously in a number of different places; and they would not necessarily spread, even though there was constant traffic between the afflicted area and the rest of the city, or the nearby countryside. People were attacked by fever, he claimed, 'not in proportion as the inhabitants of the affected mix with the inhabitants of the unaffected places, but in proportion as the inhabitants of the unaffected expose themselves to the AIR of the affected places'. The room of a fever patient

in a small and heated apartment of London, with no perflation of fresh air, is perfectly analogous to a stagnant pool of Ethiopia, full of the bodies of dead locusts. The poison generated in both cases is the same; the difference is merely in the degree of its potency. Nature with her burning sun, her stilled and pent-up wind, her stagnant and teeming marsh, manufactures plague on a large and fearful scale. Poverty in her hut, covered with her rags, surrounded by her filth, striving with all her might to keep out the pure air and to increase the heat, imitates nature all but too successfully; the process and the product are the same, the only difference is in the magnitude of the result. Penury and ignorance can thus, at any time and in any place, create a material plague.

Although Southwood Smith's hypothesis was later shown to be incorrect, it represented a significant advance on the straightforward contagion theory, which discounted the possibility that housing, or living conditions in general, could be held responsible for epidemic disease. If his views were accepted, the logical step would have been to accept his recommendation for an enquiry into 'what circumstances in the modes of life, in the habits of society, in the structure of houses, in the condition of the public streets and common sewers . . . favour or check the origin and propagation of this great curse of civilised, no less than uncivilised, man'. But his recommendation was ignored—not surprisingly, as in the articles in which he expounded the theory, in Bentham's new *Westminster Review*, his chief concern had been not so much to warn society of the dangers of allowing a proliferation of slums, as to discredit the quarantine laws, resented alike by industrial interests and by the political economists.

Every ship arriving in Britain from a port in a plague area had to bring a certificate from the local British consul. A foul bill of health, indicating that the port was not clear of fever at the time the ship sailed, meant a period in quarantine of forty days: and even if the ship had a clean bill, it had had to wait twenty-one days before unloading. By slowing down the turn-around of ships in port, critics argued, this was hampering commerce. They had tried before to produce medical proof that it was also unnecessary, but the evidence had not been of a kind to carry conviction. It had been claimed, for example, that epidemics were unknown north of Cape Finisterre; but the records of the Great Plague of London remained a warning that this geographical limitation could not entirely be relied upon. Now, however, Southwood Smith's theory gave the commercial lobby just what it needed. If he were right, quarantine was not merely futile; it was actually dangerous, as keeping a ship in port might create the atmospheric conditions in which plague bred. A committee of the House of Commons, set up to investigate the subject, was sufficiently impressed to recommend the reduction of the quarantine period to fifteen days, for ships with foul bills of health. Those with clean bills, it was suggested, need no longer be quarantined at all.

But slums were a different matter. To reduce the period of quarantine was only another step in the direction the Government was coasting, towards the repeal of all measures through which the State was committed to interfering in industry and commerce. To improve the condition of the slums would, on the contrary, require legislation to extend State powers to regulate housing and sanitation. Southwood Smith's plea for an enquiry into the subject was ignored.

'For uncertain and precarious benefit'

Not that Parliament set its face against slum clearance; its support was forthcoming for the proposal that houses should be demolished to make way for Nash's projected new Regent Street. But this, it was explained, was to encourage the carriage trade; by bringing money to London, it would eventually benefit London's poor. And, as things turned out, in the 1820s, London's poor did seem to be better off—or at least less obtrusive. 'There is not now one beggar where there were ten', Francis Place noted complacently in 1825; anybody who was too young to remember 'the horribly disgusting state' of the war years could have no conception, he felt, of the contrast.

Place had good reason to feel satisfied, with himself as well as with the conditions of his London. He had just pulled off a coup beside which even the Westminster election seemed unimportant: with the assistance of Joseph Hume, he had persuaded Parliament to repeal the Combination Acts.

The existence of these Acts had been a standard radical grievance ever since Pitt had imposed them. To prosecute workers for combining, while permitting employers to do so with impunity, seemed manifestly unfair.

If the workers were allowed to form trade unions—the old radical assumption had been—they could bargain with the employers on more nearly equal terms to secure higher wages and better working conditions.

But this was not the view of the political economists. As McCulloch put it, in an article written in 1823, it was possible that the wage level in a particular trade might be 'improperly reduced' by the employers; but in that case, higher profits would accrue to them; capital would flow in; they would need more labour; and they would have to offer higher wages. As precisely the same process would happen, in reverse, if wages were improperly increased by the workers—say, by a strike—there was no point in trade unions adopting such tactics. 'Hence the fundamental principle, that there are no means by which wages can be raised, other than by accelerating the increase of capital as compared with people, or by retarding the growth of population as compared with capital; and every scheme for raising wages which is not bottomed on this principle, and which has not an increase in the ratio of capital to population for its object, must be completely nugatory.'

Nevertheless, the political economists felt that the trade unions should be legitimised precisely because, apart from removing a source of justified grievance, it would demonstrate to the workers the futility of combining for the purpose of higher wages. They might try, but they would fail; and although their trade unions would perhaps survive as clubs and friendly societies, they would cease to be a worry to employers—which was a good reason why the employers should welcome the repeal of the Combination Acts.

Place did not go quite so far. He believed from his own experience that small groups of craftsmen could exercise pressure to push wages up, just as small groups of employers could, to push them down. But he shared the economists' view that trade unions on a national scale, of the kind that some workers had envisaged, were impracticable. 'He knows nothing of the working people', he wrote in 1823, 'who can suppose that when left at liberty to set out for themselves, without being driven into permanent associations by the oppression of the laws, they will continue to contribute money for distant and doubtful experiments, for uncertain and precarious benefit.' It happened that Peter Moore was planning to introduce a bill which would make wage contracts between employers and workers enforceable in law. The idea was so far ahead of its time that it stood no chance of acceptance; on the contrary, Place feared, it would only antagonise the industrialists, who had been induced to accept him as an ally, partly through Ricardo's persuasiveness, partly because of their shared irritation with the landowning element in Parliament. Place realised he must act quickly; and he enlisted Hume's support.

Joseph Hume was a man of diverse talents. He was the inventor of a way to dry gunpowder safely, and he had translated Dante's *Inferno*, while busy making a fortune in India. His interest in finance had prompted him, on his return to England, to seek and hire a parliamentary seat; and once established at Westminster, he quickly made his name as a relentless critic of Government expenditure. Place found him invaluable as a parliamentary go-between; with his help, Moore's measure was railroaded out of the way, and in its place, a bill was brought in to repeal the Combination Acts. A select committee, appointed to investigate, was ingeniously stage-managed to produce a favourable report; ministers, though they would have objected to new measures, were not averse to getting rid of old ones; and in 1824, almost without M.P.s realising it, the Combination Acts were repealed.

It was a remarkable achievement; and it held out the hope that if the workers behaved with circumspection—or, as Place would have put it, if they listened to him, rather than to Cobbett or Hunt—their future was bright. With industry and commerce still enjoying their prolonged boom, the setbacks of 1817 and 1819 could now safely be attributed to post-war disequilibrium. The corner, it could confidently be hoped, had been turned.

2. SLUMP

In the winter of 1825 a speculative boom developed of a kind that had not been seen in England since the South Sea Bubble; and at Christmas, it burst, almost bringing down the Bank of England. If the financiers in the City had not rallied round, the Duke of Wellington, who did not like them, had to admit, it would have crashed. Capitalists (the term was then more narrowly used to describe the men who lent money to industry, as distinct from industrialists, who utilised it) called in their loans. Industrialists, to find the money, had to sell off their stocks cheap. The market was glutted with commodities of all kinds; and many an employer who had not speculated was bankrupted along with those who had, because his goods were left unsaleable in his warehouses. Workers all over the country lost their jobs, or were compelled to accept lower wages to keep them. The beggars swarmed back on to the streets—sent there, in some cases, by the

Character, Robert Owen insisted, was the product of environment: drunken, quarrelsome parents created delinquents; the good home (*below*) produced the model child.

Robert Owen's New Lanark, 1825.

guardians of the poor, who preferred that they should take their chance of charity, rather than add to the demands on the rates; and the workhouses were crammed. In 1826 the *Norwich Mercury* described the local workhouse as presenting, in every part,

> a scene of filth, wretchedness and indecency, which baffles all description, without regulations of any kind. Imagine, too, paupers who for weeks, months and years together breakfasted, dined and supped, without any order or regularity; who had neither knife, fork nor plate; they were to be seen in groups with their hot puddings and meat in their hands, literally gnawing it. Imagine 600 persons, indiscriminately lodged, crowded into rooms seldom or never ventilated, the beds and bedding swarming with vermin; single and married, old and young, all mixed without regard to decency; I say, imagine this, and you will have a tolerable idea of the workhouse as it was.

Many similar stories came that year from London. The poor law doctor in Islington reported to his parish that owing to overcrowding in the workhouse, he could no longer segregate the sick from the healthy; the ventilation system was inadequate; and the corpse of a dead boy, for want of anywhere to put it, had had to be left in a ward for forty hours. And the following year he added a further cause for concern—a significant increase in the number of pauper suicides. With the falling off in trade the handloom weavers, too, were again in distress. During the early 1820s, the number of power looms in use had begun to increase more rapidly, as they became more efficient, and less liable to breakdowns. During the slump, their owners were able to continue working them by reducing profit margins—which meant that the handloom weavers, competing for work, were again reduced to desperate straits. In the north, the economist Nassau Senior noted in 1826, 'thousands, and tens of thousands, of hand-weavers' were working fourteen hours a day 'for what will scarce support normal existence'. It was the beginning of the period of the weavers' misery that was to be recalled by Disraeli in *Sybil*; all the more depressing in that they had nothing to look forward to but the gradual and painful extinction of their livelihood, unless the Government could be roused to do something for them.

The Liverpool Government was still in office; and ministers were still determined not to intervene—though such was the shock the slump gave that they were persuaded to do as private individuals what they refused to do as a government: contribute to a fund for the relief of distress. The Lord Mayor of London set up a committee to collect and administer it.

G

George IV gave £2,000; Sir Robert Peel, £500; his son, £300; Canning and Huskisson, £100 apiece. In ten weeks, £125,000 had been subscribed, and was being distributed. As a clergyman put it to the relief committee which was set up in Manchester, such charity was not only a Christian duty; 'he held it to be the best policy; for when the poor saw their wealthier neighbours sympathising with them in their sufferings, the edge of envious feeling became blunted, and they perceived that they had an interest in the funds reserved in the pockets of the rich, who were as stewards for the poor'. This was how ministers felt, too. At Blackburn, the distress was particularly acute: more than half the population, it was claimed, had to be kept alive on relief for two months; but the Home Secretary informed the town magistrates that they could expect help, if at all, only from the Lord Mayor's Committee, not from the Exchequer, as the Government was 'strongly impressed with the conviction that direct interference of the Government for the relief of the unemployed poor would be much less effectual than the exertions which are made locally, in concert with the Committee.'

Having given so liberally, ministers evidently felt able to resist the inevitable demands for Government intervention with more confidence. By this time, too, the strength of their resolve was so generally known that little attempt was made to argue them out of it. And the few attempts which were made locally to use the rates to better advantage came to nothing. In Burnley, John Fielden, who had himself worked in the mills as a boy, persuaded his fellow manufacturers to offer a minimum wage to all their workers, provided that the guardians would agree to support those workers who remained unemployed. Any chance the scheme had of being adopted, though, was spoiled when some aggrieved handloom weavers began to smash power looms in the area.

The only positive step the Government allowed itself to take was to set up a committee to investigate the possibilities of emigration, as a solution to the surplus labour problem. Here, it was safe from the attacks of the political economists, as State-aided emigration was an expense which they were prepared to allow that a government might legitimately incur.

The evidence presented to the Committee left no doubt, if any had existed, of the continuing distress of the poor, particularly in the cotton industry, which was 'bordering on actual famine'. In an interim report they lamented the 'disastrous consequences to a portion of the community that must follow upon every new invention by which labour is abridged'; and they paid a tribute to the handloom weavers, most of whom had continued law-abiding; 'those who in the present instance are the chief sufferers, appear to manifest a juster idea, and a more ready acquiescence in the general principle, than could have been expected from their situation in life and from the personal feelings with which their view of the case must be mixed up'. But the Committee, though attracted to the idea of assisting emigrants to go to the colonies, had to admit that in practice it could not work: 'it is vain to hope for any permanent and extensive advantage from any system of emigration which does not primarily apply to *Ireland*; whose population, unless some other outlet be opened to them, must shortly fill up every vacuum created in England or in Scotland, and reduce the labouring classes to a uniform state of degradation and misery'. This was Malthus's opinion, given in evidence to the Committee; and it was repeated in its final report. So long as the Irish continued to have free entry into Britain, and so long as their living standards remained as low as they had become, so long would they continue to drag down the standards of the British labourer; and nothing—Malthus said, and the Committee obviously agreed—but depopulation could prevent the decline continuing.

3. RADICALS DIVIDED

In 1827 Lord Liverpool had a stroke, and retired after almost fifteen years as Prime Minister. So long as he was in office, the hostile groups within the Tory party had been kept under some control; but when Canning succeeded, the 'ultras', not caring to serve under him, resigned—leaving him to form a government which might be expected to be less illiberal, particularly as he would have to rely on Whig support. The hope for a new alliance was soon extinguished. A few months later, Canning himself was dead; his successor could not hold the coalition together; and the Tories came back into office under Wellington.

That Wellington on many issues held 'ultra' views, however, was not necessarily to be taken as an indication that he would revert to the ways of his predecessors. Surprisingly, he was keenly interested in the subject of the poor laws; he regarded the inefficiency of the whole system with something of the same irritated intolerance as he had once displayed with incompetent Army methods. And in 1828, yet another select committee was appointed to examine the working of the poor laws. It came to the same general conclusions as its 1824 predecessor, expressing itself even more forcibly in its recommendations; in particular, urging discontinuance of 'the mischievous custom of making up wages and allowing for children from the poor rates'. Allowances of any kind, to able-bodied paupers, it suggested, ought to cease. But as this would be harsh, there was a case for temporary provision of work by the parish, provided it was *real* work. When confronted with the logical outcome of the Ricardian/Malthusian thesis—the starving off of the population surplus—the prospect was still too harsh for M.P.s to contemplate.

By this time, in any case, even Wellington was reluctant to do anything which might stir up trouble among the labouring poor, faced as he was with Daniel O'Connell's massive campaign for Catholic emancipation. Whatever course the Government took, Wellington realised, would involve risks. If, as his 'ultra' supporters demanded, he refused emancipation, the Irish were ripe for rebellion; with a religious cause to unite them, and a recognised leader, they would be much more dangerous than they had been thirty years before. If he accepted emancipation, though, not merely would he antagonise many of his supporters—perhaps opening the way for a Whig government, pledged to electoral reform; he would also be revealing that he was prepared to give way to the threat of force. The labouring poor in England could hardly fail to draw the obvious conclusion: force was the way to get grievances remedied. And if they were too ignorant and down-trodden to realise the significance of what had happened in Ireland, there would certainly be radicals ready to enlighten them.

The radicals, in fact, were presented with a unique opportunity. The old order was crumbling. In town and country, there was misery and dis-content. All that was needed, surely, was a cause, and a leader, for a revolutionary movement to arise of a kind which could not be so easily suppressed as its predecessors had been. But what would be the cause? And who would be the leader?

It could be assumed that the new movement would be radical. But when the term 'radical' was employed in this period, it was still not used in any closely defined sense. During the 1820s four main radical move-ments, or groupings, developed: the traditional, or old radicalism, of William Cobbett; the social radicalism of Robert Owen; the Tory radicalism of Southey and Coleridge; and the new, later to be called philosophic, radicalism of Place and Hume. The supporters of each felt that only their brand held out any prospect of restoring the country's prosperity, and relieving the distress of the poor. The chances of their being able to prove themselves would depend upon their ability to win sufficient support to take over when the Tory Government finally fell—or at least, to have a decisive influence with whatever government succeeded it.

'We must, and will, have that'

From the Government's point of view, it was still the old radicals who appeared to be the danger: and especially Cobbett. Admittedly Cobbett's following was much less strong in the towns than in the country; in London, and in many provincial towns, Hunt was the radical hero; and by this time Hunt and Cobbett detested each other. But Hunt had no national newspaper behind him; his views went largely unreported outside the local radical press. Cobbett's *Register* continued to have a national sale; and even people who, like Ricardo, were constantly being abused in it, felt compelled to read it.

For Cobbett, the solution was a return to old values, old ways. He was far from being a Merrie Englander, in the sense of seeing the past bathed in a romantic glow. Work on the land, he knew, had always been hard; the material rewards, small. But at least, he argued, the cottager before enclosures had enjoyed a decent sufficiency, with his small plot of land, his access to the common, and his craft, supplemented by wages at harvest time or whenever the local farmers were in need of labour. Above all, the old system, however inefficient, gave the cottager a degree of independence. His earnings might be low, but he was his own master. If he chose to work long hours on the land, or at a craft, that was his own affair. Nobody could compel him to, because at a pinch he could fall back on the bare living that his plot, and his common rights, and his odd jobs would provide.

What was needed, Cobbett argued, was a restoration of this former way of life, so far as that was possible. The poor, he insisted, had the same fundamental rights as the rich; where those rights had been taken away they should be restored—in particular, access to the land. Occasionally this was provided, as he found on an estate near Tutbury, where every married labourer was allowed a quarter of an acre, which his wife could look after if he was kept too busy. This idea, Cobbett suggested, could be more generally adopted; 'and then, the *agriculturalists*, as the conceited asses of landlords call themselves at their clubs, and meetings, might (and they would, if their skulls could admit any thoughts except such as related to high prices and low wages)—they might, and they would, begin to suspect that the "dark age" people were not so very foolish when they had so many common fields, and when almost every man had also a bit of land, either large or small'.

That Cobbett so rarely came across estates on the Tutbury model, though, was itself an indication that the 'agriculturalists' were not paying any attention to the sermons in his *Register*; and although parishes had the authority to reclaim waste land and let it out to the deserving poor, the hostility of ratepayers, farmers and shopkeepers to such expenditure meant that the Act was rarely invoked. He was in any case suspicious of projects of this kind; he wanted the labourer to have his land as of right, not as a form of poor relief.

But what could be done? All that Cobbett could suggest was a kind of informal passive resistance on the part of the labourers, designed to compel the farmers to accept their terms. From time to time, on his rides, he would come across a district where there were signs of this spirit, which pleased him; the cottages would be neat, with small kitchen gardens filled with vegetables, indicating that the tenants enjoyed a varied diet. 'You do get some bacon, then?' he asked a young turnip-hoer he found having breakfast; and when the lad replied 'Oh yes, sir!' Cobbett interpreted his emphasis as meaning 'We *must* and *will* have that.' If all labourers could act with the same resolution, he fondly believed, they could achieve their aims without violence, and without changed laws.

Passive resistance apart, though, the ideas he threw up on his rides never settled down into a coherent social creed. As Hazlitt shrewdly observed, 'Cobbett was a very honest man, with a total want of principles.' He relied on his observation, which was uncommonly accurate, and his feelings about what he observed, which were uncommonly shrewd; but he lacked the ability to link the two into a philosophy, let alone a policy of a kind which could attract mass support. He could not even—or perhaps it would be fairer to say, he did not even try to—rouse mass support for particular campaigns. Although his influence was feared by ministers, he was not, and could never have been, a leader like O'Connell.

'The happiness of all, knowing no exceptions'

By this time, in any case, radicalism on the Cobbett pattern was already ceasing to be relevant to the needs of society as a whole, because of its rural bias. The majority of workers were still countrymen, but the proportion of the population which was employed in agriculture was steadily dwindling; and in the towns, Owenism was potentially the more powerful radical force.

Owen had remained convinced it was no use trying to persuade people his communities could work, in theory; he must establish a community, and demonstrate that it *did* work in practice. But where was the money to come from? The 1819 committee had failed to raise it; the Government would certainly not try to do so; and as for the capitalists, they could hardly be expected to be enthusiastic about investing in a project which, if it succeeded, might discredit the profit system in which they operated, and if it failed, would lose them their investment. There was only one other source, and Owen had imperiously cut himself off from it. Had he been able to tap the wealth of any religious sect, Southey suggested, 'though it had been as visionary as Swedenborgianism, and fabulous as Popery, as monstrous as Calvinism, as absurd as the dreams of Joanna Southcott—or perhaps even as cold as Unitarianism—the money would have been forthcoming'. But, as it was, even the Bible Society every year raised larger sums from the public than Owen was able to collect.

A few disciples who tried to establish communities in the early 1820s along the lines Owen prescribed were consequently under-capitalised, and unsuccessful; and Owen began to dream, as Coleridge and Southey had done, of a community in the New World. He was lucky enough to find a ready-made village, Harmony, which had been established by the Rappites on the banks of the Wabash. They had decided they would like a change; and Owen's New Harmony community took their place.

The outcome fulfilled Ricardo's expectations. New Harmony was not an organic commercial growth, as New Lanark had been; some of those who joined were impractical idealists; some were chronic dissidents, doomed always to dissatisfaction with their lives: others were loafers. But the fundamental weakness was that without the halter of profit-making as a restraint Owen proved hopelessly unbusinesslike. The community failed to provide the shining example which, he had hoped, could convert the sceptical world.

But while Owen remained preoccupied with his co-operative communities, theories derived from his were beginning to attract followers among the English working classes—chiefly among the artisans, from the same background as Francis Place, and originally sharing his brand of radicalism.

In his *Report to the County of Lanark*, published in 1820, Owen had finally abandoned the attempt to reconcile his view of society as he would like it to be with society as it existed; and in its place he had produced an alternative type of economy. If labour was the true source of wealth, he argued—as Adam Smith and Ricardo agreed—there could be no conceivable reason why labour, properly directed, should not be able to produce enough to maintain every worker and his family in comfort. The prevailing economic system could not do this, because of its basic fault—competition. Competition for jobs pulled down wage levels, and thereby removed the purchasing power that was necessary to make the system work. In its place, Owen offered his co-operative communities, but with the added inducement that payment for work done should be based not on an arbitrary standard, like gold, but on a labour standard. Workers would be paid by 'labour-notes', related to the quantity and the quality of the work done. As the co-operative communities would be able to provide jobs for all who were capable of working, everybody would be guaranteed a reasonable income; and involuntary poverty would disappear.

But why should it be necessary to wait for co-operative communities to —in Owen's phrase—'let prosperity loose upon the country'? Might not other, more easily established, forms of co-operation be tried out in the meantime, with a view to gaining experience? During the 1820s, these questions were being discussed in many an ephemeral journal, and debated in many a workman's club.

The pioneer of the new Owenism in England was George Mudie, a Scots journalist who got a job on the London *Morning Chronicle* in 1820, thanks to an introduction from James Mill. Mudie's study of political economy turned him away from Ricardian abstractions; and in his *Economist*, which he began to edit the following year, he expounded Owenite principles. Poverty, he insisted, 'was not necessarily the lot of civilised societies, but afflicted them merely from their ignorance of true principles and the influence of other principles based on error'. While that ignorance prevailed, poverty must necessarily increase, and human misery grow; but if correct—Owenite—economic principles were followed, they 'would assuredly banish poverty, and place mankind above the fear and danger of want'.

The first full-scale effort to provide a theoretical framework for these principles appeared in 1824: William Thompson's *Enquiry into the Principles of the Distribution of Wealth most conducive to Human Happiness*. As an Irish landowner, Thompson had first-hand knowledge of the effects of the economic system at their most disastrous; and with Godwin and Owen as his inspiration, and Bentham's theory of utility as his philosophical measuring rod, he had proceeded to investigate what had gone wrong. In general, he accepted Ricardo's analysis; but he could not accept that distribution must be left to look after itself. As things were, he argued, capital took not only its own share, but also too much of the share that ought by rights to go to labour. The workers could do nothing about it, because they were not free agents—as Adam Smith had prescribed; they were at the mercy of the owners of the means of production, who offered the choice only between a subsistence income or no income at all. It was this failure to secure equitable distribution of the nation's available resources, Thompson felt, that was responsible for the grosser manifestations of poverty. To eliminate them, a system must be introduced by which distribution was regulated not to the vagaries of supply and demand, but by the needs of the community as a whole.

The following year, Thomas Hodgskin carried the argument a stage further in his *Labour defended against the claims of Capital*. Hodgskin was one of the founders of the London Mechanics Institute, where he lectured on political economy to audiences which included some of the future Chartist leaders, William Lovett and the journalist Henry Hetherington among them; his influence was more immediate than Thompson's. It was also more revolutionary. Hodgskin took the economists at their word. There was indeed, he said, an iron law of wages, which meant that labourers were condemned to dire poverty; they could not hope to get more than a subsistence wage, the rest of the country's wealth going to the capitalists. All the remedies proposed to ease the conditions of the poor—reduced taxation, abolition of the corn laws, reduction of rents—were as futile as Ricardo said; they would simply lead to a readjustment of prevailing wage rates; if the workers were to pay, on balance, sixpence a week less in rent, they would only find themselves being paid, on balance, sixpence a week less in wages. They should not, therefore, waste their time advocating or supporting any such palliative measures. Instead, they should realise that the control of the economic system lay with the capitalists. The workers had only one possible remedy: to become capitalists themselves.

Hodgskin, in fact, anticipated Karl Marx (as Marx was to acknowledge) in pointing out how Ricardo's ideas might be exploited for working class benefit. The difference between his ideas and Ricardo's, Hodgskin felt, was simply over the sacredness of private property. He agreed that it should be safeguarded—but only against predators; not against the just claims of the worker to enjoy his own property—his right to the free use of his own mind and limbs, and to whatever he created by his own labour:

> The power now possessed by idle men to appropriate the produce of labourers seems to me the great cause of bloated and unhappy weakness in the former who, having their natural wants provided for, necessarily live having no useful aim and object – and of poverty and wretchedness in the latter, who . . . have no time and no thought, but how to obtain the means of preserving an existence so filled with toil and care as to be scarcely worthy of preservation.

It was in this period that the term 'socialism' was first used (at a meeting of an Indiana history society) to describe the views, or aspirations, of the Owenites. Its meaning, though, was vague, varying according to the pre-conceptions of the user—Owen characteristically defined it as 'truth, unity, progressive and increasing prosperity, universal charity and kind-ness, and the happiness of all, knowing no exceptions'. That vision cer-tainly served for the ends; on the means, there was less agreement; to Thompson, for example, Hodgskin's project of the workers becoming their own capitalists seemed calculated to perpetuate jungle law. But the principle was established that the poor might not be inextricably in the grip of uncontrollable economic forces—that ways could be found to provide work for all at a living wage. The reviving trade union movement began to be attracted to the idea. Its leader, in so far as it could be said to have one, was John Doherty. Doherty had begun work as a boy of ten in an Ulster mill, quickly learning the limitations of disorganised labour, and coming to the conclusion that to be effective, it must be unionised on a regional, preferably a national, scale. He cherished the hope that when the trade union movement became powerful enough, it would be able to exert itself to introduce Owenite ideas. But first, it would have to build up its strength; and until it could do so, Owenism must be regarded as a distant hope, rather than an immediate social objective.

'But a people may be too rich'

Cobbett was too involved with a lost past, and Owen with a visionary future, to provide the basis for an effective radical alliance; the two movements hardly made contact. Yet a curious philosophical link between them was provided, in this period, by Southey and Coleridge.

'Have you seen Cobbett's last number?' Coleridge had written in 1819, at a time when Cobbett was still in exile. 'It is the most plausible and the best written of anything I have seen from his pen.' He went on to express his general dislike of Cobbett's writings; but he had to admit that Cob-bett had 'given great additional publicity to weighty truths as, say, the hollowness of commercial wealth'. And 'from whatever dirty corner or straw moppet the ventriloquist Truth causes her words to proceed, I not only listen, but must bear witness that it is Truth talking'. The comment was revealing of the difficulty in which he and Southey were constantly finding themselves. By inclination they were radicals in the Cobbett tradition; but they were repelled by what they regarded as his vulgarity, and by the echoes of Jacobinism which they detected in his writings. They felt a similar affinity with Owen—but again, there was a fatal obstacle: his mistrust of religion. Both of them clung tenaciously to the belief that the Church of England ought to be, and could again be, *the* Church. In Southey's *Colloquies*, conducted in the form of a dialogue between his *doppelganger* 'Montesinos' and the spirit of Sir Thomas More, 'Montesinos' actually rated Owen as one of the only three men of his generation who could be claimed to have given 'an impulse to the moral world'—but went on to regret that his expressions of anti-religious opinions, by alarming the better part of the nation, had ruined the chance of his ideas winning acceptance.

The *Colloquies*, which appeared in 1829, provided what could almost be taken as a synthesis of Owen and Cobbett, with the asperities removed. 'Montesinos', for example, had come to the conclusion that in any consideration of the effects of wealth, it would be necessary to make a distinction between a people and a state:

> A state cannot have more wealth at its command than may be employed for the general good, a liberal expenditure on national works being one of the surest means for promoting national prosperity, and the benefit being still more evident of an expenditure directed to the purposes of national improvement. But a people may be too rich, because it is the tendency of the commercial, and more especially of the manufacturing system, to collect wealth rather than to diffuse it . . . great capitalists become like the pikes in a fish pond, who devour the weaker fish; and it is but too certain that the poverty of one part of the people seems to increase in the same ratio as the riches of another.

Coleridge agreed. 'Half the wealth of this country', he argued, 'is purely artificial—existing only in and on the credit given to it by the integrity and honesty of the nation. This properly appears, in many instances, a heavy burden to the numerical majority of the people.' And in his *Church and State*, published in 1830, he set out in detail his view on what had gone wrong with society, and why. In front of him as he wrote, he observed, lay a book he had recently read describing the marvels of modern invention—public improvements, docks, railways, canals. 'We live, I exclaimed, under the dynasty of Understanding: and this is the Golden Age!' But what then?

> O voice, once heard
> Delightfully, increase and multiply!
> Now death to hear! For what can we increase
> Or multiply, but woe, crime, penury?

Wealth, Coleridge went on, had not brought prosperity. The country had game laws, corn laws, cotton factories: 'the tillers of the land paid by poor rates, the remainder of the population mechanised into engines for the manufacture of new rich men; yea, the machinery of the wealth of the nation made up of the wretchedness, disease and depravity of those who should constitute the strength of the nation'. The whole history of the making of wealth in the new society, he complained, represented a vulgar-isation of thought and politics; policy was in the hands of a Cyclops with one eye 'and that in the back of his head; our measures become either a series of anachronisms, or truckling to events'.

When it came to a solution, however, all that Coleridge could offer was a spiritual rebirth, brought about by the efforts of what he liked to call the clerisy—the members of a truly national Church. He could not see that this vision was utterly remote from the reality of the Church as it was established, with its bishops in the House of Lords, its tithes, and its livings in the gift of landowners. His influence, and Southey's, over con-temporaries, was limited by their devotion to the Church—and by their antipathy to electoral reform, which cut them off from joining what might have been a broadly-based radical movement, embracing Owenites and Cobbettites. None of these groupings could provide the dynamic needed; and to fill that vacuum, a radicalism of a very different kind had appeared, also based on a heterogeneous collection of principles, but transformed by events into an unprecedentedly powerful social force.

'The steam engine has fought our battles'

In the 1820s the new radicalism could not be said to have a leader, in the usual sense of that term; but it was organised largely by two men: Francis Place and Joseph Hume. Place was still the ward boss, in his con-stituency: and he still believed that the first call on a radical's political loyalty was to the cause of electoral reform, so that all other constituencies might share Westminster's advantages. But after the setbacks of the early 1790s, and of the post-war years, he had decided that straightforward radical agitation was ineffectual; it merely closed the ranks of government and opposition against reform. In the 1820s he had set himself to conquer Parliament from within.

Here, Hume was invaluable. Other radical M.P.s made more of an impression on the public—Sir Francis Burdett, and John Cam Hobhouse; but they lacked Hume's dedication—and his industry. Self-important, and at times downright silly, Hume burrowed away assiduously, and very

effectively—as Ricardo noted; Hume, he wrote—after attending a com-
plimentary dinner given to him by Hereford radicals in the winter of
1821—'has been of essential service in rousing the public feeling to a
conviction of the wasteful expenditure which is going on; and I really
believe it is a better class of people that are now active, than that which had
previously been operated on by Cobbett and Hunt.' It was to Hume, in
particular, that the press owed its growing freedom. He had been able to
extract information about the sums spent by the Government on suborning
newspapers—and, more to the point, to show what little benefit the
Government got out of it, in terms of circulation figures; the reduction of
this expenditure in the 1820s was largely owing to his discoveries.

One of the beneficiaries, and destined to be a significant one, was *The
Times*. It had originally been a Government journal, relying for its circulation largely on Government 'leaks'; and for its profits, on Government
subventions from advertisements, and from secret service funds. Growing
unhappy about this arrangement, its owner, John Walter, decided to
break away; and he had the good sense and good luck to appoint an editor
of genius, Thomas Barnes, to run the paper. Sensing the strength of public
opinion about Queen Caroline, Barnes exploited the case to give *The Times*
a commanding lead in circulation over its rivals; and he was able to use
Hume's revelations about the Government papers, to help kill off some
competitors. Although Barnes did not allow *The Times* to become closely
identified with the new radicalism, it was a powerful supporting influence.

But apart from devotion to the cause of electoral reform, the new
radicalism bore startlingly little resemblance to the old, because the
policies which Hume and Place sought to persuade radicals to accept,
during the 1820s, derived from political economy.

In view of the bleak image that political economy was later to acquire
among English workers, as a latter-day Giant Despair, Place's adoption of
its principles as radical policy might seem eccentric; yet at the time, his
decision was logical enough. He had been introduced to James Mill, then
the leading exponent of the principles laid down by Adam Smith, and still
suffused with Adam Smith's optimism, in 1808. The end of mercantilism, the liberation of industry and commerce from their legislative
shackles, Mill had assured him, could only bring benefit to employer and
worker alike. And later, when Place was introduced to Ricardo, he was
given similar reassurance. 'The steam engine has fought our battles,'
Ricardo claimed, 'and paid the interest on our debts'; it was only the
expense of the prolonged war, coupled with misguided financial policies,

which had delayed the spread of prosperity throughout the community. When that prosperity came, the workers would be the beneficiaries, as well as their employers.

Had Place merely read political economy, he might have remained detached about it. But as things turned out, he had become socially as well as intellectually involved in the remarkable coterie that developed. The common background of the Scots was initially a help—Hume and Mill had been schoolfellows—but the essential base was provided by the friendship which had sprung up between Mill, when he came to London, and Jeremy Bentham. Like Malthus, Bentham was not quite in the main stream of political economy; but the manual which he had written on the subject had shown that he shared the prevailing attitudes. To increase the national wealth, he had written, 'or to increase the means either of subsistence or enjoyment', the rule, unless there was some special reason, was that 'nothing ought to be done or attempted by government. The motto or watchword of government, on these occasions, ought to be—*Be Quiet!*' But still more important, Bentham's utilitarianism provided political economy with a valuable moral sanction. 'I am a selfish man,' Bentham would explain, 'as selfish as any man can be. But in me, some-how or other, selfishness has taken the shape of benevolence.' Selfishness taking the shape of benevolence was precisely how the economists envis-aged their system working, if it were allowed to; on the walks they used to take together in Hyde Park, Bentham and Ricardo also found themselves in agreement that society as an abstraction had no rights, no values, the interests of the community being 'nothing more nor less than the sum of the interests of the several members who compose it'. 'My motto,' Ricardo wrote, 'after Mr Bentham, is the greatest happiness of the greatest number.' In the 1820s there was no clear distinction, of the kind that was later to emerge, between utilitarianism and political economy.

The economists and their circle of friends, too, had an intense enjoy-ment in each other's society, and a store of personal affection for each other which differences of opinion did nothing to disrupt. Never, surely, can an intellectual movement have been cemented by so many close personal ties. Bentham had provided Mill with his house in London, and used to bring him and his family down to the country for holidays. Mill regarded him-self as Ricardo's spiritual father; after Ricardo's death he was to recall that for twelve years they had enjoyed 'the most delightful intercourse, during the greater part of which time he had hardly a thought, or purpose, respecting either public or private affairs, in which I was not his confidant and adviser'. Bentham, on hearing of Mill's claim, said that he must in that case be Ricardo's spiritual grandfather—such was the *épanchement* that had arisen between them, on their Hyde Park walks. In spite of differences over the interpretation of the laws of political economy, the friendship that sprang up between Ricardo and Malthus became equally close: 'I have never loved anybody,' Malthus claimed, 'out of my family, so much.' And from the agreeably intimate tone of Ricardo's correspondence with McCulloch, it was hard to realise that the men did not actually meet until a few weeks before Ricardo's death in 1823; their differences of opinion did not diminish its cordiality.

It must have been a heady experience for Francis Place, the journeyman tailor, after a life of sometimes fearful poverty, to be taken up in this exalted circle—and not simply welcomed, but actually deferred to. 'From his knowledge and probity,' Bentham said of him, 'and from his energy, he ought to be Home Secretary'; and whenever Mill left London, it was to Place that he entrusted his financial affairs. What had originally been an agreeable social circle, too, became in 1820 something that for Place and Hume, with their political ambitions, was more important. From time to time informal meetings were held at Ricardo's home to discuss vexed issues of political economy; and one of his friends, Thomas Tooke, proposed that they should constitute themselves into a formal society. The rules of the Political Economy Club, drawn up by James Mill, were revealing:

> The members of the Society will regard their mutual instruction, and the diffusion amongst others of first principles of Political Economy, as a real and important obligation.

> As the Press is the grand instrument for the diffusion of knowledge or error, all the members of this Society will regard it as incumbent upon them to watch carefully the proceedings of the press, and to ascertain if any doctrines hostile to sound views of Political Economy have been propagated; to contribute whatever may be in their power to refute such erroneous doctrines, and controvert their influence; and to avail themselves of every favourable opportunity for the publication of seasonable truths within the provision of this science.

> It shall be considered the duty of the Society, individually and collectively, to aid the circulation of all publications which they deem useful to the Science, by making the merits of them known as widely as possible, and to limit the influence of hurtful publications by the same means.

The Club had its vicissitudes, but there could be no question that it performed the function which Mill planned for it, as a college of propaganda, a ginger group and a parliamentary lobby. With its help, Place and Hume were able to bring effective pressures to bear on M.P.s, and on newspaper editors, on whatever issues their strategy required.

The political economists also lent radicalism respectability; and that, too, was essential. After the war, radicalism had come to be identified with violence; Charles Dickens, born in 1812, was to recall that when he was a small child, 'Radicals' were equated in his mind with the banditti—in his prayers, he would beg God to save him from them. Ricardo had for a time been reluctant to describe himself as a radical, for fear that this would link him with the likes of Henry Hunt. But Place had gone to work on his new friends, soothing their fears, and in particular taking care to remind them that there was not the slightest chance of their achieving the economic and social changes they felt were necessary so long as they were confronted with an unreformed Parliament. By accepting the radical label, they in turn made it harder for Whigs, and even Tories, to continue to think of Place as a dangerous Jacobin, waiting to overturn the constitution.

4. MEN AND MACHINES

If these diverse radical groups could have achieved unity, and if they had acquired a leader—an English equivalent of O'Connell—they could have won mass support, and conducted a revolution (or compelled reforms to avoid it). But, from the start they were disunited. Even on the need for electoral reform, there were differences. The Tory radicals rejected it; Ricardo wanted only a limited measure, designed to ensure adequate representation to all the property-owning classes, and to reduce the influence of the landowners; Owen felt that no political change really mattered, beside the social and moral revolution which he had in contemplation.

'The poor drink no wine'

Effectively, though, the struggle for supremacy had lain between the old radicals on the Cobbett model, and the new—the followers of Place. Owen was out of the country for much of the 1820s; his following remained unco-ordinated. And the radical Tories—they began to be known by that description at this time—could hardly be said to constitute even a pressure group; they were still critics, rather than performers.

So far as the general public were concerned, the divisions between old and new radicals might appear as of little account, as on most issues they seemed to agree. But their unity was illusory, because even where they did agree, it was usually from different reasoning.

Their attitude to taxation was one example. A number of attempts were made in this period to work out just what proportion of the poor man's income was absorbed in taxes; but even John Barton, one of the most assiduous of investigators into poverty, had to admit that the calculation had defeated him. It would have been simple enough to estimate roughly how much a labourer paid in excise duty on tallow, by finding out how many candles he used in the year, and working out the duty paid. But it would have been much more difficult to estimate how much more he had to pay for, say, sugar, because of Government regulations affecting the sugar industry. The cost of sugar was materially increased not merely by the bounties provided for the growers, which had to be met by the tax-payer, but also by the protection afforded to them, which enabled them to charge higher prices—and allowed them to continue with slave labour, which, being economically inefficient, pushed up production costs un-necessarily. The cost of bread was similarly raised by the corn laws, and by the bounties on the export of corn.

How much would the labourer have been saved, other things being equal, if all indirect taxation, palpable and concealed, had been taken off? Pitt was reputed to have said that the Exchequer was responsible for two-thirds of the cost of labour; but even the more modest estimate which Cobbett used to quote—ten pounds a year—was a formidable amount in a period when any labourer who earned twenty-five pounds a year could consider himself fortunate.

Old and new radicals alike condemned duties on essentials—tallow, soap, salt, leather, tea and beer (Cobbett, though he usually drank milk, always insisted that every labourer should be able to afford to drink beer if he wanted to); and in the early 1820s several attempts were made to persuade the Chancellor of the Exchequer to remove or reduce them. Criticising the beer duty, the radical John Maberley—who had made his fortune as an army contractor—actually used the same argument as Tom Paine, thirty years before. In 1825, it was still not safe to print the works of Paine, as Richard Carlile, the printer of Southey's *Wat Tyler* had found; the two years' term of imprisonment he was given in 1819 for bringing out *The Age of Reason* had stretched to six before he was released, as he refused to pay the fine. But Paine's argument could safely be borrowed; and Maberley pointed out that the rich man could have his own beer brewed for him, 'but the poor man, who had neither premises, capital, skill or time, could not . . . the beer duty was, in fact, a tax on the poor individual, from which the wealthy individual was excepted'. As a result, the poor had to pay a halfpenny a pint more than the rich, though beer was 'one of the necessities of life'.

A similar point was made that year by another M.P., Daniel Sykes, over the duty on soap. Ministers, he said, prided themselves on what they felt were their commendable efforts to reduce taxation; but how was he going to be able to face his poorer constituents when he came to explain to them what was actually being done? If he told them the duty on wine had been lowered, they would reply, 'The poor drink no wine.' As for a reduction in the duty on spirits, they would tell him, 'We have no wish to burn up our livers: give us clean hands and clean linen, and we leave to others red noses and bloated bodies.' But it was difficult for them to keep their hands or their linen clean, with a 120 per cent *ad valorem* duty on soap; and the duty on tallow was even more unfair, as, like the beer duty, it had become discriminatory against the poor; 'by the invention of gas, the use of wax, and other means, the upper ranks felt this duty very slightly,' which meant that there was 'an injurious distinction between the different classes of society'.

The Chancellor of the Exchequer had not even bothered to reply to the Maberley proposal for a reduction of the beer duty; he now intervened to say that the duty on tallow was light. This was true; but he had not answered the point about its being discriminatory—nor, as another M.P. pointed out, had he explained why, if he were really so concerned about the state of the nation's finances, he should just have agreed to throw away £6,000 a year in a grant to a royal duke.

But Ricardo—although he disliked excise duties, and agreed that the tax on beer was unfair because it was discriminatory against a class—did not believe, as the old radicals did, that reducing the excise would bring any direct relief to the poor. His complaint was that excise duties amounted in practice to a Government tax on wages, 'and a tax on wages is wholly a tax on profits'. If the tax were removed, it would simply mean that the labourer's wages could be reduced by an equivalent amount; all the direct benefit would go to the employer, though the workers could benefit indirectly if the employer put more money into his business.

There was a similar division between the old and new radicals over tithes. Tithes were not, strictly-speaking, State taxes, as they were taken by the clergy. But the clergy were part of the Established Church; so far as Cobbett was concerned, it came to much the same thing. Among his diverse interests, he was an amateur historian; and in his *History of the Protestant 'Reformation'* he had put forward the thesis that the property of which the Old Church had been despoiled by Henry VIII had been held in trust for the poor. Poor rates, therefore, should not be regarded as charity: the State was making up for the appropriation. With the introduction of poor rates, many of the clergy had, in fact, relinquished their right to exact their ten per cent. They had settled with farmers that their tithes should be compounded for, or a token payment substituted. In many cases, tithes had simply lapsed. But the massive increase in farmers' incomes as a result of the Napoleonic wars had not gone unobserved by the clergy, whose stipends had failed to rise commensurately. Some of them had employed lawyers to find out what were their legal rights, and to serve notice that in future they would be enforced. The kind of clergyman who was prepared to set lawyers on to making tithe claims, though, did not necessarily, having secured the income, use it for the parish poor. The clergy of the period, as a species, were little concerned with poverty. Even when they had a vocation, like Edmund in Jane Austen's *Mansfield Park*, they were usually far removed in background and in sympathies from their poor parishioners. To Cobbett, therefore, tithes levied to provide a relatively well-off parson with an addition to his stipend were simply another form of legalised robbery; if they were abolished, the farmer would have more to spend—and could spend some of it improving the wages of his labourers.

Ricardo, too, disliked tithes—'this most oppressive and irritating tax'. But abolishing them, he believed, would not add a penny to the income of the farmer—let alone of his labourers. The landowner would receive the full amount, in increased rent. And that, Ricardo felt, was how it should be; for the landowner could then lay out the money productively either in improving his estates, or by judicious investment.

Only on one aspect of taxation, in fact, were old and new radicals in full agreement. Both resented the way in which it was used to enable what Hazlitt called the 'State paupers'—place men—to supplement their private incomes, so that they could 'live in palaces, and loll in coaches'.

'Wages, therefore, decline'
But the differences of opinion on electoral reform and taxation were minor obstacles to political unity. An English O'Connell would have had

no difficulty in resolving them. The fundamental divergence between old and new radicals lay in their attitude to political economy.

'I have never been able to comprehend', Cobbett complained,

> what the beastly Scots feelosofers mean by their 'national wealth'; but as far as I can understand them, this is their meaning: that national wealth means, that which is *left* of the products of the country over and above what is *consumed*, or *used*, by those whose labour causes the product to be. This being the notion, it follows, of course, that the *fewer* poor devils you can screw the products out of, the *richer* the nation.

The true test of national wealth, Cobbett insisted, should not be the amount of the surplus, but how it was distributed. If a wagon left a village one morning laden with wheat and came back full of cloth, or other commodities, equal in value (except for the distributor's fair profit):

> then, indeed, the people might see the waggon go off without tears in their eyes. But now, they see it go to carry away and to bring next to nothing in return. What a *twist* a head must have before it can come to the conclusion, that the nation gains in wealth by the Government being able to cause the work to be done by those who have hardly any share in the fruit of the labour.

Again and again, Cobbett returned to this charge: that though the new radicals might believe they were working for the interest of the labouring poor, they were, in fact, working against it. Why, they were even objecting to labourers claiming traditional public holidays because, as production would be reduced, so would the national wealth! How anybody could conceive that the national wealth was increased 'by making these people work incessantly' passed Cobbett's comprehension.

One of the basic assumptions of the political economists had been that the introduction of labour-saving machinery, and the freeing of the economy from mercantilist fetters, must eventually liberate such vast productive potential that all would benefit, rich and poor alike; Cobbett, therefore, was talking nonsense. Francis Place could never have been induced to enter into alliance with Mill and Ricardo, had they not been able to reassure him on this point. The slumps of 1817 and 1819 had been disturbing, but they could be attributed to post-war dislocation, and to the fact that the economy had not yet been wholly freed—the corn laws and various trade restrictions remained. 'It could not be denied', Ricardo assured the Commons in 1819, 'on the whole view of the subject, that machinery did not lessen the demand for labour.' But like so many of the propositions which Ricardo had introduced with an 'it cannot be denied', or some similar assertion, it could be. The following year, the ranks of those who denied it were joined by an unexpected recruit: Malthus, in his long-awaited *Principles of Political Economy*. In his *Principles*, as in his *Essay on Population*, Malthus had an ulterior motive. Just as he had earlier wanted to preserve the social division of society from the threat of Godwin's egalitarianism, so he now wanted to protect it from the new radicalism. 'It is an historical truth,' he asserted, 'which cannot for a moment be disputed, that the first formation, and subsequent preservation and improvement, of our present constitution, and of the liberties and privileges which have so long distinguished Englishmen, are mainly due to a landed aristocracy.' Somehow—he had come to realise—not merely the landed aristocracy but their dependents, including gentlemen of private means, clergymen, and domestic servants, must be shown to have their legitimate place in the economic system. To Ricardo and the new radicals, many of the aristocracy were simply spongers on society, soaking up wealth that could otherwise have been productively employed. This might be a dangerous view, Malthus feared, should the radicals ever acquire political power. So he had been searching for another argument, as effective as the 'ratios', to undermine their case.

He had found it in 1817, in a tract written by John Barton: *Observations on the Circumstances which influence the condition of the Labouring Classes of Society*. Barton had observed that in spite of what the political economists thought, an increase of capital did not invariably lead to the employment of more labour:

> Let us suppose a case. A manufacturer possesses a capital of £1,000, which he employs in maintaining twenty weavers, paying them £100 per annum each. His capital is suddenly increased to £2,000. With double means he does not, however, hire double the number of workmen, but lays out £1,500 in erecting machinery, by the help of which five men are enabled to perform the same quantity of work as twenty did before. Are there not then fifteen men discharged in consequence of the manufacturer's having increased his capital?

The demand for labour, Barton concluded, depended on an increase of circulating, not of fixed, capital. This was just the argument Malthus was looking for; and he seized on Barton's idea, though this time he was careful to acknowledge the source. Labour-saving machinery, he argued, could only benefit the workers if its introduction created a demand for labour larger than the amount of labour it saved. In theory this could happen: some additional labour would certainly be needed to make the new machinery; and the reduced cost of the goods would increase demand for them, or leave more money spare to buy other goods. Nevertheless in practice, Malthus claimed, new machinery *did* save labour; the workers who became redundant ceased to earn the wages with which they could buy the goods; and, as a result, more goods were produced than could be sold. That, Malthus explained, was the reason for the periodic gluts, which the political economists had believed could not happen (except locally and temporarily). And the gluts would be worse, but for the fact that the aristocracy, the men of leisure, and the domestic servants, as well as the soldiers, judges, doctors, writers and clergy, acted as the—derided— sponge of effective demand, soaking up the surplus produce. If everybody worked—quite apart from the fact that society would lose the benefits it received from the existence of a leisured class—over-production would become unmanageable.

Ricardo had accepted Malthus's enthusiasm for a landed aristocracy as a Tory quirk which need not be taken too seriously. The theory that over-production could be caused by the introduction of machinery, though, was a different matter. It carried the unwelcome implication that a free economy might not be self-regulating; and that, he wrote at once to tell McCulloch, was 'clearly not true'. If the same amount of goods could be made with less labour,

> One of two things must happen: either you will give employment to the same or a greater number of people, and still further increase your means of enjoy-ment, or you will by the payment of the same or even less wages in money, enable the employed to command more commodities, and if they prefer indolence to the rewards of labour they may with less labour command the same quantity of enjoyments. How an abundance of production can lead to a less demand for labour, I cannot make out. Mr. M. appears to me to confound two things which ought to be kept distinct.

Once again, Ricardo appeared to have vindicated the principles upon which the radical alliance was based. But re-examining the whole issue in the light of Barton's ideas, Ricardo came to the conclusion that he had himself been wrong to believe that the introduction of labour-saving machinery would necessarily, other things being equal, benefit workers as well as employers. And in the third edition of his *Principles*, published in 1821, he included a new chapter on machines and their effects, in which he admitted that their substitution for human labour had been 'injurious to the interests of the class of labourers'.

The reason, Ricardo explained, was that with the help of labour-saving machinery, the net income of a society—the income derived from rent and profits—might increase, at the same time as the gross income—wages—was reduced; and it was the size of the gross, rather than the net income, which concerned the labourer. A capitalist who wanted to make, say, £2,000 a year profit might make it either with the help of a large turnover and a small profit margin, or a smaller turnover with a larger profit margin. As it was only the net profit that concerned him, he had no incentive to keep up the turnover, even if it provided more jobs; so 'there will necessarily be a diminution of the demand for labour, population will become redundant, and the situation of the labouring classes will be that of distress and poverty'. It followed, Ricardo concluded, that 'the opinion entertained by the labouring classes, that the employment of machinery is frequently detrimental to their interests, is not founded on prejudice, and error, but is conformable to the correct principles of political economy'.

To Place, this admission was all the more damaging because it appeared to be what Owen had said—and Cobbett was still saying. Although Cobbett had no objection to the introduction of labour-saving machinery, he was concerned to point out that it could benefit society as a whole only when the labour which it saved could be utilised elsewhere. If, for example, by installing a machine in the home, a family could make their bedding more cheaply (or earn enough to buy it more cheaply), that machine would be an asset both to the family and to the community. But if it were installed in a factory, and worked by child labour, leaving the family unemployed, to be maintained on the rates, 'then the machine is an injury to us, however advantageous it may be to those who use it, and whatever traffic it may occasion with foreign states'. The example might be home-spun; but it provided a reasonable hypothesis why the labouring poor had not benefited from the country's great increase in material wealth, and why some of them were much worse off than they had been half a century before, when factories had been scarce, and machinery had not been powered by steam.

Now, here was Ricardo admitting that Cobbett was right, and Malthus was right, and that he himself had been wrong. Or so it seemed to McCulloch: 'little did I expect', he wrote to Ricardo, 'after reading your triumphant answer to the arguments of Mr. Malthus, that you were so soon to shake hands with him, and give up all'. Ricardo, however, insisted that there was a distinction between his argument and Malthus's:

You surely must forget that Mr. Malthus's objection to machinery is that it
adds so much to the gross product of the country that the commodities produced cannot be consumed; that there is no demand for them. Mine, on the
contrary, is that the use of machinery often diminishes the quantity of gross
product and although the inclination to consume is unlimited, the demand will
be diminished by the want of means of purchasing. Can any two doctrines be
more different? And yet you speak of them as identically the same.

Machines, in other words, did not—and in a free economy, could not—
produce more than was necessary to meet the available demand. But the
effective demand might be coming from fewer people, if some workers had
been displaced by the machines. It was an ingenious hypothesis; but to
radicals, it would be utterly destructive to their earlier confidence that the
introduction of a free economy must benefit the workers. Ricardo was now
arguing that in order to preserve the economy's freedom, it would be
necessary to sacrifice that part of the labour force which machinery made
redundant—for if Malthus's law of population was accepted, redundant
workers would have to be denied poor relief, let alone compensation. And
to Cobbett, or to Owen, or to Southey, to call an economic system 'self-
regulating' which could regulate itself only by condemning a segment of
the population to starve, was to reintroduce the morality of Moloch.
Ricardo, however, did not flinch from pursuing his new theory to its
logical conclusion. If the process continued, he told McCulloch, so that
'machinery could do all the work that labour now does, there would be no
demand for labour. Nobody would be entitled to consume anything who
was not a capitalist, and who could not buy or hire a machine.'
   Pessimism was taking over political economy. Even James Mill, who
in spite of his acceptance of the Malthusian theory had remained optim-
istic, was affected. His *Elements of Political Economy*—the lessons on the
subject which he had given to his son, John Stuart, which also appeared in
1821—was in some respects hardly less discouraging than Ricardo's. At
any given time, Mill noted, there were a certain number of capitalists; a
certain quantity of food, raw material and instruments.

Let us next suppose that the labourers have increased in number by one half,
without any increase in the quantity of capital. There is the same quantity of
the requisites for the employment of labour; that is, of food, tools and material,
as there was before; but for every 100 labourers, there are now 150. There will
be 50 men, therefore, in danger of being left out of employment. To prevent
their being left out of employment they have but one recourse; they must

endeavour to supplant those who have forestalled the employment; that is, they must offer to work for a smaller reward. Wages, therefore, decline.

The reverse, admittedly, was also theoretically possible. If the number of labourers fell there would be more competition for their services, and wages would rise. But the number of labourers was rising, with the steady increase of population; apparently confirming the accuracy of Malthus's theory that population had a tendency to increase faster than the means of subsistence—or, as Mill now put it, to increase faster than capital. And in such circumstances, wages must be 'reduced so low that a portion of the population will regularly die of want'.

But how could anybody professing to be a radical accept such propositions? How could Place, in particular, continue to advocate the introduction of an economic system offering so gloomy a prospect? Recognition how bleak the future was that political economy offered could only, McCulloch felt, 'arm those who have contended that political economy is a fabric without a foundation'—the Owens and the Cobbetts—leaving Place without a working-class following.

Yet the alliance held together. Place was not a philosopher. He was primarily a political manipulator; and it was Ricardo, even more than Hume, who had provided the new radicals with their chance to use their skill where it could most effectively be employed: in Parliament. From the moment he took his seat, Ricardo managed to establish a remarkable ascendancy over the Commons. This was a little surprising, as he did not feel at ease there; but when he took a line on an issue, he seemed to be able to convince M.P.s, if not that the line must necessarily be the correct one, at least that it would be unwise to oppose him. 'It is not universally known', Mill wrote after his death, 'how signal a change has taken place in the tone of the House of Commons, on subjects of political economy, during his short parliamentary career'—a verdict which could be confirmed from Hansard. On economic questions, Lord Londonderry told the House in 1822, 'it was impossible to have higher authority'; and George Philips called him 'one of the most original and wisest writers, and one of the soundest thinkers'. At the Board of Trade, Huskisson was clearly in awe of him; Brougham was later to assert that in Parliament, few men had had more weight.

And Ricardo, although most of his contributions to debates were on economic issues, was prepared to speak and vote in favour of radical notions—one of the terms of his agreement with his borough owner being that he would have freedom to oppose the Government. Only on one issue did caution deter him from voting with his allies: Catholic Emancipation —that might have been too much for the electors of Portarlington. But he spoke up for parliamentary reform, in spite of the chance it gave Tories to mock him (he had never been in Portarlington, one of them observed, or indeed in Ireland, to consult the electors on the issue); and he made some forthright and effective speeches against the Government's abuse of its powers under the Six Acts.

To have Ricardo as an ally, then, was of immense value to Place and Hume. Nevertheless, he was beginning to make their position difficult, if they wished to preserve working-class support for the new radicalism. In May, 1823, he set out his views on machinery in the Commons, opposing a motion to help the handloom weavers. It must, he felt, 'in great degree, operate prejudicially to the working classes'; but that was not an argument against the machine. It was the workers who must adapt to it. They had the remedy in their own hands: 'a little foresight, a little prudence (which probably they would exert, if they were not made such machines of by the poor laws), a little of that caution which the better-educated felt it wise to use, would enable them to improve their situation'.

That workers ought to facilitate the introduction of machinery, though it brought them no benefit, by learning to remain celibate, was a doctrine unlikely to appeal to the handloom weavers, or to any class of worker whose future was threatened by machinery. In time, Ricardo was bound to become an embarrassment to Place and Hume. But that winter, Ricardo had performed a final service for them; at the age of barely fifty, he died. This left, as the two most influential members of the Club—apart from Malthus, whose standing as a political economist was not high among its members—James Mill and McCulloch. Mill, for all the growing pessimism of his economic opinions, was a staunch radical. 'In the great struggle between the two orders, the rich and the poor,' he insisted, 'the people must in the end prevail.' And on the machinery issue, McCulloch had refused to allow himself to be overawed by Ricardo. He continued to assert that labour-saving machinery did not put men out of work; they were absorbed, he explained, into jobs—making new labour-saving machinery. And in time, though less work would be necessary, this would be allowed for. In a properly managed society, workers 'should not be engaged twelve or fourteen hours a day in hard labour, nor would children be immured from their tenderest years in a cotton mill. The labourer would then be able, without endangering his means of subsistence, to devote a greater portion of his time to amusement, and to the cultivation of his mind.' Wherever wages were high, he went on, and not subject to severe fluctuations, 'the labourers are found to be active, intelligent and industrious . . . they are able to enjoy their intervals of ease and relaxation, and they would be censurable if they did not enjoy them.' To argue that high wages made the worker lazy was the reverse of the truth: it was where wages were low, and the workers miserably poor, as in Ireland, that laziness would be found: 'the experience of all ages and nations proves that high wages are at once the keenest spur—the most powerful stimulus to unremitting and assiduous exertion, and the best means of attaching the people to the institutions under which they live'. With political economy thus returning to its old course, the new radical alliance could again be consolidated.

5. ON POPULATION

There was one other principle which had been accepted by the political economists, and endorsed by Place, which was anathema to the old radicals: Malthus's theory of population, with its corollary (or so the assumption was) that the poor laws should be abolished, and that any attempt to relieve poverty was foredoomed to failure, because it would only encourage the poor to breed.

The old radicals, much as they disliked the way that the poor laws had come to work in practice, and anxious though they were to found a society where the need for poor laws might cease, took it for granted that so long as there were destitute men and women, or families whose earnings were insufficient to provide a decent living, some form of poor relief must continue. It used to infuriate Cobbett to hear the beneficiaries of the tax system—the relatively well-off—moaning about the only form of taxation which did not bring some benefit to themselves and their friends: the rates. 'We hear loud cries against the poor rates,' he wrote, 'the ENORMOUS poor rates, the ALL-DEVOURING poor rates; but what are the facts? Why, that in Great Britain, six millions are paid in poor rates; seven millions (or thereabouts) in tithes; and sixty millions to the fund people, the army, placemen and the rest . . . and yet all of this outcry is made about these six millions, and not a word is said about the other sixty-seven millions!' To Coleridge, too, though he also disliked the idea of any able-bodied worker subsisting on relief, the care of the aged, infirm or sick was a civic duty which 'must have been foreseen as arising from the institution of individual

properties and primogeniture'—in other words, the right of private ownership in land was contingent on the obligation to look after all those
who lived on it.

But the new radicals believed that poor relief ought to be abolished,
on two grounds. One was Ricardian—that the money collected from the
ratepayers would be put to better use, from the point of view of providing
jobs for the poor, if it were left to the ratepayers to spend. This argument,
though, was less often used, even by Ricardo himself, than the other,
derived from Malthus's law of population. To try to help the poor, except
through the operation of a free economy, would simply encourage them to
breed at the ratepayers' expense.

The Malthusian principle, John Stuart Mill was to recall in his
autobiography,

> was quite as much a banner, and point of union among us, as any doctrine
> specifically belonging to Bentham. This great doctrine, originally brought
> forward as an argument against the indefinite improvability of human affairs,
> we took up with ardent zeal in the contrary sense, as indicating the sole means
> of realising that improvability by securing full employment at high wages, to
> the whole labouring population, through a voluntary restriction of their
> numbers.

The political economists might mistrust Malthus's economic theories,
but they rarely referred to his theory of population, or the inferences based
on it, without a humble genuflection. Ricardo, for example, was so
appalled by his first reading of Malthus's *Principles of Political Economy* that
he deemed it wise to defer comment; but he got out of his difficulty tact-
fully by lavishing praise on Malthus's section on the poor laws: 'I wish
you could succeed', he wrote, 'in ridding us of the obstacles to the better
system which might be established.' And shortly before he died he
reiterated, in a letter to Maria Edgeworth, that the only way in which the
condition of the poor could be improved would be to remove their
improvidence—'the early and inconsiderate marriages of which Malthus
has so well treated'.

McCulloch, too, though even more contemptuous of Malthus as an
economist than Ricardo had been, nevertheless accepted almost unquestioningly his theory of population. The principle of increase in the human
race, he wrote in his *Principles of Political Economy*:

> is so very strong as not only to keep population steadily up to the means of
> subsistence but, generally speaking, to give it a tendency to exceed them. It is

true that a peculiar combination of favourable circumstances may occasionally cause capital to increase faster than population, and wages will in consequence be augmented; but such augmentation is rarely permanent; for the additional stimulus it is sure to give to the principle of population seldom fails, by proportioning the supply of labour to the increased demand, to reduce wages to their own level . . . the soil is of limited extent, and still more limited fertility; and it is this limited fertility that provides the only real check – the only insuperable obstacle – which prevents the means of subsistence, and consequently the inhabitants, of every country, from increasing in a geometrical progression, until the space required for carrying on the operations of industry should become deficient.

McCulloch was not unaware of the possibility that new techniques, or new machines, might improve productivity, enabling it to keep pace for a time with the population increase; but in the long run, he felt, the Malthusian principle was sound. He was also in agreement with the stock deduction from it: that the poor laws ought to go. Were they to be abolished, it could be presumed 'that most tolerable well-educated workmen, on finding their wages insufficient for the proper support of a family, would be deterred from marriage; and the check thus given to population, by reducing the supply of labour, would have the effect to raise its price to the proper level. The poor laws teach the labourer to consider it as indifferent whether his wages will suffice for the support of a family or not—that, if they are insufficient, the deficit will be made up from the parish funds, and thus remove the natural and most powerful check to over-population.' And this view was frequently echoed by political economy's camp followers: to deny the correctness of the Malthusian theory, the historian Henry Hallam claimed, was like disputing the multiplication table.

To Francis Place, though, the theory was a little embarrassing. Place had married at the age of nineteen, at a time when his financial future was very far from secure; and his wife had borne him fifteen children. 'Rare fellows we,' he wrote to a similarly situated friend, 'to preach moral restraint!' To have to tell his fellow workers that they must practise it, while the rich man could enjoy all the sexual self-indulgence he desired, would be embarrassing, particularly if Cobbett got to know about it. Casting around for a way out of this difficulty, Place came upon an idea of Bentham's, that some artificial means might be found to keep down the birth rate, and he decided to write a treatise, ostensibly to rebut Godwin's reply to Malthus, but really to show that the population might be kept down by the use of physical, rather than moral, restraint. When it was finished he sent a copy to Ricardo, who was relieved to find it 'a complete and satisfactory answer to all Mr. Godwin's objections to the theory of population', and who recommended the book, to his publisher, John Murray. Murray, however, was shocked by its contents. He kept the manuscript 'a shameful length of time', according to James Mill, 'and at last returned it without any answer at all'. Eventually a publisher was found, and *Illustrations of and Proofs of the Principles of Population* appeared in 1822.

Married couples, Place urged, should not consider it disreputable 'to avail themselves of such precautionary means as would, without being injurious to health or destructive of female delicacy, prevent conception', for if these means were accepted, 'a sufficient check might at once be given to the increase of people beyond the means of subsistence; vice and misery, to a prodigious extent, might be removed'. So, Place could accept the theory of population. Considered as a practical proposition, admittedly, birth control could not at that time be expected to do much to restrain the population increase. The condom had come into use during the previous century, but it was far beyond the means of the poor; and Murray's attitude to the book gave some indication of what the reaction would have been to a suggestion that a campaign should be mounted to popularise its use. Still, the book served Place's main purpose. It showed, to his own satisfaction and Ricardo's, that although the theory of population was correct, the poor need not be prevented from enjoying the same sexual pleasures as the rich.

Place might differ from Malthus over the desirability of birth control by artificial means; but he did not dispute that the poor laws were encouraging the increase of population, and thereby prolonging the distress of the poor. The only point on which the new Radicals were in doubt was on the practical issue of how, and how quickly, the poor laws could be got rid of. Two problems would arise—had already arisen, in fact, as the debates on the Sturges Bourne recommendations had shown. One was moral: how to get around the difficulty that poor parents who already had children had given birth to them in the belief that they would always be entitled to poor relief, as part of the law and custom of the land. The other was practical: deciding what to do about the men, women and children who would be left to starve if and when the poor laws were repealed.

Malthus's idea—that relief should continue to be available for all people born until a year after the Act abolishing it—would have entailed keeping the poor rates, though on an ever-decreasing scale, for a century;

and writing to Trower in 1817, Ricardo had questioned the value of such gradualism. Ought not the process of getting rid of the poor laws to be expedited

> by gradually limiting their application, by encouraging the poor man to depend on his own exertions only? Is not this to be done by refusing all relief in the first instance to any but those whose necessities absolutely require it – to administer it to them in the most sparing manner, and lastly to abolish the poor laws altogether? . . . It is a painful reflection, but not less true on that account, that we can never get into a good system, after so long persevering in a bad one, but by much previous suffering of the poor.

Sydney Smith, however, disagreed. Madness though it had been to call the excess population into existence—he wrote in his *Edinburgh Review* article on poverty in 1820—'it would be the height of cold-blooded cruelty to get rid of them by other than the most gradual and gentle means'. And to claim the poor had the remedy for their poverty—moral restraint—in their own hands, Smith argued, was a little unrealistic. Suppose they exercised it; years must elapse before its benefit, in the form of a reduced population, began to show; in the meantime, the opinions and habits of the labouring class might undergo a change. They were already suffering from the effects, direct and indirect, of excessive taxation, which had subjected them to long-continued want.

> . . . men placed in such circumstances, and cut off, as they must be, from all hope of rising in the world, naturally sink into a state of indolence and insensibility. They may not be discontented; but it is not in the nature of things that they should be either active or industrious . . . and it is but too evident that it is only by the terrors of the criminal law, that such persons can be prevented from breaking down those institutions which, however essential to the maintenance of society, must appear to them, not as bulwarks raised for the public benefit, but for the support and protection of a favoured few.

Sydney Smith was echoed by McCulloch, in his *Principles of Political Economy*. It was foolish, he said,

> to imagine that those who have nothing would quietly submit to suffer the extremity of want without attacking the property of others. And hence, if we would preserve unimpaired the peace, and consequently the prosperity, of the country, we must beware of allowing any considerable portion of the population to fall into a state of destitution. But without the establishment of a compulsory provision for the support of the unemployed poor, it is difficult to see

how they could avoid occasionally falling into this state. Through its instrumentality they are sustained in periods of adversity without being driven of necessity to attack the property of others and commit outrages.

It did not occur to McCulloch that there was any incongruity in referring to the 'prosperity' of a country so many of whose inhabitants were in a state bordering upon destitution; like Ricardo, he tended to equate prosperity with commercial development. But he had a more acute sense than Ricardo of the difficulties which would accompany the ending of poor relief.

'Men will work or save rather than starve'

It happened, though, that doubts about the practicability of getting rid of the poor laws were eased in this period by what appeared to be a most convincing demonstration that poor relief could be abolished, without leading to any alarming increase of beggars, and without causing civil disturbance. The evidence was provided in Glasgow by a man who more than any other contemporary—Malthus alone excepted—was to leave his mark on the history of the poor law: Thomas Chalmers.

Chalmers had made his reputation as a preacher, and it was in this capacity that he had first attracted attention in England. When he was invited to London in 1817, huge congregations came to hear him. 'All the world wild about Chalmers', Wilberforce reported; even Canning was observed to be in tears. Chalmers had a mission, as he thought of it, on behalf of the poor. He began to use his oratorical gifts to convince listeners that their relief should be regarded as the duty not of the State but—as it had for so long traditionally been—of Christians. As he wrote in the *Edinburgh Review* in 1818, his object was to show 'that the poor laws of England are the result of a very bungling attempt, on the part of the legislature, to do that which would have been better done had Nature been left to her own free processes, and man to the unconstrained influence of such principles as Nature and Christianity have bestowed upon him.'

This was all very well, but what would happen—Chalmers was asked—if the poor rate was abolished? In Scotland, he was reminded, although it was indeed left to members of the Kirk to make provision for the poor, their contribution was not strictly voluntary: each member of the congregation was expected to contribute in proportion to his means. Coleridge was to claim in his *Table Talk* that the Scots had managed to do without poor laws only 'till Glasgow and Paisley became great manufacturing places, and then people said "We must subscribe for the poor, or else we shall have poor laws." That is to say, they enacted for themselves a poor law in order to avoid having a poor law enacted for them.' Where— Chalmers' critics wanted to know—lay the advantage in such a system?

But this was not, in fact, the system that Chalmers was advocating. He, too, disliked what was being done in Glasgow, and he believed that it was unnecessary—or, at least, that the sum required to look after the poor could easily be reduced until it could once again be met by genuinely voluntary contributions. Existing poor rates, he felt, whether imposed by Church or State, were based on the assumption that people would starve if relief were not available. But this was to ignore certain facts of nature:

> First, that very generally men will work or save rather than starve; second, that generally relatives will help those of their own kindred rather than see them starve; third, that pretty generally, too, neighbours when told of the distress of a family within a few steps of them, will lend a hand to any generous proposal which might be set on foot for relieving them; and fourthly, should these experiments fail, that many, very many are the gentlemen, especially in or about towns, who would most gladly meet by their handsome donations any urgent or crying necessity which had been brought authentically to their knowledge.

These were not utopian assumptions, Chalmers insisted, they were facts; and, as he was still confronted by scepticism, he had decided—like Owen—that what he needed was a working model, to prove his point. So, in 1819, in his parish of St. John's, Glasgow, he abandoned levying a poor rate, relying instead on voluntary collections. To ensure that the money was wisely distributed, the parish was divided into twenty-five parts, each with about fifty families, and each in the charge of a deacon—a lay worker. The deacon was to be primarily concerned with the spiritual welfare of his charges, but he was also to investigate every request for relief. With only fifty families to deal with, this presented no great difficulty (one of the deacons told Chalmers that it occupied only about three hours of his time a month); and although getting to know all the families in the initial stages naturally took longer, this was properly part of a deacon's function anyway. Whenever a request for relief was received, the deacon responsible for the family was informed; his duty was to go to the home and check that the need was real—sympathetically, Chalmers insisted: 'ours was a strict, but in every case a friendly investigation'. Whether or not it was sympathetic, it was certainly effective; within a month, requests for relief had fallen by

H

four-fifths, and the parish expenses for looking after its paupers dropped to little over fifty pounds a year.

To Chalmers' annoyance, his scheme still did not commend itself to the Kirk authorities in other city parishes. They made various excuses—for example, that all he had done was compel the paupers from his parish to look for relief in other parts of the city. When he produced statistical evidence to show this was untrue, they fell back on the argument Ricardo had used against such experiments: that the success of his venture was a reflection of his energetic, dedicated personality, not of the merits of his system. There was only one way to refute them, and in 1823 Chalmers took it, leaving his parish for the Chair of Moral Philosophy at St. Andrew's University. As he had predicted, his scheme continued to work satisfactorily without him. But it was no use. Of the natural and the political difficulties of introducing it, Chalmers was later to recall, the former had all been conquered; but 'the latter have stood the assault alike impregnable to facts and to reasonings, and so abide as stoutly invincible as before'.

The success of Chalmers' experiment, though, made a considerable impression in England, and a lasting one; it was to be cited again and again, as a model, throughout the century. But the difficulty remained that the Established Church would certainly be unable to provide the inspection machinery—and the dissenting churches would be indignant if it tried to do so. There was, however, an earlier model which might have suggested a way to get round this difficulty. In 1818—the year Chalmers' anti-poor law manifesto appeared in the *Edinburgh Review*—a pamphlet was republished in London describing the operation of a similar, though secular, scheme which had been introduced in Hamburg just before the end of the eighteenth century, by Baron von Voght.

Voght had lived for some years in England; it was a country most of whose institutions he greatly admired—but not the poor law, as he observed it in operation. A few people, he realised, became paupers through incapacity, folly or vice, but 'by far the greatest number of poor in Europe are of a very different description'—they were poor because society gave them no chance to be anything else. It followed, Voght decided, that what was needed was not relief, but a system by which the deserving could be helped to find work; and to this end, he had designed a scheme not unlike Chalmers', though with a lay staff, dividing Hamburg into sixty districts, each with three 'gentlemen overseers'. Where an overseer reported that there were able-bodied paupers who needed work, work was provided for them—usually spinning, because it was simple, cheap, and had the advantage that the amount of work done could easily be measured. At the same time, to discourage the shiftless, all almsgiving was forbidden; anybody giving money to a beggar could be fined the equivalent of two pounds. But the Voght plan did not attract the same interest as Chalmers'. One reason, perhaps, was the common belief that England, the country which had introduced the poor law, had nothing to learn from any continental nation. Such was the national egocentricity on the subject at the time that even people who detested the poor laws felt a kind of pride in them, as an essentially English institution. But, in any case, under the Voght plan able-bodied paupers had to be provided with work; and to Ricardo and his followers this was unacceptable.

Chalmers' scheme, on the other hand, even if it were impracticable in English circumstances, at least was working in the United Kingdom; and it made no call on the public purse. To the new radicals, this afforded proof not merely of the rightness, but of the relevance, of their Malthusian case. All that was now needed was some scheme on similar lines, suited to English needs; and surely, they felt, one would in due course present itself. In the meantime, the important thing was to secure general recognition for the principles that Malthus had expounded, so that at least there would be no further backsliding.

And during the 1820s, the Malthusian principle had won acceptance by politicians of all parties: the opposition Whigs, in particular, and the Canningites. Certainly the report of the select committee which examined the poor laws in 1824 was Malthusian, in the general tendency of its conclusions. By out-relief in aid of wages, it said, and family allowances,

> a surplus population is encouraged; men who receive but a small pittance know they have only to marry and that pittance will be augmented in proportion to the number of their children; hence the supply of labour is by no means regulated by the demand; and parishes are burdened with thirty, forty or fifty labourers for whom they can find no employment, and who serve to depress the condition of all their fellow labourers in the same parish.

Every such report was an encouragement to Place and his allies. They could argue, with justification, that as the views they had propounded were coming to be accepted even in the unreformed House of Commons, the prospects for the supporters of their brand of radicalism were demonstrably brighter than those of the followers of Cobbett, or Hunt; and the Chalmers' experiment provided them with exactly the kind of quotable example that they needed, when they wanted to rebut the old radical accusation that to abolish the poor laws would be cruel in its effects.

'Salt and buttermilk their luxuries'

Yet during this period, the Malthusian theory was coming increasingly under fire—and not just from the old radicals. To Cobbett, Malthus was simply 'the monster': throughout history (he had written while in exile in America) priests had been remarkable for their cool and unrelenting cruelty; but 'it seems to have been reserved for the Church of England to produce one who has a just claim to the atrocious preeminence'. The abuse was misapplied: the picture did not fit. Malthus, his acquaintances felt, was an amiable soul, who genuinely wanted the labouring poor to achieve higher living standards. And if Cobbett had to fall back on vilification, that in itself could be interpreted as showing that he could not answer the Malthusian case. But there were other critics who could not so easily be brushed aside: William Hazlitt among them. After the publication of the 1817 edition of Malthus's *Essay* he had returned to the attack; in particular, finally demolishing the very part of Malthus's theory which had first attracted approval—his geometrical/ arithmetical ratios. The ratios, Hazlitt showed, were a convenient fiction. 'A grain of corn or of mustard seed has the same or greater power of propagating its species than a man, till it has overspread the whole earth'; to talk about population having a tendency to outstrip subsistence was as meaningless with man as with mustard.

By this time, not even Malthus's most devoted supporters took the ratios seriously. They simply insisted that his theory would remain valid even when the ratios—a poetic fancy, designed to capture the public imagination—were forgotten. This assumption, though, was questioned by John Barton—from whom Malthus had borrowed his theory of overproduction. Barton did not disagree with the population theory; but he doubted whether Malthus was justified in assuming that the poor laws necessarily encouraged population growth. Did the poor really need the inducement of family allowances, to procreate? Poverty alone—Adam Smith had noticed—appeared to be favourable to procreation: 'a half-starved highland woman frequently bears more than twenty children, while a pampered fine lady is often incapable of bearing any, and is generally exhausted by two or three'. And the half-starved highland woman got no family allowances. To argue, as Malthus did, that 'men would have avoided forming imprudent matrimonial connections much more carefully had those laws never been enacted' was consequently mere supposition. 'Surely,' Barton suggested, 'a very slight degree of observation may show that a state of extreme indigence is generally accompanied by the utmost thoughtlessness and improvidence.' The labourer was generally less prudent than the small trader, the beggar than the labourer; 'the pressure of want debases, stupefies and enfeebles . . . that comprehensiveness of mind which sacrifices present enjoyment to attain a distant good, dies under the harsh and stormy prospect of savage penury, no less than in the enervating sunshine of luxurious indulgence.'

Then, in 1820 a potentially formidable critic of Malthus reappeared: William Godwin. Godwin had not previously attempted a full-scale refutation of the theory of population; but now, in *On Poverty*, he dissected it, basing his criticism on two main grounds. The first was that the theory did not fit the known facts. How, for example, could Malthus account for the fact that Turkey, say, or Persia, were more thinly inhabited in the nineteenth century than in their renowned periods of ancient history? Certainly it was not because their soil was exhausted. The reason, Godwin thought, must be looked for in the way such countries had been governed; and this could be changed. If a beneficent sovereign were to appear 'to apply all his energies to make his country what it formerly was, then it seemed to be the granary of the world . . . the energies of the inhabitants of the country would be called for, and men from other regions would be invited to settle on this advantageous soil.' What mattered, in other words, was efficient government; given that, a far higher population could be absorbed.

But Godwin had reason to be aware of Malthus's remarkable ingenuity in taking criticisms of this kind and, by judicious rewriting of what he had said before, making it appear that he had already refuted them. More dangerous, Godwin went on, than the fallacies in his theory were its implications if it were accepted as correct, and adopted by society.

Would there be private charity, for example? Oh, no! said Malthus, because where provided, it would 'necessarily lead to pernicious consequences'. Frugality, then? But no—frugality brought the poor no benefit; and 'waste among the rich and the horses kept by them merely for their pleasure, operate like granaries, and tend rather to benefit than to injure the lower classes of society'. Marriage? Not for the poor: 'they should not have families, if they cannot support them'. And if a poor man refused to heed this warning, he should be left 'to the punishment of want. He should be taught to know that the laws of Nature, which are the laws of God, have doomed him and his family to suffer for disobeying their repeated admonitions.' What havoc—Godwin remarked—'do these few maxims make with the old received notions of morality . . . if we embrace his creed, we must have a new religion, and a new God.'

And, in a sense, this was what they now had: political economy. Until Malthus's *Essay* appeared, Godwin sadly recalled, writers on the subject had displayed courage. They had said 'the evils we suffer are from ourselves; let us apply ourselves with assiduity and fortitude to the cure of them . . . let us endeavour to remedy the evils of political society and mankind may then go free and contented and happy.' But Malthus had said no. 'He has proclaimed, with a voice that has carried astonishment and terror into the hearts of thousands, the accents of despair.'

On Poverty (it should really have been called *On Malthus*) was an earnest and at times moving indictment; but it was diffuse, and it made little impression. Godwin himself was all but forgotten; where he was known, it was more likely to be as the widower of Mary Wollstonecraft, and the father-in-law of Shelley, rather than as the author of *Political Justice* and *Caleb Williams*. What he needed, to re-establish himself, was a book which would make an impact in its own right. *On Poverty* was a commentary on theories which few people had read, in their original form—or wished to read. The great virtue of the Malthusian case, in the pre-digested form it was usually purveyed, was its simplicity; readers did not care to confuse themselves by trying to follow the author's own tortuous arguments in its favour, let alone by trying to follow some critic's attempts to refute them in detail. Soon, Godwin again returned to obscurity.

He was supported, though, by an admirer who proved more adept at seeing, and exposing, the fallacies inherent in the Malthusian position: William Thompson, who devoted a section of his *Enquiry into the Principles of the Distribution of Wealth* to an examination of the theory, along similar lines to Barton's, but concerned with the condition of the poor in his own home country, Ireland.

There could not be a more obvious test-bed for the whole theory. Since their country became part of the United Kingdom, the Irish had come to be a more direct responsibility for Parliament; and after 1815, a source of continual worry, as their standard of living was wretched beyond anything that could be found in England. Their condition was described to the Commons by Curwen, following an extensive tour he had made of Ireland in 1817; 'their clothing scanty and worn, their cabins mean and in disrepair; an earthen floor; a few boards and a wretched straw pallet, their bed. A stool or two, and an iron pot forms their whole menage; their sole food, potatoes; salt and buttermilk their luxuries.' By English standards, these peasants were living far below accepted subsistence levels, and in conditions which should have rendered them an easy prey to epidemic disease. Here, if ever, was a case where the labouring classes were not obtaining Malthus's declared minimum, 'that quantity of the necessities of life which climate and custom have rendered essential to their healthful existence'; and here, consequently, his theory could be tested against the realities.

The general assumption had been that Ireland provided the perfect example of the correctness of Malthus's theory. Place, for example, claimed in his work on population that 'Ireland furnishes proofs in refutation of every one of Mr. Godwin's positions'. Yet a mystery remained. In spite of the restraints imposed on the growth of population by vice, misery, and moral restraint; in spite of frequent famines, and devastating epidemics of fever; in spite of extensive emigration, the population of Ireland was increasing even more rapidly than England's, and it was rising faster in those regions where living standards were lowest. Yet in Ireland there was no poor law, no family allowances, to encourage the poor to breed.

Malthus's explanation was that the Irish were in so degraded a state that they could not really be considered as human; they were apt to 'propagate their species like brutes', and it therefore mattered little whether poor relief existed or not—'no stretch of human ingenuity and exertion could rescue the people from the most extreme poverty and wretchedness'. But was this true? To Thompson, who naturally was much better acquainted with conditions in Ireland than Malthus or Place, the evidence pointed to a very different explanation. In many parts of Ireland the peasantry did indeed live, and propagate their species, like brutes. But how to account for the fact that in other parts, notably in the north of Ireland, the peasants were conspicuously more prosperous? Although their farms might be small, they enjoyed a markedly higher standard of living, with better homes and a more varied diet. Yet, in these areas, the population was relatively stable. Why?

The usual explanation was that the Ulstermen were descendants of Scots Presbyterian families 'planted' two centuries before; and that they were energetic and efficient, compared to the lazy, feckless Catholic Irish. But, when they emigrated to Britain, the Catholic Irish had the reputation of being extremely hard-working. Could it be, Thompson asked, that there was some other reason for the contrast between the two types? He believed that there was: the difference in the land tenure system.

In the south, the peasant had no rights over his holding, and no security on it. If, for example, he drained a field, increasing his revenue from it, the landlord (or—as the landlord was often an absentee, living in England—the agent) could simply raise the rent, to cream off the benefit; and if the peasant refused to pay, he could be evicted. If he built a wall, or added a room to his cottage, they belonged to the landlord. He consequently had no incentive to attempt to improve his condition; and 'rack-rents' had gradually forced him down to the extreme limit of subsistence living, which the potato provided. The potato could be grown cheaply, a small plot providing enough for a family; and very little else was needed for survival, except a mud cabin, and the right to cut turf from the local bog, for fuel.

In Ulster, on the other hand, a tradition of tenant right had been established, giving relative security against eviction, and allowing tenants to improve their land without the landowner raising the rent on them. Naturally this gave them an incentive to improve their living standards; and also, Thompson believed, to 'restrain immediate inclination for the sake of greater preponderant good'—which kept down the birth rate. In the south, on the other hand, the advent of another mouth to feed required no more effort than the cultivation of a few extra square yards of land to grow some more potatoes. Restraint brought no benefit, and the lack of it, only slight additional inconvenience.

The moral, to Thompson, was clear. To solve the problem of pauperism in England, it was necessary to think in terms not of getting rid of the surplus population by refusing to relieve it, which experience in Ireland showed was futile, but of raising the living standards of the poor—and, still more important, improving their prospects—with the help of legislation. If this were done, the population might continue to rise, but it would assuredly rise far less rapidly, and could be kept in proportion to the increased production of the comforts and necessaries of life.

Obviously Thompson's diagnosis, if it were correct, was of fundamental importance. Should it be necessary—as Malthus insisted, and as members of all political parties were coming to accept—to reduce the surplus population, it was useless to think only in terms of reducing it in England, so long as the Irish population continued to rise. If vice, misery and moral restraint were not acting as population checks in Ireland, something else needed to be tried there. Why not tenant right?

There was nothing in the principles of political economy to rule out consideration of this proposal. Ricardo himself had blamed the Irish landlords for the condition of the people; 'any stimulus which should rouse the Irish to activity', he felt, 'which should induce them to dispose of their surplus time in procuring luxuries for themselves, instead of employing it on the most brutal pursuits, would lead more to the civilisation and prosperity of that country than any other methods which could be recommended'. Malthus, too, giving evidence to the emigration committee of 1826–7, agreed that the Irish landlords practice of encouraging the subdivision of farms had contributed very much to the population increase there—an increase which, he asserted in his answers, was wholly to be deplored.

> Q. If it be an admitted fact, that there are a great number of labourers for whose labour there is no real demand, and who have no means of subsistence, does not it necessarily follow that as far as the wealth of the country is concerned, these labourers are of no advantage?
>
> Malthus: Certainly.
>
> Q. In point of fact, therefore, if a thousand labourers, supposed to be under those circumstances, were to die, the wealth of the country would not be diminished by their decrease?
>
> Malthus: I think not.

The Irish population increase was also fatal, Malthus agreed, 'to the happiness of the labouring classes in England, because emigration to England lowered wages'. But when he was asked whether the Government ought to take steps to remedy the situation, he was adamant that it should not. The land tenure system in Ireland was responsible? Yes. It needed to be changed? Yes—but only by the landlords; 'I do not know how the Government can interfere to force them.'

The reason why Malthus was prepared to accept that the land tenure system was responsible (he could not blame the poor law, as the Irish did not have one) and refused to allow that the Government could do anything about it, was obvious. To accept the need for intervention of the kind Thompson urged would have been to admit that the condition of the labouring poor was not entirely in their own hands. To agree that society could intervene on their behalf would have been an admission that Godwin had been right all along. And as nothing could be done by the State, and nothing was likely to be done by the landlords, things must be left— Malthus' implication was—until the day arrived when there was no more land on which to grow potatoes, so then any further population increase would be offset by sheer starvation.

'The difference between us is almost entirely verbal'

It had hardly been necessary for Malthus to take his early critics very seriously, because none of them was a political economist. Occasionally, members of the circle had expressed small doubts about the theory of population; Trower, for one—writing to Ricardo in 1821—accepted Hazlitt's point that the increase of vegetable life was infinitely more rapid than that of population: what was lacking was not the capacity to reproduce, but the land to do it on. But Trower was careful to add 'of course, this is what Malthus *means*, but it is not what he *said*': the law of population remained virtually unquestioned.

The first indication that it might be challenged from within the ranks of the political economists did not come until 1823, and then only in an article in the *London Magazine*, which had not acquired the formidable reputation of the *Edinburgh* or the *Quarterly*. Besides, it was by Thomas de Quincey, better known for his *Confessions of an Opium Eater*, which had appeared in the magazine two years earlier, than for his views on political economy. Nevertheless de Quincey was a disciple of Ricardo, and a keen amateur economist; he was later to write a *Logic of Political Economy*, which won praise from McCulloch. He certainly was not a hostile critic.

It was clear from the article that de Quincey had read very little of the earlier controversy on Malthus; if he had, he might have been more circumspect. From his own judgment, he had formulated two main criticisms of the *Essay*; one concerning the ratios; the other drawing attention to a fallacy in the author's reasoning 'which I verily believe is the greatest logical blunder that has ever escaped any author of respectability'. In order to refute Godwin's theory of the perfectibility of man, de Quincey recalled, Malthus had endeavoured to prove that even if a perfect society were to be established, it would be overthrown by the pressure of population, leading to a re-establishment of an imperfect society in which misery and vice would be required to keep the population down. But, de Quincey triumphantly pointed out, 'vice and misery can have no existence in a state of perfection'. Malthus, in other words, had been guilty of a simple logical error. He had not believed in the possibility of a perfect society, but he had accepted it, to refute it: if he accepted it, though, his refutation collapsed!

De Quincey was concerned only with the *Essay*'s logic; the fact that it was false made no difference, he felt, to the validity of his theory of population, which remained an integral part of political economy. But the criticism was in fact much more damaging than de Quincey realised, because Malthus's law of population happened to be founded on the very fallacy which de Quincey had exposed. Whether or not society was perfectible was unimportant; what mattered was whether it could move in that direction. Malthus had claimed to show that it could not do so without creating the additional population which would drag it back to its former level again. But if this claim were based on false logic, then it became necessary to re-examine the whole theory. Suppose, for example, that in moving towards higher standards, society began to find new ways to control population? Then not only the law of population, but all the principles which Ricardo had borrowed from it to incorporate into orthodox political economy—for example, the objections to poor relief, and to the use of State funds to provide work for the unemployed—would cease to be applicable. But de Quincey did not realise the significance of his contribution; and through his neglect of the earlier stages of the controversy, he had left himself open to a demolition by Hazlitt, so crushing that de Quincey's view was unlikely to be taken seriously by either side.

McCulloch's *Principles*, when they appeared two years later, included nothing to suggest any doubt about the theory of population. Critical though McCulloch was of Malthus as an economist, he was prepared to accept that the only way by which the workers could improve their condition was 'by increasing the ratio of capital to population'—and the only way that could be done would be by moral restraint. But McCulloch's supremacy as the interpreter of political economy, after Ricardo's death, was now to be challenged by a newcomer: Nassau Senior, appointed in 1824 to the first Chair of Political Economy at Oxford University. Senior was younger than most of the members of the Political Economy club; he was not one of the Ricardo circle; he was Whig, rather than radical, in his political affiliations; and he liked to go his own way. One of the subjects on which he had chosen to lecture was population; and in 1826, he published his views in an essay.

It was written with the breezy confidence of one who believes he has had the advantage of first-hand experience on the subject; his initial resolve to become an economist had arisen out of a youthful impatience with the poor laws, as he observed them in operation in his father's parish. He accepted that the three restraints of vice, misery and moral restraint kept population growth in check; but experience had taught him that moral

restraint was ineffective, except before matrimony. As he saw it, when a
married Englishman was hesitating between love and prudence, the
prospect of an addition to his family was 'not one of his terrors'; but if he
could be caught before he was married, he might be persuaded to realise
that 'the income which supported his social rank while single, may be
unable to give his children the advantages which he himself enjoyed—in
short, he may lose his caste'.

Up to this point, there was nothing in Senior's argument that was likely
to offend Malthus; but he went on to draw an inference from his argument
which, if accepted, could only be destructive of one of Malthus's most
cherished beliefs. For the fear of loss of caste to be effective, Senior argued,
there must be some caste to lose. The destitute, in their degraded state,
had no such fear to restrain them from indulging an inclination to get
married. It followed that the poor must be given some ground for hope
that if they did try to better themselves, they could improve their living
standards, and thereby achieve caste. The followers of Malthus had denied
the poor this hope, by claiming that any improvement in their condition
must encourage them to breed more, and force them back to the subsistence level. But was this really true? Senior thought not.

Senior was an optimist—a disciple, in this respect, of Adam Smith
rather than of Ricardo; and he had no difficulty in finding arguments to
justify his thesis. Look at the English! he would tell his students: look at
the improvements that the common people of England enjoyed which were
unknown in Caesar's time, 'the warm and dry cottage of the peasant
labourer, its chimney and its glass windows (luxuries not enjoyed by
Caesar himself) . . . and, above all, his safety from personal injury, and his
calm security that tomorrow will bring with it the comforts which have
been enjoyed today!' Many an English labourer at this time might have
found it hard to recognise himself in Senior's mirror, but the point which
Senior was making could hardly be controverted; in certain respects, the
poor clearly enjoyed higher living standards than their ancestors. On the
prevailing interpretation of the Malthusian theory, this could not have
been accomplished without a population increase dragging the standards
down again. That had not happened.

The Malthusian process, therefore—Senior was saying—was not
inevitable. It was possible for the poor in a well-regulated community to
begin to enjoy, and to keep, higher standards than their forebears.
Society's aim should be to encourage this. 'Knowledge, security of
property, freedom of internal and external exchange, and equal admis-

sibility to rank and power, are the principal causes which at the same time promote the increase of subsistence, and by elevating the character of the people, lead them to keep at a slower rate the increase of their numbers.'

Senior clearly had no idea of the reaction that his thesis would provoke. With due deference, he pointed out that Malthus's error, 'if it be one', did not affect the practical conclusions which placed him 'as a benefactor of mankind, on a level with Adam Smith'. He was consequently disturbed when he heard that Malthus had been annoyed by the essay; and he sat down to write a soothing explanatory letter. All he had been concerned to do, he explained, was to clear up a misunderstanding, for which Malthus's disciples were undoubtedly responsible, about the meaning of the word 'tendency'. That population had a tendency to increase faster than the means of subsistence was undoubtedly true, wherever there were artificial forces, such as the poor laws, at work to encourage breeding among the pauper population. This, obviously, was what Malthus had meant. But his followers were interpreting 'tendency' to mean that population *invariably* outstripped food production unless some check was opposed; and this, Senior argued, was contrary to the historical evidence. His belief was that 'in the absence of disturbing causes, food has a tendency to increase faster than population because in fact it has generally done so'—with which Malthus would surely agree; 'if I rightly understand you, the difference between us is almost entirely verbal'.

But Senior had not rightly understood, as Malthus's reply made clear. Malthus was prepared to concede that there were checks which could operate to prevent the population from outstripping its food supplies; he was not prepared to accept that they could be described as constituting a 'tendency'. On the contrary, the tendency was, as he had stated, for the population to increase faster than the food; as had been 'distinctly proved by the universally acknowledged fact that wherever improvements in agriculture, or the effects of some disruptive plague, loosened the restraints which kept down the population, it made a start forward at the greater rate than usual'. This was hardly a reply to Senior's argument; but it was certainly a reaffirmation of the central Malthusian position. Senior might choose to interpret 'tendency' as meaning 'it can happen, if allowed'; Malthus was determined to stick to his own interpretation, 'it does happen, if not prevented'.

But Malthus went further. Senior's historical view, he claimed, was fallacious. The desire of people for any betterment of their standards was quite unimportant; it was 'perfectly feeble, compared to the tendency of population to increase.' And once again, Malthus formally set out his own opinion. As the labouring classes had no access to capital, they could not materially help to increase the means of subsistence. Admittedly, they could in theory help to increase it relative to the population by restricting population growth:

> But as this cannot be effected without restraint and self-denial, to which there is certainly a much less tendency than to marriage, the practical result is such as might be expected, namely, that although this restraint and self-denial may prevent more misery and vice at one period than at another; though they are often more efficient in civilised and populous countries, than in ignorant and thinly-peopled countries; and though we may hope that they will become still more efficient as knowledge advances; yet so far as we can judge from history, there never has been a period of any considerable length, when premature mortality and vice, specifically arising from the pressure of population against food, has not prevailed to a considerable extent; nor, admitting the possibility, or even the probability of these evils being diminished, is there any rational prospect of a near approach to their entire removal.

Senior could no longer escape by claiming that he was simply refuting the error of Malthus's followers. Here was Malthus spelling out his own pessimistic interpretation of his theory; and in the process, bluntly intimating that Senior's optimism was ill-founded. The temptation to hit back must have been strong. But Senior was in an embarrassing situation. The past doctrine of orthodox political economy would be cited against him if he repudiated Malthus. Worse: he himself had said in his essay that Malthus's propositions, though 'formerly assailed by every species of sophistry and clamour, are now so generally admitted that they have become rather matters of allusion than of formal statement'. Was he now going to admit that he had been wrong?

To have done so would have been made still more humiliating by the fact that, as Senior well knew, the critics of the Malthusian theory had not in fact been silenced. Apart from Thompson, there was still Cobbett, diligently collecting examples on his rural rides to refute Malthus—examples which fitted in very well with Senior's views. The inhabitants of the prosperous Avon valley produced, by Cobbett's computation, about twenty times as much food and clothing as they consumed, and they had done so for generations; but there had been no observable increase in their numbers. Where, then—Cobbett asked—was 'their natural tendency to increase beyond the means of subsistence'? So long as the land was properly cultivated, he claimed, and its produce distributed fairly among those who worked on it, the tendency did not operate: it was only when a landowner took too large a share in rent, as in Ireland, and persuaded the tenants and labourers to switch from bread, because it was more expensive, to oatmeal or to 'Ireland's lazy root', that the poor began to breed too rapidly.

The political economists preferred to behave as if Cobbett did not exist; but this would become difficult, if Cobbett were able to tell the *Register*'s readers that Senior had now come round to the view he had been putting forward for years. Senior's old friend and mentor Thomas Whately, soon to succeed him in the Oxford Chair, and later to become Archbishop of Dublin, begged him to be conciliatory, so as not to give comfort to the common enemy; and Senior allowed himself to be persuaded.

He made one last effort to paper over the fissure. At least, he wrote, they could reach agreement on the basis of Malthus's own statement, that population is always 'ready and inclined to increase faster than food, *if the checks which repress it are removed*'. It was Malthus's followers, Senior reiterated, who were at fault, for accepting the proposition without the qualification; as a result, they were denying the efficacy of *any* measures to improve the condition of the poor—including emigration. Why, they were even being cynical about repeal of the corn laws! 'If food were more abundant', their reasoning ran, 'there would be a proportionate increase of population, and we would be just as ill-off as before.' Demonstrably this was false, for otherwise, how could the world ever have emerged from a state of savagery? Would not Malthus at least concede that mankind operated like a snail, 'who climbed four feet up a wall, but fell back only three'? Malthus, however, would concede nothing; and the correspondence ended.

But the controversy continued. Another political economist was defecting—McCulloch. An article in the *Edinburgh Review* suggested a change of mind; and in 1830, giving evidence to a committee on the state of the poor in Ireland, he confessed that he had modified his earlier opinions. He had formerly opposed the poor laws, but further consideration had led him to realise that he had been wrong; 'poor laws may be administered so as to be productive of good, rather than evil'. They were necessary, he now believed, to make landlords and farmers aware of their responsibilities; 'if you once give to all people of fortune, to all those in fact who have property in the country, a strong direct pecuniary interest in repressing the spread of pauperism, and in taking care that the poor are not improperly multiplied, you will do more than you can do by anything else to improve the condition of the people'. And he went further:

> Q. Do you rely, as a mode of permanently improving any country, upon a forced diversion of any portion of the resources of the State, rather than upon the natural development of industry and the operation of natural causes?
> McCulloch. I do, in so far as respects the management of the poor.

It was a staggering admission. For a decade, ministers had been refusing to allow any expenditure of the taxpayer's money on public works to relieve unemployment on the ground that it was contrary to the principles of political economy. The report, for example, of the select committee which had been set up in 1828 to examine the working of the poor laws had unhesitatingly accepted the Malthusian theory, in spite of some reservations about how to put it into practice. Yet here was the man who was generally regarded as the repository, since Ricardo's death, of economic orthodoxy, repudiating not merely Malthus, but Ricardo himself.

It was a difficult moment for the new radicals. The campaign to get rid of the poor laws was a useful vote-catcher, because it appealed to the class which was likely to provide radicalism with its main support—the rate-payers. That support was likely to be even more valuable, too, when Reform gave more ratepayers the vote. And the Whigs, who were likely to form the next government, were attracted to the idea of poor law reform on Malthusian principles. It would be foolish to throw away such alluring political prospects simply because those principles had been challenged. The new radicals decided to stick to them.

6. THE OLD ORDER CHANGETH

As the 1820s drew to their close, the Tory Government's difficulties increased. The 1827 harvest was poor; its successor, worse. In 1829, industry, which had been recovering after the slump, suffered another set-back. 'The distress in the country is frightful', Creevey's friend Lord Sefton wrote to tell him. So wretched had the condition of the agricultural labourers become by 1830 that an American visitor came away with the impression that the term 'pauper' was applied in rural areas of England 'to that numerous class of society who depend for subsistence solely on the labour of their hands'. That this was not simply an isolated impression was also made clear to Wellington in his correspondence: 'pauperism', one writer told him, 'which forty or fifty years ago, was scarcely felt, except as to the impotent poor, is now a general system'.

As discontent mounted Lord Eldon—the John Scott of Pitt's administration—began to feel that society was in danger; and he was inclined to blame Wellington. All the signs, he feared, pointed to a repetition of the events of the early 1790s, but 'of a more frightful kind'. Then, at least, republicanism had been avowed; now, the language of revolution was more subtle, which made the culprits harder to detect and prosecute. 'They are, of course, more dangerous. The sacrifice, too, of the Test Act, and the passing of the Roman Catholic Emancipation Bill, have established a precedent so encouraging to the present attempts at revolution, under the name of Reform, that he must be a very bold fool who does not tremble at what seems to be approaching.'

If revolution was approaching, the new radicals had little to offer to attract support among the disaffected. The nearest approach to a radical manifesto had been presented by Place in 1822: electoral reform, the repeal of the Combination Acts, the removal of restrictions on emigration, and the repeal of all remaining State restrictions on industry and commerce. These were hardly calculated to inspire a starving agricultural labourer, who could not expect a vote, was not a member of a trade union, did not wish to leave his home, and might be even worse off if the corn laws were repealed. Cobbett had scoffed at the proposals—particularly those for State-aided emigration. There were indeed plenty of people in England, he conceded, that the country would be better off without; but the campaign which Place and others were conducting had as its aim to get rid 'not of the idlers, not of the pensioners, not of the deadweight, not of the parsons, not of the soldiers—but to devise means of getting rid of these working people, who are grudged every morsel they get'.

Nevertheless Place had one distinct advantage: one of his aims had actually been accomplished. The legalised trade unions had had a hard time of it in the slump of 1826, but they had been recovering; and although their growing national strength was not entirely welcome to Place, as he had believed that they could not operate except on a local basis, he was not averse to taking the credit. How much more radicalism could achieve, he was able to argue, if his policy of working by constitutional means, in alliance with the Whigs, was continued—especially now that the Tory party was split, and could hardly last in office much longer.

All would depend on whether Place could hold his radical following and, at the same time, impress on the Whigs the vital necessity of helping him to hold it by concentrating their political energies on the campaign for Reform (as it was by this time usually called, without any prefix). Most Whigs would have preferred to retain an electoral system in which the landowning interest predominated, as of old. But they had been out of power for close on half a century, apart from the brief intermission of 'All the Talents'; and if Reform was the price of returning to power and keeping it, they were reluctantly prepared to pay. And although most of them felt uncomfortable at the link with radicalism, a few influential members of the party had radical sympathies; among them Lord Durham, Grey's son-in-law, and Brougham, who for a time had been one of Bentham's circle. Grey himself had been one of the 'Friends of the People' in the early 1790s; his ardour for Reform might have cooled, but he had not lost hope of putting a reform measure through, and he would not spurn radical help. Most important of all, he supplied what radicalism lacked; he was an accepted leader. He might not be ideal, but he would do.

'The most wretched upon earth'

In the summer of 1830 George IV died; and his successor, William IV, was known to be less hostile to Reform. The succession necessitated a general election; and while the campaign was in progress, the news came in of the July revolution in France. This time there were no excesses, no Terror, merely a change to a constitution more democratic, in many respects, than Britain's. Thus encouraged, the Whigs campaigned more boldly for Reform; and the results of the voting showed that the electors, where there were enough of them to exert an influence, were increasingly in favour.

It remained uncertain, however, which would come first; Reform or revolution. In the autumn of 1830 outbreaks of violence were reported from the south-east: machine-breaking, rick-burning, threatening letters to farmers who used threshing machines. At first sporadic, the outbreaks began to spread up towards the country districts area around London, and round the capital to the north and west. Such was the precision with which some of the forays were executed that ministers began to suspect some master-mind must be at work—as Peel put it, there must be 'some ulterior object in view beyond the redress of mere local grievances'.

In a sense he was right: there was. The landowners had helped to create one themselves, as a result of their enclosures, and of their passion for the preservation of game.

The game laws were of long standing—the only oppressive part of the feudal system, Sir William Elford had pointed out in a treatise on the subject published in 1817, which had remained on the statute book. They had been designed to restrict the right to shoot game to the aristocracy. A farmer, unless he had an extensive property, was not merely debarred from taking game on his own land, but could be fined, imprisoned, and sentenced to corporal punishment if he were found to have the means of taking game in his possession—and they might be found on the strength of a search warrant signed by the same magistrate who would be on the bench to pass sentence.

The first quarter of the nineteenth century had seen a general reduction of the penalties for crime, but not for breaches of the game laws. It was easy to see why. The *battue*, in which game birds were driven by beaters towards the waiting guns, was superseding 'walking up'; far more birds had to be bred to meet the demand; and the opening of the shooting season was beginning to become a great social occasion—for many people, then as now, the occasion most looked forward to in the whole year, awaited with the expectation that a child has for Christmas.

Among the advantages that cottagers had been accustomed to enjoy from their access to commons were rabbits, hares, and the occasional game bird. It might be against the law, but the law was difficult to enforce. With enclosures, though, merely to set foot on the old common was to risk prosecution for trespass; and to be found with a gun or a trap was to invite prosecution. Penalties for poaching were increased until by the 1820s a man who snared a rabbit on enclosed land, though he might have been snaring rabbits on it all his life before it was enclosed, could be sentenced to seven years' transportation. The judiciary had further held that in common law, the use of spring guns against trespassers was legal (when in 1827 their use was banned, it was as a result of the mortality among game-keepers and children, rather than of any change of heart about using them against poachers). And as in local courts the magistrates were usually the local landowners, the laws, common or statute, were rigorously enforced; by 1825 one out of every four commitments to jail on criminal charges—it was revealed in the Commons—was for an offence against the game laws.

Sydney Smith—who had plenty of leisure in his humble rural parish to observe what was happening, while he waited hopefully for the return of a Whig government which, he assumed, would present him with the

ecclesiastical preferment which his talents and his social contacts merited
—was among those who were shocked by this manifestation of what he
regarded as aristocratic callousness. He felt little sympathy with the
agricultural labourer, whom he regarded as little better than an animal; 'a
ploughman marries a ploughwoman because she is plump; generally uses
her ill; thinks his children an encumbrance; very often flogs them; and,
for sentiment, has nothing more nearly approaching to it than the idea of
broiled bacon and mashed potatoes'. But he was appalled at the treatment
that the ploughman who was caught poaching could receive under the
game laws, and repelled by the callousness of the people who invoked
them. 'How any human being, educated in liberal knowledge and Christian
feeling, can doom to certain destruction a poor wretch, tempted by the
sight of animals that naturally appear to him to belong to one person as
well as another, we are at a loss to conceive. We cannot imagine how he
could live in the same village, and see the widow and orphans of the man
whose blood he had shed for a trifle . . . there rests upon his head, and
there is marked in his account, the deep and indelible sin of blood-
guiltiness.'

Sydney Smith might be disregarded as a babbling humanitarian; but
there were a few landowners who viewed the effects of the game laws with
alarm for a different reason. They saw, much as opponents of the Prohibi-
tion laws in the United States began to see a century later, that not merely
were the laws failing as a deterrent; they were creating a criminal network
of a kind that could have destructive consequences for society. 'The
receipt to make a poacher', Lord Suffield—a former Tory who had horrified his friends and relations by beginning to entertain Whig, and even
radical, notions—told the House of Lords in 1825

> will be found to contain a very few and simple ingredients, which may be met
> with in every game county in England. Search out (and you need not go far) a
> poor man with a large family, or a poor man single, having his natural sense of
> right and wrong . . . give him little more than a natural disinclination to go to
> work; let him exist in the midst of lands where the game is preserved; keep
> him cool in the winter, by allowing him insufficient wages to purchase fuel; let
> him feel hungry upon the small spare pittance of parish relief; and if he be not
> a poacher, it will only be by the blessing of God. In the poacher thus easily con-
> cocted, my experience justifies me in asserting that we have at least a fair
> promise, if not the absolute certainty, of an ultimately accomplished villain.

The next step—according to the anonymous author of an article on the
game laws in the *Westminster Review*, the following year—was equally

inevitable. It was well known, he pointed out, that over a great part of England, the most an agricultural labourer could earn was a shilling a day. 'In comparison with this the gains of the poacher must be enormous. A gang of poachers has been known to take as much as three sacks of game in one night.' And, as game was not normally available for sale in the open market, the price a gang could command for such a haul was very attractive. A gang, too, could afford a high degree of protection from a gamekeeper by the simple expedient of setting guards, to give the alarm if he approached; or, not infrequently, by terrorising him into keeping away.

As a result, poachers in many areas had formed themselves into disciplined bands of the kind Harriet Martineau was soon to describe in one of her poor law tracts; and it was a short step for them to turn from organised poaching to organised rick-burning and machine-breaking. Their nocturnal habits, too, made them hard to detect; in the morning they might appear to be respectable farm labourers. And so it came about that insurrectionary forces, though without leaders or a political cause, nevertheless displayed what appeared to be the common purpose of a well-organised resistance movement.

Confronted with the spreading violence, the Government seemed paralysed. In a debate in the Commons on November 5, 1830, speaker after speaker rose to describe the distressed and discontented condition of the poor in rural areas, and to warn the Government to act before it was too late. Peel—following the death of his father, he was now Sir Robert Peel, Baronet—could offer no course of action. He could only protest against 'this course of asking, day after day, questions with regard to the measures contemplated by the Government', and he begged members to desist from uttering warnings, as they would only aggravate the 'excitement and inflammation'.

Peel's helplessness was understandable; he had found that so far from reprobating the unrest, and taking firm measures to put it down, magistrates and—still more surprisingly—farmers and shopkeepers in many districts were openly sympathising with the labourers. In some places wages settlements were arrived at, and sanctioned by the magistracy; Cobbett would report them, triumphantly, in his *Register*. And by this time the machinery of repression, disused since 1820, could not easily be put back into working order; certainly not without incurring considerable expense, which would be unwelcome, as the Government was in chronic financial difficulties. It would hardly be possible to increase indirect taxation—the burden it imposed on the poor was one of the labourers' main grievances;

and ministers could not agree on which of the alternatives, a property tax, or the reimposition of income tax, was the more objectionable. The only expedient they were able to find to raise money without unpopularity was a Beerhouse Act, licensing anybody who wanted to sell beer to do so for two pounds a year. This, the Chancellor of the Exchequer hoped, 'would conduce at once to the comfort of the people, in affording them cheap and ready accommodation; and to their health, in procuring them a better and more wholesome beverage'—more suitable, that is, than spirits. According to the Act's critics, all that the new beershop did was encourage labourers to neglect their families, and get together to drink, brood on their grievances, and plot violence.

Ministers did not lack advice about what they should do. It poured in on them in the form of letters, private and open. And the remedy most commonly presented was far from revolutionary: the provision of a plot of land and of a living wage for every labourer. But this would have required legislation; and it had the further disadvantage that as a policy, it was identified in the public mind with radicalism—Cobbett's radicalism. He had continued to urge farmers to ensure that every labourer in their employment had a living wage, and some land; because only by such means could the labourer's distress, and consequently his discontent, be removed. And it was in the farmers' own interest, he reiterated, that they should remove the sources of discontent; for 'unless their flocks were as safe in their fields as their bodies were in their beds, their lives must be lives of misery; if their stacks and barns were not places of as safe deposit for their corn as their drawers were for their money, the life of the farmer was the most wretched upon earth, instead of being the most pleasant, as it ought to be'. Now, the accuracy of this forecast was being verified; but it brought little credit to Cobbett. Because it had been accurate, ministers preferred to think he must in some way be responsible for the trouble.

At this point, the Tory Government was finally released from its difficulties—it was defeated in the Commons. Wellington resigned, and William IV called on Grey to form a government. It would be pledged to Reform: and this, Place and Hume could claim, would give the new radicalism its great opportunity. But to have any chance of making good use of it, radicals must avoid becoming identified with the cause of the agricultural labourers, especially as they were threatening to get out of control. Cobbett must be repudiated, and Hunt, and all radicals who were not prepared to abandon old loyalties, and come in with the Whigs to work for radicalism's all-important first objective: Reform.

5

RING OUT THE OLD

I. CAPTAIN SWING

'JUST NOW THERE is a belief in universal suffrage,' Princess Lieven wrote to her brother, a few days after her old friend Lord Grey had taken office; 'just imagine what would become of England if it were obtained!' At the same time, she had to admit

> it is quite certain that the wrongs of the lower classes need a remedy. The aristocracy rolls in wealth and luxury while the streets of London, the highways of the country, swarm with miserable creatures covered with rags, barefooted, having neither food nor shelter. The sight of this contrast is revolting, and in all likelihood were I one of these thousands of poor wretches I should be a democrat.

But it was not simply distress which confronted the new ministers; they found they were faced with what, in many areas of the south-east and the midlands, amounted to an insurrection. Rick-burning and machine-breaking spread; the labourers were becoming more militant, bolder, presenting themselves in daylight to make their demands—usually, a minimum wage (two and threepence or two and sixpence a day) and greater security of employment. The rebels were not irresponsible youths or ne'er-do-wells; most of them were men in their twenties and thirties, many with wives and families. If the farmer complied, he was safe; if not, his barns might burn, or his threshing machine would be found smashed. The labourers were often supported by small farmers and craftsmen; and they appeared not to think of what they were doing as illegal, any more than they thought poaching illegal: they felt that they were merely reasserting their rights. And although their threatening letters were often signed by a mythical figure, 'Captain Swing', they were not directed by any leader or central organisation—though locally, the experience they had won in poaching gangs might provide them with a semblance of military discipline.

The Government was pledged to electoral reform; but the promise of it could do nothing to pacify the labourers, who stood no chance of gaining the vote from Parliament as it was then constituted. And the new ministers were, if anything, less sympathetic to the labourers than Wellington's had been. Grey's cabinet consisted of eleven peers, a baronet, and only one commoner; most of the junior ministers were either peers or peers' sons; all were landowners. The insurrection represented a direct threat to them. Indirectly, too, it menaced their political future, because the continued existence of their coalition—as in effect it remained— depended on keeping their support in the unreformed House of Commons —on the men of the rotten boroughs, and the nominees of peers who owned seats. They would not tolerate what appeared to be a weak administration. The electors, too, who had voted the Tories out were composed of men of property—as were the voters who, by passing a reform bill, the Whigs hoped to attract. They would expect the Government to take a firm hand if property was threatened.

There was nothing positive that ministers could do, though, while they believed the poor laws were responsible for what had happened. As Princess Lieven explained to her brother, 'a pauper goes to the parish for relief; if he is unmarried the pittance is quite inadequate, if he marries he gets twice as much—so he gets married, begets ten children, draws double relief for himself, and allows his children to die of starvation'. The intention of the poor law, she thought, was doubtless philanthropic, but its result was inhuman. Ministers shared her view; at the very time that the political economists were repudiating the Malthusian theory, it had consolidated itself as ministerial orthodoxy. But Grey was not anxious to involve himself in reform, let alone repeal, of the poor laws, before he had carried his measure of electoral reform. In the circumstances, there was nothing that could be done for the labourers; their movement must simply be suppressed.

'In brotherly love towards each other'

The fact that the followers of 'Captain Swing' appeared to be well-disciplined was in one way convenient; it was easy to maintain that they were highly organised. Even the fact that the movement was so controlled —in spite of the widespread violence, no fatalities were reported—could be claimed as evidence of some sinister guiding hand. And the fact that the agricultural labourers attracted the sympathy of Cobbett and Carlile was, to most Whigs, merely additional proof that the cause must be wicked. Cobbett took an 'I told you so' line. 'I knew that English labourers would not lie down and die in any number, with nothing but sour sorrel in their bellies (as two did at Acton at the beginning of this summer); and I knew that they would never receive the extreme unction and die of hunger, as the poor Irish did . . . O God! With what indignation did I hear the unfortunate Irish *praised* because they died of want, while their country abounded in the means of subsistence!' But Cobbett, though he was prepared to argue that necessity knows no law, did not go so far as to welcome the rioting. Carlile did. Undeterred by the memory of the years he had spent in gaol, unable to pay the fine imposed on him for printing the works of Tom Paine, he risked his liberty again to congratulate the labourers for what they had achieved: 'you are much to be admired for everything you are known to have done during the last month . . . were you proved to be the incendiaries, we should defend you by saying that you have more just and moral cause for it than any king or faction, that ever made war, had for making war.'

But in Parliament, the cause of the agricultural labourers had no spokesman—except Henry Hunt; and his support was unlikely to be of much use to them. He, too, had served out a jail sentence following his arrest after Peterloo; but on his release he had been given a hero's welcome by his supporters, and in London and a few other urban areas he enjoyed a reputation almost as great as Cobbett's. When Edward Stanley, the future Prime Minister, was made Chief Secretary for Ireland in the Grey Government—and under the then prevailing system, had to resign to contest his seat again—Hunt decided to oppose him. Preston shared with Westminster the advantage of an unusually wide franchise; and Hunt was returned. But Hunt was an old-fashioned demagogue; his speeches more attuned to the hustings rather than to the intimacy of the House of Commons, with its club atmosphere. His knowledge of rural conditions, too, was slight. Nor was there any chance of his forming on this issue the same kind of alliance with Cobbett that Hume had with Place: Hunt and Cobbett loathed each other. Old radicalism consequently made no impression in Parliament. And to the new radicals the rebellious farm workers, however real their grievances, were a nuisance; their violence might imperil the cause of Reform.

The fate of the farm workers would therefore depend largely on the character and the capacity of the new Home Secretary, Lord Melbourne. A Canningite, he had Canning's dislike of cant, and fear of revolution. He was shrewd enough, on the basis of reports from Government agents and magistrates, to dismiss opposition allegations that the unrest was being fomented by foreign agents—that it was part of a new Jacobin plot. But he could not accept that the explanation of the unrest was simply that the labourers had been driven beyond endurance. Rick-burning, he decided, arose 'from a pure, unmixed and diabolical feeling of senseless malignity'; so there was nothing for it but oppose force with force. Dragoons were sent to the troubled areas; and, in case local magistrates might be insufficiently stern, a special commission of judges was appointed to try all cases arising out of the disturbances, with orders to exercise whatever severity they decided was necessary.

The commission proceeded to follow this instruction with a vigour unmatched since Judge Jeffreys and his 'bloody assizes', a century and a half before. Nearly 2,000 men and women were put on trial, before the commission and other courts; and of these, 252 were sentenced to death for arson and other crimes then capital offences. Only eighteen were actually executed, but most of the rest were transported; and of nearly 500 who were sent to Australia or Tasmania, few were to return (though that, it seems, was only partly due to the fact that when their sentences had been served, or remitted, they had to find their own fares back; most of them had come to prefer the life which they would have as settlers, to what they could expect to find at home). Hunt made an effort to secure clemency for them before they sailed; but only three M.P.s—Hume was one of them—supported him. The relatives of the convicted men were left the consolation of a prayer, composed by the Archbishop of Canterbury at the request of the Privy Council, and read out in the churches:

Restore, O Lord, to Thy people the quiet enjoyment of the many and great blessings we have received from Thy bounty; defeat and frustrate the malice of wicked and turbulent men, and turn their hearts; have pity, O Lord, on the simple and ignorant, who have been led astray, and recall them to a sense of their duty; and to persons of all ranks and conditions in this country vouchsafe such a measure of Thy grace, that our hearts being filled with true faith and devotion, and cleansed from all evil affections, we may serve Thee with one accord, in duty and loyalty to the King, in obedience to the laws of the land, and in brotherly love towards each other.

The crisis past, ministers then turned to revenging themselves on the men who, they were sure, had helped to cause it, by encouraging the labourers: Carlile and Cobbett. To prosecute them seemed safe enough, as the Tories were unlikely to raise any objection, and the Government's radical allies had been unsparingly critical of them—as had *The Times*, which was by this time a useful barometer of new radical opinion.

Carlile presented no difficulty. His reputation had been won as a free-thinker, a fighter for the liberty of the press; he had little working-class support, or indeed support of any kind, outside the circle of his disciples. He was tried, convicted and—when he again refused to pay the fine—imprisoned. But the outcome was not at all what ministers had expected. Place was furious. Not since Castlereagh, he wrote angrily to Hume, had anybody even been prosecuted, let alone given so barbarous a sentence, for such words as Carlile had been found guilty of. That was precisely the kind of action, he feared, which would lose the Government the radical support he had so painstakingly won for it.

Perhaps chastened by Place's wrath, ministers hesitated before bringing Cobbett to trial. He was far more influential than Carlile, and his *Register* still had a big circulation by the standards of the time. It would also be less easy to prove to a jury, however well packed, that what his *Register* had said was seditious. Admittedly he had suggested that if there was food available, the labourer who had grown it could not be expected to starve, simply because in law it was not his property. 'What is his homely reasoning upon the case? "I work twelve hours a day to produce this food; I do all the real labour, and you, who stand by and look me over, deny me even subsistence out of it; if you give me none of it, you shall have none yourself, at any rate." And to work he goes, burning and destroying.' But Cobbett had been careful not to express any gratification that his gloomy forecast had been justified. 'There is no man', he had written, 'not of a fiend-like nature, who can view the destruction of property that is now going on in the southern counties without the greatest pain.'

When eventually the trial opened, the prosecution's case was that Cobbett, by his support of the labourers, had helped to foment the violence which he pretended to repudiate. Because of the delay in bringing him to court, though, he had been able to prepare an ingenious defence, which he conducted himself with considerable skill. Brougham, in one of the many indiscretions with which his ministerial life was littered, had written to him during the uprising to ask him for permission to reprint his earlier *Letter to the Luddites*—for the benefit of the Society for the Diffusion of Useful Knowledge, of which Brougham, the founder, was president. Subpoenaed as a witness, Brougham had to admit having made this request, which he had neglected to mention to his ministerial colleagues. The trial almost collapsed there and then; the jury ultimately disagreed;

and the Government did not care to take the risk of embarking on fresh proceedings.

'It is time to search beyond'

Out of office, the Whigs had been regarded as the party of melioration; they had been largely responsible for reducing the savagery of the penal code. Yet as soon as they had come into power they had ruthlessly exploited it to stamp out disaffection. They had, however, one excuse, which they now used freely, in connection with disturbances in England as well as in Ireland; conciliation could only become possible after tranquillity had been restored. It sounded reasonable, so long as there was some reason to hope that conciliation would prove a meaningful term: that they would have some plan ready, to raise the labourers out of the depressed condition into which they had sunk. But they gave no sign, in 1831, that they had any clearer idea what to do than had the Tories.

In the meantime, however, a committee of the House of Lords, set up in 1830, had been examining the subject; and some of the evidence given to it had been striking. It left no possible room for doubt that the insurrection had not, as Melbourne claimed, been motiveless. The condition of the labourers in the regions where there had been outbreaks had indeed been desperate. Nassau Senior, who was hardly likely to sympathise with rebels, admitted that although the evidence given to the Sturges Bourne committee had painted a picture which, at the time, 'it seemed scarcely possible to make darker', that period was 'looked back to by some of the witnesses as one of comparatively good management'.

From the evidence, too, it emerged that in those parishes where the general pauperising trend had been resisted, there had been little or no violence. Captain Swing's letters had not been received by farmers in the north, where the demand for produce and, in good times, for labour had led to more regular employment and better wages for farm workers. And those landowners in the south-east who had taken the trouble to ensure that the labourers on their estates had land—either legally, in compensation for enclosures, or by private agreement—were not troubled.

The most telling evidence on this issue came from the Reverend Stephen Demainbray, rector of a Wiltshire parish, and Chaplain-in-Ordinary to the King. Demainbray explained how in 1806, when an Enclosure Act had been passed affecting his parish, he had refused the offer of land for himself in lieu of tithe, arguing that the function of tithe was to make provision for the poor, and it would be better to do that direct.

So, the Act included a clause giving every cottager half an acre. And the effects? 'I fear I shall appear an enthusiast upon the subject,' he told the committee, 'but I do most sincerely from my heart feel that they are most beneficial.' The labourers, he claimed, worked their land well, and paid their rent (and their tithe) punctually, to the benefit of the landowner and the clergyman—and the ratepayer. Later, Demainbray was to come back before the committee with more detailed evidence, to show just how much better off the parish was as a whole than it had been before the scheme was established.

Why, then, if it worked so well, had the expedient not been more generally adopted? In a tract, *The Poor Man's Best Friend*, in which he elaborated on his evidence to the Lord's committee, Demainbray explained that the system could only work where there was a will to work it. With the slump in farm prices of the early 1820s, many farmers had taken advantage of the allowance system to get rid of their regular labourers, and hire paupers, at less than a subsistence wage, knowing that it would be made up out of the rates. In that case, the cottager with land was at an actual disadvantage. 'If he be the owner of a cottage, or of an acre or two of land, he has no legal claim on his parish so long as he retains it; and therefore, when burdened with a family, must part with it, before he can obtain a fair remuneration for his labour, or that part of it which is paid from the poor rate; and while his honest pride is struggling against resorting to the parish pay table, he is often in a worse condition than the actual pauper.' When to this was added the deprivation the labourer had suffered from the loss of his grazing rights on the local common, it was no wonder, Demainbray felt, that distress was so prevalent. But it need not be, if farmers could be persuaded to pay a living wage, and keep their labourers in all the year round employment.

The Lords committee, therefore, did not lack evidence that there was a way in which the labourer's grievances could be remedied, if some means could be found to encourage the system which Demainbray had instituted to spread. But here, the influence of political economy began to make itself felt. What was the use of making arrangements which would artificially lead to greater production—the implication of some questioners was—when the increase would simply pull down prices, and make things more difficult for other farmers?

Among the witnesses who appeared before the committee, however, there was one who was prepared to repudiate this by now widely accepted assumption. Richard Bacon was a versatile journalist; for a while he had run a musical review, and he was now editor of the Norwich *Mercury*, a friend of Lord Suffield's, and a student of agricultural economics. The whole principle, he told the committee, was founded upon error:

> If you keep a great quantity of the population at the minimum of subsistence, and if at the same time you keep them idle, you prevent their producing any article which they can exchange for other productions; and at the same time you subtract just as much as their subsistence costs from the earnings of others, and by that means you saddle the real producers of the country with the food of the idle labourers, so that the poor rate, in point of fact, is a total abstraction from the production of others. At the same time, you reduce all those who subsist as paupers to the very minimum of subsistence, and prevent them from producing that which would give employment to the labours of others.

In the name of political economy—Bacon was arguing—society was actually preventing the principles of political economy from working; for how could the law of supply and demand operate freely if demand could not make itself effective? Like Demainbray, he elaborated on his evidence to the Lords in a tract—an *Open Letter* to Lord Suffield, in which he exposed the fallacies of the political economists in greater detail. Their mistake, he felt, was to think only in terms of rent, when they were considering agriculture, because they assumed that no land which could not be made to yield rent would be farmed. Where land was in private ownership, this was certainly the case: there was no point in the landowner letting it for no return. But if society was presented with an alternative—keeping a pauper at the expense of the community, or turning him loose on a small farm reclaimed from waste land (or land not in cultivation), with a spade and some seed, where he would earn a subsistence living—common sense pointed to the second alternative. At least he would be self-supporting; and his produce, when he came to sell it in the market, would give him the money to buy shoes, or clothes, thereby stimulating the economy in general.

But the members of the Lords committee, all themselves landowners, could not grasp the point. Look—they replied—at what was happening to the Irish, with their small subsistence farms! And Bacon was not knowledgeable enough about Ireland to realise that what was happening there was in fact another argument in his favour. The Irish did indeed use spade husbandry—the term then in common use to describe subsistence farming, where the farmer employed no labour but his family's, and could afford no machinery, not even a plough. But they did not live rent free; and if they improved their land's productivity they could not better themselves, because to do so simply meant the rent would be increased.

The essential point, though, that Bacon was concerned to make was that where the political economists were in error, on agriculture, it was because they had based their science on the assumption of the inevitability of private property in land. Because of this assumption, land was out of cultivation not because it could not provide a living for the population 'surplus' but simply because it could not provide rent for its owners. The law of the political economists, therefore, must be considered fallacious: 'it is in truth not the law which governs the circumstances of a state situated like our own', he concluded; 'it is time to search beyond it'.

Suffield knew this himself; he had already searched beyond it. In the ten Norfolk villages of which he was owner or part owner, he had instituted a system whereby the labourers had their plots of land; and when the rioting spread to the area, they were not affected. But he already realised that any attempt to convince the Government that this was the solution they were looking for was futile. He knew Melbourne socially; and when the Whigs came to office had been quick to present him with a scheme, based on his own experience, for remedying the labourers' grievances by providing them with land. The provision of such plots, he explained, would 'make the labourers independent of the farmers, and substitute the competition of employers for the competition of employed'. Wages would rise, and the rates would fall. Receiving no reply, he waylaid Melbourne a few days later to ask what he had thought of it. Melbourne replied that he hadn't. Why? Suffield asked; because he had not understood it? On the contrary, Melbourne said, he had understood it perfectly, and that was why he had said nothing about it; he considered it hopeless. Such projects would only increase the population: 'the evil is in numbers, and the sort of competition that ensues'. And with that, he turned away.

It was an early indication of how completely the new Government was hypnotised by Malthus, and political economy. Brougham, the new Lord Chancellor, had long been a disciple; Lord Althorp, appointed leader of the party in the House of Commons, was a member of the Political Economy Club; and Melbourne, though he did not mix in such circles, used to boast that he had read enough of the political economists to know that they were right. For their guide on economic issues they had Senior; and Senior assured them that there was nothing they could do for the labourers except reform the poor laws. This, they decided they would do; but they realised it would be a formidable operation, and they felt that it must be postponed until they had reformed the electoral system. Until then, discussion of individual remedies was pointless. 'The fact is,' Suffield sadly remarked, 'with the exception of a few individuals, the subject is deemed by the world a bore; everyone who touches it is a bore.'

The last peasant revolt, then—as it came to be called—achieved nothing —unless the happier lives that many of the transported convicts ultimately found in the Antipodes could be placed to its credit. In some districts, where wages had risen, they did not fall back quite to their former levels; farmers who had had their machines smashed were in no hurry to replace them; and anybody who contemplated buying one tended to postpone making the purchase. But that was all. The Lords committee contented itself with publishing the evidence given to it, making no recommendations; and there was no sign that what had happened had made any impression on ministers—except, perhaps, to confirm them in their belief that the old poor law must go. And one of the ministers who gave evidence to the Lords committee—yet another clergyman, the Reverend Thomas Whately, Rector of Cookham and Maidenhead—pointed the way. In future, he thought, parishes should be more ruthless, refusing— as his own did—any outdoor relief to the able-bodied, and offering the alternative of either harder work and lower wages, or the workhouse, with a diet of bread and cheese. And it was this principle that ministers were to favour, when they began to turn their mind to poor law reform.

'Insults barbed by past recollection'

So even when reports began to come in, towards the end of the summer of 1831, that the plight of the agricultural labourers was as bad as ever, the Government made no move; and this led a newcomer to the Commons, Michael Sadler, to make the first of the speeches by which he won his reputation there, short though his parliamentary career was ultimately destined to be.

As a young man, Sadler had been attracted to Methodism, and had learned what it was like to be stoned by a hostile audience. Later, he became an Evangelical, and a Tory; using his business, which did not much interest him, to further his philanthropic designs. By 1827 he was sufficiently well known and esteemed in Yorkshire for Anne Brontë, playing the old game of 'desert island company', to select him as one of three companions she would choose, if she were a castaway.

Sadler's social philosophy sounded utilitarian; he wanted 'to extend the utmost degree of human happiness to the greatest number of human beings'. But he did not believe that end could be achieved through political economy, as then expounded; and in particular, he was horrified at the acceptance of the Malthusian theories. As a writer he was turgid, and diffuse; a book which he wrote to prove that they were false was gleefully eviscerated by the young Macaulay in the *Edinburgh Review*. As a speaker, though, Sadler could be very effective; his denunciations of Catholic Emancipation had attracted the admiration of a Tory peer—an 'ultra'; and this led to the offer of a nomination borough, to enable Sadler to display his talents to better effect, at Westminster.

In October 1831, Sadler asked leave of the House to bring in a bill to remedy the wants of the agricultural labourers; and he used the occasion for a tirade against those who blamed paupers for their condition. How could a pauper be held responsible for the squalor in which he so often had to live, when it was the systematic demolition of cottages which compelled him and his family to crowd into a hut, 'often unfit to stable even quadrupeds'? And to show that this was not simply idle rhetoric, Sadler brought forward evidence collected by the vicar of a Lincolnshire parish, who had taken the trouble to conduct a statistical survey of fifteen neighbouring parishes with a view to finding out why the labouring poor were so often wretchedly housed. From the survey, the vicar had found that since 1770, although the population had greatly increased, only nine cottages had been built, while 176 had either been demolished, or had their land taken away from them. In such circumstances, the pauper could not be expected to live decently—especially as the system prevented him from negotiating his wages.

> Wages, did I say? Parish pay! He is, perhaps, sold by auction, as in the case in certain parishes, and therefore reduced to the condition of the slave, or driven to the workhouse, where he is often treated worse than a felon. Labour, meant to degrade and insult him, is often prescribed to him; or, wholly unemployed, he sits brooding over his miserable fate; winter labour, whether for himself or his wife and children, having been long since taken away. Perpetually insulted by false and heartless accusations – for being a pauper, when his accusers have compelled him to become such – for being idle, when his work has been taken from him – for improvidence, when he can hardly exist – he feels these insults barbed by past recollection.

Even the feelings common to man's nature, Sadler complained, were regarded in the labourer as if they were an offence; his marriage was criminal, his children nuisances, and he himself was pronounced

I

'redundant'. Finally, after being despoiled of his belongings, he was kindly advised that his best, and indeed only course, was 'to transport himself for life, for the good of his oppressors'. Yet the people who gave him this advice, the authors of his suffering, were the very people who wanted him to remain quiet and grateful, cheerful and contented.

What was needed, Sadler claimed, was for Parliament to make provision for the rebuilding of cottages, each with some land, or at least a kitchen garden; and perhaps access to a common meadow. Wherever this had been done, the results had been satisfactory for all concerned; for example, in the parish of Lyndon, in Rutland, where the poor rate had been reduced to a halfpenny in the pound. Why did M.P.s not realise, he concluded, that Parliament could help, and should? 'Let the House then assume its noblest character, that of the protector of the poor . . . let the law once more interpose its sacred shield, and protect the defenceless and wretched from the miseries they have too long endured.' And, unused to being appealed to in such terms, the House gave leave for the introduction of the bill.

Ordinarily, ministers might have been expected to resist the proposal; but they knew it was too late in the session for there to be any chance of the bill being debated. And the following February, before the subject could be brought up again, they announced that they were going to take action themselves. The subject of the labouring poor was of such importance, however, that they would not employ the usual device of a select committee. A royal commission, no less, was to be appointed to conduct a detailed and comprehensive investigation, with a view to a reform of the poor laws.

In an earlier age, royal commissions had been commonly used; but as they were instruments of the crown, and apt to be exploited for authoritarian purposes, they had come to inspire mistrust. Except for mainly administrative functions they had fallen out of common use. Now, the Government could claim that it had acquired the right to exercise the crown's old prerogatives; and any fear of authoritarianism could be put aside, as the commission would be under parliamentary control. In any case, this commission was being set up simply to investigate, and make recommendations; Parliament would be free to decide whether they should be accepted and enacted.

A royal commission had one valuable advantage, so far as the Government was concerned, over a parliamentary select committee. The members of a committee to a great extent chose themselves; and although the Government could theoretically ensure that its views were presented, the tendency was for only those M.P.s with an interest in what the committee was investigating to join, and only those M.P.s who were deeply concerned to remain active members. M.P.s who were deeply concerned might hold views very different from those of the Government; and even when they were on the Government's side, as in the case of the Sturges Bourne committee, their proposals might appear to ministers to be impracticable, or untimely.

The members of the royal commission, on the other hand, could be hand-picked by the Government. The names of two of them were significant: Sturges Bourne—who had been Home Secretary for a short time under Canning; he had retired from politics in 1831, but agreed to serve on the commission; and Nassau Senior. Their views on the poor laws were common knowledge. So were the views of the two bishops, London and Chester, who were on the commission. Both had publicly stated that the poor laws should be abolished. Nobody of Sadler's, or Owen's, opinions was included. Even more significantly neither Torrens nor McCulloch was on the commission. Torrens's views were diverging further and further from Ricardian orthodoxy; and McCulloch was heretical on the subject of the poor laws. Their views—and, perhaps, their minority reports—would be unwelcome.

2. TEN HOURS

Even before the Government had disposed of the farm workers, though, it found itself confronted with a new threat; less immediately dangerous, as there was little violence; but in the long run likely to be embarrassing, because the workers concerned were in a better position to organise themselves effectively, and to back their demands by strikes.

Throughout the 1820s, in spite of trade setbacks, the north of England had been growing more industrialised. The cotton industry had continued to expand, following the setback of 1826; imports of the raw cotton which fed the factory machinery had almost doubled during the 1820s. But the development of the woollen industry had been even more striking. In the same period, imports of raw wool had quadrupled. For wool, too, the factory system had become dominant, concentrated in the West Riding of Yorkshire in Leeds, Bradford and other rapidly growing towns; and as with cotton, children supplied the bulk of the labour force. The youngest, from around seven years old, were employed to clean up waste off the floor; as they grew older, they became 'piecers', or 'pieceners', mending broken strands. Their wages were very low—around fourpence a day, rising to fivepence at nine years old. But even this meant that the child was self-supporting; and that might be sufficient to save its parents from destitution.

In October 1830, a letter appeared in the Whig Leeds *Mercury*, ostensibly in connection with the anti-slavery campaign. At one of the meetings organised by the campaigners, the anonymous correspondent said, the usual assertions had been made: that it was 'the pride of Britain that a slave cannot exist on her soil', and that 'the air which Britons breathe is free'. These were sentiments which he applauded; unfortunately, they were untrue. At that very moment, thousands of people in that very county, Yorkshire, were

> in a state of slavery more horrid than are the victims of that hellish system of colonial slavery . . . the very streets which receive the droppings of an 'Anti-Slavery Society' are every morning wet by the tears of innocent victims at the accursed shrine of avarice, who are compelled, not by the cartwhip of the negro slave-driver, but by the dread of the equally appalling thong, or strap, of the over-looker, to hasten, half-dressed, *but not half-fed*, to those magazines of British infantile slavery – the worsted mills in the town of Bradford!!!

The writer was Richard Oastler; and for the next decade he was to be the most striking figure in the series of campaigns on behalf of the labouring poor, employed or unemployed, which were to arouse so much fervour in the north of England.

Oastler's grandfather had been a yeoman; his father, compelled to leave home on becoming a convert to Methodism, had become a prosperous merchant. Richard, trying to follow in his footsteps, had been less successful, and eventually he had returned to country life, as an agent for an absentee landlord who owned estates in Yorkshire; becoming known locally as an Evangelical, an energetic supporter of Wilberforce, and a Tory. In 1827, however, he had been caught up in a campaign to resist the demands for tithe that a new vicar, seeking to take advantage of his legal rights, was making on the local farmers. His efforts attracted the hostility of the Leeds *Intelligencer*, the *Mercury*'s Tory rival, which surprised him by denouncing him as a radical; it also led to a meeting with another Evangelical Tory, John Wood, the owner of what was thought to be the largest worsted spinning mills in the country. When Oastler came on a visit to him in the summer of 1830, Wood told him of the lives that children were forced to lead in even the best-run—as he considered his own to be—of mills. They had to attend from six in the morning to seven at night, six days a week, with only a forty-minute break for a meal in the middle of the day. Less humane employers, Wood told him, made them work longer hours, with a shorter break, their overseers using thong or strap to keep the children awake.

'The system which impoverishes, enslaves, and brutalises'

Oastler had lived for years within sight of woollen mills, without concerning himself about the conditions in them. The shock was all the greater because the description came from Wood, who could not be suspected of wishing to deceive him. He recalled with embarrassment the hours he had spent agitating on behalf of slaves in the West Indies—whose hours of work, he knew, were regulated, and far shorter. Before he left, early the next morning, he went to say goodbye to his host, to find that Wood had had no sleep, having spent the night reading his Bible. 'On every page', he told Oastler, 'I have read my own condemnation', and he refused to let his guest go until Oastler had promised that he would use the talent he had revealed as a campaigner against the unjust tithe exactions, 'to remove from our factories system the cruelties which are practised in our mills.' Oastler gave the pledge; and the letter to the *Mercury* was his first instalment.

The editor of the *Mercury*, Edward Baines, was an old friend of Oastler's father—they had toured New Lanark together—or he would hardly have considered publishing such opinions. He had bought the *Mercury* at the beginning of the century and made it the leading Whig journal in the north of England; it was regarded, and was pleased to regard itself, as the mouthpiece of the Leeds middle classes, of which the factory owners were the most important element. Knowing no more about mill conditions than Oastler did himself, Baines charitably thought he must have been misled; and he had enquiries made, with a view to excusing himself for declining to publish the letter. To his astonishment, he found that Oastler's facts were correct; and he published it, deploring its tone in an editorial, but admitting that if the facts really were as Oastler alleged, something ought to be done.

The letter had the effect Oastler desired; it revived the controversy, languishing since the failure of Hobhouse's 1825 measure, over whether factory children required protection. After the prevailing Eatanswill fashion, the *Intelligencer*, delighted to be able to score off its rival, opened its columns to Oastler's critics, who denied his charges. 'The occupation of the children', a mill-owner wrote, 'is far from laborious, and consists chiefly in the quickness and attention given to the machine, allowing them abundant time to take refreshments during mill hours'; so far from being slavery, child employment in the mills was 'rendered a comfort by the regular hours of rising from, and retiring to, bed, and by the most systematic regulation by which refreshments are brought to them.' From evidence which came in from other sources, though, it was soon apparent that Oastler had understated the case. In many mills, it was admitted, a fourteen-hour working day was the rule, rising even to sixteen in times when demand was heavy, children as well as adults having to work those hours. And although opinions differed on the unhealthiness of working conditions, and the extent to which the overseer's thong was in use, it was clear that the only effective protection that the child worker enjoyed from them was the conscience of the individual mill-owner—not the law.

Many prominent Yorkshire mill-owners shared Wood's views. They would have liked to reduce the hours the children had to work, but they could not do so unless competitors were compelled to do the same. They would be happy for Parliament to lay down regulations for the employment of children in woollen mills, on the lines of those observed—in theory—in the cotton industry. In November 1830 a meeting of mill-owners who shared Wood's views carried a motion calling for legislative action, with only one dissentient vote; and Hobhouse, approached, agreed to bring forward another bill to limit the hours of work for all children in factories.

But at this point, Oastler began to take a new course. It was no longer just the long hours that children had to work that appalled him; it was the fact that very young children were compelled to work in mills at all. Like Owen, he felt that they ought to have to work only at whatever schooling might be provided for them. More than that: Oastler was coming round to the view that there must be something inherently wrong with an economic system which had allowed this English variety of slavery to come into being: 'a system which drags in the train of the remorseless tyrant, the man of benevolent mind; and compels the kind-hearted master either to relinquish business altogether, or in some measure to copy the cruelty of the oppressor. The system which impoverishes, enslaves and brutalises the labourer can never be advantageous to any country. The nation's strength and stability is built, if built for perpetuity, on the solid basis of a contented and happy population. The constitution of this country and the present factory system cannot long exist together; their principles are as opposite as light and darkness.'

So Hobhouse's measure, when it was presented to Parliament in February 1831, did not go nearly far enough to satisfy Oastler. It left the minimum age at which children would be allowed to work in the mills at nine; and they might then have to work a twelve-hour day. But when Oastler insisted that this was too long, he found himself confronted with the argument that when the children stopped, the machines had to stop, too. And statutory limitation of adult hours of work, the implication was, was unthinkable.

But why, Oastler began to ask himself, should it be unthinkable? Wood himself, after all, had once contemplated the restriction of adult working hours, as the only feasible way to secure a reduction of children's hours. And in the spring of 1831, when Parliament was dissolved in the course of the Reform controversy, Oastler published an appeal to the workers of the West Riding of Yorkshire, urging them to try to secure a pledge from each of the candidates at the coming election that he would support a bill to introduce a ten-hour working day.

In 1825 George Philips had warned that adult workers, for their own ends, were behind the campaign on behalf of children; but he had produced no evidence for this allegation, and in fact the idea had been slow to catch on. By 1831, though, independently of Oastler, 'Short Time' committees had been established in many parts of Yorkshire, with the aim of campaigning for regulation of working hours. They had had no contact with Oastler; but his 'Ten Hours' gave them just what they needed, a simple, effective rallying cry. The members of the Huddersfield Short Time committee decided to send a deputation to him, to try to enlist his co-operation with their movement. The project almost fell through when the deputation arrived on a Sunday; he could not, he felt, allow the Sabbath to be broken. Only when he realised that Sunday was the one day of the week on which they, as six-days-a-week factory workers, could come to see him, did he relent. It could be regarded as a work of charity, he told himself, to receive them.

Oastler had been astonished by Wood's description of conditions in the mills; now, he was still more amazed at, and delighted with, the 'intelligence and civility' of the mill workers. He had not met working men on business matters before, and they impressed him 'by the knowledge which they communicated and the sensible manner in which they conveyed that knowledge'. Although as a Tory, and an Evangelical, he was still reluctant to encourage radicals and dissenters, he allowed them to persuade him not simply to join the Short Time campaign, but to undertake to lead it, with 'Ten Hours' as its rallying cry.

Anxious though Wood and his friends might be to secure the regulation of factory hours and conditions for children, the prospect of the pace being forced by adult workers made them uneasy. And by this time, a break-away movement had been organised by Simeon Townsend, the single dissentient at the meeting when it had been resolved to ask Hobhouse to bring forward his bill. Many of the smaller mill-owners, he had found, shared his dislike of legislation which would control the hours worked by children. As machinery improved it was growing simpler for children to operate; in fact 'the great object of such improvements', as a group of Bradford woollen merchants put it, had become 'to adapt the machinery to the youngest class of workers'. If the labour of the youngest class of workers was restricted, they would lose their competitive advantage.

At a meeting in March, Townsend's following decided to oppose the Hobhouse bill, and set out the arguments against it. They were revealing, because they presented the case against State intervention of any kind in industry; the first comprehensive avowal of the principle *laissez nous faire*. Disdaining the shelter of the argument which had commonly been advanced against factory bills—that children might need protection, but that it was impracticable to provide it—they insisted that unfettered private enterprise was best for the children, the industry, and the nation.

Among the committee's resolutions were:

That the condition of those employed in worsted mills does not warrant the conclusion that the present usages of the trade are injurious to the health and comfort of this class of operatives; and that the present term of labour (viz. twelve hours per day) is not attended with any consequence injurious to those employed and is not more than adequate and necessary to provide for their livelihood . . .

That an enactment which will abridge the hours of labour, or limit the hours of children employed in worsted mills, will produce the following effect:

1st: It will cause a proportionate reduction of the wages of this class.

2nd: It will materially cripple the means of those who have large and young families, who, in many instances, are the main support of their parents.

3rd: It will raise the price of goods to the consumers, which will affect the home trade considerably, and will produce the most serious effects upon the prosperity of this district, by tending to foster the manufacturers of foreign nations, our trade with whom depends on the cheap and advantageous terms on which we now supply them with goods, and whose manufacturers would be enabled by an advance of price successfully to compete with the British merchant.

4th: It will throw out of employment and means of existence numbers of children now beneficially engaged, and a corresponding proportion of wool-sorters, combers, weavers and all those other classes necessary to produce the present supply of goods.

5th: The agriculturalists will also feel the effects of the diminished consumption of wool in no slight degree . . .

That the character of the generality of master worsted spinners in respect to humanity, kindness and considerate attention to those in their employ is unimpeachable, but though there may be exceptions to this general and well-known fact, which this meeting is unacquainted with, yet no legislative enactment can effectually protect innocence and poverty from the fraud and tyranny of the unprincipled . . .

That this meeting is convinced of the pernicious tendency and effects of all legislative enactments . . .

Just as the Lancashire cotton manufacturers had objected to Peel's bill on the ground that it singled them out for attention, while ignoring the worse conditions in the Yorkshire woollen industry, these Yorkshire owners now also claimed that their workers were far healthier than those in the cotton industry—or anywhere else: 'Experience proves that the health and general comfort of the population employed in worsted mills is equal, if not superior, to that of any other extensive class of operators.' The work, too, was most suitable for boys between the ages of seven and fourteen, because they were particularly 'capable of undergoing long-continued labours'—an opinion, they felt sure, that doctors practising in the region would uphold.

'Health! Cleanliness! Mental improvement!'

They were unlucky, however, with their timing. It happened that a Leeds doctor, H. Turner Thackrah, had been investigating the effect of different types of employment on the workers' health; and although he had been more concerned with craftsmen than with workers in factories, his findings and recommendations, published in 1831, were very relevant to the controversy over whether the State had a right, or a duty, to intervene to protect the worker.

Science, Thackrah observed, had effected wonders. 'We see wool converted into cloth, in establishments so numerous and extensive as almost to supply the civilised world. We see the slight blue-flowered product of the field formed, in the same mill, into the thread which passes through the eye of the needle, and into the canvas which bears our ships to every region of the globe.' Such works, he reiterated, were assuredly wonderful.

> But while we admire, let us examine. What are the effects of these surprising works – effects, I mean, physical and moral? I say nothing of the wealth they produce or have produced, for wealth is good or evil according to its application: I refer to the health of fifty thousand persons, who spend their lives in the manufactories of Leeds and its neighbourhood, or in allied and dependent occupations. I ask, if these fifty thousand persons enjoy that vigour of body which is ever a direct good, and without which all other advantages are comparatively worthless?

It was the first time that an attempt had been made to answer that question with the help of statistics, as well as of observation. Thackrah was able to show that the West Riding—the manufacturing area—had a considerably higher mortality rate than the rest of Yorkshire, which was predominantly rural; and that if the average rate in a country village were taken as the standard, about 450 people died annually in Leeds, in excess of it, 'from the injurious effects of manufacture, the crowded state of population, and the consequent bad habits of life'.

It was sometimes argued, Thackrah noted, that children seemed to be less affected by long hours of strenuous work in bad conditions than adults. He agreed. But this, he felt, was due to their life force; and he hated to see those years when that force was at its most vital squandered in ceaseless toil:

> The employment of young children in *any* labour is wrong. The term of physical growth ought not to be a term of physical exertion. Light and varied motions should be the only effort – motions excited by the will, not by the task-master – the run and the leap of a buoyant and unshackled spirit. How different the scene in a manufacturing district! No man of humanity can reflect without distress on the state of thousands of children, many from six to seven years of age, roused from their beds at an early hour, hurried to the mills, and kept there, with an interval of only forty minutes, till a late hour at night; kept, moreover, in an atmosphere impure . . . Health! Cleanliness! Mental improvement! How are they regarded? Recreation is out of the question. There is scarcely time for meals. The very period of sleep, so necessary for the young, is often abridged. Nay, children are sometimes worked even *in* the night.

Thackrah was not critical of factories as such (except those which manufactured flax, which he singled out for severe disapprobation). But he felt, like Oastler, that the system was compelling the humane factory owner to treat his workers in a way that on his own account, he would never have dreamed of treating them. Because the employers felt helpless in the system's grip, too, they preferred not to think about its results; and as a result they were often unaware of what was happening in their own establishments. Even when they knew what was going on, they might be unmoved; 'we underrate evils to which we are accustomed'. This, Thackrah thought, was how the period allotted to breaks from work had been reduced:

> Formerly an hour was allowed for dinner; but one great manufacturer, pressed by his engagements, wished his workpeople to return five minutes earlier. This abridgement was promptly adopted at other mills. Five minutes led to ten. It was found also that breakfast might be taken while the people were at work. Time was thus saved; more work was done; and the manufactured article could be offered at a less price. If one house afforded it at a lower rate, all other houses, to compete in the market, were obliged to use similar means. Thus what was at first partial and temporary had become general and permanent. And the unfortunate artisans, working before in excess, have now to carry labour to a still greater and more destructive extent.

In the form it originally appeared, Hobhouse's bill would have made that process a little less destructive; but when he reintroduced it, in the new Parliament which followed the spring election of 1831, it was Townsend rather than Thackrah who had allies at Westminster, and Hobhouse was able to get it through only by allowing it to be emasculated. Although it laid down that children were to work no more than twelve hours a day, and nine on Saturdays, employers were allowed various excuses to lengthen the working day; and the precautions for ensuring that children of less than nine years old were kept out of the mills were actually less strict than in his earlier Act. In any case, as no provision was made for inspection, there was no prospect that it would be any more effective than earlier measures. Before it had passed into law, it had been repudiated by Oastler and the Short Time committees, as Peel's bill had been repudiated by Owen; and the indications were that the new Act, which the Government had allowed to be passed in the hope that it would allay discontent in the north, had only succeeded in fomenting it.

3. CHOLERA

By this time, however, the working conditions of the labouring poor in the towns were of less immediate concern to the Government than their living conditions. In spite of occasional warnings from investigators like Southwood Smith, they had attracted little attention until a cholera epidemic, which had broken out in India, reached Europe in 1831. It was soon observed both that the disease was most destructive in towns, and that it appeared to exercise social discrimination, concentrating upon the poor, and rarely afflicting the rich. The rumour actually gained credence that the cholera had been introduced *by* the rich, on Malthusian principles, as a simple way to get rid of the surplus population; in Hungary, some peasants rose against their aristocratic oppressors, on that assumption.

By that summer the approach of the disease, which could be followed on the map of Europe like the march of an invading army, had begun to cause alarm in England. 'The great topic now in London', Macaulay wrote to his sister, 'is not, as you perhaps fancy, Reform, but Cholera. There is a great panic; as great a panic as I can remember, particularly in the City.' As a member of the Southwood Smith anti-contagionist school, Macaulay was able to boast that he was not himself alarmed; but ministers were, as they feared that if the disease followed the same pattern as it had in Europe, and struck in the towns, the urban poor might be stirred to follow the example of the agricultural labourers, and turn to violence.

Precautions, it was agreed, must be taken. But what precautions? As the experts could not agree on how the disease was transmitted, it was not easy to decide what to do. In the past the Government might have been expected to order a tightening of quarantine arrangements simply to be on the safe side; but the new Vice-President of the Board of Trade, Poulett Thomson, was a friend of Bentham and an amateur of political economy, and anxious to do nothing which would offend commercial interests, or jeopardise the country's trading position. He was relieved to be able to report to his colleagues that the President of the Royal College of Physicians was sure that cholera could not be communicated in imported goods. But a committee of the College insisted that it could be communicated by infected persons; and in that case, quarantine would be essential. Reluctantly, ministers allowed themselves to be persuaded; in June 1831 a Proclamation was issued, urging scrupulous observance of quarantine regulations whenever they had to be put in force, and setting up a central Board of Health to advise on whatever further measures might be required.

The members of the Board might not be able to agree on how cholera spread, but they realised the necessity of setting up machinery locally to handle the problems an epidemic would certainly cause. At that time there were few borough councils capable of effective action. Local authority, such as it was, was ordinarily exercised by the parish vestries; otherwise there were often only *ad hoc* bodies, established by individual Acts of Parliament to provide water or drainage or street lighting, and as they were profit-making concerns, they confined their activities to the wealthier districts of towns. They would be unlikely to be ready to operate in the districts where, if continental experience was a guide, cholera could be expected to strike—in the slums.

The central Board of Health therefore recommended that every town and village should set up a local board, to take all the necessary precautions, such as designating certain buildings for the reception of cholera patients, and arranging for the cleaning of infected premises. And hardly had these recommendations been published than the first case of cholera was reported, from Sunderland. There had probably been earlier cases; but the local doctors, with one exception, had never seen a case of the Indian, or Asiatic cholera, and were cautious about committing themselves to a positive diagnosis. But by the end of October they felt there could be no further doubt, and notified the central Board of Health in London.

When the Sunderland businessmen heard of the notification, they were furious. Sunderland at this time was the fourth biggest port in the country; its prosperity might be destroyed if a board in the capital decided to meddle. The new Lord Londonderry, who derived a considerable income from the port, issued a flat denial that cholera had been found there. The Sunderland Board of Health, taken over by the businessmen, took the same view. Leading local doctors were called to a meeting in the Town Exchange, held to reassure the public that Sunderland was 'in a more healthy state than it has usually been in the present season of the year'; and that 'as to the nature of the disorder which has created unnecessarily so great an excitement in the public mind, the same is not the Indian cholera, nor of foreign origin'. Statements in the London press to the contrary were described as 'wicked and malicious'; the imposition of quarantine on ships using Sunderland as a port was consequently 'perfectly unnecessary and uncalled for'. Regret was expressed that the authorities in London should have been informed without the sanction of the town's principal inhabitants; and doctors who had reported cases were called upon publicly to disavow what they had done. Many of them, aware that their future employment prospects were at stake, recanted—including one who had actually been at the bedside of the first victim, but who went so far as to say that to describe what he had seen as the Asiatic cholera was a 'farce'.

So far as the cholera victims were concerned, the delay caused by the dispute mattered little; without the necessary knowledge how the disease was transmitted, the local board would have been powerless to check it even if they had not been obstructed. And inexorably, it spread to other towns, reaching London in February 1832. There, too, its existence was for a while denied; but again the mounting death rate soon confirmed the sceptics, and ministers felt compelled to pass a Cholera Act.

It was a modest measure, but a significant one, because it laid down that the cost of combating cholera, as it was a disease of the poor, should be defrayed out of the poor rate, with the Exchequer repaying such sums as parishes might be unable to afford. It also made provision for a committee of the Privy Council to give orders—as distinct from mere advice—to local Boards of Health; and the committee was to prove less dilatory and inhibited than the Government. On July 18, Poulett Thomson tried to reassure the Commons that the ravages of the disease had been grossly exaggerated by rumour, and that the only reason the Government did not publish the official figures was that other countries might place fresh restrictions on trade with England—a sacrifice, he felt, which the circumstances did not warrant. Yet two days later, the Cholera Committee proceeded to give local Boards of Health unprecedented powers.

The Englishman's home, it had long been claimed, was his castle; and except for such purposes as searching for illegal weapons (like game traps), or making an arrest on a criminal charge, it had been held to be inviolate. Now, local boards were given the right not merely to authorise entry into any home, but to arrange for it to be washed, fumigated and whitewashed, if deemed desirable. The cholera had forced recognition of what came to be known as the sanitary idea; that the State had not merely a right but a duty to its citizens to try to protect them from health hazards arising out of bad living conditions, even at the cost of interfering with the property rights of individuals.

'He sinks into sensual sloth . . .'

A by-product of the epidemic was that for the first time, the public was made aware of how bad those living conditions were, in the new industrial towns. In December 1831 a reporter from the Leeds *Mercury*,

who had been sent to investigate the poorer districts of the town, gave a
vivid description of the unpaved, undrained streets through which he had
walked, 'almost filled with ashes and filth, which filth oozes into many of
the cellar dwellings'; and his account caused more than a local sensation.
When the Manchester Board of Health were making their preparations
for the arrival of the disease, they decided to conduct a survey of the conditions in which the poor were living; and it showed that out of almost
7,000 dwellings inspected, 1,400 were damp; over 2,000 had no privy
(water closets were virtually unknown) and over 2,500 needed washing
and whitewashing. Of the streets in which the houses were situated, over
half had no drainage; they were filled with refuse, stagnant pools, and
ordure.

The Secretary of the Manchester Board of Health was Dr. James Kay—
later, through marriage to an heiress, to become Kay-Shuttleworth, and to
be knighted for his services to education. He was horrified at what the
inspection disclosed; and he described it in *The Moral and Physical Conditions of the Working Classes employed in the Cotton Manufacture in Manchester*,
published in 1832. Kay was in no doubt where the chief responsibility lay:
with the influx of Irish. The population of Lancashire had doubled since
the beginning of the century, largely through Irish immigration. And
from the Irish, the inhabitants of the country had learned a pernicious
lesson: 'debased alike by ignorance and pauperism, they have discovered,
with the savage, what is the minimum of the means of life upon which
existence may be prolonged. They have taught the fatal secret to the
population of this country.'

As a result, the Lancashire labouring population had been demoralised.
The need to compete for jobs with the Irish left them a prey to exploitation by their employers, who imposed on them a dull routine of ceaseless
drudgery. 'To condemn man to such severity of toil', Kay argued, 'is, to
some extent, to cultivate in him the habits of an animal.' And an animal
he had often become. 'Impotent of all the distinguishing aims of his
species, he sinks into sensual sloth, or revels in more disgusting licentious-
ness. His house is ill-furnished, uncleanly, often ill-ventilated, perhaps
damp; his food, from want of forethought and domestic economy, is
meagre and innutritious; he is debilitated and hypochondriacal, and falls
the victim of indiscipline.'

Kay's revelations were the more notable because they were the work of a
man who was not in any sense a hostile witness. He repudiated Sadler as
'deluded by a theoretical chimera'; accepted political economy; and was to

go out of his way to insist that the evils which he had described were not the necessary consequence of the commercial system, but 'evidence of a disease which impairs its energies, if it does not threaten its vitality'. But it was impossible, if Kay's descriptions were believed, to continue to believe that the commercial system was regulating itself as satisfactorily as the industrialists' spokesmen maintained; and, as it happened, confirmatory evidence was provided the following year by a surgeon, Peter Gaskell, in *The Manufacturing Population of England*, with its descriptions of slum dwellings:

> filthy, unfurnished, deprived of all the accessions of decency or comfort, they are indeed but too truly an index of the vicious and depraved lives of their inmates. What little furniture is found in them is of the rudest and most common sort, and very often in fragments; one or two rush-bottomed chairs, a deal table, a few stools, broken earthenware such as dishes, tea-cups, etc.; one or more tin kettles and cans, a few knives and forks, a piece of broken iron serving as a poker; no fender; a bedstead – or not, as the case may happen to be; blankets and sheets, in the strict meaning of the words, unknown – their place often being made up of sacking; a heap of flock, or a bundle of straw, supplying the want of a feather bed; and all these cooped up in a single room which serves as a place for domestic and household occupations.

The slum streets, Gaskell found, were particularly repulsive. As the houses lacked plumbing, refuse had to be thrown into them; and as they were unpaved, and undrained, they cut up into deep ruts, interspersed with stagnant pools. Even where there was a communal privy, as it might have to serve fifty people 'it is in a very short time completely choked up with excrementitious matter; no alternative is left to the inhabitants but adding to the already defiled street'.

But the conditions in which the urban poor were living were a matter for concern only while the epidemic lasted—hardly even as long as that, for cholera proved to be indeed socially circumspect. A few members of the upper classes succumbed—among them, Godwin's son; but, as a commentator noted in one of the medical journals of the time, it was soon realised that the great majority of its victims were among 'the poorest of the poor', and consequently 'there was never a real panic'—particularly as the epidemic was rather less destructive in London, for some reason, than in any other towns. And as the provisions of the Cholera Act were designed to last only as long as the epidemic, they were allowed to lapse as soon as notification of new cases ceased.

7 & 8. — SOHO:

The light and dark side: the view of the Soho factory in Birmingham which the public saw – the façade – contrasted with a view from the rear.

THE LIFE OF A LABOURER

CONTENT HAVING FOOD & RAIMENT

(*Above and following four illustrations*) The decline and fall of an agricultural labourer in 1830, in five scenes: the victim not of his vices but of his times.

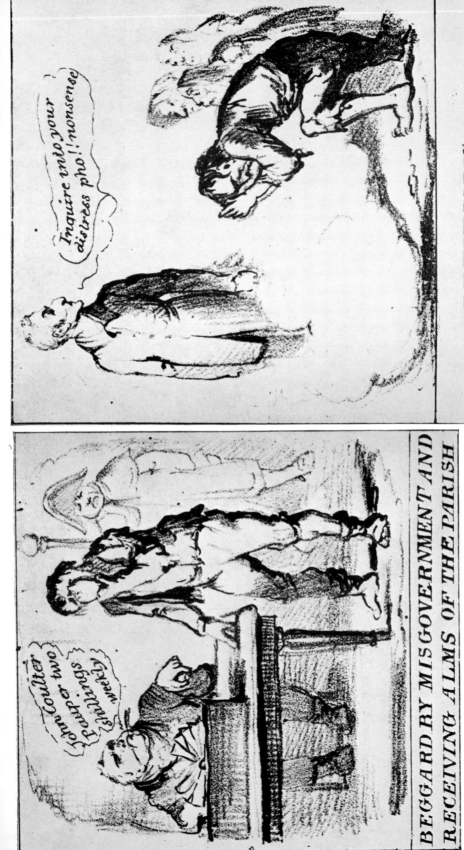

IN IGNORANCE TRIES TO
RIGHT HIMSELF AND GETS

PUNISHMENT IN ENGLAND FOR
A BLOODLESS RIOT.

4. THE WHOLE BILL

The revelations about the condition of the agricultural workers, following the revolt of 1830; the descriptions of the lives of children working in factories, given by Oastler and Thackrah; and the reports of Kay and Gaskell on the living conditions of the labouring poor in the new industrial towns—all pointed to the existence of some grave defect in the social system, but the Whigs could reasonably insist that they should not be held to blame. It was almost a quarter of a century since they had last held office, and then only for a few months. Nor was it possible for them—they could plead—to introduce whatever measures might be needed to put the economy to rights, until they had taken the vital preliminary step, and put the Reform bill through Parliament.

This was just what Francis Place wanted: the chance to reunite radicals of all persuasions under their old banner. True, the bill fell far short of Cartwright's specifications. The vote was to be given only to owners of property with a rateable value of ten pounds, which few artisans, let alone labourers, possessed; and there was to be no secret ballot. Still, the rotten boroughs and the nomination boroughs would disappear; and the seats would be redistributed among the counties, and the new industrial towns. It was an instalment of electoral justice, Place argued, and the most that could be hoped for, at that time.

Once more, Place was in a position of considerable influence. The Government, he knew, needed him. Soon after he had come into office, Melbourne had actually sent round his brother, George Lamb—the prototype of a later species, the contact man—to find if Place would help by issuing an appeal for an end to violence. He had no reason to trust Melbourne—rather the reverse; years before, Melbourne had failed to pay the bills for some breeches Place had made for him. Place also despised George Lamb, commenting on his 'vulgar air of frankness, which may put some people off their guard'. He accordingly replied that the Government was in difficulties through its own mistakes—its policy of savage repression of the farm workers, and of press prosecutions. What was needed, he explained, on the strength of his own information, was not a reign of terror, but a reform of the poor laws. Place's information—Melbourne perceptively remarked, when his brother reported back—always supported policies which he was advocating at the time.

Still, one of the ways, and perhaps the only way, ministers could hope to get the Reform bill through would be to convince the Tories that the danger of revolution if they resisted it was greater than if they permitted it to pass; and Melbourne was shrewd enough to realise that Place was the man to direct and control the disposable mob, to that end. Place went to work again, as he had in the old Westminster elections, but this time on a national scale. The Birmingham banker and currency reformer, Thomas Attwood, had revived an older radical organisation in his home town— the Political Union, designed to fuse middle-class and working-class support behind Reform; and unions on the same model were appearing in other towns. Place began to link them into a National Union, under the slogan minted by the new *Spectator* magazine: 'The bill, the whole bill, and nothing but the bill.'

Ministers were grateful for this support; but there were times when they became a little uneasy about their ability to exercise adequate control over it, should the need arise. It was all very well for Place to boast that he had brought radicals of all shades of opinions into line; he had, but this only meant that individuals could exploit the Reform campaign for their own purposes—for example, to stir up resentment against the factory owners, or to preach socialism. After the ignominious outcome of the Cobbett trial ministers were warier about prosecutions; but it would in any case be difficult to proceed against a writer or speaker who was careful to mask his seditious opinions under the disguise of attachment to Reform. As a result, the months during which Reform was being fought out in Parliament were a period of intellectual ferment, during which social issues were discussed with a vigour and freedom unknown since the early days of the French revolution.

'Knowledge is power'

Of the journals which appeared to cater for the appetite for new ideas, some did not even pretend to support the Whigs. Of these, the most influential was the *Poor Man's Guardian*, brought out by one of Owen's disciples, Henry Hetherington. Other editors had campaigned on behalf of the poor, but none had previously identified himself with their cause— Cobbett regarded himself as a yeoman farmer, even to dressing the part. Hetherington insisted that his life was at the service of the poor—and his liberty. As they obviously could not afford to buy any paper which had to pay the fourpence stamp duty, he must defy the law, and sell his *Guardian* unstamped; or, rather, with a mock stamp on it, bearing the inscription, 'knowledge is power'. The first number appeared in the summer of 1831; and the authorities, who might have been reluctant to prosecute for the opinions expressed in it, were glad of the excuse to proceed against Hetherington on a charge of failing to pay the stamp duty. They could not find him: he had arranged to move from town to town, bringing out the paper whenever he could persuade somebody to risk printing it, and moving on before the law caught up with him.

This was hard on those who printed and sold the *Poor Man's Guardian*; they could be arrested and convicted. Still, before he was caught, two months later (his mother had fallen ill, and he was arrested when he returned to see her) he had shown there was a market for it, and publication continued while he was in jail. The circulation might be very small, but its continuing existence was an embarrassment to the Government. In opposition, Whigs had denounced the stamp duty; they were leaving themselves open to the charge of hypocrisy when they prosecuted Hetherington for refusing to pay it. Place was also embarrassed, but for a different reason: the politics of the paper. Its chief writer, Bronterre O'Brien, was a caustic critic both of the Government and of the Reform bill; all it would do if it were passed, he argued, would be to throw power into the lap of the middle class; 'and of all governments, a government of the middle class is the most grinding and remorseless'.

The danger, Place knew, was that this attitude would spread among radicals who had been reluctantly persuaded to support the bill, in default of anything better. Increasingly, radical voices were heard taking the same line—Cavie Richardson, for example, denounced the bill in Leeds on the ground that it would 'deprive the poor of every vestige of political existence'. Such opinions might begin to make headway among those who were supporting the campaign not so much out of enthusiasm for reform, as because it offered them the opportunity to propagate their own social theories: in particular, trade unionists, whom Doherty was seeking to inspire with his vision of working-class solidarity, achieved through a union of all trades; and the members of the co-operative movement.

The trade unions, after the setback in the depression period of 1826, had begun to recover their confidence. A few effective strikes had been undertaken; and in 1830 Doherty had been able to form a National Association for the Protection of Labour—a Trades Union Congress in embryo. The following year, the co-operative movement held its first national conference in Manchester. Although none of the communities set up in Britain on Owen's model had been any more successful than his New Harmony experiment, co-operatives on a small scale for marketing purposes had been started in many areas, and by the time William Thompson convened the conference, there were about 500 of them. Owen, who had returned to England financially the poorer but in no way the humbler for the failure of his New Harmony experiment, was at first inclined to be a little contemptuous of the co-operatives as he found them. He had changed his mind when a resolution was passed 'That this congress considers it highly desirable that a community on the principles of mutual co-operation, united possessions, and equality of exertion, shall be established in England as soon as possible', because he believed he had found a way in which this might be achieved.

All wealth, Owen reasoned, 'proceeds from labour and knowledge; and labour and knowledge are generally remunerated according to the time employed'. Why not, then, 'make time, the standard, or measure, of wealth'? With this aim, he set about establishing a National Equitable Labour Exchange in London, using its own currency based on labour time. Goods brought to the Exchange were paid for at a rate calculated on the cost of the materials and the hours spent on making them up (less a penny in the shilling to pay on the Exchange's running costs); and with this currency the producer (or his wife) could buy what he wanted at the Exchange—a notion then less strange than it would later sound as private currencies were common. The Exchange, set up in the Gray's Inn Road, was a success, and was soon paying its way; and there seemed a reasonable possibility that it would revive an interest in Owen's ideas.

'Selected passages of social life'

But in the event it was not to be Owen's social philosophies which attracted attention in this period. Instead, the imagination of the reading public was caught by a woman writer, virtually unknown until her *Illustrations of Political Economy* appeared in 1832.

Harriet Martineau came of prosperous Huguenot stock; her father had been a reasonably successful merchant, but like so many others, his business had been destroyed when the slump in the winter of 1825 left him with no reserves, and unsaleable goods. His daughter lacked feminine charm; she was deaf; and life appeared to hold no better prospect for her than, perhaps, becoming a companion to some rich old lady. But she could write, and she began to produce and sell short stories; fiction, with a realistic background, set among machine-breakers or trade unionists. Then, in 1827, she came across Mrs. Marcet's *Conversations on Political Economy* and found, to her astonishment, that she was preaching in her stories almost the same economic doctrines that Mrs. Marcet had presented in her dialogues. 'It struck me at once', she was to recall in her *Auto-biography*, 'that the principles of the whole science might be conveyed in the same way—not by being smothered up in a story, but by being exhibited in their natural workings in selected passages of social life.' So she began to write some stories along these lines, each illustrating a set of economic principles, with a summary of them at the end.

The *Illustrations* presented as orthodox a version of political economy as she could make it; but, not surprisingly, it was old—Ricardian—orthodoxy, with no hint of the doubts that had begun to afflict the econo-mists; for example, over the Malthusian theory of population. Malthus, in fact, had no more devoted disciple than Harriet Martineau. By some quirk of her auditory nerves, Malthus was the only person whose conversa-tion she could follow easily without having to use her ear trumpet—all the more curious in that he was not an easy man to understand; Malthus's speech 'was hopelessly imperfect, from a defect in the palate; when I con-sidered my own deafness, and his inability to produce half the consonants in the alphabet, and his hare lip which must prevent my offering my tube, I feared we should make a terrible business of it. I was delightfully wrong.' She felt it her business and her pleasure, 'in illustrating Political Economy, to exemplify Malthus's doctrine among the rest. It was that doctrine pure and simple, as it came from his virtuous and benevolent mind, that I presented.' So the stock Malthusian phrases bespattered the *Illustrations*—'there is a perpetual tendency in population to press upon the means of subsistence'; 'the ultimate checks by which a population is kept down to the level of the means of subsistence are vice and misery'; 'the only way out is restraint of population—if possible by preventive checks, to avert the horrors of any positive check'.

Although she might have been disconcerted to hear it, Harriet Martineau was also recognisably a new radical, in her political attitudes. There was little of the humanitarian about her; where she sympathised with the poor, it was usually because she regarded them as the victims of some State interference upsetting the nice mechanism of supply and demand. Indirect taxes, for example, she considered unfair, because they left the rich man, with his disposable income, free to decide how much he wished to contribute to the State, 'while the man whose whole income must be spent in the purchase of commodities has no such choice'. But her real objection to them was to their stultifying effect on trade: the shop-keeper in *The Farrers of Budge Row* found his profits declining because the common people ('and they are the customers who signify most, for their number') were reluctant to buy the taxed goods: 'they go without tea and sugar, and save more in soap and candles than you would realise'. And although Harriet Martineau objected to slavery, it was primarily because she regarded it as an inefficient form of labour, which meant that the sugar plantations she described, in her story about Demerara, had to be subsidised by the English taxpayer. She had no patience with those who complained of slavery in English factories—factory legislation to her was an unjustified interference in free wage bargaining.

Like Gaskell, she was under no illusions that the principles of political economy had as yet brought benefit to the poor. 'A rich and noble country is yours', one of her characters, the kindly and observant Monsieur Verblanc, observed; 'and the greater the wonder and the shame that it contains so much misery—such throngs of destitute.' But this, she insisted, was not the fault of political economy. 'Enormous as has been and now is the expenditure of your government', Monsieur Verblanc went on, 'while the nation has been growing rich, whole crowds of your people have been growing poor'—making her point that the money which the Government had been abstracting in rates and taxes was being wasted; stricter adherence to the principles of political economy would have brought more benefit to the poor than they got from the rates.

Harriet Martineau was prepared to countenance State help for the poor only through aid for emigration, to reduce the labour surplus; and also for education, in order to teach the poor the moral restraint they would require in order to prevent themselves from providing an addition to that surplus when they grew up. Otherwise, she insisted, the State should cease to intervene. The old poor law must go. If this seemed harsh, the remedy was in the worker's own hands; he should not marry and have a family unless he earned an income adequate to keep it, and until he could be sure there was no risk of losing his employment through some stagnation of trade.

Nor, if he did, should the public help. If there was one subject on which she went further than her mentors, it was in her objections to organised almsgiving. It could be doubted, she wrote, 'whether the most profligate tyranny ever depraved so many hearts as the charities of our Christian nation. If our practices are to be judged by their fruits, there are none, next to slavery, for which we need so much pardon as for our methods of charity.' The reason, she explained, as that 'in a society where capital abounds in proportion to the consumers, individuals are fully justified in giving away in whatsoever form and to whomsoever they please, as they give away that which leaves nobody destitute. But in a society where population abounds in proportion to capital, to give food and clothing to the idle, while the industrious are debarred from earning it, is to take subsistence from him whose due it is, to give it to one who has no claim.'

Earlier writers, notably Hannah More, had emphasised the desirability of selective almsgiving; but Harriet Martineau took the argument off the moral plane on which it was ordinarily presented—that care should be taken to ensure that the alms went to deserving cases—and instead, examined it in the light of the law of population. 'The small unproductive consumption occasioned by the relief of sudden accidents and rare infirmities' might justifiably, she thought, be provided for, because 'such charity does not tend to the increase of numbers.' But with this single exception, 'all arbitrary distribution of the necessaries of life is injurious to society, whether in the form of private almsgiving, public charitable institutions, or a legal pauper system'. And she could claim that this sweeping judgment followed logically from the principles of political economy; the money distributed annually in charity to the poor would be far more productive if it were spent, or invested, providing employment. The only way to lessen the increasing number of the indigent 'was to let capital and labour take their natural course, but to proportion the number of the consumers to the subsistence fund'. Charity did precisely the opposite—it encouraged the growth of a population surplus, and anything which did that was to be deplored. Lying-in hospitals for the poor, for example, were 'a bounty on improvidence', and should be stopped. Even 'the gift of coals and blankets to the poor at Christmas', she felt, 'creates more misery than it relieves'.

Having embarked on the series, the next step was to find a publisher. James Mill, asked for his advice, was discouraging; he was sure that she was wasting her time. Publisher after publisher told her the same thing; that what with Reform and the cholera, the public was in no mood for such instruction. She was eventually able to have stories published only by accepting terms very disadvantageous to herself; and the publisher lugubriously assured her that the 1,500 copies he was having printed could not hope to sell. Ten days after publication she received a letter from him to say that the demand had justified increasing the print order to 2,000. In a postcript, he added that 'since he wrote the above he had found that we should want 3,000. A second postscript proposed 4,000; and a third, 5,000.' Reviews were enthusiastic; and almost overnight, at the age of thirty, Harriet found herself the literary celebrity of the day.

How far the *Illustrations* were influential in the promotion of a better understanding and appreciation of the principles of political economy is impossible to assess; but it is hard to believe that they would have enjoyed so spectacular a success if the reading public had not been anxious to learn, and ready to accept what she taught. And this was learning made easy, for the stories were by no means negligible in their own right; she had quite a vivid imagination, and although some of the characters were simply mouthpieces, and the dialogue contrived, she was always readable—particularly in the first story, *Life in the Wilds*, which not merely demonstrated some of the simpler economic principles, such as the advantages of the division of labour, but was also a good yarn in the Robinson Crusoe tradition; and this helped to ease her readers into the more complex issues she discussed later. But she never forgot it was the economic issues which mattered. She might make some of her Tory characters sympathetic—like old John Armstrong, who hated seeing an iron works set up in his quiet Welsh hills; but this was only to help make his wrong-headedness more striking. In her industry, machines made work for the labourer; on her enclosed land, the cottagers who had been deprived of their rights found regular and more renumerative employment than they had previously enjoyed—and so on.

The *Illustrations* had an enthusiastic reception from most of the critics, as well as from the public: the *Edinburgh* was not embarrassed to use the term genius about her. In one journal only was the glibness of much of her reasoning systematically dissected: the Tory *Quarterly*. By her own account, its review of her *Illustrations* was a combined operation between the editor, Walter Scott's biographer J. G. Lockhart, and the reviewer, the Tory politician and essayist John Wilson Croker—himself the victim of what was perhaps the most savage of all Macaulay's essays in the *Edinburgh*; and Poulett Scrope, she heard, provided the criticism of her political economy. Croker and Lockhart, she was warned in advance, had made up their minds to tomahawk her; they did. Most of the review was gently feline, but exasperation kept breaking through, particularly over her advice to the worker not to marry and have children until he could be sure that a slump would not take away his job. How could any worker, the review asked, with the best of intentions, make such a forecast about his future prospects when the political economists themselves were baffled by trade fluctuations? At this time, trade happened to be picking up—but look what was the consequence! The northern employers were advertising for labour in newspapers in the south. How could the worker know whether he had a safe job, in such circumstances? And was his destiny doomed 'to remain in the hands of men who have the imbecility to listen with reverence to such "principles" as these—or the quackery to pretend they do so'? What kind of a 'principle' was it on which the political economists welcomed the introduction of machinery, yet at the same time insisted that every increase in the number of human machines was 'a cause of unmitigatable want and woe'?

The review would have been more damaging if it had stuck to economic issues; but the writers could not resist the opportunity to goad Harriet Martineau personally. Could it be, they wondered, that she had sat for the Tom Moore's *Portrait of a she politician*?

> Tis my fortune to know a lean Benthamite spinster
> A maid who her faith in old Jeremy puts
> Who talks with a lisp of 'the last new *Westminster*'
> And hopes you're delighted with 'Mill upon gluts'.

But no—the review continued—the portrait did not fit Miss Martineau —such a character could not be ascribed 'to a *female Malthusian* who thinks child-bearing a *crime against society*! The *unmarried woman* who declaims against *marriage*!! A *young woman* who deprecates charity and a provision for the poor!!!' It was unnecessary, Harriet Martineau convinced herself, to reply to such 'low-minded and foul-mouthed creatures'; she simply awaited her opportunity, and 'cut' them at a social function. She could afford to; she was famous; the *Illustrations* had won her more adulation even than Hannah More had received.

5. SADLER'S COMMITTEE

Before the Reform bill reached its final stages, in 1832, the Government had to face one further challenge to its authority: a factory bill designed to replace Hobhouse's. It was put forward by Michael Sadler, who had met Oastler years before when both were engaged on a charitable enterprise, and who had given informal help to the Short Time campaigners at Westminster during the passage of the Hobhouse bill. Disgusted at the concessions Hobhouse felt compelled to make to get it through, Sadler obtained leave to bring in a bill of his own, incorporating the Short Time demands.

'To liberate children . . .'

No child should in future be employed in any factory, the bill proposed, under the age of nine; and nobody under eighteen years of age should work for longer than ten hours a day, or forty-eight hours a week. There was to be half an hour off for breakfast, and an hour off for dinner. As a precaution against evasion, every employer was to keep a time book entering the hours that both children and machinery were working, to be made available for inspection by the magistrates, who could impose penalties for incorrect entries. The responsibility for seeing that the child's age certificate was correct was to remain with the parents; but they could be penalised if it was false. The purpose of the bill—Sadler claimed, in his introductory speech to the second reading in March—was:

> to liberate children and other young persons employed in the mills and factories of the kingdom from that over-exertion and confinement which common sense, as well as long experience, has shown to be utterly inconsistent with the improvement of their minds, the preservation of their morals, or the protection of their health; in a word, to rescue them from a state of suffering and degradation which, it is conceived, the industrious classes in hardly any other country endure, or ever had experienced, and which cannot be much longer tolerated.

Sadler judiciously mixed statistics with appeals to the heart. 'Our ancestors could not have supposed it possible,' he told the Commons, 'posterity will not believe it true—it will be placed among the historic doubts of some future antiquary—that a generation of Englishmen could exist, or had existed, that would labour lisping infancy, of a few summers old—regardless alike of its smiles or tears, and unmoved by its unresisting weakness—eleven, twelve, thirteen, fourteen, sixteen hours a day, and through the weary night also, till in the dewy morn of existence, the bud of youth faded, and fell ere it were unfolded.' To show the effects of such labour on lisping infancy he cited, as well as Thackrah's survey, a detailed study by two Stockport doctors of six local cotton mills. Of over 800 people employed, most of them children, the doctors claimed that only 183 could be regarded as healthy; 240 were delicate, 258 unhealthy, forty-three very much stunted, 100 suffered from enlarged ankles and knees, and seventeen from postural distortions. The list did not include accidents; but Sadler also had a report from a Manchester physician which stated that out of 106 children he had examined in a local Sunday School, forty-seven had had accidents in the course of their mill employment. And this suffering, Sadler reminded the House, was experienced by girls as well as boys; the mills made no distinction of sex.

Nor, he went on, did they make any distinction of sex in administering punishment. Children working such long hours inevitably found it difficult to keep awake. 'Sir, children are beaten with thongs prepared for this purpose. Yes, the females of this country, no matter whether children or grown-up—I hardly know which is the more disgusting outrage—are beaten upon the face, arms and bosom, beaten in your free market of labour, as you term it, like slaves! These are the instruments . . . '— 'these' being a selection of black, heavy leather thongs; when he struck one of them on the table, the smack of it resounded through the chamber. They were quite capable, he went on, of breaking an arm; but 'the bones of the young are, as I have said before, pliant'.

Only a few months earlier, Sadler recalled, Parliament had taken upon itself to regulate the employment of negro slaves. Henceforth, it had been decreed, no slave on English colonial territory was to be compelled to work except between the hours of six in the morning and six in the evening; and in that period slaves were entitled as of legal right to an hour's break between eight and nine, and two hours between twelve and two. Adult slaves, in other words, were limited to a nine-hour working day. Was the House to say that it was right to limit the hours of labour for African children—but monstrous to suggest any such limitation for an English child?

It had happened before, Sadler knew, and it could be expected to happen again, that M.P.s would be shocked by such revelations into voting for the bill on its second reading; but then would allow themselves to be persuaded on a variety of economic grounds to permit the piecemeal destruction of the bill in committee. He must be careful, he realised, to demolish the chief argument which, experience had shown, would be used against him—that he wanted to flout the principles of political economy. Those principles, he pointed out, were already being flouted, because the majority of workers in the factories were not free agents; they were children. In any case, to describe adult workers as competing on equal terms with their employers was nonsense. The political economists, he went on,

seem, in my apprehension, too much to forget the condition of society, the unequal division of property, or rather its total monopoly by the few, leaving the many nothing whatever but what they can obtain by their daily labour;

which very labour cannot become available for the purpose of daily subsistence without the consent of those who own the property of the community, all the materials, elements, call them what you please, on which labour is bestowed being in their possession. Hence it is clear that excepting in a state of things where the demand for labour fully equals the supply (which it would be absurdly false to say exists in this country), the employer and the employed do not meet on equal terms in the market of labour; on the contrary, the latter, whatever his age, and call him as free as you please, is often entirely at the mercy of the former. He would be wholly so were it not for the operation of the poor laws, which are a palpable interference with the market of labour, and condemned as such by their opponents.

The political economists and their radical allies found themselves in a difficult position. They disliked Sadler's evangelical Toryism; they resented being lectured on political economy; and they were reluctant to admit that labour was a seller's market, though they knew very well that it was, in case this should be used as the excuse for more Government intervention to redress the balance. But they could not unite against Sadler, because on the main issue, child labour, some of them were on his side.

At the time when the elder Peel's second bill was being debated Malthus, moved by the plight of the children, had supported it; and although Ricardo appeared unwilling to encourage any precedents for further factory legislation, the tendency among the political economists had been to echo Malthus's view—as did their allies, particularly Sydney Smith; in his 1820 *Edinburgh Review* article on the poor, he had gone so far as to blame the extensive employment of children in factories for counterbalancing the good effects industrialisation must otherwise have produced; 'we indeed strongly suspect that the present redundancy of labour has been in no inconsiderable degree owing to this cause'. And when Sadler first introduced his bill in the Commons, Robert Torrens gave it his support on the ground that it was impossible for the principles of political economy to be 'opposed to those of humanity'.

Hume, however, with his political training, had an inkling where this was going to lead. It was not just a case of protecting the young and helpless, he told the House; 'it was bound up with the interests of the manufacturers'; and though he insisted that he did not want to oppose the bill, he could not disguise his uneasiness about it. Out of Parliament, Francis Place was more explicit. The Ten Hours campaign might have been initially designed for the benefit of children working in factories, but it would affect adult working hours too. He did not like the idea of making children—or women, for that matter—do such work, but for adult men, 'all legislative interference is pernicious. Men must be left to themselves to make their own bargains; the law must compel the observance of compacts; there it should end.'

By this time, too, another argument was being used against State interference on behalf of children. In the past, the wages they could earn had been accounted a useful supplement to the family's income. Now, in many families, what the children brought in made the difference between subsistence and destitution. Any attempt to reduce their working hours, an M.P. pointed out, must also reduce their wages; and as adult wages were already so low that they were barely sufficient to keep a family supplied with food, 'starvation must be the consequence'. The suggestion was even made that to try to prevent evasion of the minimum age regulations was futile because, as earlier experience had shown, the law would be 'completely evaded by the parents'. Nearly fifteen years before, Stanley had argued that parents by their nature could be relied upon to afford better protection to their children from exploitation than the State could hope to do; now, it was being claimed that the parents had become so much the accessories to breaches of the law that State protection for their children was impracticable.

Althorp was left in a quandary. Political economy had given him an intellectual prop: now, it was speaking with two voices. His instinct, as always, was against any proposal which might require legislative interference; on the other hand, he was a kindly man, and—like many other M.P.s who had not previously given the subject much thought—he had been disturbed by Sadler's revelations. If the facts were as Sadler stated, he had to admit, there was certainly a case for legislation. But 'some of his statements appeared to be absolutely incredible'. Would it not be wise, therefore, to refer the matter to a select committee?

This was just what Sadler had feared. The committee was being suggested, he complained, 'to postpone, if not defeat, the measure'. But, just as Owen had done, he realised that if he could not prevent the delay, he could at least ensure, with the help of the Short Time committee, that it was put to a good purpose.

First, as the mill-owners were arguing that the Short Time campaign was the work of only a few irresponsible agitators, it was desirable to prove that in fact it enjoyed mass support; and for this purpose Oastler, in the spring of 1832, organised a meeting in the Castle Yard at York, to which delegates marched from all the main industrial towns. The rally had many of the ingredients of farce. Torrential rain fell on the marchers as they neared York; beer was laid on there in plenty, but the food which had been ordered was mysteriously lost; and the marchers were again drenched on their way back. Yet in spite of ridicule from bystanders, and in the columns of the local newspapers, something in the event caught the imagination of those who attended it, so that it was soon to take on the aura of a legend. Certainly nothing comparable had been seen, apart from some of O'Connell's meetings in Ireland; and it banished any notion that the Ten Hours campaign was not supported by the workers. Well satisfied, the Short Time committee set to work to collect witnesses and evidence for the select committee.

'The most shocking cases of lacerations'

The evidence was similar to, but more professional than, that which had been provided for Peel. On most issues, it left no room for doubt that Sadler's allegations in his speech had not been exaggerated. Samuel Smith, for example—a member of the College of Surgeons, who had been for thirteen years with the Leeds Infirmary—said that from his experience the hours worked by children in factories were generally twelve; he had never known of any instance where they were less than eleven hours and a half; he knew 'that in a great number of instances they have to labour fourteen, fifteen, sixteen and seventeen hours a day'. When business was good, factory owners felt compelled to increase the hours in order to capture, and keep orders: if they declined to do so, such orders would in future go to less scrupulous competitors.

The evidence also revealed what was less widely realised, the length of time that a child might be away from home, each working day. Not all mills were close to housing districts; often the children had to walk a couple of miles or more, there and back; and they could not risk being late, as this meant a fine, deducted from their wages. And a fine of even a penny was severe, taken as it was from a pay packet of less than sixpence per day. As a result, Oastler claimed in his evidence,

> It is almost the general system for the little children in these manufacturing villages to know nothing of their parents at all excepting that in the morning early, at five o'clock, very often before four, they were awakened by a human being that they are told is their father, and are pulled out of bed (I have heard many a score of them give an account of it) when they are almost asleep, and

lesser children are absolutely carried on the back of the older children asleep to the mill, and they see no more of their parents, generally speaking, till they go home at night, and are sent to bed.

It had been suggested, Oastler added, that the children of handloom weavers had had to work as hard; but this, in his experience, was rubbish. When he was a boy in the West Riding the weavers there had been able to make a good living without endless labour; and at least the children had been at home. But now the parents, themselves deprived of an income, had to rely on the earnings of children to whom they were strangers, except on one day of the week.

The evil effects of the system on family life were also described by George Stringer Bull, one of the few Church of England clergymen to support Short Time, and destined to become an influential figure in the campaign. Parents, he complained, had to pull the mill children out of bed, and 'shake them till they awoke'; that was virtually all the family life the mill children got, six days of the week. As for the seventh day, the thought of it made Bull, as a clergyman, feel guilty: 'for we—while they are "stowed up", if I may use the expression, in the mills during six days of the week—then confine them in our crowded Sunday Schoolrooms'. In the circumstances, they could hardly be expected to imbibe Christian precepts, or acquire much of an education. How, then, could they be expected to grow up into decent citizens?

On how harmful work in the mills was for the children, there was more diversity of opinion. Whether factory work was laborious, for example, as Sadler believed, or was agreeably easy, as some mill-owners claimed, had already provoked controversy—and was to continue to do so, for many years to come. Yet it was really, as Samuel Smith pointed out to the committee, an irrelevance. He did not himself believe that strenuous exertion was required of mill children; but they were not spared extreme fatigue, because they were not allowed to sit down. Years before, when he had been an officer in the local militia, he had observed that simply having to stand to attention on the parade ground was more tiring than exertion: and in the same way, for children, he felt sure, that 'merely having to sustain the erect position of the body for so long a period of time is harrassing in the extreme, and no one can have an adequate idea of it unless he had himself been subjected to it'. A Manchester doctor echoed his view, adding an illustration which was more likely to impress members of the committee than reminiscences of the parade ground, as many of them must regularly have had the opportunity to experience it for themselves. The simplest acts, he told them, when protracted, can be extremely fatiguing: 'for instance, the short period which is passed in the celebration of public worship would be passed in a much less satisfactory manner, in the kneeling, or the standing, or the sitting posture, than it is by the judicious admixture of the three. And the reason is obvious, for the muscles which are called into action to maintain for a long time any particular position, or to perform continuously the same act, become fatigued from the want of due alternations of activity and repose.'

Various health hazards to children were described as arising from work in the mills. The most frequently noticed were deformities. 'Ossification not being complete at that early age'—a Bolton physician, Thomas Young, argued—'the bones yield under the weight of the body, and distortion is thus produced.' The tortuous positions and actions required of mill children at their work were also blamed. The overseer at John Wood's Bradford factory, who thought it one of the best in the country, admitted that the activity of a 'piecer' in a worsted mill—throwing the left shoulder up and the right knee inward, and at the same time having to stoop—often led to deformities of the right knee. Joseph Hebergam of Huddersfield was shown to the committee: he had been straight and healthy, it was claimed, until he was seven; but then, his widowed mother being poor, he had been sent to work in the mills, and deformity had followed. Had this not, he was asked, made his mother unhappy? 'I have seen her weep sometimes,' he replied, 'and I have asked her why she was weeping; she would not tell me then, but she has told me since.'

Respiratory disorders, too, were commonly encountered; partly because the children were continually inhaling dust and cotton flue; partly, some of the doctors giving evidence believed, because of the extremes of temperature to which children in mills were subjected. And there were many references to the high accident rate. 'I have seen every extremity in the body broken', Samuel Smith told the committee: 'I have very frequently seen the most shocking cases of lacerations it is possible to conceive.'

The evidence which made the greatest impact, though, concerned the punishments inflicted in the mills. Some of the allegations obviously arose out of the sadism of an individual employer, or his overseer; in other cases, though, overseers who gave evidence claimed that they disliked having to use the strap, but found themselves compelled to, out of necessity. As one flax mill overseer explained, the speed of the machinery was calculated by the employers; he had to see that it was maintained; and unless the children were 'driven or flogged up' the required quantity of work could not be got out of them.

Up to this point, the bill's opponents had made no attempt to call witnesses. They were evidently in no hurry to do so; and Sadler realised why. It would have been difficult, in view of the evidence already given, to deny that in some mills, children were worked excessive hours; that they were subjected to harsh treatment; and that their health might be impaired. The best Townsend and his supporters could say would be that these mills were the exception; and this was unlikely to impress Members of Parliament, who could reply that if such exceptions existed, the law must ensure that they should exist no longer. But with luck, the bill's opponents knew, if they waited long enough, they might not have to give evidence. The Government was at last on the verge of victory; Reform was almost through. And on June 7, which happened to be the day that Sadler reported on the committee's progress to the Commons, the Reform bill received the royal assent.

Sadler could plead that there was now ample proof that his bill was needed. To the life of a beast of burden, he reminded the House, a value was attached; the lives of slaves, even of felons, was protected by law; 'but in the case of the rising generation, no such protection is rendered'. Althorp, however, declined to facilitate the passage of the bill. At the end of June, Lord Morpeth presented a petition in its favour from his York-shire constituents which, it was found, measured no less than 2,322 feet in length; with a gesture, he let it unfurl part of its length on the floor of the Commons. Althorp remained unmoved; and before the measure could be taken any further, Parliament was dissolved.

Twelve years later, Friedrich Engels was to disparage the work of the Sadler committee in his *Condition of the Working Class in England*, describing its findings as 'a very partisan document, which was drawn up entirely by enemies of the factory system for purely political purposes'. Sadler, Engels continued, 'was led astray by his passionate sympathies into making assertions of a most misleading and erroneous kind. He asked questions in such a way as to elicit answers which, although correct, nevertheless were stated in such a form as to give a wholly false impression.' But here, Engels was allowing his own sympathies, or antipathies, to lead him astray. His knowledge of parliamentary procedure was slight, and he appears to have been under the impression that Sadler did all the question-ing. In fact, at least six members of the committee, including Poulett Thomson of the Board of Trade, were hostile to factory legislation and

K

could at any point intervene to ask whatever questions they liked. That they made much less use of their opportunity than they had done during the Peel committee's investigation was a matter of tactics. As for Sadler himself, his claim that the evidence had demonstrated the accuracy of his allegations was not disputed—except, inevitably, by spokesmen for the mill-owners.

For Engels to say that evidence was collected for purely political purposes, too, merely served to indicate how little he understood the political scene in the pre-Reform days. He was prejudiced against Toryism of the Sadler variety. The Radical Tories—Oastler, J. R. Stephens and others—were more successful in attracting working-class support than the new Radicals, the Peelite conservatives, or the bourgeois liberals; first for Short Time; then, in the late 1830s, for the campaign against the new poor law. Engels found their 'altar, throne and cottage' a threat to his own vision of a working-class movement; and he reacted accordingly.

6. NOTHING BUT THE BILL

The Government had had some uneasy moments before the Lords gave way; and so had Francis Place. Had the Tory opposition been less obdurate, in fact, Place would have been in danger of losing control; for there were many Whigs, and a few cabinet ministers, who would not have been averse to making more concessions, to get an agreed Reform bill through without the need—which at times appeared imminent—to coerce the House of Lords by the creation of new peers. If there had been any compromise of this kind, the radical movement would have split; Place himself could hardly have continued to support the Government. He had to use all his powers of persuasion to convince his Whig contacts— who would, he knew, report back to ministers—that the choice lay between the whole bill, and revolution.

All the ingredients of revolution had in fact been present; a further trade recession, in the winter of 1831, adding to the workers' distress and discontent. In some areas, the authorities actually lost control; Bristol was taken over by the mob; Nottingham castle burned; Derby jail sacked. All that Place had been able to do was to keep the rage of the crowds directed against the Tories, the House of Lords, and the bishops; and to show that the new radicals were as militant as their allies—Robert Torrens' language about the House of Lords was so violent, in fact, that William IV wanted to have him cashiered.

Eventually it was the Duke of Wellington, whose intransigence had brought the reform ministry into power, who had made it possible for them to pass the bill. When in May the king refused to create new peers, Grey resigned; and Wellington, by trying to form a new ministry, gave Attwood and Place the excuse they needed to put radicalism in the fore-front of the campaign. Place invited the public to refuse to pay taxes, and to withdraw their savings: 'To stop the duke, go for gold!' The duke, however, was stopped by his own inability to form a government; Grey returned to office, and the bill went through. Attwood received Grey's formal thanks for what the political unions had done; and the new radicals could fairly claim that their influence had been decisive. It remained to see how effectively they could use it in the coming elections which, Hume expected, would present him with a sizable party, not just a group, in the reformed Parliament.

6

RING IN THE NEW

1. CHILDREN IN FACTORIES

THE GENERAL ELECTION provided the Government with the majority for which it had been hoping; the Tories lost 100 seats, leaving them with only about 150 supporters in the Commons. Ministers could no longer claim any excuse for delay in embarking on their promised programme to sweep away the inequalities and injustices left from years of Tory misrule; a programme in which 'dispauperisation'—a term painfully in vogue at the time—was to have an important part.

But when Parliament reassembled, the royal commission on the poor laws was not ready to present its proposals; and in the meantime, ministers found themselves confronted with widespread destitution, in town and country. The first business, in fact, to which M.P.s were asked to give their attention, when the reformed House of Commons met, was a request that they should do something, as a matter of urgency, to relieve the distress of the handloom weavers.

Their condition had improved slightly after the slump in the winter of 1825; but the effect of even small trade setbacks was sufficient to reduce their earnings to the point where they could not provide for their families. It was difficult to estimate precisely how badly off they were, because of regional and local variations—and also because estimates of their average income were apt to be coloured by the sympathies of the investigators. An enquiry in 1830 had appeared to show that the average income of a group of weavers was only twopence a day; but when this was checked, the vigilant *Manchester Guardian* reported that the figure ought to have been nearer fivepence. Still, fivepence a day was not going to keep a weaver above the subsistence level, let alone his family. John Fielden, one of the new M.P.s, begged the Commons to take action. If they were of the opinion that the legislature was powerless to relieve distress, he said, he 'would take his hat and walk away, and not come within the walls again'. Ministers were not prepared to admit anything so derogatory to Parliament. But they could not think of anything they could do.

Accordingly, they appointed a select committee. To allow the condition of one group of workers to be singled out for investigation might create a precedent for endless further enquiries; the committee was therefore asked to make a more general enquiry into the state of manufactures, commerce, and shipping in the United Kingdom. This had the advantage that it would take more time; there would be no risk of a report being made, and proposals presented, before the session ended.

'By guilty neglect'

A more serious threat to the Government's peace of mind, when Parliament reassembled, was the Short Time campaign. Unable to complete the work of his committee before the old Parliament was dissolved, Sadler had decided to publish the minutes of evidence. They caused much the same shock that the Peel report had done, fifteen years before—greater, if anything, because there had been an impression that Peel's and Hobhouse's factory Acts must have been giving some protection to the children. Now, it was clear they had failed to do so.

The report received extensive coverage in the press. Newspapers were by this time more independent, and they had more space available; a growing income from advertising was enabling them to expand, in spite of the continuing stamp duty. Naturally, the grislier details from the report were singled out for attention—except in a few papers, where they were omitted with an editorial note to the effect that they were too appalling for readers' sensibilities. Southey, after reading the evidence, found his sleep disturbed for two nights; something, he claimed, that had never happened to him before in his life; and Harriet Martineau, though far from sympathetic to Sadler, had to admit that 'by guilty neglect we have brought ourselves into an inextricable embarrassment'. Even the Leeds *Mercury* conceded that, making every allowance for exaggeration,

> there remains an overwhelming and irresistible mass of proof that cruel overworking has in many places been practised, and that it has been excessively injurious to the health of the children, crippling their limbs, stunting their growth, and often shortening their lives . . . it is horrible, and an outrage on humanity, and decency, to work children of 7, 8 or 9 years old such a length of time. And the fact that such overworking has been practised, without the child's consent, for the joint benefit of the master and the parents, seems to us now, as it has always seemed to us, to call imperatively for legislative interference.

It happened, too, that in 1832 John Doherty had published the *Memoir of Robert Blincoe*, a description of what mill life had been like at the turn of the century, by a boy who had been 'apprenticed' out of a London work-house to a northern cotton mill. It was a horrifying tale of ill-usage. The children had had to adapt their actions to the pace of the machines; any boy who was too slow, and held things up, was savagely beaten. Accidents were common; and when one of Blincoe's fingers got crushed in a machine, he was not allowed to stop working. If the children's hair grew verminous, it was treated by pitch-capping—a technique in common use at the time by the forces in Ireland, as a means of intimidating rebels; hot pitch was put on the scalp, allowed to set, and then jerked off, removing the lice with the hair. On one occasion a sadistic overseer had hung Blincoe above a machine so that he had to lift his leg, to avoid losing it, every time the machine turned. The compiler of the memoir, John Brown, was no longer alive; but he had been able before his death to find a couple of other children who had been in the same mills as Blincoe, and who testified to the accuracy of his account; and although the shift of mills to factory towns, and the diminishing use made of pauper apprentices, had changed conditions in the mills, enough evidence of ill-usage and brutality was provided in the Sadler evidence for people to wonder whether there might not still be Blincoes suffering in silence.

The combination of the memoir and the Sadler evidence provided the Short Time movement with just what they needed to stir up feeling in the West Riding against the manufacturers; and with the Reform bill through, ministers would no longer have the excuse to delay taking action. Here, then, was Sadler's opportunity. But it came too late for him to exploit. As a member for one of the nomination boroughs which Reform had swept away, he had to look for a new constituency; and although there were several where the Tories would have welcomed him as their candidate, his choice was rash—Leeds, one of the strongholds of the new middle-class Whigs, who preferred to be called Liberals. It had two seats to be filled; and one of the two Liberals standing against him was his old adversary, Macaulay—who owed his invitation to stand for Parliament to the delight with which an influential peer had read his scathing criticism of James Mill and the utilitarians in the *Edinburgh Review*. Macaulay realised that few of the Leeds workers—vociferous though they might be in favour of the Ten Hours campaign, and consequently in favour of Sadler, Tory though he was—had votes; and the electors could be made nervous about anybody who threatened to interfere with the rights of factory owners. 'Without the slightest hesitation', he told them at an election meeting, 'I venture to declare that I am a fitter object for the choice of this great community than one who had laboured to deprive that great body of their privileges. You will not be deceived by the profession of a convenient philanthropist! Gentlemen, we have heard—you have heard—of a certain wild beast called the Hyena who, when it wishes to decoy the unwary into its den, has a singular knack of imitating the cries of little children . . .' The 4,000 electors of Leeds (out of a population of close to 100,000) took the point: Macaulay and his colleague were elected, and Sadler was out of Parliament.

With the Liberals in the ascendant, there was no immediate prospect that another, safer, constituency would be found for Sadler; and he had left no obvious successor—a serious matter for the Short Time campaigners, as they needed to exploit the sympathy that had been aroused by the publication of the evidence given to the Commons' committee. It was not even clear from which political party, or group, he should be chosen. The affinities of the Short Time campaigners were with radicalism; and by this time, Oastler and Sadler were becoming accustomed to hear the epithet radical applied to them. When Baines had tired of printing Oastler's frenetic letters in the *Mercury*, Oastler had found them welcomed not only by his old antagonist, the *Leeds Intelligencer*, but also by the radical Leeds *Patriot*. As for Sadler, 'What am I now?' he had asked a friend on the day the Reform Bill became law, 'a Tory? No. A Whig? No, no, no! I don't know . . . every man will have to raise his hand to his face before he can call his nose his own.' They might have raised no objection, if a suitable radical had been found at Westminster; but suitable radicals proved elusive. Hunt had lost his seat; Hobhouse and Burdett were too half-hearted; Hume, hostile. The only possibilities were two newcomers to Parliament, both elected for Oldham. John Fielden would, in many ways, have been ideal, with his experience both as mill-hand and employer; but he was a Lancashire man; Short Time had been very much a Yorkshire campaign. The other new M.P., though far better known, was even less suitable; Cobbett.

In their political philosophies, admittedly, Cobbett, Oastler and Sadler had much in common. But Cobbett was in his seventieth year; and he was still largely identified with the problems of the country ('A FARMER ', he assured the readers of the *Register*, 'I WILL LIVE AND DIE'). His continuing faith in Cartwright's programme for electoral reform did not commend him to Sadler and Oastler; nor did his methods. When the new session of Parliament opened he took his seat among the ministers on the Treasury Bench—leaving it only for the Opposition front bench opposite, much to the discomfiture of Peel, who found Cobbett sitting next to him. From Cobbett's point of view, there might be method in his eccentricity; he took his duty to his electors more seriously than his duty to the Commons. But the Commons predictably replied by refusing to take him seriously. 'It seems to be put beyond doubt', Creevey was soon to report, 'that Cobbett can do nothing. His voice and manner of speaking are tiresome, in addition to which his language is blackguard beyond anything ever heard of.' The Short Time campaigners might welcome his support, but they did not consider him when they came to choose a parliamentary spokesman.

As there was no obvious successor to Sadler, a meeting was held of representatives of Short Time committees from a number of Yorkshire towns to discuss the matter; and it was decided to send somebody to take soundings in and around Westminster. The choice fell on the man who happened to be secretary at the meeting—George Bull. Bull had originally joined the campaign because he believed that people, and particularly children, needed to have leisure 'to reflect, to improve their minds, to instruct their families, and to worship their God'; but he also, which at that time was unusual, felt that the campaign was important for the Church, which he wanted to become Christ-like again; 'she must be cleaned, and that promptly, from her real abuses, or she must fall, and no one can save her. Let her be made the Poor Man's Church, and then the God of the Poor will bless us.' That he was the chosen emissary helped to explain why a young, deeply religious evangelical Tory was approached to become Sadler's successor: Lord Ashley, heir to the earldom of Shaftesbury.

'Most disgraceful to the nation'

Ashley had refused to serve under Canning, on the ground that 'no one would be Prime Minister of this great country, unless deeply imbued with religion'; but while still in his twenties he had accepted office under Wellington, as a Commissioner of the India Board of Control. He had thereupon embarked on his first task, in what was to be a lifetime of philanthropic endeavour: a scheme to make better provision for pauper lunatics. He had made a favourable impression in the Commons for his obvious integrity and dedication—as well as for 'those manly good looks', as his friend Lord Granville described them, 'and that striking presence which, I believe, help a man more than we sometimes think'. He was, however, a diffident and often inaudible debater; and so much of his time was devoted to good works that it was hard to take him seriously as a politician.

While Ashley was at the India Board, he found that it left him, as such posts usually did, with some patronage at his disposal; and true to his principles he decided that instead of offering any jobs which became available to a relation, or friend, he would seek out some genuinely worthy recipient. His choice fell upon the Poet Laureate; he wrote to ask Southey whether he had a son, or nephew, who would like to find employment in the East India Company. He did not even know Southey at the time; the offer was made as '*due* to a man who has done so much by his writings to extend the knowledge of true philosophy, and impress upon the world the consolation and practice of Religion'. Southey had, in fact, a nephew of suitable age for such advancement; and the offer also began an epistolary friendship in which he from time to time gently prodded Ashley to espouse the cause of factory children. If their condition were not improved 'physically, morally and religiously', Southey felt, 'we shall be in more danger from them than the West Indian planters are from their slaves'.

After Sadler's defeat in the 1832 election, Southey returned to the subject. 'Those who grow cotton', he wrote to Ashley, 'are merciful in comparison with those who manufacture it'; and he cited as an example the attitude of Macaulay's fellow M.P. for Leeds, who had explained that the reason children in his mills looked delicate was because the 'flew' in the air rendered them consumptive: 'he spoke of this with as little compunction', Southey complained, 'as a general would calculate the probable consumption of lives in a campaign'. The cruelty in mills, he reiterated, might not be so excessive as in a slave plantation, 'but it is more unmitigated; the system is more uniformly and incorrigibly evil'.

Ashley agreed. He had read in *The Times* some of the extracts from the Sadler committee's minutes of evidence, which had left him 'astonished and disgusted'; and when he heard of Sadler's defeat, he had written to him offering his services 'in presenting petitions or doing any other small work that the cause might require'. George Bull came to see him, sized him up, and told him it would not be small work that would be required of him; he was to take Sadler's place. When Ashley asked for some time to reflect, Bull told him that he must make up his mind at once. The Short Time campaigners had heard that, as they had feared, a rival bill was being prepared by Lord Morpeth; and Morpeth, though a sympathiser with the movement to control the employment of children in factories, was not a Ten Hours supporter. After seeking guidance through 'meditation, and prayer, and "divination" (as it were) by the word of God', Ashley agreed to take up the cause.

Early in March 1833 Ashley introduced a bill along the same lines as Sadler's, though increasing some of the penalties. As no provision was made in the bill for inspection, it could have been argued that the measure was likely to suffer the fate of earlier factory legislation; but there was one substantial difference. Assuming that the mill-owners were right, and that adults could not work longer hours than were permitted to the children, it would be obviously easier for the adults to ensure that the regulations were obeyed—if they wanted to.

But would they want to? The mill-owners insisted that it was often the adults who compelled the children to work longer hours, to increase their earnings. But any doubts whether the adult workers really desired the Ten Hours limitation were quickly removed. Irritated to hear about Ashley's bill, Morpeth decided that he would proceed with his own measure—only to find that he could muster no support for it. *The Times* jeered at 'his—or rather the masters'—bill'; the masters were divided on whether they wanted the bill at all; and among the workers, Morpeth found himself the object of execration—'the sleek and oily Morpeth like Judas enters,' Oastler wrote, 'supported like his great and wicked prototype by bands of murderers (mill-owners), and would betray the infant's sacred cause—like Judas, with a kiss'. Reports from the north soon showed that this was not just Oastler's view; the Ten Hours campaign was gaining strength.

It was also beginning to pick up support in London. Ashley was introduced as the new parliamentary leader of the movement at a meeting of the London Society for the Improvement of the Condition of Factory Children, with the Lord Mayor presiding, and with contributions by speakers as diverse as Daniel O'Connell, Robert Owen and Colonel Robert Torrens. Torrens had formally announced his adherence to Sadler's cause in a letter to the *Bolton Chronicle* in January 1833; it had become imperative, he felt, for Parliament to intervene to reduce working hours 'to save the infant labourer from the cruel oppression of excessive labour'. And Torrens was not the only political economist to give his adherence. At the end of March, McCulloch wrote to Ashley to express the hope that his cause would prosper. 'A motion is entertained', he wrote, that political economists are, in all cases, enemies to all sorts of interference, but I assure you that I am not one of those who entertain such an opinion. I would not interfere between adults and masters; but it is absurd to contend that children have the power to judge for themselves as to such a matter. I look upon the facts disclosed in the late report as most disgraceful to the nation and I confess that, until I read it, I could not have conceived it possible that such enormities were permitted . . . if your bill has any defect, it is not by the too great limitation, but by the too great extension of the hours of labour.

Ministers began to grow uneasy. They had hoped to watch the progress of a bill brought in by a respectable Whig—Morpeth—with much the same detachment as their predecessors had been able to watch the earlier Hobhouse measure. It might not achieve much, but it would give little trouble, and would help to damp down unrest in the north. Now, feeling in the Commons, still influenced by the Sadler committee revelations, appeared likely to favour Ashley's measure,—involving State regulation of working hours. Yet to oppose it might bring them unpopularity. They would certainly be held up to execration for being more generous to slaves than to children . . .

'Ne'er be still, ne'er be still'

At this point, however, ministers were rescued by a mill-owner M.P., Wilson Patten. A few days after Ashley introduced his bill, Patten presented petitions from some northern industrialists asking for a further committee on the factory bill, 'for the purpose of clearing the characters of the masters from those imputations which seemed to be cast upon them by the friends of this measure, but which further evidence would prove to be utterly unjustifiable'. When Ashley suggested that this was merely a delaying device, Patten was able to reply that Sadler's committee had not heard evidence from the masters; and that, surely, was unfair. The Government, grateful for the respite, accepted Patten's proposal: early in April, a motion was introduced proposing that a fresh enquiry should be held into the conditions in which children were employed in factories; and although several speakers complained that this was only a device to ensure further delay, the Commons passed it, by a single vote.

The method which was to be used to investigate the subject, however, was different; not a select committee, but a royal commission—on the same principle, though on a smaller scale, to the one which was investigating the poor laws. Again, this had the advantage that the Government was able to handpick the commissioners; and when, on April 19, the names of the three men chosen were announced, the worst fears of the Ten Hours campaigners appeared to be confirmed. Thomas Tooke had been Ricardo's close friend—a 'very useful and able ally', Ricardo called him; it was at his suggestion that the Political Economy Club had originally been formed. Edwin Chadwick, a young barrister, had been Bentham's secretary; a protégé of Nassau Senior's, he was also Secretary to the Royal Commission on the poor laws. As for Southwood Smith, he had been Bentham's closest friend, chosen when he died in 1832 to make the funeral oration; Bentham had even left his corpse to him for medical research.

Southwood Smith, too, had shortly before won an unenviable reputation for callousness. He had campaigned against the quarantine laws, much to the satisfaction of the manufacturers (and thereby—it was hinted—perhaps helped to let in the cholera); he had also demonstrated his insensitivity to the feelings of the poor by urging that teaching hospitals should be given the bodies not merely of executed criminals, for medical students to dissect, but also of workhouse inmates, unless relatives claimed them. In a period when there was an obsession among the poor about the need for decent interment, whatever the expense (burial societies did much better than companies which offered insurance policies designed to give the poor something in their lifetime) the attempt to link paupers with criminals sounded repellent; and, unluckily for Southwood Smith, this was the time in which the activities of the 'resurrectionists', Burke and Hare, came to light. Medical schools fell under the suspicion of having encouraged the gruesome trade; and some of the obloquy brushed off on to him.

Southwood Smith was, in fact, very far from callous. That utilitarianism took the course it later followed, towards scientific philanthropy, was to be largely his doing. But at the time, the prevailing view of him and his fellow utilitarians was expressed by the radical barrister-journalist, George Condy, in *Fraser's Magazine*: that they 'had no idea of people except as tax-producing and money-gathering animals of the unplumed bi-ped species'—and in Wordsworth's poem *To the Utilitarians*, not published till over half a century later, but written in 1833:

> Avaunt the Economic rage!
> What would it bring? An iron age
> When fact, with heartless search explored,
> Shall be Imagination's Lord
> And sway with absolute control
> The god-like functions of the soul
> Not thus can knowledge elevate
> Our nature from its fallen state . . .

In the north, political economy was identified with the version accepted by industrialists, though they regarded themselves as orthodox, they were really only appropriating as much of orthodoxy as they required for their own purposes. 'They have learned a few words of French,' John Wilson remarked in *Blackwood's*; 'and each parrot from his perch, as he keeps swinging himself to and fro, in his glittering cage, ejaculates *"Laissez nous faire"*!' In the circumstances, it was inevitable that the membership of the commission, when it was announced, should have excited anger. 'Here are three Government hirelings and their secretary', an anonymous pamphleteer introduced them, 'with most philosophical coolness, sitting in judgment upon a cruel, murderous system—the criminal party whispering in their ears, and guiding their pens all the while.' Condy agreed: the commissioners, he claimed, had been chosen 'because of their supposed indifference to the questions of infant suffering, and their great capacity for political calculation, without any liability to any misgivings on the score of human kindness'.

Although it was certainly true that the commissioners were not the men to allow sentiment to affect their judgment, the reaction was unjustified. They might all be adherents of political economy, but their version of it was not *laissez nous faire*. They were genuinely anxious to elicit the facts about the employment of children in factories; questionnaires were despatched to magistrates, doctors and clergy, as well as to mill-owners and workers; and assistant commissioners were sent to all the industrial areas to gather the information required at first hand. And as individuals, they were far from indifferent to questions of infant suffering.

Still, appearances were certainly against them. Had there been even one member of the commission known to be sympathetic to the Ten Hours movement—or at least known not to be hostile to it—the assistant commissioners might have been accorded a different reception on their round of visits; but as it was, they met with a virtual boycott from the workers. Wherever they went, hostile demonstrations were held, organised by the Short Time committees. In Leeds, the children working in the mills came out to demonstrate, and to sing Condy's *Song of the Factory Children*:

> We will have the Ten Hours Bill
> That we will, that we will;
> Or the land shall ne'er be still,
> Ne'er be still, ne'er be still;
> Parliament say what they will
> WE WILL HAVE THE TEN HOURS BILL.

Almost the only assistance the Commissioners received from the Short Time campaigners, in fact, was a brochure, *The Commissioners' Vade-mecum*, ostensibly giving them guidance on how to proceed. They should tip the postillion extra to drive them into towns by a back route, the writer advised, and not to say who they were: 'if you come by coach, book yourself by false names . . . by the by, have you all made your wills?' Thomas Chalmers, who happened to be on a visit to England at the time, was to confirm that this question was not merely facetious. From the window of his hotel room in Huddersfield, he listened to Oastler whipping up hatred of the commissioners, and watched them being burned in effigy: 'the figures were fearfully like men; and being now dark, the conflagration lighted up the whole square, and revealed the faces of the yelling myriads' —the spectacle leading Chalmers to fear that the demonstration was 'fitted to prepare the actors for burning the originals instead of the copies'.

The fact that the visits of the assistant commissioners were mapped out in advance was itself taken as an indication that the whole enquiry was a put-up job. Bull had warned the Sadler Committee that inspection would always be useless if the date and time were known beforehand; the mill would be cleaned up, the children told to come in their best pinafores. Sadler now echoed this criticism, adding that manufacturers who had been remiss about sanitation or safety were being given the opportunity to improve their premises before they were inspected. There would be no occasion, *The Commissioners' Vade-mecum* suggested, for the commissioners to be very particular about asking a mill-owner how recently he had installed certain improvements 'such as boxing off machinery—removing cripples—ventilation—cleaning—the speed of the engine. All they need do was ask some of the men, "I suppose all things are going on in the usual way?" "Oh yes, sir!" "You swear that?" "Oh yes, and anything else you please, sir."'

If the Short Time campaigners had required further evidence that their suspicions were justified, the members of the commission proceeded gratuitously to provide it. Spies, set to watch them on their tours, were able to reveal not merely that they regularly lunched and dined with the owners of the mill which they were inspecting, but on occasion were actually entertained by the mill-owners as weekend guests. And what appeared to be the conclusive proof that the commission was no more than a Government trick was given by the haste with which its investigation was terminated. The reason was obvious: the Ten Hours bill was due to come up in the Commons in June, and ministers knew that they must have the report ready for use against it. As things turned out, the report was not quite ready; but when Althorp promised that it would be, before the end of the month, the Commons allowed themselves to be persuaded to defer consideration of Ashley's bill until it appeared.

When it came up, the report could immediately be seen to represent— in some respects, at least—a decided improvement on the reports of the earlier select committees. In spite of the difficulties under which they had worked, the assistant commissioners had collected a mass of first-hand evidence of a kind that had not been available to Peel, or to Sadler; and there was also detailed statistical information. For example, there were figures for the age and sex, and wages, of workers in a group of Lancashire cotton mills.

	Male workers		Female workers	
Ages	Numbers	Wages	Numbers	Wages
Below 11	246	2s. 3d.	155	2s. 5d.
11–16	1,169	4s. 2d.	1,123	4s. 3d.
16–21	736	10s. 2d.	1,240	7s. 3d.
Over 21	1,629		1,326	

Out of every four factory workers, in other words, only one was an adult male; and it was admitted that in other types of factory—in mills making silk, for example—the proportion of juvenile workers was considerably higher.

The figures for adult wages were not included because they varied according to the nature of the work; but the evidence showed that they ordinarily amounted to between fifteen and twenty-five shillings a week— roughly twice as much as unskilled labourers got, and enough to provide a fair standard of living, for the time. But from this wage, various deductions could be made. The worker might be expected to provide his own tools; there were fines, for lateness and errors; and in some areas, there was 'truck' —part of the wages were paid in the form of vouchers which could be exchanged only at a shop which the employer ran, or had an interest in. At New Lanark, the system had been used to provide the worker with better quality goods, cheaper than he could get them locally; but most employers regarded it simply as a useful way of making money on the side. Truck, or 'tommy', had come to be synonymous with extortion; and an Act designed to control it, passed not long before, had proved a failure. The figures on wages which the evidence provided were not, therefore, a wholly trustworthy indication of the amounts the worker took home.

The assistant commissioners, though, were able to provide a few representative family budgets, which were more revealing. One was for a family of a Manchester cotton spinner. As the eldest daughter was fourteen, she was old enough to work as her father's 'piecer'; thus saving him having to pay four and sixpence to another child; he could bring back twenty-five shillings a week to his wife. Twenty-five shillings a week was an income beyond the dreams of a handloom weaver, or a labourer; yet, the budget, when broken down, revealed a sparse enough existence. The chief item of expenditure, four and sixpence, was for bread, which the housewife made herself. The family ate fresh meat—one pound between them—only on Sunday; for the rest of the week, a pound and a half of bacon had to suffice. Each week they consumed half a gallon of oatmeal, a pound and a half of sugar, a pound and a half of butter, an ounce and a half of tea, and a couple of score potatoes—no other vegetables. Then there was the rent, and coal, and candles; education (threepence a week for each child to be taught reading, though not writing); insurance (one penny a week for each child—to a funeral society); and sundries. As a result, although the family home had four rooms—the conventional two up, two down,—they could not afford to furnish them properly; they had only two beds, one table, and four chairs; no cupboards, no chest of drawers.

Still, the family lived in relative affluence, considering how many agricultural labourers received seven shillings—and how many handloom weavers received less—for a week's work. Besides, another factory worker to whom the assistant commissioner had spoken had been inclined to think that the family were, if anything, living a little below the usual standard; most families thus circumstanced, he thought, would have fresh meat more often. But—the factory worker had added—there were two classes of family: 'those in which the parents work in mills as well as the children, and those in which only the children work in mills'. The first class, he said pointedly, 'live better than the second'.

So the evidence provided for the commission stopped just short of the stage at which it would have been really revealing about how the poor fared in industrial areas. It showed the income of a family in the first class, where the father had a job; what it did not show was the proportion of first to second-class families: the number, in other words, of children working in the mills who were providing a small though welcome addition to the family income, as compared to the number who were the family breadwinners. Nor did it give any indication of the effects of trade fluctuations —of what proportion of workers suffered a severe reduction of income or lost their jobs during recessions. Such calculations were not within the commission's terms of reference. It was concerned only with the conditions under which factory children worked; not with how they fared when they, or their parents, could not find work.

'To beat her till she screamed again'
The main purpose of the commission, though, had been to establish whether or not the evidence given to the Sadler committee, and subsequently published, was as one-sided and unfair as some manufacturers had claimed. A surprise was in store for those Short Time campaigners who had predicted that the report would be a coat of whitewash. Broadly speaking, the evidence collected by the commission on the conditions in which factory children worked was a repetition, and a confirmation, of Sadler's.

In some ways, the picture that the report presented was even uglier. One of the main criticisms of the Sadler investigation, for example, had been that its attention had been directed exclusively to children working in factories. What about children who were employed in small workshops, in Birmingham, and other industrial towns in which the factory was not yet dominant? Might not they be even worse treated? The commission had investigated, and found that working hours for children other than those employed in mills, were ordinarily much shorter—usually not more than nine a day. In mills, the working day was from twelve to twelve and a half hours, 'while in several districts they are not less than thirteen'; and there were various excuses which employers could use to make the children work still longer. Where a shorter day was worked by agreement on Saturday, the hours lost might have to be made up during the week. To regain time lost by stoppages—through the breaking of machinery, say, or inadequate water power during a drought—it was the custom 'to work sometimes half an hour, at other times an hour, and occasionally even as much as two hours daily, until the whole of the lost time be made up'. When the children did not have to clean the machinery during their mealbreaks, they had to clean it out of their working hours. And when local custom dictated that a day should be observed as a holiday, the adult workers were given the option of making up the time, or having the pay deducted from their wages; 'generally they choose the former'. The children, in such circumstances, were not consulted. They had to work the longer hours, too.

Some of these excuses to increase working hours were legal; the concession in the event of drought had been granted to stop steam-powered mills gaining what seemed to be an unfair advantage over their older competitors. But legality, the evidence showed—even more clearly than Sadler's—was not an important consideration to the mill-owners. The provisions of earlier Factory Acts had simply been disregarded. In any case, they applied only to cotton mills; and in other factories, hours and conditions of work for children were at the whim of the owner, or his manager. 'We have forty-five children', the overseer of a Nottingham factory had told one of the assistant commissioners.

> Our regular day is from six to seven. It should be an hour for dinner, but it is only half an hour. No time allowed for tea or breakfast; there used to be a quarter of an hour for breakfast; it is altered now. We call it twelve hours a day. Overtime is paid for extra. When we're busy we work over-hours. Our present time is still half past nine (beginning at six). It has been so all the winter, and since to this time. We have some very young ones, as young as eight . . .

Such conditions, the evidence showed, were not exceptional. An assistant commissioner reported a case he had found:

> Worked all night (I found her working at a quarter before six); worked from a quarter before six yesterday morn; will work till six this evening; thirty-four hours, exclusive of two hours for meals; did this because the hands were short, and she could gain an additional shilling.

In other cases, the children spoke for themselves:

> 'Have worked here two years; I am now fourteen; work sixteen hours and a half a day. I was badly, and asked to stop at eight one night lately, and I was told if I went I must not come back.'

> 'I have worked till twelve at night last summer. We began at six in the morning. I told the book keeper I did not like to work so late, and he said I must. We only get a penny an hour for overtime.'

The regulations governing meal breaks had also been generally ignored. Time allowed for meals varied, but—the commission found—it was generally less than an hour; in Leeds, 'they sometimes stop half an hour for breakfast, one hour for dinner, and half an hour for drinking; but this is very unusual. It is seldom that they stop more than forty minutes for dinner, and often not at all for breakfast or drinking.' In some factories, it was pretty evident that practices had been resorted to, to cheat the work-people of a portion of their meal hours—by tampering with the factory clock, for example, a practice which 'cannot be too strongly reprobated'.

Occasionally, too, 'the work continues without intermission during the whole of the meal hours; the engine never stopping excepting about ten minutes to be oiled, and the workpeople "eating how they can".' The report quoted several examples given by children of how they fared, in such conditions:

'Did not stop for meals; used to eat how we could . . .'

'Never stop to take our meals except at dinner; has gone on so this six years and more . . .'

'Sometimes the breakfast would stand an hour and a half; sometimes we'd never touch it. Many a time I've brought mine our and never touched it because I hadn't time. All in my room would rather stop, because the breakfast had got so covered with lint . . .'

'No time for breakfast or tea; took it as they could, a bite and a run; sometimes not able to eat it from its being so covered with dust.'

As the report pointed out, eating 'how they could' was not necessarily imposed by the management; if adult workers preferred it that way, so that they could earn more, the children also had to have it that way.

On ill-treatment of factory children, too, the evidence given to the commission confirmed that given to the Sadler committee. The mill-owners had denied that the strap was as freely used for disciplinary purposes as had been suggested; but the commission's investigators heard many stories of harsh punishments.

'When she was a child too little to put on her own clothes, the overlooker used to beat her till she screamed again . . .'

'The boys are often severely strapped; the girls sometimes get a clout.'

'Has often seen the workers beat cruelly. Has seen the girls strapped; but the boys were beat so that they fell to the floor in the course of the beating, with a rope with four tails, called a cat.'

'The boys were very badly used. They are whipped with a strap until they cry out.'

'The other night a little girl came home cruelly beaten; wished to go before a magistrate, but was advised not.'

Such an existence, the commissioners felt, could not but produce evil effects. The regular hours were excessively long, and the irregular additional hours deplorable: 'to the young persons, and especially to the young female workers, this extra labour is often extremely irksome and harassing; and the younger the age, the more injurious the consequences'. There was admittedly less evidence of deformity resulting from factory work than in earlier enquiries: this, Althorp was later to explain, could be attributed to better-designed machinery. And the medical evidence to the commission on the whole painted a less gloomy picture than had been given to the Sadler committee. Still, the commissioners were in no doubt that the long hours could seriously impair the children's health, sometimes leading to 'serious, permanent and incurable disease'. The children's minds also suffered, as even where education was provided, they were too fatigued to benefit from it.

'It does not protect children'

There could be no question; Sadler had been vindicated—and the vindication was all the more impressive in that it came from a source which could not conceivably be suspected of bias against the factory owners. But the fact that the evidence was, in general, the same as Sadler's did not necessarily mean that the commissioners would place the same interpretation on it. Although his committee had not been able to make a report, he had shown—by continuing to identify himself with the Short Time campaign—that he believed the evidence had confirmed the case for a general limitation of factory working hours to ten a day. The commissioners in their report disagreed; they not merely derided the Ten Hours bill, but went out of their way to cast doubt on the sincerity of those who supported it; 'we should not feel ourselves warranted in suppressing our conviction that the interests of the children, which alone supply materials for popular excitement on the subject of the proposed measure, are that which appears least to enter into the counsels of the operative agitators for that measure'.

The way in which the commissioners had reached this conclusion was ingenious. The evidence, they conceded, revealed a disgraceful state of affairs in some factories; but this did not necessarily mean that there was anything wrong with the factory *system*. For one thing, the worst conditions were almost invariably found in the smaller mills (a point which had also been made clear in the Sadler evidence). And even in them, it was not necessarily, or even usually, the mill-owners who were responsible. The long hours, the working meal breaks, the punishments, were often imposed by the adult workers, trying to increase their earnings.

This revelation, however—though it acquitted the mill-owners of some of the responsibility—would not in itself have been sufficient to refute the argument of the Short Time campaigners. A Ten Hours Act, if enforced, would effectively control the adult workers' rapacity. So the commissioners in their report concentrated on another aspect of the evidence:

> We have been struck with the perfect uniformity of the answers returned to the commissioners by the young workers in the country, in the largest and best regulated factories as well as in the smaller and less advantageously conducted. In fact, whether the factory be in the pure air of the country, or in the large town; under the best or the worst management; and whatever the nature of the work, whether light or laborious; or the kind of treatment, whether considerate and gentle, or strict and harsh; the account of the child, when questioned as to its feeling of fatigue, is the same. The answer is always 'sick-tired, especially in the winter nights'; 'so tired when she leaves the mill that she can do nothing'; 'often much tired, and feels sore, standing so long on her legs'; 'often so tired she could not eat her supper'.

Numerous illustrative examples were given in the report. 'Many a time', one child had told an assistant commissioner, 'I have been so fatigued I could hardly take off my clothes at night, or put them on in the morning. My mother would be raging at me, because when I sat down I could not get up again.' And an overseer described how he had actually seen children fall asleep, after the machine had stopped, when their work was over. 'I have stopped and looked at them for two minutes, going through the motions of piecening, fast asleep, when there was really no work to do, and they were doing nothing.'

At first glance, it might appear that the commissioners were doing no more than reiterate, even more forcibly, a point which had emerged from every earlier factory enquiry. But the emphasis was designed to serve a particular purpose. There was little the matter with the factories, their implication was, which could not be put right by a single, simple reform: an enforced limitation on the hours which young children could work.

The long hours—they were in effect saying—were not only objectionable in themselves; they were also responsible for the other objectionable features of factory life—for example, the brutality. As it happened, a number of witnesses had emphasised to the Sadler committee that most of the punishments in the mills arose from this cause; Bull had said that children told him they were usually strapped at the end of the day 'when they get tired and fatigued, and cannot work so well'. But this was not remembered; the impression left by the Sadler evidence had been almost of brutality for brutality's sake. Now, the commissioners insisted that if the hours were reduced, the need for the strap would disappear; and case after case was cited to prove the point. 'I used to beat them,' a former mill hand told an investigator, 'I am sure that no man can do without it who works long hours; I am sure he cannot. The master expected me to do my work, and I could not do mine unless they did theirs.' An overseer described how, very often, at the end of the day, the children

> were nearly ready to faint; some were asleep; some were only kept to work by being spoken to, or by a little chastisement, to make them jump up. I was sometimes obliged to chastise them when they were almost fainting, and it hurts my feelings; but the last two or three hours were my hardest work, for they then got so exhausted.

'I have known children', another witness said, 'hide themselves in the stove among the wood when the work was over, so that they should not go home when the work was over . . . I have seen six or eight children fetched out of the stove, and beat home; beat out of the mill, at least. I do not know why they should hide themselves unless they were too tired to go home.'

The children would not be so tired, the commissioners argued, if they did not have to endure the full adult working day. With shorter hours, there would be no need to take the strap to them, except for flagrant indiscipline. With shorter hours, too, they could get out into the open before and after work; their twisted bodies would unwind, their lungs fill with fresh air. They would be able to attend school, without falling asleep over their lessons. And limiting children's hours of work would leave employers and adult workers free to fix their own terms, without the State interfering—except, perhaps on such matters as factory sanitation, and safety precautions; but they were side issues. All that was needed, in short, was acceptance by the Government and the manufacturers that, as children were not free agents, their working hours must be regulated; and that would be the end of the Short Time campaign.

On this basis, the Commission put forward its formal findings.

> 1st That the children employed in all the principal branches of manufacture throughout the Kingdom work the same number of hours as the adults.

> 2nd That the effects of labour during such hours are, in a great number of cases:

> Permanent deterioration of the physical constitution. The production of disease often wholly irremediable. The partial or entire exclusion (by reason of excessive fatigue) from the means of obtaining adequate education and acquiring useful habits, or of profiting by those means when afforded.

3rd That at the age when children suffer these injuries from the labour they undergo, they are not free agents, but are let out to hire, the wages they earn being received and appropriated by their parents and guardians.

We are therefore of the opinion that a case is made out for the interference of the legislature on behalf of the children employed in factories.

It remained only to suggest the form the interference should take. Children under nine years of age, the report suggested, should not be employed in factories; and from then on until their fourteenth year, their working day should be limited to eight hours, during the period between five in the morning and ten at night. At puberty, however, 'the body becomes more capable of enduring protracted labour'; and for this and other reasons, the fourteenth birthday should be accepted as the natural period when young persons could be placed on the same footing as adults.

To avoid dislocation in industry, the commissioners suggested a shift system should be instituted for children. Admittedly, some manufacturers had insisted this was impracticable, and impossible: 'we find, however, in the course of our enquiry, that the words "impracticable" and "impossible" are too commonly attached by many of the manufacturers to any regulation which may subject them to expense or to temporary inconvenience'. Whatever the expense, or the inconvenience, the commissioners concluded, there was no other solution. The convenience of employers could not be allowed to outweigh 'the enormous evil, at present existing, of excessive labour imposed during the period of childhood, and permanent injury thereby entailed on so large a class of the population'.

The employers might get away with this gentle chiding: not so the Short Time campaigners, whose Ten Hours bill came in for another denunciation: 'Its professed object is the protection of children; but it does not protect children. For the same evidence which shows that the legislative protection of children is necessary shows that the restriction of the labour of children to ten hours a day is not an adequate protection.' All that the Ashley bill would lead to, if enacted and enforced, would be a reduction of hours for adults, ultimately resulting in a general reduction of profits and wages, to the detriment of industry and commerce, of the workers themselves, and of the country.

The commissioners clearly had a case. Although the Ten Hours bill was ostensibly designed to protect factory children, and although many members of the public might assume that was its only purpose, the Short Time campaigners by this time were well aware of the advantage it would also bring to adult workers—or so, at least, they were hoping. But what the commissioners did not mention was why the campaign had taken that form. From the time of the debates on Peel's bill, fifteen years before, the manufacturers had steadfastly opposed any reduction of the hours worked by children, on the ground that adults would necessarily be restricted to the same working day. If the children stopped, the argument ran, the machines had to stop too. All that the Short Time campaigners had done, therefore, was to take the employers at their word. Assuming that the hours of both adults and children would have to continue to be the same, they had settled on ten hours a day as an acceptable compromise. If this was deception, they could reasonably claim that the employers had taught it to them. But the commissioners did not concede them this point.

The commissioners' interpretation of the evidence, too, impressively dispassionate though it appeared, was not free from the bias of their pre-conceptions. For the report, they had selected whatever evidence would help to justify their thesis that the factory problem could be solved without doing violence to the principles of political economy. But the report's bland assumption that so long as children were protected, adults could look after themselves, was hardly borne out by a study of the evidence as a whole. Little direct attention had been paid in collecting it to adult working hours and conditions, but enough indirect information had accumulated to suggest that if children were in need of protection, so were women. As an M.P. was later to point out, the medical view at the time was that although for boys puberty might be held to mark the period at which they were fit to do a man's work, women at that stage could reasonably be said to be at their most delicate. And as the majority of factory workers were female, the possibility of making differentiation between the sexes ought at least to have been considered in the report.

The evidence had also given some indication of the hardship suffered by the wives of unemployed or underpaid workers, forced to go into the mills for far lower wages than men doing similar work; and by expectant mothers, who were compelled to work up to the day, even up to the hour, of their confinement. But the commission did not need to bring these to Parliament's attention; they were not directly in its terms of reference. And the commissioners were doubtless relieved not to have to consider the position of women. Spinsters were free agents; wives were their husband's property; political economy dictated that even with the best of intentions, the State ought not to try to intervene on their behalf.

'Infants' blood has been sold for nought'

These were not, however, the kind of limitations that were likely to worry the Government. To ministers, the factory commission's report represented what was almost the perfect answer to their requirements. On the one hand, it presented proposals which could be introduced with the minimum of State intervention in industry; bargaining between employers and adult workers would not be affected. On the other, they made Ashley's measure look hypocritical. The only immediate risk was that the report, worded as it was, might produce a violent reaction in the north; and for a time it threatened to do so. Apart from their resentment at the charge of hypocrisy, the Short Time campaigners at once realised what the passing of a measure based on the report's recommendations would mean; the removal of any meagre protection they, as adults, had enjoyed from the Factory Acts. It represented, they felt, an open invitation to the employer to work children in two eight-hour shifts—and make adults work a sixteen-hour day. The demonstrations held in the West Riding to signify disapproval of the report dwarfed their predecessors. On July 1 a meeting was called at Wibsey Low Moor, near Bradford, along the same lines as the York Castle affair, but far larger and better organised. 'Infants' blood has been sold for nought,' Oastler told the crowd, 'but if we are despised now, it shall be a question of blood in another sense'—the first intimation of violence impending, which led the Leeds *Intelligencer* to warn that the meeting showed 'a mighty physical power which may easily be called into adverse exercise'.

The slight delay before the Government announced its intentions, how-ever, was probably due less to ministers' alarm over what was happening in the West Riding—the threat of violence in the industrial north still left them unmoved, compared with the concern which they felt about country districts—than to traditional inertia, which they were finding hard to throw off. When Ashley proposed to proceed with his bill, Althorp temporised by suggesting that it should be referred to yet another select committee. The Commons were in no mood to allow such tactics to con-tinue. From the opening of the Reformed Parliament, for all the size of the Whig majority, ministers found things being made difficult for them; not so much by the Tory opposition—which under Peel's guidance was restrained, even co-operative—as by dissident Whigs, linking up with radicals and with O'Connell's Irish following. The proposal for a select committee was defeated—even Hume spoke against it; and the house prepared to proceed with Ashley's bill. The Government realised that it had no alternative but to present a bill of its own, based on the commission's recommendations.

Ministers, though, did not merely propose in their bill to forbid the employment in factories of children under nine, and restrict the working hours of children to forty-eight a week, as the commissioners had recommended. Aware they would be criticised for assuming that boys and girls became fully adult at fourteen, they added a further limitation: children between the ages of fourteen and eighteen would not be allowed to work more than sixty-nine hours a week. This at one stroke upset Tooke's and Chadwick's calculations; for if the working hours of children between those ages were limited, in all probability adult hours would perforce be restricted, too. It could no longer be claimed, though, that this would flout the principles of political economy; for by this time the divergence of views among the political economists had become apparent. Torrens told the Commons that of the two bills, he had a decided preference for Ashley's, precisely because it *would* limit adult hours—whereas the Government's, by encouraging the introduction of the shift system for children, would increase them. If workers were really free, he argued, the principle of free wage bargaining would hold: but they were not. The corn laws loaded the scales against them; and so long as the State discriminated against them, in that way, it must also protect them.

Ministers also had their first indication that their own bill was not going to please the employers, either. George Philips, who by this time had acquired a knighthood, could not accept the interpretations that had been put on the commission's report; it was well-known in Lancashire, he claimed, that delicate people were sent to work in factories *because* they were delicate, and in factories, they would be sure to be 'well-clothed and warm'. But what would happen to them if the Government's proposals were made law? Two-thirds of the country's exports would be affected; wages would have to be lowered; the consequences for the factory workers would be terrible. Torrens denied that there was any justification for such pessimism. England had so great an advantage over its foreign rivals in machinery that it could afford to compete with fewer workers—or with the same number of workers, and shorter hours of work. If the corn laws were only abolished, the ten hour limit could be imposed without any risk. The irrepressible Cobbett added that during his lifetime, he had heard the Navy described as England's bulwark against the foreigner; then, her commerce—her colonies—her banks. Now, it was being admitted 'that our great stay and bulwark was to be found in 300,000 little girls'—or, rather, in one eighth of that number, for it was being asserted that 'if those little girls worked two hours less per day, our manufacturing superiority would depart from us'.

But to the ordinary M.P. with little knowledge of factory conditions, the Government measure clearly offered the better protection for factory children. A ministerial amendment to Ashley's bill was carried by a substantial majority; and Ashley, withdrawing it, handed over responsibility for the care of the factory children to the Government.

On past performance, the Government might have been expected to allow modifications to the bill in committee, or by the Lords. But this, unlike the earlier factory bills, was Government-sponsored; and Althorp was to prove unexpectedly tough. A few exceptions were permitted: the silk trade was to continue to be allowed to employ children under nine; and lost working hours could still be made up—though with added time limited, for children, to one hour a day. The Lords also rejected a clause which would have given authority to establish schools—which meant that although the Act provided for the education of factory children, there were unlikely to be many schools in which they could obtain it. But Althorp, though admitting the measure might bring inconvenience— factory legislation of any kind, he felt, was likely to cause mischief— insisted that if it was agreed that children were not free agents, Parliament must give them protection. With this argument, he held out against all pleas for further amendment; and the bill went through substantially unchanged.

Even more important, as time was to show, was the fact that it included clauses designed to provide for effective enforcement, to spare the new measure from the ignominious fate of earlier Factory Acts. Four inspectors were to be appointed, and they were given remarkably wide powers. They could enter a factory at any time, to examine the prescribed register of hours worked by each child employed; they could examine witnesses under oath and levy fines for obstruction; they even had the power to imprison recalcitrant witnesses for contempt.

In ordinary circumstances, it would have seemed inconceivable that even the Reformed Parliament would have been prepared to permit such powers to be given to Government-appointed inspectors; yet the proposal was not seriously challenged. For this the mill-owners could only blame themselves. The evidence given both to the Sadler committee and the royal commission had shown how they had flouted Parliament's wishes in the past, by evading or ignoring successive Factory Acts. Few Members of Parliament had much sympathy with the mill-owners, and the revelations in the two sets of evidence were still fresh in their memory. There was also still a division among the mill-owners themselves—between those who, little though they might care for State interference, were anxious that any laws passed should be obeyed; and those who regarded it as their duty to resist State encroachment by any means. In its enquiries, the commission had naturally received more co-operation, and advice, from the former class of mill-owners—like Oastler's old friend Wood. They had emphasised that whatever the law might be, they would endeavour to keep it; but they explained that to have kept it in the past, when unscrupulous competitors were evading it with impunity, would have been to lose their business. It was consequently in their interest, they admitted, that the new Act, whatever its terms, should make adequate provision for inspection and enforcement. For this purpose, they had suggested, local officials should be given special powers to enforce those regulations which were 'not directly conducive to the immediate interests of masters or operatives'. But the commissioners had decided that it would not be easy for local officials to maintain their independence. They had recommended, instead, a centralised inspectorate; and, although this was not what the established mill-owners had wanted, it would have been difficult for them to object without leaving the impression that they wanted local inspectors only because local men would be easier to manipulate.

Poulett Thomson, on behalf of the Board of Trade, went far out of his way to reassure the mill-owners. When, for example, an amendment was proposed that those children who were old enough to work a twelve-hour day should at least be secured a break of an hour and a half for meals, he replied that if it were carried 'the hours of labour would be only ten and a half per day, and he was sure that was not the wish of the house'. Later, he was revealingly to sum up his attitude when he described the measure as 'an evil forced on the Government and the house'. He looked upon its operation as very doubtful indeed; but the public and the workers themselves had declared in favour of legislative intervention to control the hours of infant labour in the factories, and for the Government to leave the issue open, any longer, he feared, 'would be productive of the greatest possible evil to the trade itself, and to the public'. The Commons accepted this proposition; the Lords were not disposed to make difficulties; and on August 29, 1833, less than three weeks after it had been introduced, the factory bill became law. After over thirty years of half-hearted measures, with the guarantee of their own failure written into them, Parliament had suddenly accepted a bill which not merely went farther, in some respects, than the Short Time campaigners had attempted to go, but also provided machinery for enforcement which, potentially at least, was much more powerful than they had believed possible.

Still, although the measure had been taken out of their hands, they could claim most of the credit for it. The publication of the evidence given to the Sadler committee had been decisive; after it appeared, the Government could no longer continue to prevaricate. The established mill-owners had also played an important part; the hospitality which they had extended to members of the royal commission, in so far as it had helped them to convince the commissioners of the need for effective enforcement, had been well-directed, after all. And political economy had provided the final sanction. Melbourne, for example, had been sufficiently horrified by the Sadler committee revelations to surprise himself by offering to sponsor Ashley's bill in the Lords; yet, at the same time, he felt convinced that factory legislation of any kind was a futile exercise, because it attempted the impossible—State interference with economic laws. But the report of the royal commission, and the support for factory legislation given by Torrens and McCulloch, had provided reassurance that the principles of political economy were not being flouted—the justification which he, and Althorp, and many M.P.s of all parties had needed.

Even for Ashley himself, though the repudiation of his bill was a setback, there was the consolation—as Southey pointed out to him—that ministers had been compelled to do more for children than he could have ventured to ask. He should now direct his mind to other things; Southey knew, from his own experience, 'what effects are produced upon the health and happiness of those who suffer one great subject to take full possession of them'. Ashley took his advice, and went on a six months' tour of the Continent, spending Christmas in Rome, where he went to the Santa Maria Maggiore—'the church lighted up and decorated like a ballroom; full of people, and a bishop with a stout train of canons listening to the music, which was fine, but, as usual, precisely like an opera. In such rites as these, the soul has no share.' Oastler and the Ten Hours campaigners were denied the consolation of travel. They tried to organise a protest campaign against the new Act, but they were soon forced to realise it was not arousing the response they hoped for. The Government had been too clever for them; and the Short Time campaign died away—for a while.

2. TOLPUDDLE

No sooner was the Ten Hours campaign undermined than ministers found themselves faced with a potentially more serious threat to their authority; one which neither a royal commission nor a select committee could hope to deal with to their satisfaction.

In the final stages of the campaign for Reform, industrial workers, particularly craftsmen, had begun to feel a sense of their power. Encouraged by the radicals to denounce Tories, peers and bishops, they had also been tempted to organise in favour of causes likely to bring them more direct benefit than Reform; and this had brought new strength to the trade union movement. In October 1833 Doherty's vision of a union of unions at last became reality, with the formation of the Grand National Consolidated Trades Union; and in the *Poor Man's Guardian*, Bronterre O'Brien could look forward to the time when the workers would be able to use their power to change society—'a change amounting to the complete subversion of the existing order of the world. The working classes aspire to be at the top, instead of at the bottom of society—or, rather, that there should be no top or bottom at all.'

At this point, however, Robert Owen again intervened. For a while, his Labour Exchange had been a success; it actually made a profit on its first year's operations. But it had been under-capitalised; there were difficulties in disposing of goods surplus to the Exchange's own requirements; and having to go to the Exchange was inconvenient for many workers—and still more for their wives, who found it easier to continue to shop locally even if the shops were more expensive. The project did not satisfy Owen's requirements; soon, he was referring to it as 'a mere pawnshop', and looking around for some more elaborate scheme to which he could attach his aspirations.

He found it in a new version of the old guild idea—the forerunner of what was later to become known as syndicalism. What sparked his imagination, apparently, was seeing a resolution taken by the Birmingham builders' union, after its members had been sacked by the city's largest contractors. The men must be reinstated—the union had told the contractor; and he must open his books for inspection, so that an equitable agreement could be reached 'which will not only remunerate you for your superintendence, but us for our toil'. This was just the solution Owen had been groping for. Let the building workers everywhere unite to form their own guild, and in future, employ themselves! Within a few weeks, the Grand National

Guild of Builders made its appearance, aiming to give the citizen all the services for which he had previously relied on a contractor; and, at the same time, to provide work for guild members who were unemployed, old age pensions on retirement, medical treatment for their families, and education for their children.

To Owen, inevitably, this was only a beginning. All trades, he decided, ought to have their guilds; and only a month after the formation of the first of them, he formed a Society for National Regeneration, the better to spread this gospel. The attendance at the inaugural meeting made it clear that he was looking for wider support than he could expect in the confines of the trade union movement: Fielden was there, and Cobbett, and Condy, as well as Doherty and Hetherington. For a time, there seemed a possibility of a link-up between old radicalism, the factory movement, the trade unions, and the guilds.

Their combined forces, had they been shrewdly directed, would have been very powerful. But with Owen now in charge, the direction was unlikely to be shrewd; and from the start, his plans began to go awry. Anxious to attract factory workers, he called for the establishment of an eight-hour working day—'enough', he felt, 'for any human being, and under proper arrangements sufficient to afford an ample supply of food, raiment and shelter'; the remaining sixteen hours could then be apportioned, according to the taste of the individual worker, between education, recreation and sleep. A message was accordingly sent to the Short Time movement, informing them of this decision, and requesting them 'to desist from soliciting Parliament for a Ten Hours Bill, and to use their utmost exertions in aid of the measure now adopted'.

To the obvious criticism that Parliament would never be persuaded to vote an eight-hour day, the reply was that very soon the matter would be taken out of Parliament's hands. 'See into what a position this mode of pursuing things resolves itself', the Builder's Guild journal claimed: 'Every trade has its internal government in every town; a certain number of towns comprise a district, and delegates from the trades in each town form a district government; delegates from the districts form the annual parliament; and the King of England becomes President of the trade unions.' But the Tories in the Short Time movement, Sadler, Ashley, and Oastler, had little sympathy with the trade unions and none at all with a campaign—as they would certainly regard it—to subvert the constitution; all Owen succeeded in doing was disrupting the Short Time movement.

There was also little effective unity of purpose between the guilds and the trade unions. The builders did not join Doherty's Grand National Consolidated; nor did Owen. Still, even on its own, the Grand National Consolidated, claiming a membership of over half a million—more than the number of citizens on the nation's electoral register—could be regarded by ministers as a danger to society. The political economists had given assurances that a national trade union movement could not develop; but here were unions, guilds and strikes to show it was developing with disconcerting rapidity. Melbourne, who had expressed the view that trade unions were 'inconsistent, impossible, and contrary to the laws of nature', now found himself pestered by employers to suppress them.

But how? As always, Melbourne was reluctant to legislate, if he could help it. If the employers acted with sufficient resolution, it should not be necessary. 'You may rely', he told the nervous Yorkshire manufacturers, 'that the Government will take the most prompt and efficient measures to repress disorder, to punish crime, and to secure the effectual execution of the law; but the local knowledge and experience of the memorialists themselves will better suggest to them the precise measures which they should adopt, and the course which it will be most expedient for them to pursue'. Encouraged by this broad hint, the employers came to an agreement to employ no workman unless he would sign 'the document'—a promise not to join, or help, any trade union.

The Grand National Consolidated found its member unions inadequately prepared. They had not had sufficient time to build up their resources; and their leaders had no experience of sustained industrial warfare of the kind the employers now nerved themselves to face. Even without Government help, the employers would have had little difficulty in breaking the union. But at this point something happened which decided the Government that the time had come to intervene. To the alarm of Melbourne and his colleagues, reports began to come in that the Grand National Consolidated was recruiting agricultural workers.

Melbourne asked the law officers of the crown what they could suggest; and they came up with an ingenious idea. New members were commonly admitted into trade unions by swearing an oath of allegiance; and the ceremony was usually in private, partly from fear of reprisals, but also because unions often had developed masonic-type induction rituals. Under an Act passed before the end of the previous century, the crown lawyers pointed out, the administering of oaths in secret was a criminal offence. Melbourne reminded the magistracy of the existence of this law, suggesting that perhaps they would be able 'to make an example by such means'. In March 1834, six farm workers from the village of Tolpuddle, in Dorset, were arrested on the charge of administering an oath in secret to men intending to join the Grand National Consolidated. Again, Melbourne felt it would be unwise to trust to the local magistracy; the accused were tried before a special commission. They were found guilty, and given the maximum sentence under the Act: seven years' transportation.

The trade union movement erupted in protest. Guild members and radicals of all kinds denounced the sentences. A demonstration in London culminated in a march of an estimated 30,000 people to Whitehall, to petition for a pardon. Melbourne was in a difficult situation. He had taken the precaution of enquiring about the characters of the six men when sentences had been passed on them; and he had confirmed the sentences when he had been assured that they were known to be bad characters. It now transpired that they were not bad characters. Their employers testified that they were industrious and sober. Melbourne, however, did not dare to go back on his decision, for fear it would be interpreted as a sign of nervousness on the Government's part. The men were duly transported to Australia.

For a time it seemed as if the Tolpuddle affair would unite the trade union and guild movements. Owen joined the Grand National Consolidated; as Grand Master of a newly formed branch, he was actually chosen to conduct negotiations with the Government. But he had not wanted the demonstration, rightly believing that Melbourne was more likely to respond to a quieter approach; and he was disgusted when he found trade union journals using the departure into exile of the 'Tolpuddle Martyrs' to advocate class war. He determined that such articles would appear no more; he would now lead the trade union movement over to guild socialism.

But there was no effective movement, he found, left to lead. 'The document' was having its effect. With improving trade making more jobs available, workers were thankfully taking them; and having got work, they were reluctant to risk losing it by being identified with a trade union. Owen made one last characteristically grandiloquent attempt at reorganisation, founding yet another of his all-embracing societies—the British and Foreign Consolidated Association of Industry, Humanity and Knowledge; but it turned out to be little more than a debating club. He quickly grew dissatisfied with it; and soon it suffered the ultimate indignity when the treasurer absconded with what little remained of the funds.

L

3. THE NEW POOR LAW

The factory commissioners had been allowed only a few weeks in which to finish their allotted task; the members of the royal commission on the poor laws were allowed to proceed at their leisure. Never in history had so extensive an investigation been attempted into the condition of the poor— or, indeed, into any other subject. Yet it could be questioned—and was, by Cobbett—whether the volumes of evidence were going to serve any useful purpose, except to give the impression of assiduity. Why go into such detail, when the Sturges Bourne report and its successors in the 1820s had shown the failings of the old law—the depression of wages due to the allowance system, the evils of the Act of Settlement, and so on? It would have been a different matter if the commission had been investigating the causes of poverty; but since they were investigating the poor laws, it was futile to duplicate the work of earlier enquiries.

Cobbett had another reason for his mistrust. The commission was less blatantly packed with political economists than the factory commission, but their influence predominated. Sturges Bourne had retired from active politics, but he could be relied upon to support Nassau Senior. So could Walter Coulson, a member of the Political Economy Club, and a friend of Place and John Stuart Mill. Coulson had been Bentham's secretary, a job in which he had been succeeded by Edwin Chadwick; and Chadwick was Secretary to the commission. So impressed had Bentham been by Chadwick that he had tried to persuade him to take over the responsibility for the preservation and propagation of the utilitarian creed; and although Chadwick had refused to allow himself to be tied down—in spite of the prospect of being recognised as Bentham's financial, as well as spiritual, heir—he was generally regarded as the residuary legatee of utilitarian wisdom. He was also a forceful personality; and very quickly, he and Senior had begun to dominate the commission's proceedings. In a letter to Alexis de Tocqueville, Senior was to claim that he wrote three-quarters of its reports himself, and revised the rest; but he admitted that it was Chadwick who had been responsible for framing the remedial measures which the report recommended.

Their task, Senior and Chadwick knew, was to find a system which would provide an acceptable compromise between the extreme abolitionist attitude, which allowed the poor no right to subsistence, and the belief of ministers that although allowances should go, subsistence must be provided to the genuinely destitute. The Chalmers system would not do;

but if the destitute were to have a right to subsistence how could abuses be prevented? What was required, clearly, was some objective test for destitution—the equivalent of a litmus test in a laboratory. And the commissioners did not have far to search; it was provided for them by one of their own assistants, George Nicholls.

'The resort of the idle and profligate'

Nicholls had been a bank manager: a worthy, industrious man whose personality was encapsulated in a story told of him that when he was taken to *Don Giovanni*, his comment was 'What a shocking state of society!' His interest in the poor law had been aroused by reading the Sturges Bourne report: the seed then sown, he was to recall in his *History of the Poor Laws*, might have been slow to fructify, but the report had been 'the means of first opening his mind to the consequences of the existing system, and had awakened in him the earnest desire for remedying the evils it portrayed', and to the fulfilment of this desire, he had 'subsequently devoted the best years of his life'.

If the opportunity presented itself, Nicholls had decided, he would investigate the workings of the poor law at first hand, to see if there was anything that could be done; and when in 1821, his bank job took him to Nottingham, he became a parish overseer in the nearby town of Southwell. It had 3,000 inhabitants, and was quite prosperous; but its poor rate—just over fifteen shillings per head of the population—was high, for the area. The reason, he found, was that the workhouse which had recently been built there had become 'the resort of the idle and profligate of both sexes', and, as the local magistrates were disposed to be lenient in their allowances, 'the circle of pauperism embraced nearly the whole labouring population'.

According to his own account, Nicholls had been allowed by the local guardians to take over. First, he had reorganised the workhouse, bringing in a new master and matron to impose discipline, and segregating the sexes. Then, he had persuaded the guardians to cease offering outdoor relief; anybody who applied for it was, instead, 'offered the workhouse'—a term which was to become official jargon. Because the Southwell workhouse ceased to be attractive to the idle and profligate, or indeed to anybody, the local labourers preferred to look for work; and because the local farmers could no longer obtain labour subsidised by the rates, they were compelled to provide it at a living wage. As a result, the Southwell poor rates had been reduced from £2,000 a year to £500. Although Nicholls' bank career had then taken him away from Nottingham, the parish vestry had continued to operate along the lines he had laid down; and nowhere else in the entire country, the commissioners agreed, was 'anything discovered so simple and complete, or of equal efficiency as a corrective, or that was so susceptible of universal application, as the workhouse principle developed and established at Southwell'.

'Susceptible of universal application'—that was the essential point. Southwell provided the commissioners with the chance to preserve the basic principle of Elizabethan legislation—that the destitute should be relieved—with the principle they themselves wanted to establish—that *only* the destitute should be relieved. In Nicholls' words, 'no person in actual want will reject the relief proferred therein; and a person not in want will not submit to the restraints by which relief is accompanied'. It seemed the perfect answer—provided, of course, that it did not provoke insurrectionary tendencies among the poor; and on that point, Nicholls was able to ease the commissioners' (and the Government's) mind. When he returned to Southwell, to see how this experiment was going, 'he was greeted in the market place by a number of labourers with expressions of hearty goodwill, and with declarations of having been their best friend, for that he had compelled them to take care of themselves'. How gratifying this had been, Nicholls concluded, 'will be readily imagined'. He preferred to leave entirely to the commissioners', and to posterity's, imagination what kind of reception he got when he visited the Southwell workhouse—if he did.

With Southwell available as a pilot model, the rest was comparatively simple; all that was needed was an administrative framework so that the system could be extended throughout the country. Clearly the parish was too small a unit; there would have to be groups of parishes, each with its workhouse and its board of guardians. But could the boards be trusted to carry out the Southwell principle rigorously? Past experience suggested no —and even if they tried, their efforts might be undermined by the local magistracy. So a central board must be set up, the commissioners agreed, with power to instruct the guardians in their duty, and if necessary to compel them to do it; and the powers of the magistrates must be curbed.

As soon as the outlines of the scheme were agreed, it was submitted for scrutiny to the parties most concerned, the cabinet, and the Political Economy Club. The club performed one of the functions James Mill had designed for it; frequent meetings were held, with Senior in attendance, at which the proposals were discussed; Chadwick was also invited, though he was not yet a member. Although there were serious reservations over the wisdom of the projected central authority, to run the new poor law, members in general approved of what Senior and Chadwick were doing. Ministers sometimes attended—including Poulett Thomson; the cabinet also held special sessions to which Senior was invited, and he had little difficulty in persuading them that the report would be on lines they would welcome.

Yet they remained uneasy. The contemplated abolition of outdoor relief, the reduction of the powers of the magistracy, and the setting up of a central board of control, would represent a drastic departure from traditional practice. How would Parliament and the public react? That question, Senior suggested, could easily be answered, by providing an interim report, indicating the lines along which the commissioners were thinking. It was duly written by Chadwick, and presented to the Reformed Parliament when it began its sittings in April 1833; published as *Extracts of Information*, it sold the remarkable number of 15,000 copies, and won a generally favourable response from the press. Chadwick himself was singled out for approbation, and as his reward was promoted a full member of the royal commission—which incidentally enabled him to be spared to join the factory commission, too, when it was appointed.

Chadwick's popularity derived from the fact that the *Extracts* said precisely what ministers wanted to hear. He was mainly concerned to demonstrate the deplorable effects of outdoor relief, particularly in the form of allowances from the rates in aid of wages; but he also gave telling examples of the absurdity of the poor law's effects in general. In Gosport, for example, he was able to show—with the help of tables—that the worst fed men were the independent farm labourers, who were not receiving poor relief. Paupers were rather better off; then—in ascending order on the dietary scale—soldiers; then convicts; then—best-off of all—*transported* convicts. In some workhouses, too, the inmates were getting two and a half pounds of meat a week; outside them, the labourer was lucky if he could afford half a pound.

It was just what ministers wanted: not simply theoretical evidence against outdoor relief, family allowances, and inefficient workhouses, but evidence illustrating their failings, of a kind that would undoubtedly circulate over dinner tables. Yet they still had doubts. It was not enough simply to test the public response, though that had been gratifying. Ought not the new ideas to be more fully expounded, so that they would not seem new and strange when they appeared? And at this point Brougham—

the minister most closely identified with poor law reform—had an inspiration. He would enlist the help of Harriet Martineau.

'I must be reduced to a state of beggary'

In an age when literary lion-hunting was becoming a recognised social sport, Harriet Martineau had become the most sought-after of the capital's big game. She was, perhaps, the first woman to experience on a small scale the treatment later to be given to film stars; crowds would gather outside the door of a house when she was known to be visiting, and would cluster round her, to gape at her in the street. Within months of the publication of the first of her *Illustrations*, she had met, or was in a position where she easily could arrange to meet, the leading political, as well as literary and social, luminaries of the day. Still, it was flattering to be approached by a Lord Chancellor.

Brougham, whose book on the same subject for the Society for the Diffusion of Useful Knowledge had not managed to arouse the reading public's interest, had a dual reason for making the approach. If Harriet Martineau wrote up the new poor law proposals in the same way, and with the same success, as she had written up political economy, she would help the Government; and she might also help the Society, who would be the publishers. Only she could write the stories, he told her—warming to his flattery after recovering from the surprise of having to pour it into an ear-trumpet. The Government needed her. The country needed her!

Harriet Martineau was weighed down by other commitments; but, as it happened, she had already studied the old poor law for her *Cousin Marshall*, acquiring her information from a brother who was a guardian; so she would not be required to break new ground. Realising that she was weakening, Brougham told her that because of their respect for her, ministers were willing to show her the evidence, as it came in, which was being collected for the poor law commissioners. And for six poor law stories, he said, he could offer her an advance of no less than £600, three-quarters of it to be paid by the Society, the rest—to show how important he considered her help would be—by himself. When he was able to assure her that the commissioners had real hopes of presenting a cure for pauperism—adding that his own hopes would be doubled, if she would undertake to help the scheme—'the temptation to overwork was irresistible'. She held out, though, for four stories only; and the payment was adjusted accordingly (by her account, the Society paid its share: Brougham defaulted).

The confidential material promised was duly sent to her, and she was relieved to find that she had reached much the same conclusions as the commissioners, independently. She was therefore able to express her opinions without inhibitions. Her poor law tales had two main aims; to show the evils of the old poor law, and to indicate where the system was at fault so that the reader, as soon as he saw the commission's proposals, would realise that that they were precisely what was required.

The stories described the old poor law in fictional terms, but many of the episodes were taken from the evidence; some were eventually to appear in the commission's report. In *The Parish*, for example, she described how a worthy farm labourer, Ashley, had managed to put aside some savings; but they did him no good, because they rendered him ineligible for poor relief. As a result, the local farmers would not give him a job; why should they when, if they needed labour, they could employ paupers, part of whose wages would be found out of the rates? So, honest Ashley's only reward for his past frugality was the rejection by the guardians of his application for relief, and the loss of any chance of getting another job until he had spent all that he had saved.

The parallel case, as given in the report, had been related to the commission by a farmer who had been the employer of a 'hard-working, industrious man', William Williams:

> He is married, and had saved some money to the amount of about £70, and had two cows; he also had a sow and ten pigs. He had got a cottage well furnished; he was a member of a benefit club at Meopham, from which he received 8s. a week when he was ill. He was beginning to learn to read and write, and sent his children to Sunday school. He had a legacy of about £40, but he got his other money together by saving from his fair wages as a waggoner.

But then, Williams' employer had been compelled to dispense with his services:

> The consequences of this labouring man having been frugal, and saved money, and got the cows, was, that no one would employ him, although his superior character as a workman was well known in the parish. He told me at the time I was obliged to part with him 'Whilst I have these things I shall get no work: I must part with them all. I must be reduced to a state of beggary before anyone will employ me' . . . He has not yet got work, and he has no chance of getting any until he has become a pauper; for until then, the paupers will be preferred to him. He cannot get work in his own Parish, and will not be allowed to get any in other Parishes.

This was the main theme of the Martineau stories: that poor relief, so far from helping the deserving poor, only tempted them to become un-deserving. 'Nothing astonishes me so much', the respected local clergyman in one of the tales commented, 'as the patience of the honest poor. They rise up early and go weary to bed (when bed they have) while their less scrupulous neighbours get what they want from the parish by asking . . . they find their spirit of independence despised, their virtuous toil con-temptuously pitied, and their mutual charities ridiculed by their com-panions.' And it was their companions, the idle, the feckless, and the unscrupulous, who were the grateful recipients of the ratepayers' money.

Harriet Martineau was also careful to justify the reforms which she knew that the commission were going to advocate not by presenting them as her own conclusions—which might have been regarded as a little presumptuous—but by revealing the necessity for them. Knowing that the power of the magistrates was to be reduced, for example, she introduced her readers to Mr. Weakly, J.P., an amiable but indolent man who could not be bothered to sift appeals which came to him. Because he got the reputation locally of being lenient, appeals were more likely to be taken to him, rather than to other magistrates; he would sign just to be rid of the applicants.

The reception of the poor law tales did not quite match Brougham's, or Harriet Martineau's, expectations—because, she thought, of the connec-tion with the Society for the Diffusion of Useful Knowledge, and with Brougham. Still, praise poured in from all quarters—the most gratifying coming from Elizabeth Fry, who had devoted so much of her life to the care of the criminal poor: she invited Miss Martineau to visit the New-gate, and there explained that she was now convinced by the stories that, ultimately, the poor could only be helped by a radical reform of the poor law. Miss Martineau was flattered, too, when a peer asked for an introduc-tion to her at a reception, to tell her that it had taken her work to show him how his generosity to the poor through almsgiving, which he had prided himself on for years, had really been productive only of mischief. Soon afterwards her pleasure was diminished when she heard that he had become deranged.

'A burden on other parishes'

The Poor Law Commission report, when it appeared early in 1834, was a most authoritative-looking compilation. It was divided into two parts: the first, in which the commissioners described in grim detail the deficiencies of the old poor law; the second, in which they put forward their proposals for its amendment.

The first part made, by this time, familiar reading. Although it was more comprehensive than the Sturges Bourne report, and backed by a wealth of examples, the picture presented was the same. But there was one vital piece of new evidence. It was obviously very much in the commissioners' interest to be able to show that Sturges Bourne's often-quoted dire warning—that the poor rate would continue to increase 'until it should have absorbed the profits of the property on which the rate might have been assessed, producing thereby the neglect and ruin of the land'—was being borne out. But as they had to admit, a little shamefacedly, the amount of money spent on the relief of the poor was actually less than it had been fifteen years before, in spite of the population increase. The inevitable excuses were made: that 1819 had been a year of particular distress; that in the meantime, the cost of bread had fallen. Nevertheless they could hardly claim that there was any sign of the cumulative process that the Sturges Bourne report had forecast. But they had what was almost as useful: one parish where the process had been observed, the Buckinghamshire village of Cholesbury. 'We are happy to say', the commissioners remarked, 'that not many cases of the actual destruction of estates have been stated to us'; but from the use to which they put Cholesbury, it was obvious that they were even happier to have found that single example.

At the beginning of the century, the evidence showed, the Cholesbury rates had amounted to only ten pounds eleven shillings a year—all expended on one pauper. In 1816, they had risen to just under a hundred pounds: in 1831, to £150. In 1832, when they had reached £367, the rate suddenly ceased 'in consequence of the impossibility to continue its collection; the landlords having given up their rents, the farmers their tenancies, and the clergyman his glebe and tithes'. One October day that year, apparently, the parish officers had closed their books; and the paupers had gone round to the clergyman, to ask him for advice and food. He was still in bed, when they arrived, but he had got up, and organised charity for them as best he could, with the help of neighbouring parishes; and on that, the paupers had since been compelled to rely. In Cholesbury, therefore—the commissioners concluded—'the expense of the poor has not merely swallowed up the whole value of the land; it requires even the assistance for two years of rates in aid, from other parishes, to enable the able-bodied, after the land has been given to them, to support themselves; and the aged and impotent must even then remain a burden on other parishes'.

'Repugnant to the common sentiments of mankind'

The commissioners were aware that in spite of the priming of the interim report, and of Harriet Martineau's stories, the public would still require to be eased gently into acceptance of the proposed new poor law. They accordingly took considerable pains to make the second section of the report sympathetic as well as authoritative. Even the title, 'Remedial Measures', had a reassuring look.

The first essential, they asserted, was to restore the distinction between poverty and indigence. In any large community, there must always be some whose means of subsistence has failed; and to refuse them relief, leaving them to starve, was 'repugnant to the common sentiments of mankind'. The commission actually went further: it was repugnant to punish the indigent for begging, in such circumstances—repugnant, even, to punish them for depredations, if committed as the only resource against starvation. The provision, compulsory or voluntary, of poor relief, was therefore reasonable in cases of genuine *indigence*—'the state of a person unable to labour, or unable to obtain in return for his labour, the means of subsistence'. But nowhere else in Europe, the report continued, had it been deemed expedient to relieve *poverty*, 'that is, the state of one, who, in order to obtain a mere subsistence, is forced to have recourse to labour'.

But how to preserve the distinction, in practice? In the past, overseers had notoriously had great difficulty in deciding where to draw the line— all the more so when trying to apply the criterion whether the applicant was 'deserving'. Such judgments were necessarily subjective; what the commissioners had looked for, therefore, was a sound and well-defined objective test. And they had found it in a principle which, they claimed, was already generally accepted, even by those who did not practise it: that if anybody was to be granted relief, 'his situation on the whole shall not be made really, or apparently, so eligible as the situation of the independent labourer of the lowest class'. This, they felt, should be considered the first and most essential of all conditions under which poor relief was given.

The principle of 'less eligibility', as it came to be known, was the foundation upon which the rest of the commission's report rested. In future (if the recommendation was accepted), no outdoor relief was to be given to able-bodied workers. They would be told to look for work. If they could not find a job, or if the job that they did find did not give them a subsistence wage, they could return to the guardians, and ask for relief— but it would be given to them only if they consented to enter a workhouse, designed and run so that their existence in it would be 'less eligible' than the existence of the poorest class of self-sufficient labourers outside.

The way in which 'less eligibility' would work appeared beautifully simple—very similar, as was later to be noticed, to the standard army practice of 'either come on parade, or go sick'. All the trouble of ascertaining whether an applicant needed or deserved relief would be eliminated; for if workhouse life was kept less bearable than the most poverty-stricken existence outside, nobody but the really destitute would enter the workhouse. But anybody who was really destitute would be saved by the workhouse from starvation. He would also be removed from the labour market, thereby reducing the labour surplus. This, by helping to adjust the labour supply to the level of the demand, would raise wages. And there was no need for alarm on Malthusian grounds, because the sexes in the workhouse could be segregated, to prevent paupers from continuing to breed.

It remained, though, to convince the public that so drastic a remedy was necessary—for obviously people might wonder why outdoor relief should not continue to be provided for deserving cases, so long as it left them in a situation less eligible than that of the lowest class of independent labourer. In theory, the commissioners conceded, this might be possible. But, in practice, to permit out-relief would be to jeopardise the prospects of the new system. Out-relief had proved a literal illustration of the legal maxim, hard cases make bad law. 'The bane of all pauper legislation', the commissioners explained, 'has been the legislating for extreme cases. Every exception, every violation of the general rule to meet a real case of unusual hardship, lets in a whole class of fraudulent cases, by which that rule must in time be destroyed.' So the hard, or sad, cases must submit to relief in the workhouse; and, after all—the commissioners felt—to the really destitute, 'relief in a well-regulated workhouse would not be a hardship; and even if it be, in some rare cases, a hardship, it appears from the evidence that it is a hardship to which the good of society requires the applicant to submit'. Besides, where the hardship was real, the remedy was to hand—individual charity, 'a virtue for which no system of compulsory relief can be or ought to be a substitute'. Public charity was a different matter; the report echoed the Martineau view, calling for a parliamentary investigation into established charities. But where feeling was strong enough locally that a family deserved better than the workhouse, then there was no harm in allowing voluntary endeavours to keep them out of it.

For the rest, the report was chiefly concerned to provide justification for the administrative changes that would have to be made; particularly for the new central authority. How important this was to the commissioners could be gauged by the amount of space they gave to the subject. History, they argued, had shown that permissive poor laws were futile: 'there is scarcely one statute connected with the administration of public relief which has produced the effect designed by the legislature; the majority of them have created new evils, and aggravated those which they were intended to prevent'. Local overseers served too short a term to master the problems which faced them; and the job was not well enough paid to attract the right people. Inevitably, too, local interests and pressures were at work to encourage administrative laxity, or evasion of the regulations. That was why it was essential to have a central board, with extensive powers to guide and control.

'That they who toil should not live worse than they who are idle'

The report was as favourably received as ministers could have hoped. Cobbett derided it, but that was inevitable. The only unexpected adversary of any consequence was *The Times*. This was the more disconcerting in that, by 1834, *The Times*, under Barnes' editorship, had grown more prosperous, and more influential, than any newspaper had ever been before. In circulation it far exceeded all its serious rivals put together; and it was treated with grudging respect even by those who, like Wellington and Peel, had been accustomed to regard the press with contempt. Its support over the Reform bill had been valuable to the Government and on balance, though critical of ministers' handling of factory legislation, it had remained friendly to them. According to Harriet Martineau, they had taken soundings, and been assured of *The Times*' support for amending the poor law — to their relief, and hers: 'how the other newspapers would go there was no saying, because the reform was not a party measure; but with *The Times* on our side we felt pretty safe'. She was consequently much vexed when, opening her *Times* one morning at the breakfast table, she found in it a vehement and total condemnation of the proposed new poor law.

The explanation she heard at the time was that *The Times* had learned of the anger of the country magistrates—'a most important class of customer' —over the impending loss of their powers. Then, as it became clear that *The Times*' disillusionment with the Government went deeper, another story found favour: that it had been bought by the Tories. Barnes's own explanation was more credible. He had realised, like everybody else, that the poor laws needed to be changed; and *The Times* had tempered criticism out of a desire to assist reform: 'as in the case of a frightful epidemic, everybody eagerly seizes the first remedy offered, whether by a quack or by a man of sense and science'. The more closely he studied the proposals, though, the more aghast he had been at their acceptance of 'the monstrous assumption that there is no such thing as temporary distress which temporary aid may relieve'. The policy of refusing relief to the able-bodied in any circumstances, except in the workhouse, would be 'enormously expensive, degrading to the honest pauper, and ruinous to fathers of families who will not any more receive that temporary relief which might set them on their feet again, without their being torn from their wives and children, who will all be pauperised and imprisoned under the new system'.

Probably, too, *The Times'* owner, John Walter, helped to change his editor's mind. As a Berkshire landowner, Walter knew more about the condition of the labouring poor in the country than Barnes; and he was to be one of the new poor law's most persistent critics.

In spite of *The Times'* desertion, the report on the poor laws was sufficiently well received for the Government to allow Senior to draft a bill based on it; and he was invited to attend the Cabinet meetings at which the draft was discussed. Only on two issues was there any serious difference of opinion, Melbourne being the minister concerned. The proposal that outdoor relief should be abruptly terminated was rejected; better, it was agreed, that poor law officers should be dissuaded from giving it, rather than ordered not to. As a compromise, they were to be allowed to continue to grant it in special cases; but to ensure that this privilege was not abused, they would have to make out a report each time, to the central board, justifying their decision; and in due course the board would name a day for the practice to cease. Melbourne was also worried about the powers given to the central board. But here, Senior was adamant; if the board did not have the powers called for in the report, the new poor law would inevitably go the way of the old. Reluctantly, Melbourne gave way; though when the time came for him to cast his vote for the bill, he was overheard in the lobby muttering objurgations about it, under his breath.

Asking leave of the House to introduce the poor law amendment bill, on April 17, 1834, Althorp claimed that it dealt with as important an issue as any that the House had ever had submitted to its attention—a statement with which even the bill's opponents were unlikely to disagree. But when he said that the bill was needed not for the benefit of the landowner or the capitalist, but to rescue the labouring population from its

state of 'deplorable misery and distress', Cobbett was roused; and he was
to be the measure's most implacable opponent. There was little that could
be done in the second reading, in view of the overwhelmingly favourable
reception given to the bill from both sides of the House; only twenty
M.P.s voted against it. But in the committee stage, he fought it clause by
clause.

His opposition was based on two main contentions. Historically, he
argued, the poor had the same right to their subsistence as the rich had to
their property. The bill, admittedly, promised subsistence; but on such
degrading terms that it amounted to a breach of contract. And in practice,
the bill was misguided, because it attributed pauperism to defects in the
old poor law, which with all its faults was not really to blame. Pauperism
was the consequence of the Government's fiscal mismanagement, and of
the uprooting of the labourer from the land by enclosures—as many a
parish would bear witness. In one Sussex parish he knew of, every cottage
except one had been owned, half a century before, by its occupier. Now,
only two were owner-occupied—and there were nearly 200 paupers. That
was what the Government ought to be thinking, and legislating, about.

But Cobbett attracted little support. Poulett Scrope, a new M.P., disliked the workhouses: as envisaged in the report, he thought, they bore a
suspicious resemblance to jails. Torrens, though like Scrope he felt legislation was needed, agreed that the workhouse system might be too
stringent; and he was also concerned about the powers of the central
board; he actually persuaded the Government to accept an amendment
that its members should be appointed for only five years. But this was one
of very few amendments to be incorporated in the measure; the great
majority of Whigs favoured it, and Peel gave it his tacit support. Whenever Cobbett or one of the other opponents of the bill divided the House
on an amendment, they were lucky if their tally reached two figures.

More difficulty was expected with the Lords, where the bill was introduced by Brougham—Grey had resigned from the premiership a few days
before. Brougham was at his most orotund. The bill's principle, he assured
the House, was simple: 'that men should be paid according to the work
they do—that men should be employed and paid according to the demand
for labour, and its value to the employer—that they who toil should not
live worse than they who are idle—and that the mere idler should not run
away with that portion which the industrious workman had earned'. All
this appeared as self-evident, he suggested, 'as if a man were to say two
and two make four, and not fourteen'. The men who were responsible for

the 43rd Elizabeth were not to be blamed, 'they could not see that a Malthus would arise'; but the time had now come to revise the whole wretched system. And to those who, like Eldon, were complaining that so important a measure should have been brought in towards the close of the session, giving them insufficient time to study it, Brougham issued a grave warning: time was what they did not have. Everything betokened the approach of agrarian war, if something were not done quickly. The issue before them was simple: did they want to keep their properties? Or didn't they?

They clearly did. A few amendments were presented: the Archbishop of Canterbury wanted workhouse chaplains to be provided for the religious instruction and consolation of the poor—but when he insisted they must be from the Established Church, dissenters objected; and the Duke of Richmond claimed that if paupers were allowed leave of absence to go to whatever service they liked, they would employ it by going to a beershop. Only one amendment of any substance was passed. Lord Ellenborough, son of the former chief justice, proposed that the magistrates ought to be left with the discretion of affording outdoor relief to children under three years of age, and to the aged and infirm over the age of sixty. Melbourne pointed out that parents ought on principle to be compelled to look after their children, and that part of the amendment was lost; but the rights of magistrates to order relief for the old was allowed to remain.

In general, however, the Government's fears that the Lords might find the bill's changes too much to accept proved unfounded. Much of the House's time, in fact, was spent in argument about the new bastardy provision, which took away the former right of the mother to obtain maintenance by 'swearing' the child on to the putative father. In the past, unless he could prove his innocence, he had been compelled to provide maintenance. In future the mother must provide, or go to the workhouse. This, the Earl of Falmouth complained, introduced a new principle of 'giving the most perfect impunity to the man, while it visited the woman with heavy punishment'. The House was against him, the Bishop of Exeter reminding him that a witness had assured the commission that the female in these cases was generally to blame. The clause on which the Government had expected most opposition—concerning the powers of the new board—excited relatively little criticism. Wellington expressed the general view when he said that although he would have preferred Parliament to retain more control, he was not prepared to use that as an excuse for opposing a measure which he believed would prove to be, as a remedy for the evils of the old law, 'unquestionably the best that had ever been devised'.

When the bill was returned to the Commons, however, so that the Lords' amendment could be considered, uneasiness about it had begun to spread; and it was increased by an unguarded remark of Althorp's, in reply to a question whether husbands and wives must be separated in the new workhouses. That would be necessary, he claimed, 'to ensure proper regulation'. Three days later, realising that this statement had caused concern, he changed his line: in principle, he said, husbands and wives would not be separated, though instances might occur where it was necessary. This, in fact, was the already prevailing practice; but some M.P.s who had not previously examined the measure began to scrutinise it more carefully; and others who had already expressed their doubts, felt justified in expressing them more forcibly. Was the discontinuation of out-relief really so desirable as the commissioners in their report insisted? What, for example —Scrope asked—was going to happen 'in the case of the sudden stoppage of any large manufactory, from the failure of the owner, or from any sudden revulsion of trade?' Althorp could only reply that in such cases out-relief could still be given, provided that it was reported to the central board; and when Scrope demanded a vote, it was found that the number of dissidents had risen to forty.

But forty M.P.s were not enough to alarm the Government at this stage of the bill. It went through substantially unchanged; and six months to the day after it had been introduced, it received the royal assent.

4. CHOLESBURY REVISITED

Althorp was right: reform of the poor law was indeed as important a social issue as any that Parliament had been called upon to deal with. Parliament appeared to have dealt with it in a singularly enlightened, scientific way. An enormous quantity of evidence had been collected, and sifted; from it, the commissioners had produced a massive report, and recommended changes of the law; and Parliament had accepted their advice, in spite of the fact that it cut across some cherished preconceptions.

But why, in that case, did the report excite the contempt of McCulloch? Admittedly his relations with Senior were not cordial; he might well have been envious of the authority Senior wielded. He was also implacably hostile to the idea of giving any central authority such extensive powers; Adam Smith, he was to recall in a criticism of the report, had once said that it was the highest impertinence in kings and ministers to instruct private people how they could best employ their capital and industry; but that mercantilist pretension 'appears to be modesty itself, compared with the pretensions put forward by the authors and abettors of the new poor law'. In the whole history of legislation, McCulloch went on, even in the least enlightened and most despotically-governed nations, he doubted whether any instance could be pointed out 'in which the rage for interference (influenced no doubt by the sense of patronage it was to bring along with it) had been carried to such an extreme, not to say offensive, extent'. But McCulloch went further. He accused the commissioners and their assistants of having falsified the evidence for venal purposes:

The reports of these commissioners, and the evidence taken before them, fill several folio volumes; and contain a curious mixture of authentic, questionable and erroneous statements. The commissioners, with very few exceptions, appear to have set out with a determination to find nothing but abuses in the old poor law, and to make the most of them; and this was no more than might have been expected, seeing that this was the most likely way to affect its abolition, and to secure employment for themselves under the system proposed to be adopted in its stead. Hence the exaggeration, one-sidedness and quackery so glaringly evident in most of their reports. But, such as they were, they became the foundation of, or rather the pretext for, a measure of the most sweeping description by which, with a few exceptions, every vestige of the old system for the administration of the affairs of the poor was wholly abolished.

No statute had ever been passed, McCulloch concluded, 'that appears to be more contradictory of the best-established principles, or more likely to be productive of mischievous results'.

'It is the price'

The justness of McCulloch's verdict was only gradually to become apparent: the poor law commission report had told neither the truth nor the whole truth; and it had certainly evaded telling nothing but the truth. At the time, though, only one aspect of its one-sidedness attracted notice: the absence of any serious consideration of the problems of the industrial areas. Even where the report mentioned the subject, as in a brief section of the effects of the allowance system on employers, it did not go into the type of destitution that was giving most trouble there. And this could not conceivably have been from ignorance; Chadwick was working with the factory commission at the same time as he was on the commission investigating the poor laws, and Senior considered himself something of an expert on the economics of industry.

Anybody reading the report who knew nothing about conditions in England might have been forgiven for assuming that allowances in aid of wages were mainly responsible for the distress of the poor, and that the problem could consequently be solved if outdoor relief were discontinued, and the destitute offered the workhouse. But this solution simply did not fit the realities of poverty in the industrial north. There, unemployment was of a different kind. Some workers were redundant, owing to machinery. Others were thrown out of work by trade recessions, or by commercial accidents like the imposition of a tariff by some foreign country on English cloth. Any attempt to enforce the rule that men out of work for these reasons could obtain relief only in a workhouse would arouse violent antagonism, not only from the men themselves, but from their employers. The poor rates in the north did not constitute a heavy burden; they were low in Yorkshire; in Lancashire, the lowest in the country. For the manufacturers, they represented a relatively cheap insurance policy, keeping in being the surplus labour force which they needed when trade was expanding —as Coleridge had realised, ten years before. Any extensive commercial and manufacturing system, he had remarked in his *Table Talk*, must be accompanied by poor rates; they were 'the consideration paid by, or on behalf of, capitalists for having labour at demand. It is the price, and nothing else.'

The commissioners, however, could not admit this in their report. The Government, Chadwick and Senior knew, did not share their enthusiasm for a unified national system of poor relief. If ministers realised that it would be difficult to impose the workhouse test in the north, and that it was quite unnecessary to attempt to do so, they would certainly take some easy way out—perhaps by leaving the establishment of Unions and workhouses to local option. But if exceptions of this kind were allowed, the Act was as good as lost from the start. Better to trust to the ignorance of ministers, and of Parliament, about the situation in the industrial areas, and hope that they would not realise the position. The ruse had worked. Scrope and one or two other M.P.s had drawn attention to this weakness in the report; but they had not been listened to.

A less surprising, but also a deliberate, omission from the report was any consideration of community schemes for the relief of destitution, such as those based on the ideas of Robert Owen. Fifteen years before they had

attracted princes, and compelled even Ricardo to take notice. Now, they
were no longer thought of sufficient importance to merit even a reference.

Yet by chance, an experimental community had been established on
Owenite principles shortly before the commissioners had begun to collect
their evidence; it was in operation while they were at work; and it was
proving very successful. True, it was in Ireland, and Ireland was technically
outside their terms of reference. But so was Scotland, and that had not
prevented them from investigating Scots methods of providing relief for
the destitute. In any case, so long as the flow of Irish immigrants continued, anything being tried in Ireland which might help to reduce that
flow merited their attention.

The Irish Owenite venture had been founded by John Scott Vandeleur,
a name which might have featured in the cast list of a melodrama—not
entirely inappropriately, as events were to show. Vandeleur came from
what was known as the landed gentry: he had been High Sheriff of his
county, Clare; and he had the reputation of being a scientific farmer. But
like most of his kind, he did not care to bury himself on his estates; he
enjoyed the social life of Dublin and, because he enjoyed it, it galled him
that the revenue from his land was so small. There was nothing the matter
with the land: why could it not yield him more rent?

He had met Robert Owen on one of Owen's proselytising visits to
Ireland in the early 1820s; visits which had aroused enormous interest and
enthusiasm but failed to attract sufficient funds to promote the cause.
When, a few years later, an outbreak of violence on one of his estates left
Vandeleur still worse off than before, the idea of setting up a co-operative
community recurred to him. He decided, though, that he would depart
from earlier models; he would provide the land and the necessary capital,
but he would put in a manager to make sure that the project was efficiently
run, at least until it settled down; and he would require an agreed rent.

Vandeleur's reasoning was that the individual Irish peasant, knowing
as he did that if he increased the productivity of his smallholding he
would simply be compelled to pay higher rent, had no incentive to
improve it, and even if that disincentive had been removed, his holding
was too small to provide more than a meagre surplus for the landowner to
claim as rent. But if a group of peasants were brought together on his
600-acre Ralahine estate—which had water-power to drive machinery, to
enable them to make better use of the resources of the land and of their
own labour—they could easily raise their own living standards, and
provide him with a larger, and more regular, income. The community was

established in November 1831; and from the start, it surpassed even Vandeleur's expectations. Once they had got accustomed to the idea, its members began to work as hard as the Irish traditionally did in England, but rarely in their own country. A mill was opened, and a school. Ralahine quickly became a show-place, attracting favourable attention not only from sympathetic visitors like William Thompson, and Owen himself, but also from neighbouring landowners and clergy.

Ordinarily, a scheme along these lines could safely have been recommended by the commissioners. It was not contrary to the principles of political economy; even Ricardo—though he would have been sceptical about the chances of the community continuing to function satisfactorily on a co-operative basis, with 'labour notes' for wages—would not have disapproved, so long as the enterprise involved no use of State capital, and was being engaged in for the landowner's profit. Why, then, did the commissioners not draw attention to the possibilities that Ralahine opened up to proprietors who were anxious to improve the standard of living of the Irish poor, and their own incomes, at the same time?

The commissioners may not have known about Ralahine; but this would not excuse their ignoring the co-operative movement, considering how it had developed. It was precisely because of this development, though, that they avoided the subject. While they were collecting their evidence, there had seemed a very real chance that the co-operative and trade union movements might merge, under Owen and Doherty; and this had presented a threat to the established political parties, perhaps to the constitution, and certainly to the reputation of the political economists, whose assertion that a national trade union movement was impossible was being shown to be false. Ministers would consequently not have welcomed any report which took co-operation seriously enough even to rebut it.

So the possibility of extending co-operatives was not considered. Experience in other countries, and eventually in Ireland, was later to show that farm co-operatives had much to recommend them as a way of raising living standards. Certainly they could have been invaluable to the Irish, offering as they did the last way out of the difficulties which in the 1840s were to engulf them. But because co-operation was not considered respectable, the chance was lost.

And after only two years, the Ralahine experiment ended—though not in the way that the critics had foretold. One day, the news came that Vandeleur had vanished. Investigation revealed that, unknown to his friends, he had been a compulsive gambler; he had lost so much at the tables that he realised he was ruined; and he fled to the United States. His friends never heard from him again. And, as his creditors would not agree to allow the Ralahine experiment to continue, the community was broken up.

'To the care of their own self-interest'

The commissioners could afford to ignore the special problems of the industrial areas, because they were still imperfectly understood at Westminster. They could afford to ignore Owen, as he no longer had influential backing. But they deemed it wise to make a show of having examined some alternative proposals to reduce pauperism—as if to prove how openminded they had been; and in the report they discussed them, to explain why they had been rejected.

One was that the labour rate system should be more systematically adopted. It had evolved to help the poor in areas where there was not enough work by apportioning it through schemes under which each ratepayer was assessed for his ability to employ labour, and allotted a quota of labourers, for whom he must find work at current wage levels, or pay the difference into the rates. It had seemed a sensible idea, spreading the load more equitably throughout the employer class, and stimulating employment (if the payment had to be made anyway, it might as well be spent on employing labour, rather than simply going into the rates); it made the poor work for their keep; and it lowered the rates. But to the commissioners, it was an admission that the poor had a *right* to employment; and it interfered with the ordinary processes of supply and demand. The fact that it could only work by enforcing the law of settlement gave Senior a good excuse to damn it, for hindering labour mobility; the labour rate, he argued, was a scheme of general pauperisation, and 'for confining all the labourers to the accidental boundaries of their parishes, without reference to the demand for their services'.

But if that was the way the commissioners' minds were turning, why not make poor relief into a national charge? With relief paid for out of national taxes, rather than local rates, it would have been possible to repeal the Act of Settlement, because there would be no further need to send a pauper back to his place of settlement in order to prevent him becoming a charge on the rates. As the law of settlement was universally detested—by the poor for its cruelty; by the ratepayers for the inconveniences to which it submitted them, and the cost of the frequent litigation involved—the commissioners did not feel any need to find excuses for it; on the contrary, they provided evidence to show how it was being abused. In some parishes, where there was either a single landowner, or so few that they could easily come to an arrangement between themselves, a regular policy had been evolved of knocking down all labourers' cottages as they became vacant, and importing labourers only from outside, for periods too short to allow them to obtain a settlement. In such parishes, the poor rates were nominal.

But to have a national charge, the commissioners explained, though it would prevent such abuses, and might temporarily prove beneficial, would in the long run lead to a weakening in local vigilance and economy; and—they added, as if from an afterthought—to pay for it 'a property tax would be called for'. A property tax would fall most heavily on landowners. It had been resisted so far; and a cabinet of landowners was unlikely to sanction it to replace the poor rate.

The only proposal, in fact, which the commissioners claimed to have considered that could seriously be regarded as an alternative to their own plan, was discussed in the report under the heading 'legislative provision for enabling labourers to occupy land'. Here, they had to be wary. They could hardly ignore an idea which had attracted such influential support, over so long a period. The Whig government had actually passed legislation to facilitate the provision of land for labourers through voluntary agreement; but it had not been effective. The Labourer's Friend Society, founded in 1833 with a distinguished array of titled backers, was seeking some better way to ensure that the land was made available. There would certainly be questions in Parliament, if the commissioners failed to provide plausible reasons for rejecting the idea.

They could not accept it because it was contrary to the principles of political economy that the State should threaten the sanctity of property rights by interfering with agreements between employer and worker; and perhaps also because for years its most persistent advocate had been Cobbett. Still, as they had no desire to arouse antagonism in the Lords— where they had expected to have criticism enough to face over their centralisation plan, and the reduction of the magistrates' powers—they had looked for a way to turn it down without giving offence. They were helped by the confusion that had arisen between what could be described as the English system, where the labourers, if they had land at all, ordinarily only had a tiny plot; and the French (and Irish) system of peasant proprietorship, where the holdings might be small, but where the tenant regarded himself as a farmer first, and a labourer in his spare time.

Peasant proprietorship had been rejected by the political economists on the ground that it prevented the division of labour, and delayed the introduction of farm machinery. It was a primitive way of life, they argued, rather than—as they thought farming ought to be—a business. They disliked it all the more because it was recommended by the Swiss economist de Sismondi—the first of the disciples of Adam Smith to defect; his heretical opinions had been the source of particular irritation to Ricardo, and to McCulloch. The commissioners had been sent a memorandum on the subject by M. Chateauvieux, a member of the French *Académie des Sciences*, suggesting—much as Bacon had done in his *Letter to Lord Suffield*—that there was scope for the introduction of peasant proprietorship in England. They repudiated the idea; the moment a labourer was given enough land to think of himself as a farmer, they were sure, 'his ultimate ruin seems certain'; and they relegated Chateauvieux's memorandum to an appendix, at the end of the minutes of evidence.

They agreed, however, that where labourers had been leased small plots of land by proprietors (though not where it had been leased by the parish) the results appeared to be very beneficial. Their enthusiasm for the project was at first sight puzzling; but it was to be explained in their conclusion: 'since it appears that land may be let to labourers on profitable terms, the necessity for any public enquiry on these points seems to be at an end'. If landowners found the system so valuable, in other words, they would introduce it without the need for State intervention. 'A practice which is beneficial to both parties, and is known to be so, may be left to the care of their own self-interest. The evidence shows that it is rapidly extending; and we have no doubt that as its utility is perceived, it will spread still more rapidly.'

It was a plausible argument. The evidence did indeed show that where an enthusiastic landowner took up the project, and began to introduce it, neighbours noticed the good effects, and began to copy it themselves. But the process was, in fact, far from rapid; farmers were in general opposed to it; Lord Carnarvon had reported that he had found them reluctant 'to give up the least portion of land for this purpose', for fear that the labourer would work less energetically on their land than on his own. And the commissioners neglected to make any reference to the reverse process, by which land was still being taken from the labourers who had previously enjoyed the use of it—from Sadler's evidence, in fact, they had been losing land far more rapidly than it was being given back to them.

'They live better in the workhouse'

The commissioners, in other words, had been devious. Wherever discussion of a proposal might be embarrassing to them, or to the Government, it had been ignored; where it could not be ignored, they had found ways to extricate themselves from the necessity of supporting it. But this was not all. The quantity of material which was provided for them in the evidence might appear to have been impartially collected, but it was tailored to their specifications; and, wherever it would not fit their thesis, they selected from it only such examples as would give the impression that it did.

If there was one point upon which there had been general agreement, for a century and more, it was that the workhouse was regarded by the poor as the ultimate degradation—worse than jail, at least when the jail sentence was for such offences as smuggling or poaching. Even Harriet Martineau in one of her poor law tales had emphasised that men and women would submit to fearful deprivations to avoid having to accept indoor relief; from time to time, cases had been reported where individuals had starved to death rather than go into a workhouse.

But this was not the impression that the commissioners wanted to convey. Their thesis was that the old poor law did not work because it was too leniently, too laxly, administered; and they consequently wanted to show that the workhouse, so far from being regarded with horror by the poor, appeared to them as an agreeable place of refuge when times were bad, where they could enjoy good food and accommodation without having to pay for it.

This proved less difficult for the commissioners to illustrate than they might have expected, for a curious reason: that the men who were masters of the worst workhouses were unlikely to give evidence which would show just how incompetent and cruel they had been. Where there was evidence given of appalling workhouse conditions, it was usually either at second-hand, or from officers who emphasised how terrible the workhouse was *before* they were elected—in order to show how active they had been in putting things to rights. Thus, the Islington officers described how when they had taken over in 1829 they had found the children suffering from lice and ophthalmia, and swollen abdomens; and they had realised that infections flourished because the children had to sleep four or five in a bed. This they had promptly remedied, with beneficial results. They might well have expected that their good work would be held up by the commission as an example of what could be done, with efficient management. But in the commission's report, evidence of this kind was ignored, and for an obvious reason: the more disgraceful the workhouses were shown to have been, in the past, the more likely it was that M.P.s might be swayed by humanitarian pleas not to enforce the workhouse test, but to leave it open to guardians to give out-relief to deserving cases.

In the three pages that the report devoted to workhouses (as compared to thirty dealing with the evils of out-relief) the commissioners therefore concentrated on seeking to prove, with the help of examples, that—as one witness put it—'parish poorhouses, as at present administered, have the effect of attracting paupers'. A London workhouse master claimed that paupers were often heard to boast 'that they live better in the workhouse than they ever lived before'; and the report even repeated the statement of a Westminster vestry clerk, who had told them that the diet and accommodation enjoyed by workhouse inmates were 'very superior to that which can be obtained by the most industrious of our independent labourers and mechanics'. It must surely have been this section of the report which Dickens, at this time a reporter in the Commons press gallery, had in mind when three years later he came to describe the attitude of the board of poor law guardians in *Oliver Twist*:

> The members of this Board were very sage, deep, philosophical men; and when they came to turn their attention to the workhouse, they found out at once, what ordinary folks would never have discovered – the poor people liked it! It was a regular place of public entertainment for the poorer classes; a tavern where there was nothing to pay; a public breakfast, dinner, tea and supper all the year round; a brick and mortar Elysium, where it was all play and no work. 'Oho!' said the Board, looking very knowing, 'we are the fellows to set this to rights; we'll stop it all, in no time.' So they established the rule, that all poor people should have the alternative (for they would compel nobody, not they) of being starved by a gradual process in the house, or by a quick one out of it.

That there were some poorhouses which had earned a sleazy reputation was not in dispute; where the officers were lax in enforcing discipline, it was not surprising that the paupers took what advantage they could. But, as Harriet Martineau had shown, it was not so much that the idle and the profligate turned to the workhouse, as that the workhouse made the honest pauper idle and profligate. Once inside, he had nothing to hope for, and behaved accordingly. The commissioners consequently had little difficulty in finding witnesses to confirm that workhouses were used by prostitutes taking a rest from their professional activities (though 'it very often happens that they go out worse than they came in, owing to their intercourse, within the walls, with older and more vicious characters'), and for the idle, looking forward to the one day a week when they were allowed to go out, to return 'in a beastly state of intoxication'. And with the help of such evidence, the commissioners were able to assert that the workhouse was 'a large almshouse, in which the young are trained in idleness, ignorance and vice; the able-bodied maintained in sluggish sensual indolence; and aged and more respectable exposed to all the misery that is incident to dwelling in such a society, without government or classification; and the whole body of inmates subsisted on food far exceeding, both in kind and in amount, not merely the diet of the independent labourer, but that of the majority of the persons who contribute to their support'.

There was one other aspect of the workhouse system that the commissioners discreetly refrained from mentioning: the source of the principle upon which paupers were in future going to have to endure it. Due recognition was given to Southwell, as the pilot model; but it was not disclosed where the idea of less eligibility had come from. The principle had been set out many years earlier by Bentham in his plan for a development of Gilbert's system by the provision of potentially profit-making workhouses. For the purposes of supervision, Bentham had suggested that they should be constructed on his Panopticon principle, with all the wards visible from a central vantage point—a development of his earlier proposal, that the Panopticon principle should be used in the construction of new jails. When he had described how the prisoners in the new jails should be treated, too, Bentham had written that the ordinary situation of a convict 'ought not to be made more eligible than that of the poorest class of subject living in a state of innocence and liberty'. 'Less eligibility' in other words, had originally been intended to apply in jails. But, just as he had adapted the Panopticon principle for paupers, so he had adapted less eligibility: 'if the condition of persons maintained without property by the labour of others were rendered more eligible than that of persons maintained by their own labour . . . individuals destitute of property would be continually withdrawing themselves from the class of persons maintained by their own labour, to the class of persons maintained by the labour of others.' The Panopticon scheme came to nothing; but less eligibility had lingered on—to be echoed by McCulloch, for example, in his *Edinburgh* article on the poor laws in 1828, 'the able-bodied tenant of a workhouse should be made to feel that his situation is decidedly less

comfortable than that of the industrious labourer who supports himself'.
So Scrope's instinct had been sound; what was now proposed for the
destitute had originally been designed for the criminal.

'This darling and selected parish'

On some issues, the commissioners did not even trouble to present
evidence to justify their conclusions. So confident were they that their
views were generally shared that they did not feel it was necessary. They
took it for granted, for example, that Malthus had been right to say that
the allowance system which had spread after 1795 had been a bounty
on improvidence, by encouraging the poor to breed, though there was
nothing in the evidence collected for the commission to justify this
assumption. The population in some counties which had not provided
children's allowances had in fact increased rather faster than in those
which did provide them. This did not, of course, necessarily refute the
Malthusian theory—there might have been other reasons, such as the
fact that allowances were not commonly given in industrial areas, where
the Irish lived, and bred prolifically; but at least it suggested that the
theory should be treated with greater caution. The commissioners also
disguised the fact that the system of allowances which had come to be
attributed to (and blamed on) Speenhamland had been disappearing.
They would not admit this, because it would have destroyed their case
against the old poor law.

The most striking example of the way the commissioners had manipu-
lated the evidence, though, was not uncovered until three years later: in
the case of Cholesbury, where the expense of maintaining the paupers 'had
swallowed up the whole value of the land'. Their aim was to show that this
process, as the Sturges Bourne report had warned years before, could suddenly become uncontrollable. 'It appears to us', they wrote,

> that any parish in which the pressure of the poor rates has compelled the
> abandonment of a single farm is in imminent danger of undergoing the ruin
> which has already befallen Cholesbury. The instant the poor rate on a given
> farm exceeds that surplus which, if there were no poor rate, would be paid in
> rent, the existing cultivation becomes not only unprofitable, but a source of
> absolute loss. And as every diminution of cultivation has a double effect in
> increasing the rate on the remaining cultivation, the number of unemployed
> labourers being increased in the same instant that the fund for payment of
> rates is diminished, the abandonment of property, when it is once begun, is
> likely to proceed in a constantly accelerating ratio.

Naturally, this dire warning was freely used by ministers to justify the passing of the Poor Law Amendment Act, and to defend it after it came into operation. 'All the farms in the parish', as Lord John Russell was to remind an audience, 'had gone out of cultivation under the old system'; and he recalled the commission's reference to the speed with which the catastrophe had taken place: 'scarcely a year elapsed between the first land in Cholesbury going out of cultivation, and the abandonment of all except sixteen acres'—again, the emphasis being on how the progress became uncontrollable, once it had begun. But eventually this constant refrain, 'Remember Cholesbury!' irritated Edward Mallalieu, a contributor to the anti-government *Fraser's Magazine*; and he decided to make enquiries. 'This darling and selected parish', he found, comprised a mere 110 acres, on which there had been only two farms. A chain reaction it might have been—but the chain had only a single link.

Senior and Chadwick could hardly have been ignorant of that fact. Were they so convinced of the rightness of their principles that in fudging the evidence, they simply blinded themselves to whatever they did not care to see? Or did they deliberately twist it—much as a priest, anxious to protect the faith of his erring flock, might arrange for the artificial lique-faction of the local saint's blood, on the saint's name day—aware of the deception, but convinced of its necessity? Whatever the explanation, it enabled the commissioners to produce the report they and ministers desired. Its proposals, though, were not based on the evidence: the evidence was selected, and presented, to justify the proposals.

5. ON WEAVERS AND CLIMBING BOYS

There remained the handloom weavers to deal with. Their requests for assistance had been successfully stalled by the Government; but early in the session of 1834 ministers found themselves confronted with a batch of petitions which could not easily be ignored. In the first place, they were signed not only by the weavers themselves, but also by many of their employers, as well as clergy, magistrates, and other respectable citizens. And the M.P. who presented them was not a Tory humanitarian, but Colonel Torrens—the last man to be impressed by a ministerial lecture on economic principles. Ordinarily, in such circumstances, the Government would have resorted to a select committee, as a delaying device. But with Torrens against them, and with Fielden and John Maxwell certain to sup-port him, its recommendations could be expected to be embarrassing, as they might well directly conflict with those of the report of the royal commission on the poor law. It was safest, they decided, to do nothing, and await events.

The Government could afford to do this, because the handloom weavers still had the reputation of being wonderfully long-suffering. They played little part in the trade union movement—not surprisingly, as the trade unionist's ultimate sanction, the withholding of his labour, was a futile weapon for a handloom weaver, whose grievance was that work was being withheld from him. And although occasionally, in bad times, groups of weavers would go on the rampage and smash power looms, on the whole they behaved with exemplary patience, as their employers and their M.P.s continually testified. They still thought of themselves as they had once been, respected and even honoured members of society, a cut above the ordinary labourer—as in education they often were. Mrs. Gaskell, later to be the author of several novels set in the industrial north, described in her correspondence how her husband, a Unitarian minister, gave four lectures to 'the very poorest of the weavers in the very poorest district of Manchester' on 'The Poets and Poetry of Humble Life'—for example, Wordsworth's *The Cumberland Beggar*.

> Man is dear to man; the poorest poor
> Long for some moments in a weary life
> When they can know and feel that they have been
> Themselves, the fathers and the dealers out
> Of some small blessings; have been kind to such
> As needed kindness, for this simple cause,
> That we have all of us a human heart.

Not merely were the lectures very well attended, Mrs. Gaskell was able to report; but also, 'two deputations of respectable-looking men waited on him to ask him to repeat these lectures in two different parts of the town'.

'Aye, drive them from the world'

With the handloom weavers so docile, there was little risk of trouble if the Government continued to do nothing for them; and now, any chance there had been of Government intervention was further reduced by an authoritative-sounding explanation why nothing could be done. The author was Edward Baines, son of the editor of the *Leeds Mercury*, now emerging as one of the most dedicated adherents of *laissez nous faire*—and a particularly effective one, in that he was able to provide what seemed to be unassailable historical justification why the principle should be observed in industry. He was working on a book on this subject, and in 1833, a pilot study he had done for it attracted McCulloch's notice and approval in the *Edinburgh Review*.

The commonly-adopted view had been that the decline in the income of the handloom weaver had been due to the introduction of the new power loom. But the power loom, Baines pointed out, was not the real reason for the weavers' distress. They were not skilled workers; they could hardly be described as semi-skilled; their job did not even require strength. A twelve-year-old boy—or girl, for that matter—could quickly learn how to weave as efficiently as an adult. Such had been the demand for the hand-loom weavers' product, up to 1805, it had outstripped supply. There-after, however, earnings had fallen because too many recruits had been attracted into the industry by the high earnings; as a result, the industry had become over-supplied with labour.

In Ricardian political economy, it was hardly material whether the labour surplus had been caused by the introduction of machinery, or by too high a rate of entry into the trade. Either way, there was nothing the Government could do about it. But the current of orthodoxy was moving towards making a distinction. Both McCulloch and Senior now were com-ing round to the view that in certain circumstances public money could and should be spent to relieve unemployment; and here was Torrens insisting that the weavers were suitable recipients. The argument might be sustained if they were the victims of a technological advance, on the ground that such advances ought to be for the benefit of the community. But he could hardly claim that the handloom weavers ought to be provided for if it was their own fault, for allowing their labour market to become overstocked. On the contrary, to provide them with relief would be the height of foolishness; for it would discourage weavers from doing what they ought to have been doing, and seeking other work. Baines went further; if the handloom weavers had been condemned—as their sym-pathisers claimed—to a lifetime of unrewarding toil, the power loom should be acquitted; for rendering that toil unnecessary, it ought to be 'hailed as a national blessing'. In the circumstances, the Government could feel, there was no need to worry.

When some weeks had passed, and ministers had taken no action, John Maxwell decided that he would himself press for a select committee, to test the feeling of the House. It was estimated, he told the Commons, that there were 800,000 handloom weavers; but to be on the safe side he would settle for a figure of 500,000. They had been the nation's mainstay, during the wars; had not Pitt, himself, warned that they must not be left to the mercy of the machines that already threatened to supplant them? The time would come, Pitt had forecast, 'when manufactures have been so long established, and the operatives not having any other business to flee to, that it will be in the power of any one man in a town to reduce the wages, and all the other manufacturers must follow'. Should this ever happen, Pitt felt, 'Parliament, if not then sitting, ought to be called together; and if it cannot redress your grievances, its power is at an end. Tell me not that Parliament cannot! It is omnipotent to protect!' How, then, did the Government propose to redeem this pledge?

For the Government, Poulett Thomson was now forced to admit that the pledge could not be redeemed. Parliament could not abrogate economic laws; and even to hold an enquiry into the subject would be useless, because it could only raise hopes on the part of the weavers which could not be realised. England was on the way to becoming the great manufacturing workshop of the world; if, to help the handloom weaver, employers had to pay more for their cloth, they would be driven from the country. 'Driven from the country?' Cobbett derisively echoed; 'Aye, "drive them from the world!" ' he would say, 'drive them down to the infernal regions, rather than that they should produce so much misery'. But, again, the Government was more concerned about Torrens' views than Cobbett's. Torrens did not have much hope that his project, local boards of trade, would work; but at least, he claimed, they would show the handloom weavers that something was being attempted for them. In any case, he had been driven to the conclusion that 'where the introduction of machinery increased production and augmented the wealth of the country, the country was bound, in some shape or form, to afford assistance to those classes who were reduced to destitution by the change'. If it was right for Parliament to sanction the retention of the corn laws to prevent distress among the agricultural labourers, he reiterated, it could not be wrong to give some help to the handloom weavers, too.

M.P.s were impressed; against Poulett Thomson's expressed wishes, they agreed that an enquiry ought to be held. As usual, in this connection, there was little difference of opinion about the handloom weavers' distress. Witness after witness described how catastrophically their living standards had declined. In Spitalfields, in the old days, William Hale recalled, he had employed men for forty years at wages, regulated under the Act, of not less than sixteen shillings a week. Now, the weavers could not earn more then seven or eight shillings, for a much longer day's work—twelve to fourteen hours; and some of them were in the most destitute, abject poverty 'without clothing, furniture, bedding and every comfort in life'. Richard Needham, a Bolton weaver, claimed that earnings there were down to five and sixpence a week; and this was confirmed by John Makin, a Bolton manufacturer. He had kept his firm's records for many years back, and they showed among other things the way that the handloom weavers' wages had declined:

1797   29s. a week
1815   14s. a week
1834   5s. 6d. a week

In its report, the committee expressed their deep regret 'at finding the sufferings of that large and valuable body of men, not only not exaggerated, but that they have for years continued to an extent and intensity scarcely to be credited or conceived, and have been borne with a degree of patience unexampled'. The committee did not feel that their investigation was sufficiently complete to justify making recommendations, but they were 'impressed with a serious conviction that some legislative enactment is imperatively necessary for the removal of existing evils, which are alike injurious to the master and the operative'; and they hoped to be able to resume their deliberations in the next session, so as to be able to put forward a plan. So the Government, which had finally made up its mind to take no action, was given a further respite.

'Sweep'

One other ghost from the Tory past remained to be exorcised. Ministers were reminded of its existence when, in June, a bill was presented in the House of Lords to regulate the employment of climbing boys.

Introducing it, the Duke of Sutherland recalled that when the subject had last been debated in Parliament, fifteen years before, there had still been some doubt whether the work done by climbing boys could efficiently and safely be done by machinery. Now, there could be doubt no longer. The chimneys of 150 public buildings were regularly swept by machinery, without any necessity for boys; and in every case, they were better swept. Fire insurance rates had fallen since machine-sweeping came to be more generally adopted, proof enough of its safety; and he could see no reason why the earlier intention of the legislature, to give protection to the climbing boys, should not now be implemented.

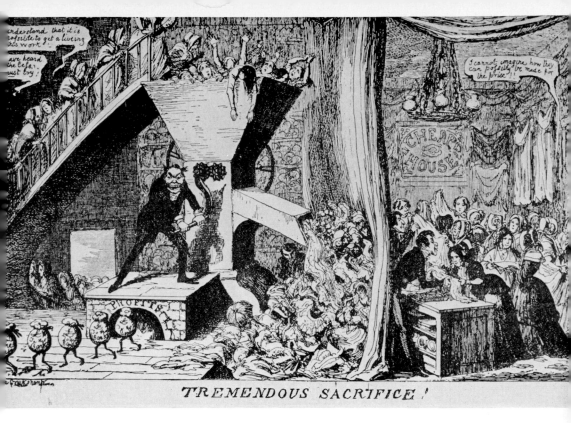

TREMENDOUS SACRIFICE!

(*Top*) Cruickshank reminds the ladies why their factory-made dresses are so cheap; and (*below*) illustrates the effects of the 1826 slump.

The yard of one of the new Union Workhouses established by the Act of 1834 on the 'less eligibility' principle.

The Duke of Hamilton disagreed. There were still some chimneys which could not be swept by machinery; and if the bill were accepted, it would be calculated to alter the whole system of building in the city of London. For individual citizens to be required by law to erect their chimneys after a particular fashion was, he thought, carrying legislation 'a little further than was necessary'. And, disconcertingly, Lord Kenyon, who had been the sponsor in the Lords of Bennet's bill to regulate the climbing boys, had now changed his mind. The subject, he thought, needed re-examination. He suggested a select committee. The Government accepted his proposal.

'When a case is fully made out for any measure', Lord Suffield observed, 'which its opponents cannot overthrow by fair reasoning, they immediately appoint a committee, as the best way of getting rid of it.' The Prime Minister intervened to deny that this was what was in the Government's mind. Although most insurance companies were not objecting to the bill, he had received objections to it from the Sun Fire Office, the Phoenix Fire Office, the Westminster Fire Office, the County Fire Office, the Globe Insurance Office, and the Royal Exchange Insurance Office; and this, he felt, justified the decision to hold another enquiry.

Hardly had the committee begun to sit when—as the publication of the minutes of evidence later revealed—it was shown one of the most striking illustrations that can ever have been presented in such circumstances; drawings, roughly to scale, of the flues in a number of public buildings, including the flue from the drying room at the newly-built Buckingham Palace, whose meanderings, horizontal and vertical, might have been designed to make cleaning impossible. The witness, John Bedford, had been one of the first sweeps to experiment with the new machinery, thirty years before—for which he had been given a testimonial by the Society for Superseding the Necessity of Climbing Boys. He never used boys, if he could help it; but there were some householders, he said, including peers, who would not allow him to use machinery; and there were some flues which the machines could not clean. One of the clauses in Bennet's measure had aimed to prevent such flues being built in future; but after its rejection, their construction had continued. Two-thirds of the flues in Buckingham Palace, Bedford estimated, were of this kind.

The usual size of the flues up which boys had to climb, he explained, was twelve to thirteen inches by nine to ten inches.* This meant that the boy had to go up with one hand above his head, to scrape off the soot; the

* Approximately the area of this book, when opened.

M

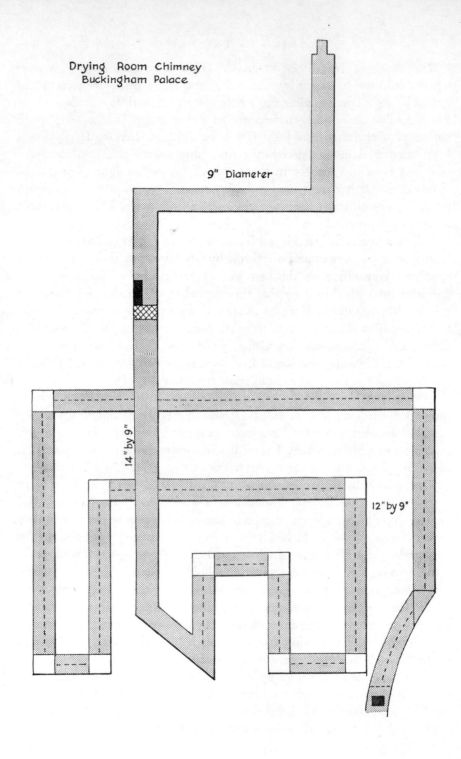

Drying Room Chimney
Buckingham Palace

9" Diameter

14" by 9"

12" by 9"

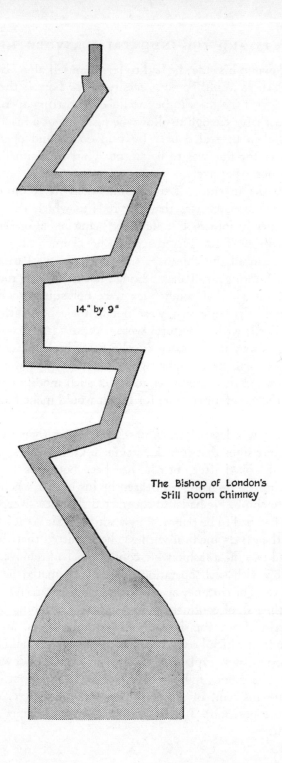

14" by 9"

The Bishop of London's
Still Room Chimney

other, pressed down to his side; he had to lever himself along by his knees and elbows. Yet there would be no necessity to use boys if the owners of the chimneys allowed the flues to be modified by cutting apertures wherever required, just large enough to allow the insertion of a machine. These apertures could then be sealed over by iron doors, and opened up for cleaning whenever the flue was to be swept. This, he claimed, would be neither difficult nor expensive.

Joseph Glass, the inventor of a machine then in common use—its advantage over predecessors was that the rods to which the brush were fixed were not merely joined, but flexible, being made of whalebone—went further than Bedford. His machine, he claimed, had been used successfully to clean all the chimneys in the Houses of Parliament, and most of those at Buckingham Palace (though not the drying room flue). It was true, he admitted, that some flues were not suited to cleaning by machinery—but in that case they were not fit for a boy, either. And he agreed with Bedford; where apertures were necessary, they could be made without damage, even if necessary in the best drawing room, or best bedroom. But servants, he thought, were the trouble. It was they, very often, who persuaded their employer to reject such modifications, and to refuse to allow the use of a machine, for fear it would make more work for them.

Although there was less evidence of ill-treatment than in the earlier enquiry, there were signs that it had continued. One witness recalled how he had been well looked after until he had been bound as an apprentice, but from that time on he had been beaten by his master when he showed any reluctance to climb. He had also contracted chimney sweeper's cancer, in the groin: it had had to be removed by a surgeon. Sir Astley Cooper was again called as the expert medical witness; he admitted that the nature of his work (he had become a fashionable consultant) had removed him from direct connection with such operations, but he estimated he must have seen a hundred cases of chimney sweep's cancer in his career.

Apart from the risk of contracting disease, too, a climbing boy still had to expect suffering from abrasions on knees and elbows, and from the contorted attitude in which he worked. He might have to hold one arm up for three hours, a witness explained, 'and when he comes down it will be in that way that he cannot tell whether he has got it or not, and it will bleed underneath his arm, by the weight of his head (here, the witness demonstrated the position). I have known the blood spurt out of the knuckles with it.'

Even master sweeps who were hostile to the bill admitted that boys
were still sent up the flue of a chimney which was on fire, to put the fire
out; and that there were still occasionally cases of suffocation. And scandals
were recalled which had received publicity in the press; in particular a case
which *The Times* had reported three years before where a householder,
intervening to prevent a sweep from maltreating a young climbing boy,
had found that the boy was in fact an eleven-year-old girl, who had been
employed on the job for the previous four years.

But there was one marked difference between this enquiry and its predecessors. The petitioners against the bill had obtained permission to be
represented by counsel; so witnesses could be gently assisted to make the
case against it with the help of leading questions. And the published
minutes of evidence showed how well the master sweeps who were
brought to speak against the bill had been briefed. John Bennet told the
committee that he could not recollect any accident to a boy in the course of
his business:

Q. No broken limbs?   A. No.
Q. No loss of life?   A. No.
Q. No casualty?   A. No: nothing more than a little illness.
Q. Now and then a cut
    of the finger?   A. Yes.

'I do not know', Bennet added, 'that I have ever seen more healthy
boys.'

The counsel for the master sweeps was also permitted to cross-examine
witnesses in favour of the bill; and he made the most of his opportunity.
James Green, for example, who had begun to climb at the age of eight,
described the repulsive conditions under which he had lived and worked as
an apprentice. 'Was it not alleged', he was asked, 'that you were habitually
given to drinking?' And Green had to admit that he liked his liquor.

Only on one issue were the opponents of the bill in some embarrassment. The master sweeps were in obvious difficulty when asked about the
'itinerant' sweeps, as they were known, who were not members of the
Master Sweeps' Society, and who earned their living by walking the
streets with their climbing boys, crying their trade, offering cut rates.
The master sweeps could not conceal their irritation with the itinerant,
who stole their custom, and by his irresponsibility brought discredit on
the trade. But they had obviously been warned that if they blackened the
reputation of the itinerant too thoroughly, the case for legislation to

The last Chimney Sweeper.

A large brush made of a number of small whalebone sticks, fastened into a round ball of wood, and extending in most cases to a diameter of two feet, is thrust up the chimney by means of hollow cylinders or tubes, fitting into one another like the joints of a fishing rod, with a long cord running through them; it is worked up and down, as each fresh joint is added, until it reaches the chimney pot; it is then shortened joint by joint, and on each joint being removed, is in like manner worked up and down in its descent; and thus you have your chimney swept perfectly clean by this machine, which is called a Scandiscope.

> Some wooden tubes, a brush, and rope,
> Are all you need employ;
> Pray order, maids, the Scandiscope,
> And not the climbing boy.

Copy of a printed hand-bill, distributed before May-day, 1826.

No May Day Sweeps.

CAUTION.

The inhabitants of this parish are most respectfully informed, that the UNITED SOCIETY OF MASTER CHIMNEY SWEEPERS intend giving their apprentices a dinner, at the Eyre Arms

Mechanics' Magazine,

MUSEUM, REGISTER, JOURNAL, AND GAZETTE.

No. 164.]   SATURDAY, OCTOBER 14, 1826.   [Price 3d

" A man's genius is always, in the beginning of life, as much unknown to himself as to others; and it is only, after frequent trials, attended with success, that he dares think himself equal to those undertakings in which those who have succeeded have fixed the admiration of mankind."

HUME.

CHIMNEY-SWEEPING MACHINES.

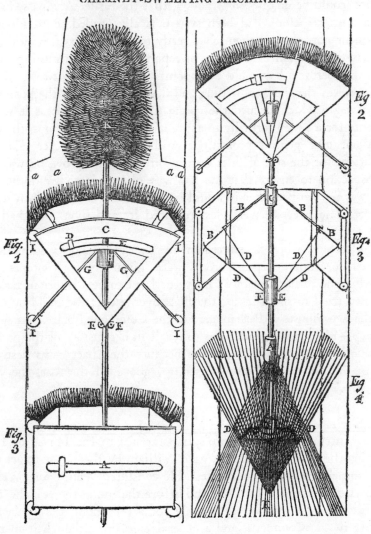

control the trade would be strengthened—and the measure might make no distinction between members of their society and outsiders. So, with an effort that emerges from the printed pages of evidence, they restrained themselves. William Duck, for example, a former president of the Master Sweeps' Society, when pressed for information about the climbing boys in itinerant service would not admit that they were ever cruelly treated: 'improperly treated' was all he would concede.

There could be no question, though, that the earlier Act, passed almost half a century before, had been systematically evaded. Both Houses of Parliament now showed themselves ready to pass, in 1834, a measure for the better regulation of chimney sweepers. Among other things, it laid down that before a boy could be apprenticed to a sweep, two magistrates must confirm that he was 'willing and desirous to follow the business'—the provision which rescued the young Oliver Twist. But as it was unnecessary for a sweep formally to apprentice his climbing boys, the clause could not give general protection. And although the Act laid down regulations for the size of flues in new buildings, no provision was made for inspection to ensure that the law was observed: so from the start, there was no prospect that it would be any better observed than its predecessor. The sweeps nevertheless resented it; and soon, they had their revenge.

In October, when a storeroom in the House of Commons was required for some purpose, orders were given for its contents to be burned in the furnaces below. This turned out to be a laborious task; the workmen tried to speed it up; the flues overheated; the building caught fire; the two Houses of Parliament and the Commons library were gutted. A sweep—Harriet Martineau was to recall in her history of the period—was among the crowd 'in high glee because the "hact" was destroyed; and, in the joy of his heart, he set up, above all the roar, the cry of "Sweep!".'

6. 1835

In the winter of 1834, Althorp's transference to the House of Lords, following the death of his father, gave William IV the excuse to get rid of a Government he had come to detest. He consulted Wellington: Wellington advised him to send for Peel; and before the end of the year the Tories were back in office. It was to be only for a few months; they lacked a majority in the Commons, and a general election, although it increased their representation, failed to provide it. But Peel's Tamworth Manifesto made it clear that he had no intention of overturning the Whigs' political and social reforms; and during his few months as Prime Minister, his government followed the policies of its predecessor. He rejected a plea that the new poor law should be modified; and although the committee on the handloom weavers was reconstituted, the new President of the Board of Trade felt no good could come of it. Even with his own party in power, Ashley realised, it would be hopeless to resume the Ten Hours campaign.

In May, Cobbett told the Commons that he could see little difference between the Whigs and the Tories—adding that the people would never be satisfied until 'they ceased to play into one another's hands'. Characteristically, he at once began to expose the defects of the new poor law in order to show that what he had predicted was coming to pass. The Duke of Richmond, he found, had persuaded one of the new poor law unions to spend £2,000 on increasing the accommodation in the local workhouse on the pretext that it would reduce bastardy. 'The noble lord seemed to forget', Cobbett remarked, 'that he was himself sprung from a bastard, and that he was only noble because he had sprung from a bastard.' In the uproar that followed, the Speaker could only with difficulty make himself heard; he was understood to say that such observations were not consistent with the decorum usually observed in the House.

It made no difference to Cobbett. A few days later, the condition of the agricultural workers was again debated. Lord John Russell—back in office in the new Whig government—did not attempt to minimise the distress they were suffering: but this was simply, he insisted, because the new poor law had not had time to prove itself. Where it was in full operation there were already signs that it was beginning to reduce the rates. 'No wonder!' Cobbett replied, flourishing a bill of fare from the workhouse in which the Duke of Richmond had interested himself. On Sunday, each boy in that workhouse was entitled for his dinner to twelve ounces of bread, half a pint of milk or gruel and seven ounces of rice; for supper, another half a pint of milk or gruel. 'A spaniel dog', Cobbett commented, 'should be allowed more.'

The Duke's brothers rose to his defence, begging the House not to accept Cobbett's word; Cobbett promised to substantiate his story. But before he could do so, he was dead. He had written his *Legacy to Labourers* only a few months before, as if aware that he could not have long to live. In it, he restated his thesis that the poor had rights which they were being denied; and reminded the working people of England, wherever and whenever they might read it, that 'they once had a friend'. Nobody would have disputed that valedictory claim. Cobbett had many failings: in financial transactions he could be unreliable to the point of unscrupulousness; his prejudices were strong and sometimes ugly,—'I see', he wrote in his *Register*, while in exile, 'that they had adopted a scheme of one Ricardo (I wonder what countryman he is?) who is, I believe, a converted Jew.' And he was temperamentally incapable of working with potential allies who were also potential rivals: Henry Hunt, say, or Barnes of *The Times*. With Barnes, Cobbett maintained a long-standing feud; the *Register* was continually denouncing the 'vile *Times*', the 'stupid *Times*', the 'bloody old *Times*'. Partly this was because *The Times* would not accept his brand of Tory radicalism without qualification; partly, no doubt, because its influence alone rivalled his *Register*'s, and by the end of the 1820s far exceeded it. Barnes usually ignored Cobbett—a standard *Times* device, even then, to infuriate other newspaper editors; at other times replied to him, indirectly, with feline banter. But now, Barnes wrote an obituary which, in spite of some contorted wording (perhaps because he was reluctant to make it sound too eulogistic) was a touching effort to give Cobbett—'in some respects a more extraordinary Englishman than any other of his time'— his due.

> Birth, station, employment, ignorance, temper, character in early life were all against him. But he emerged from, and overcame them all. By masculine force of genius and the lever of a proud and determined *will*, he pushed aside a mass of obstacles of which the least and slightest would have repelled the boldest and most ambitious of ordinary men. He ended by bursting that formidable barrier which separates the class of English gentlemen from all beneath them, and as a Member of Parliament representing a large constituency which had chosen him twice.

Barnes went on to speculate about what he clearly felt was an incongruity in Cobbett; he belonged neither to principles, nor to parties, nor to classes, and, although he was a man 'whom England alone could have produced and nurtured up to such maturity of unpatronised and self-generated power' he had never really put down roots there—or in America, which had first nourished his talents. Yet Barnes should have been well placed to provide the explanation. Cobbett, the traditionalist, had nevertheless been ahead of his time—just too far ahead to fit easily into it. It was now Barnes' own turn to grasp what the new radicalism was doing, with its poor law. Disillusioned, he was beginning to feel his way towards a Tory radicalism similar, in many respects, to Cobbett's.

But *The Times*' conversion had come too late. Its exposures of administrative incompetence in the running of the new poor law might gratify the Tories, but it could not persuade them that the law itself was a disaster, or that the whole social and economic ethos of the Whigs needed re-examination. The course was set; and, almost as if it was realised they were redundant, the men who had figured most prominently in the controversies of the immediate past were being removed from the scene. Bentham had died in 1832—the day before the Reform bill became law; and Walter Scott; and Hardy—the secretary of the Corresponding Society, who had lived on into a tranquil old age. In 1833, Hannah More, William Wilberforce, and William Thompson died; in 1834, Malthus and Coleridge; in 1835, as well as Cobbett, Sadler, Hunt and Suffield; in 1836, Godwin and James Mill. Southey, though he had some years to live, spent them in retirement, sinking into a mindless senility. Owen, too, though he lived on until 1858, ceased to exert any public influence after the debacle of 1834. His messianic urge did not leave him; he was forever founding new societies to greet the millennium, and new journals to explain why it must inevitably emerge. He also found, through spiritualism, what he believed was a way to renew old communication with the Duke of Kent and other departed acquaintances. But although his earlier teachings remained influential—most of the Chartists were his disciples at some point in their lives—none of his later projects or ideas attracted serious attention.

With Owenism routed; with the Ten Hours movement to all appearances defunct; and with traditional Toryism, of the type Coleridge and Southey had hoped to awaken, won over, the political economists could have been forgiven for displaying quiet, perhaps even exuberant, satisfaction. But by the mid-1830s they were feeling very far from satisfied. Place and Hume had seen cause after cause for which they had fought accepted; yet the political influence of their brand of radicalism was actually less in the reformed Parliament than it had been in the early 1820s—even O'Connell and his Irish 'tail' were more powerful. So far from being grateful for Senior's assistance in getting through the new poor law, the new Whig Government appeared almost to feel they could dispense with his services; certainly he was finding that his advice was much less acceptable to the new Prime Minister, Melbourne, than it had been to Grey. And Chadwick, co-architect of the new law, and of the new Factory Act, although he was appointed Secretary of the Poor Law Commissioners, found that he was not even to be given a seat on the three-man commission.

But the radicals and the political economists had more serious cause for concern. The economic system they had advocated, and watched over as it was introduced, was not working—not, at least, in the way they had expected it to work. Admittedly, they could still put some of the blame on continuing political interference; the corn laws, and excessive taxation; but this could not account for the system's manifest imperfections. Although there was no doubt that the country's material wealth had greatly increased, economic development was still painfully erratic, with booms and slumps; and the new wealth had done nothing to reduce, let alone to remove, poverty. The Old Testament prophecy appeared to have been vindicated; whatever else the revolutions in agriculture and industry had achieved, the poor were showing no signs of ceasing out of the land.

7

RETROSPECT

I. ALWAYS WITH US

IT WAS LATER to be claimed that the condition of the workers in the
period of the industrial revolution was not nearly so bad as it appeared:
that after 1820, at least, living standards began to rise. This was not
the impression at the time; the general attitude of writers of all shades of
opinion in the early 1830s was that the living standards of workers both
in agriculture and in industry had fallen.

Admittedly this was occasionally denied in the *Edinburgh Review*; but its
evidence was hardly convincing. One article in 1833 described unemployment as 'frightful'; another argued that if the cotton trade had greatly
increased—as the figures showed it had—to claim that there was distress
among the cotton workers 'is to suppose what is too contradictory and
absurd to deserve notice'; it might just as well be contended that 'the
wonderful increase of population and extension of agriculture in Kentucky
were occasioned by the growing poverty and misery of its inhabitants'.
The choice of Kentucky as an example, in view of that state's subsequent
history, was unfortunate. It was less absurd at the time, though, than
another country chosen to justify the theme that a free economy must
necessarily benefit the worker: Ireland. It had been 'proved beyond all
question', the *Edinburgh* claimed, 'that in Ireland capital had greatly
increased, agriculture had improved, manufactures were rapidly extending'.

The *Edinburgh*, though, was at this time much influenced by the young
Macaulay, who was exuding optimism. He delighted to draw up historical
balance sheets, as Senior had done in his *On Population*, to reveal how
greatly improved was the Englishman's lot. Yet even Macaulay, when he
pointed out that a greater share of wealth was falling 'to almost every
individual, than fell to the share of any corresponding class' made one
pointed omission in his list of beneficiaries. 'The serving man, the artisan,
and the husbandman', he asserted, 'have a more copious and plentiful
supply of food, better clothing and better furniture'; but he had to admit

that the 'lower orders' suffered severe hardships. All he felt justified in claiming was that they were no worse off than the labourer on the Continent—an estimate which Southey (whose *Colloquies* Macaulay was reviewing) would not have disputed; his argument had been that they ought to be much better off.

The agricultural labourers, it was universally agreed, had been the worst sufferers. On his *Rural Rides* Cobbett occasionally came across districts where they had managed to keep up their old standards, or where there were landlords like Suffield or Winchilsea; but the general picture was one of decline. Not only were the labourers worse off; they had lost caste, and dignity.

> All of you who are sixty years of age can recollect that bread and meat, and not wretched potatoes, were the food of the labouring people; you can recollect that every industrious labouring man brewed his own beer and drank it by his own fireside . . . You can recollect when every sober and industrious labourer that was a married man had his Sunday coat, and took his wife and children to church, all in decent apparel; you can recollect when the young men did not shirk about on a Sunday in ragged smock frocks with unshaven faces, and a shirt not washed for a month, and with their toes pointing out from their shoes, and when a young man was pointed at if he had not, on a Sunday, a decent coat upon his back, a good hat on his head, a clean shirt, with silk handkerchief round his neck, leather breeches without a spot, whole worsted stockings tied under the knee with a red garter, a pair of handsome Sunday shoes which it was deemed almost a disgrace not to have fastened on his feet by silver buckles. There were always some exceptions to this; some lazy, some drunken, some improvident young men; but I appeal to you all, those of you who are sixty years of age, whether this be not a true description of the state of the labourers of England when they were boys.

It was sometimes later to be suggested that Cobbett falsified history by contrasting an admittedly disagreeable present with an agreeably bucolic, but in fact mythical, past. But not even the *Edinburgh* writers, Cobbett's most unsparing critics, made this accusation at the time. Although he detested Cobbett's political opinions, Brougham eulogised his *Cottage Economy*, with its plea for a restoration of old living standards, including white bread and beer; and Sydney Smith conceded that the inadequacy of wages had compelled 'the greater part of the people of Britain to relinquish a variety of comforts, and to satisfy themselves with comparatively coarse and scanty fare'.

The rural worker in England in the period was largely mute; his sufferings did not emerge so strikingly from, say, the evidence given to the
parliamentary committees set up to consider the future of the poor laws, as
did the sufferings of the climbing boys. But from such enquiries, and from
countless books, pamphlets and speeches on the subject of the agricultural
labourer's distress, the historian Rowland Prothero (Lord Ernle) was to
conclude, half a century later, that between 1800 and 1834 their standard
of living had sunk:

> to the lowest possible scale; in the south and west wages paid by employers fell
> to 3s.–4s. a week, augmented by parochial relief from the pockets of those who
> had no need of labour; and insufficient food left its mark in the physical
> degeneracy of the peasantry. Herded together in cottages which, by their
> imperfect arrangements, violated every sanitary law, generated all kinds of
> disease, and rendered modesty an unimaginable thing . . . compelled by insufficient
> wages to expose their wives to the degradation of field labour, and to send their
> children to work as soon as they could crawl, the labourers would have been
> more than human had they not risen in an insurrection which could only be
> quelled by force. They had already carried patience beyond the limit where it
> ceases to be a virtue.

'The benignant power of steam'

But, it could be argued, the farm workers, though still the largest
segment of the labouring population, could hardly have been expected to
benefit as much from the introduction of machinery, and of the factory
system, as the worker in industry. The essential test, with the future in
mind, was his condition.

For one category of industrial worker—the largest one—the ultimate
effects of the factory system had unquestionably been disastrous. By the
1830s the handloom weavers had been reduced to a wage (when they were
lucky enough to find work at all) of less than a penny an hour; hardly
enough to keep them alive, unless they had wives and children working in
factories. When trade improved, as it was doing in 1835, they fared a little
better—but only a little; the more extensive use of power looms meant
that they were brought only temporary relief.

Again, though, it could be argued that—as Baines claimed—the power
loom had been performing a merciful function in releasing the weavers
from a lifetime of toil. The transition might be cruel, but the real test was
whether the factory worker, who was supplanting them, was better-off
than he had been—or, rather, as there had been no factories a century

before, whether he was better off than he would be if there was no factory to work in.

From the time that the condition of the factory worker was first debated at Westminster, at the beginning of the century, the mill-owners had boasted that he demonstrably *was* better off. He must enjoy a higher standard of living than he could otherwise have hoped for; because if it were not for the efficiency and economies of factory production, leading to expanding trade, there would be no job for him to do, and he would be faced by the alternative of the workhouse, or starvation. And by the 1830s, the manufacturers' case was being presented less negatively: they were claiming to be not simply job providers, but public benefactors. Following a fact-finding tour of the industrial areas, Andrew Ure returned enraptured to write his *Philosophy of Manufacture,* published in 1835:

> I have seen tens of thousands of old, young and middle-aged of both sexes, many of them too feeble to get their daily bread by any of the former modes of industry, earning abundant food, raiment, and domestic accommodation without perspiring at a single pore, screened meanwhile from the summer's sun and the winter's frost, in apartments more airy and salubrious than those of the metropolis in which our legislative and fashionable aristocracies assemble. In these spacious halls the benignant power of steam summons around him his myriads of willing menials, and assigns to each the regulated task, substituting for painful muscular effort on their part, the energies of his own gigantic arm, and demanding in return only attention and dexterity to correct such little aberrations as casually occur in his workmanship. . . . Such is the factory system, replete with prodigies and political economy, which promises in its future growth to become the great minister of civilisation in the terraqueous globe, enabling this country, as its heart, to diffuse along with its commerce the life blood of science and religion to myriads of people still lying 'in the region and shadow of death'.

Ure was prepared to admit that industry still had its problems and its setbacks; but if its early promise had not yet been fulfilled, he explained, the workers had only themselves to blame: 'had it not been for the violent collisions and interruptions resulting from erroneous views among the operatives, the factory system would have developed still more rapidly and beneficially for all concerned'. Wisely administered, he felt, the cotton industry would become 'the best temporal gift of Providence to the poor— a blessing designed to mitigate, and in some measure to repeal, the primeval curse pronounced on the labour of man: "In the sweat of thy face shalt thou eat bread."'

But was the cotton industry being wisely administered? The evidence given to both the Sadler committee and the royal commission on the factories suggested that whatever else the factory system might be achieving, it was certainly not mitigating, let alone repealing, the primeval curse. Men had to work harder—or at least longer—for their bread. And even if many adult workers were in better-paid jobs than they could have hoped for if the factories had not been built, there were tens of thousands of children working, as Sadler complained, in a way which children had never, in recorded history, been compelled to work before.

Early in the eighteenth century John Cary, no humanitarian, had felt bound to abandon his scheme for making workhouses self-supporting when he found that it would require adult paupers to work a ten-hour day. In the closing years of the century, when factories began to appear, the owners found it difficult and often impossible to persuade men and women to work in them; when Owen first went to New Lanark, for example, his predecessor there explained that he had been compelled against his will to use pauper apprentices because such was the dislike of factory work that, with few exceptions, 'only persons destitute of friends, employment and character were found willing to try'. If convicts had been compelled to work a twelve-hour day as part of their punishment, in jails, it would have provoked a humanitarian outcry. Yet the twelve-hour working day in factories had been established on commercial grounds—and not just as the norm; as the minimum. It was this, rather than the cruelty involved (it might have been claimed that the factory child was little worse off in this respect than the boys at Eton, over eighty of whom were flogged by the ferocious Dr Keate in the course of a single summer's day in 1832), which was the ugliest aspect of the factory system: that it imprisoned men, women and children, for so much of their lives.

This was the point that Shelley had emphasised in his *Philosophical View of Reform*, which he wrote in 1819. The condition of the poor in England in earlier years might not have been anything to boast about, 'yet they had earned by their labour a competency in those external materials of life' which, rather than moral and intellectual excellence, was supposed to be 'the legitimate object of the desires and murmurs of the poor'. But then, the old landed aristocracy had been joined by the new aristocracy of commerce; and since then, the poor had often worked twenty hours a day.

Not that the poor have rigidly worked twenty hours, but that the worth of the labour of twenty hours, now, in food and clothing, is equivalent to the worth of ten hours then. And because twenty hours cannot, from the nature of the human frame, be exacted from those who performed ten, the aged and the sickly are compelled either to work or starve. Children who were exempted from labour are put in requisition, and the vigorous promise of the coming generation blighted by premature exertion. For fourteen hours' labour, which they do perforce, they receive – no matter in what nominal amount – the price of seven. They eat less bread, wear worse clothes, are more ignorant, immoral, miserable and desperate.

In one respect, Shelley was wrong. The factory children did not necessarily eat less bread, or wear worse clothes. Where father, mother and children were all employed, even if their individual earnings were low, the family's total income might be higher than that of a neighbouring family where only the father worked. Naturally the factory owners made the most of the argument that families were actually better-off, where the children were working. But as Peter Gaskell noted, it was absurd to use the term 'family' about parents and children who saw each other in the home only one day a week. The slight gain from their being able to buy more food and clothes was a trivial benefit, compared to what the children were losing from lack of home life, and schooling, and recreation.

Worst of all, few of them could have any prospect in life but un-remitting labour—and labour, as a *Westminster Review* writer complained in 1833, of a debasing kind:

If no provision be made to introduce the grateful relief of variety of occupation, but the workman be constantly subjected to the same dull routine of ceaseless drudgery; if little or no leisure be permitted to him; and if during that leisure his wearied energies be neither refreshed by gentle amusements, nor his mind by more elevated pursuits, his tastes will sink to the level of the brutes to which by the process he is assimilated. A more frightful fate could scarcely be contemplated.

What further degraded the factory worker to the level of the brutes were the conditions in which, unless he was lucky, he was now compelled to live. They might be no worse than London slum dwellers had long been accustomed to, but there was a distinction; the northern slums in the 1830s were designed, in effect, as slums. They also became disease traps. The *Edinburgh* contended that the health risks in industrial areas had been exaggerated; to tease Southey, Macaulay pointed out that the English must be healthier in 1830 than they had been in the days of Sir Thomas More, three centuries earlier, because the life span was known to have increased—and 'that the lives of men should become longer and longer, while their bodily condition during life is becoming worse and worse, is utterly incredible'. But Macaulay unwisely went on to cite another piece of evidence in his favour; society was no longer troubled by the plague! A few months later, the cholera arrived.

Machinery, then, had vastly increased England's productive potential; it had made fortunes for many employers, and for those who financed them; and it had made England the foremost trading nation of the world. But it had done so—Sismondi asserted in his essay on the condition of the factory workers, written in 1834—only at the workers' expense:

> The proletarii are cut off from all the benefits of civilisation; their food, their dwellings, their clothes are insalubrious; no relaxation, no pleasures except occasional excesses, interrupt their monotonous labours; the introduction of the wonders of mechanics into the arts, far from abridging their hours of labour, has prolonged them; no time is left them for their own instruction or for the education of their children; no enjoyment is secure to them in those family ties which reflect their sufferings; it is almost wise for them to degrade and brutalise themselves to escape from the feeling of their misery; and that social order which threatens them with a worse condition for the future, is regarded by them as an enemy to combat and destroy. And this is not all: whilst their own distress is increasing, they see society overcome, as it were, by the weight of its material opulence; they are in want of everything; and on all sides their eyes are struck with what is everywhere superabounding.

A writer in _Blackwood's_ expressed the same concern. Never at any time, he thought, had there been more for man to do for man; there had been a breaking up of the entire system. 'It may be for our ultimate good, but this is certain, that the love of money is the ruling passion of the rich—and of the poor, the mere love of life.'

2. ON WEALTH

But why had the system given such disappointing results? From very different points of view, Shelley and Wordsworth reached the same conclusion. Commerce, Shelley had lamented in _Queen Mab_:

> . . . set the mark of selfishness
> The signet of its all enslaving power
> Upon a shining ore, and called it gold
> Before whose image bow the vulgar great,
> The vainly rich, the miserably proud,
> The mob of peasants, nobles, priests and kings,
> And with blind feelings reverence the power
> That grinds them to the dust of misery.
> Gold is a living god, and rules in scorn
> All earthly things but virtue . . .
> The harmony and happiness of man
> Yields to the wealth of nations . . .

Wordsworth blamed the same culprit in his *Humanity*:

> . . . 'Slaves cannot breathe in England' – yet that boast
> Is but a mockery! When from coast to coast
> Though *fettered* slave be none, her floors and soil
> Groan underneath a weight of slavish toil.
> For the poor many, measured out by rules
> Fetched with cupidity from heartless schools
> That to an Idol, falsely called 'the Wealth
> of Nations', sacrifice a people's health
> Body and mind and soul . . .

The view that political economy was basically responsible for the
nation's economic ills, and in particular for the condition of the poor, had
been held by a remarkable diversity of people. Arthur Young had expressed
it; Cobbett continually reverted to it; it became basic to Owen's philosophy, and to that of many of his disciples; it was expounded by writers in
the *Quarterly*, and in *Blackwood's*; and it frequently appeared in Coleridge's
tracts and table talk. But it had also begun to spread among economists
who were, or had once been, disciples of Adam Smith.

In the 1820s Sismondi had continued to deplore what he felt was the
wrong course that political economy had begun to take under the guidance
of Mill, Ricardo and McCulloch. He had even come round to the belief
that a form of mercantilism would have been better for the community, in
the circumstances, than *laissez-faire*. It had not been an efficient system, he
granted; 'but with regard to persons, have all the effects of destroying it
been well-calculated?' Was it really the aim of human society to give two
or three individuals in a hundred thousand the power of disposing of an
opulence which would give comfort to all those hundred thousand? Could

it be that in searching after wealth, they had forgotten how to run the home—'and the city, Political Economy'?

But apart from those who defected, like Sismondi, or who carried the Ricardian theory a stage further, like Hodgskin, there had also been writers in the 1820s who applied the rules of political economy to an investigation of its principles. In 1825 Samuel Bailey exposed the shallowness of Ricardo's labour theory of value; four years later, Samuel Read rehearsed some of the contradictions in the economists' writings; and then, in the 1830s, political economy was subjected to the most searching scrutiny it had yet received, from Poulett Scrope.

Although George Poulett Scrope—born Poulett Thomson; he was a brother of the Whig minister, but he had changed his name following marriage to a Wiltshire heiress—was still in his early thirties, he had already made his name as an expert in volcanic phenomena; he had been Secretary to the Geological Society, and, since 1826, a Fellow of the Royal Society. When he went to live in the country, he had become, as was expected of him, a magistrate; and what he saw from the bench, and on the land, had prompted him to take an interest in the condition of the labouring poor—his tracts on this and other subjects eventually became so numerous that they were to win him the punning nickname, 'Pamphlet' Scrope. To further his investigation, he had begun to study economics, coming quickly to the conclusion that it was not the science it had been claimed to be; and he presented his critique in tracts, in articles in the *Quarterly*, and in his *Principles of Political Economy*, published in 1833.

Scrope might be an amateur, but he represented potentially a more serious threat to the orthodox economists' peace of mind than any critic since the time that Sismondi had first troubled Ricardo. He was a man of wealth—and influence, with his brother at the Board of Trade; in 1833, too, he himself entered Parliament for Stroud. His diversity of interests did not make him any less formidable an antagonist; his *Principles* extorted the admiration even of the economist he most unsparingly criticised—McCulloch, who thought that although some of Scrope's theories might be questionable, the book showed 'considerable talent and acuteness'. Scrope, in short, could not lightly be dismissed along with the rest of the *Quarterly* tribe, the Southeys and Crokers.

By the 1830s, Scrope argued, it could no longer be pretended that the economic system was working satisfactorily. Knowledge was increasing, but the discoveries made in art and science were adding only to the stock of superfluities: 'food, the staff of life, seems to be stationary, not to say retrograde, in the rate of supply. This is not what it should be. There is something wrong.'

Could it be—Scrope asked—that the something which was wrong was that political economy had been accepted, not as the speculation it was, but as scientific? The proposition that it was a science, after all, had originally been advanced by the French economists in the eighteenth century; yet Adam Smith had made the same claim for the theories of *The Wealth of Nations*, which were very different. And since the appearance of *The Wealth of Nations*, there had been many accretions:

> It must, I fear, be conceded by all who are acquainted with the more recent works on political economy, that whatever the degree to which the science was advanced by Dr Smith, it has received few or no substantial improvements since his time, in spite of the volumes that have issued from the press on the subject and the tribes of authors that have successively lectured upon it *ex cathedra*. Professor after professor has brought forward his special doctrine with no small flourish of trumpets, as a newly-discovered truth; but, each having for his new erection uniformly destroyed the productions of his predecessor, and occasionally his own, the sum total of our acquisitions during this period, even in the estimation of the most enthusiastic devotees of the science, is but small. They too are divided into sects and schools, perhaps equalling in number the individual authors; and the consequence of this discordance, even on the most fundamental questions, coupled as it has been with glaring inconsistencies, and the frequent assertion of the most startling paradoxes, is a general feeling of disinclination, we had almost said of disgust, in the public mind towards a science which, during so considerable a period, has confessedly propagated so many dangerous fallacies, and established so few useful truths.

A theme emerged from Scrope's various commentaries. The political economists had assumed the existence of a science of political economy: from it, they had adduced principles; and from their interpretation of the principles, they had recommended certain courses of action. That there should have been disagreements about the interpretation was not surprising; but this had not deterred the economists from putting forward whatever version they believed at the time as if it were the only conceivable course of action, consonant with scientific reasoning and social common-sense. This was bad enough; but what was worse was that the principles themselves—which they had thought to be, and claimed to be, immutable economic laws—had often been no more than naive attempts to interpret those laws; very often they clashed; some had been discarded; and it was beginning to be doubtful whether any laws existed. Yet an economic edifice had been built on these rickety principles. The consequences for the community had been disastrous.

'It is not with happiness, but with wealth, that I am concerned'

The political economists, Scrope observed, were inclined to disclaim responsibility for what had happened by insisting that their function was simply to elucidate economic principles in the abstract; they ought not to be blamed for what politicians had done in their name. But this simply was not true. In the first place, Adam Smith himself had insisted that the object of political economy was 'to provide a plentiful revenue or subsistence for the people, or more properly, to enable them to provide such a revenue or subsistence for themselves'. If political economy were to be of such practical utility, Scrope insisted, 'it must have for its object, not merely a dry enumeration of the different modes in which the productive powers of man are in practice applied to satisfy his desires, but also a comparison of the efficiency of these different modes towards the attainment of that end . . . it is only the practical lesson to be derived from its study, that renders political economy a subject of deeper concern than the abstractions of pure mathematics or transcendental metaphysics.' In any case, Scrope continued, the political economists could not claim that they had stayed aloof from the political and social struggle. They were 'perpetually claiming for their science a paramount importance to the interests of mankind, and urging its conclusions on governments and legislatures, as the only infallible guide for securing the welfare of states'.

Yet these economists who presumed to guide the nation's destinies were so uncertain of themselves that they had not even been able to agree on terminology. Considering that all of them accepted that political economy was 'the science of the laws which regulate the production and distribution of *wealth*'; it might at least have been expected, Scrope thought, that they would have reached agreement on the meaning of that term. Yet Malthus confined it to material objects, whereas McCulloch, though defining it as 'those articles or products, useful or agreeable to man, which possess exchangeable value' allowed the talents of an author into this category. Some ludicrous confusion had resulted—as when Malthus had felt compelled to make a distinction between the third footman behind a coach (who, he felt, was not part of his master's wealth) and the livery he wore, (which was). 'The whole footman', Scrope insisted, '. . . livery, cane and all —is an object of gratification to his master's vanity; and if the livery is to be reckoned as wealth, so also must be its wearer.' If the political economists could not even agree on the first principles of their science—what they were talking about—how could they possibly claim they were being scientific?

But the economists' failure to reach an agreed definition of such terms as wealth and value was of little significance, except so far as it was the measure of the spuriousness of their pretensions. Much more serious, Scrope thought, was their acceptance in practice of a definition of wealth which excluded welfare.

Early in the century, the Earl of Lauderdale in his *Inquiry* had warned against the idea that the nation's wealth could be measured in financial terms, such as the sum of individual incomes; true wealth, he had argued, must be differentiated from riches. But he had not gone on to explain how; and later economists, whatever their theoretical definition might be, had tended to accept in practice that wealth could be measured in financial terms. Sometimes they put it a little differently: Senior, for example, in his *Essay on Wages*, claimed that he was far from disregarding the importance of human happiness; and he realised that the evils of severe and incessant labour, or the benefits of a certain degree of leisure, ought not to be left out of account when happiness was being estimated. 'But', he went on, 'it is not with happiness, but with wealth, that I am concerned as a political economist; and I am not only justified in omitting, but, perhaps, am bound to omit, all considerations which have no influence on wealth.' No sooner had he made this point, though—which at least was theoretically defensible—than Senior went on to say that in practice wealth and happiness were 'very seldom opposed'; and he tended to assume that for ordinary purposes, they were identical. Owen had challenged the assumption—and been derided by Torrens for doing so. Now, Scrope took Owen's side:

> It is utterly false, that every increase of wealth is a proportionate increase of the aggregate means of enjoyment. Nay, some kinds of wealth may be vastly augmented with little or no increase of the means of enjoyment, and a very small increase of some sorts of wealth is often more beneficial to mankind than a large increase of others. Suppose, for illustration, a race of absolute sovereigns to have a taste for jewels, and to employ several thousands of their subjects or slaves, generation after generation, in toiling to procure them. These treasures will be wealth of enormous *value*, but add barely anything to the aggregate means of enjoyment. Suppose another race of sovereigns to have employed equal numbers of workmen during the same time in making roads, docks and canals throughout their dominions, or on erecting hospitals and public buildings for education or amusement. These acquisitions to the wealth of the country,

having cost the same labour, may be of equal exchangeable *value* as the diamonds of the other sovereigns; but are they to be reckoned only equally *useful*, equal accessions to the aggregate means of human gratification?

The political economists had failed to make this distinction; their guidance had been relevant only to 'the increase of wealth *in the sense of exchangeable value, not of utility*'. If they believed, as most of them claimed to do, that the greatest happiness of the community was the true and only end of all human institutions, it followed, Scrope feared, that any government which took political economy as a guide to its legislation, 'without continually correcting its conclusions by reference to the *moral code,* or the principles upon which the happiness, not the wealth, of man depends, must often sacrifice the real interest of the people it presides over for a glittering fiction'.

As things had worked out, precisely at the time when more wealth was becoming available to promote the welfare of the community as a whole, political economy had been teaching that it did not need to be used for that end. Welfare did not have to be taken into consideration; wealth could be accumulated for its own sake. Admittedly, Adam Smith had assumed that welfare must necessarily follow wealth; and his followers clung to that belief. But welfare had not kept pace with wealth; for reasons which could be traced to faults in the economic system, and the principles from which it had been derived. Three of these principles, in particular, had been influential, because they had been accepted by successive governments: that the economy, if left by the State to regulate itself, would do so more effectively for the benefit of the community as a whole than the State could hope to do, if it tried to intervene for that purpose; that private property was sacrosanct; and that population had a tendency to increase faster than the means of subsistence.

'To increase the comforts of the South American peon'

That a free economy would both regulate itself, on the basis of Adam Smith's hidden hand, and operate for the greatest good of the community, on the basis of Bentham's enlightened selfishness, was accepted by all the political economists—except Malthus, who had some reservations. And certainly it was the principle that ordinarily came to politicians' minds when they cited political economy.

Yet the political economists had found themselves in constant confusion, both over the principle and the practice. To begin with, they realised that the hidden hand could be expected to work only in a free economy; and the English economy was not free—partly because a Parliament of landowners was in control, forever seeking to manipulate it for their own benefit; partly because in industry, the employers were allowed to combine. This had not been Adam Smith's idea of a free economy; in such circumstances, he had warned, the employers would retain restrictive practices of the kind that had enabled them to levy 'for their own benefit, an absurd tax upon their fellow citizens'; Parliament must watch for this; and if they made any protest, it should be looked on with suspicion, for it would be coming 'from an order of men whose interest is never exactly the same as that of the public, and who have generally an interest to deceive and oppress the public'. But whereas workers who tried to combine had been harassed, employers had been allowed to combine— even encouraged to do so, as when Melbourne prompted them to get together to crush the Grand National Consolidated Trades Union. What had developed in England was not even *laissez-faire*, but the employers' version, *laissez nous faire*—as put forward by Josiah Wedgwood, when he gave evidence before the Peel committee: 'I have a strong opinion that, from all I know of many factories in general, and certainly from all I know of my own, we had better be left alone.'

It would theoretically have been possible for the political economists simply to repudiate *laissez nous faire*: but it was so much closer to what they wanted than the likely alternative, State regulation of industry, that they tended to side with the employer, and to identify with him, against both the landowning interest and the worker. They began to think, and write, as if the economy *was* free, and should behave according to their principles: in particular, that it should be self-regulating, on the theory which had been developed by the French economist, Jean-Baptiste Say. Supply, Say argued, created its own demand; the processes which resulted in any commodity appearing for sale automatically provided the purchasing power which would enable it to be bought; any general glut, therefore, was impossible. When a general glut came in 1817, and again in 1819, it was explained away: the economists preferred to blame the war, or post-war dislocation of taxation, rather than to re-examine the principle in relation to the economy as it existed. In his *Elements*, for example, in 1821, Mill could still insist 'production can never be too rapid for the market; in other words, there can never be a general glut of commodities'—in spite of the recent examples.

But by this time, the principle was being challenged not only by

Malthus, whose economics could be discounted, but by Ricardo. Labour-saving machinery, Ricardo had admitted, might lead to a labour surplus; its introduction was therefore not necessarily in the workers' interest. This did not worry him; he now envisaged a society in which machines would grow more complex, capable of being managed by a smaller number of skilled workers: the rest of the labour force would gradually become redundant, except that part of it which could be absorbed by 'the increased demand for menial servants'. This might satisfy Ricardo, and leave Malthus happy; but to some of their radical allies 'self-regulating' was an odd description for an economy which was continually presenting redundant labourers with the choice between domestic service and the workhouse. It was an embarrassing situation, to which other economists had reacted predictably. McCulloch rejected Ricardo's new theory, and continued to behave as if nothing had happened—to the amusement of some of his more cynical fellow members of the Political Economy Club; as one of them put it, McCulloch 'tranquillised himself' with his own assumption that the population had never been better off. But orthodoxy also provided a substitute theory, which very quickly found acceptance: the idea of the wages fund.

Suppose—Senior was to explain—a machine had been invented which enabled one corkscrew maker to do the work of several, throwing the others out of work, or forcing them to accept lower wages. It would not matter; 'as the whole fund for the maintenance of labourers, and the whole number of labourers to be maintained has remained unaltered, that fall must have been balanced by a rise somewhere else . . . the fall in the price of cork-screws must have left every purchaser of a corkscrew a fund for the purchase of labour, rather larger than he would have possessed if he had paid the former price.' There was no need to worry about redundant labour. By the laws of economics, for each job lost, another would appear. The situation, temporarily imperilled by Ricardo's defection, had been retrieved.

The wages fund theory was presented as if it were scientific; and indeed it sounded very reasonable. Richard Bacon, however, exposed the fallacy. When the price of a commodity fell owing to the introduction of a labour-saving machine, the purchaser of that commodity certainly had more to spare to purchase labour. But what was the use of purchasing labour if the market for goods had contracted—as it had, owing to the fact that the men whom the machine had put out of work no longer had the wages to buy the goods? In such circumstances, Bacon pointed out, increased production could not be absorbed; the manufacturer could not sell his goods; more workers would have to lose their jobs, lowering demand still further until there was a general glut. By cutting down the workers' purchasing power, the manufacturers were themselves destroying the capacity of the system to regulate itself; 'the whole circulation is thus stopped in the first elements', consumption as well as production being checked 'because all the working classes are by this artificial arrangement, by the compressive force and unequal distribution of property, reduced to the lowest quantity of food and raiment that can sustain life'.

In *Blackwood's Edinburgh Magazine*, too—the *Edinburgh's* rival, higher Tory even than the *Quarterly*, and reputedly having the biggest circulation of any of the serious magazines of the time—the myth of the self-regulating economy was denounced by David Robinson in a series of articles on the social system, which appeared in the late 1820s. Again, there was the curious link between high Toryism and Owenism; Robinson took up Owen's idea that the economic system, so far from being self-regulating, was inherently unstable. Once in every three or four years, Robinson argued, there was bound to be a crisis; 'production and consumption cannot possibly be kept together; the powers of the former have been rendered gigantic by capital, machinery and knowledge, and the market must be very frequently overloaded with merchandise and manufactures'. In the circumstances, abolition of the poor laws, so far from helping the economy, would be disastrous:

> The poor laws form the great prop of wages; abolish them, and with your redundant population wages will speedily fall by half. What will follow? The body of your British labouring orders will be compelled to abandon the consumption of taxed articles, to feed on potatoes and butchers' offal, and to wear rags. In their fall they must pull down with them not only the small tradesmen, but to a great extent the larger ones.

Scrope provided yet another reason why the economy was not self-regulating. Adam Smith had based his theory on the assumption that increasing wages would maintain demand, and increasing competition would keep down profits. But in the event competition for jobs had kept down wages, and agreements between employers had kept up profits. As a result, it was not the English men, women and children, who made the clothes who benefited; ironically, it was the foreigners who wore them.

The explanation, Scrope showed, was very simple. In England, labour was heavily taxed. Apart from having to pay more for imported corn, the labourers had to pay duty on sugar, tea, coffee, tobacco, malt, hops, beer, spirits, licences, leather, printed goods, soap, tallow, and candles. But machines paid no tax at all (except indirectly, through the men who operated them). It followed that any industrialist who wanted to reach a new market by lowering the cost of his goods would do so, if he could, by installing new machines and getting rid of labourers.

But this meant that the men thrown out of work had to be maintained at the ratepayers' expense. So, the ludicrous situation had arisen whereby the ratepayers were, in effect, subsidising not only the English manufacturer (by looking after the men his machines had put out of work) but also the foreign consumers, who were getting their cotton dresses cheaper *because* of the subsidy. 'As the poor rate is chiefly paid by the owners of real property, this portion of it operates as a tax levied upon that class, and is expended in giving a *bounty* to the exportation of manufactures without an adequate return; in other words, *in paying for* the clothing of the Americans, Russians, Danes, etc'. And what was the advantage to the nation of such an extension of foreign trade, 'if all it did was fill the workhouses with idle paupers, for the sake of clothing the continental peasantry in cheap calicoes? Which occasions poverty and misery at home, in order to increase the comforts of the South American peon?'

The way in which the self-regulating theory had developed was a revealing demonstration of the process by which economic ideas hardened through doctrine into dogma. Adam Smith had contented himself with explaining why a free market *ought* to work; 'it is the interest of all those who employ their land, labour or stock in bringing any commodity to market that the quantity should never exceed the effectual demand; and it is the interest of all other people that it should never fall short of that demand'. But Say presented the principle, in condensed form, as an economic law; and because it came to be regarded as a law, various dogmatic assumptions were derived from it: for example, that it was futile of the state to provide funds for public works to relieve unemployment.

Adam Smith had assumed that the State should intervene to pay for public works where, for example, some institution was deemed necessary for society, which would not repay its expense to individuals. Bentham, in his early writings on economics, had gone further, citing unemployment as one of the legitimate reasons for the provision of public works. But Ricardo, though he agreed that governments might finance certain projects

with a view to assisting industry and commerce—docks, say, or canals—
had insisted that they must limit themselves to that. They must not
intervene to provide employment, because to use public funds for that
purpose would 'only divert funds from other employments which are
equally, if not more, productive'. Grateful for advice which absolved them
for asking the taxpayer for more money, ministers had accepted it: Canning explained to the Commons in 1826 that the circumstances could not
warrant a departure 'from that legitimate principle, which prohibited the
grant of public money towards the relief of partial distress'.

Public works were only one of many legislative devices, previously
sanctioned and eventually to be accepted as socially desirable, which were
rejected in the period of the industrial revolution on the theory that
the economy ought to be self-regulating. The 'law' was also cited as the
justification for repealing measures which had formerly given protection
to workers, or to the community; and for rejecting new measures to
provide such protection, even when the dictates of humanity or common
sense urged the necessity for them. It was used to deny the right of the
legislature to intervene in order to procure land for labourers, or to
limit the hours adults worked in factories, or to regulate the sweeping of
chimneys. By the 1830s, not merely had the theory been shown to be
fallacious, or at least irrelevant, by the course of events; the reasons why
it was irrelevant had been given by critics of political economy, and were
coming to be accepted even by formerly orthodox economists. Yet it was
still being taught as orthodoxy; and still being accepted as a guiding
principle, by politicians.

'The most horrible perversion of humanity'

The second of the main principles on which the political economists
were agreed, or believed that they were agreed, was the sacredness of
private property. In a sense, it was the principle upon which all the others
rested; for without it, they claimed, political economy could not operate.
Satirising McCulloch as McQuedy (MacQ. E. D.) in *Crotchet Castle*,
Peacock had him describe civilisation as 'a just respect for property'—a
definition which McCulloch would hardly have thought satirical, as he
himself had written that without security of property, there could be
neither riches nor civilisation. The reason, McCulloch explained, was that
in the ascent of man from poverty to affluence, the institution of private
property had been the first and most important step, because 'no one
would ever engage in any laborious or difficult undertaking without a

thorough conviction that he was labouring for his own advantage, and not for that of others, and that he would be permitted to enjoy the fruits of his labour without molestation'.

Put in this pragmatic form, the principle sounded eminently reasonable. But the economists could not make up their minds about what constituted 'molestation'. Theft, clearly; but what about taxation? Obviously there must be taxes, if only to provide for the means to protect property, the army, the judiciary, police, jails. Thus far, Adam Smith believed, and no farther. There should be no taxation for purposes other than making provision for the security of property owners; where there was, 'the sacred rights of property are sacrificed to the supposed interests of public revenue'. In practice, though, the line was impossible to draw. Suppose, for example, the Government decided to provide the capital for some public works to relieve unemployment. It might appear to be a molestation— but what if it helped to reduce unrest, and thereby remove the threat of revolution? The family allowance system had, in fact, been introduced for this purpose, as well as for humanitarian reasons. Taxes, in other words, might be levied on private property in order more effectively to safeguard private property. But, inevitably, this left wide discretion to the State; it might decide—as later governments were to decide—that the rich would have to sacrifice most of their income, to preserve the rest. The decision how much to take was not a matter of ethical principle, so much as a political judgment.

But this was not the only issue then in doubt. Even granted that private property in the form of houses, clothes, jewelry, stocks and shares ought, so far as was humanly possible, to remain the property of the rightful owner, was land in the same category? Spence had argued that it was as inherently absurd that any man should claim to own land as that he should claim to own the sea, or the air. They were the fundamentals of human life; they had been provided by God, or nature. For practical purposes there might be a need to allocate responsibility for cultivating the land; the better to utilise it, it could be rented. But the ownership, if it could be called that, must remain vested in the community, and the rent from it put to whatever uses the community thought fit. Coleridge did not go so far; but he invoked the traditional Christian ethic, which had always imposed on the well-off the duty of looking after the poor. When would society— he asked in his *Table Talk* in 1833—return to the traditional conception of the right to own land as:

implying and demanding the performance of commensurate duties? Nothing but the most horrible perversion of humanity and moral justice, under the spurious name of political economy, could have blinded men to this truth, as to the possession of the land – the law of God having connected indissolubly the cultivation of every rood of earth with the maintenance and watchful labour of man. But money, stocks, riches by credit, transferable and convertible at will, are under no such obligation; and, unhappily, it is from the selfish aristocratic possession of such property that our landholders have learned their present theory of trading with that which was never meant to be an object of commerce.

Ricardo, for one, held that theory of trading. Land to him was simply an alternative form of stock; to be bought cheap, if possible, and sold dear, relative to other stock. The use to which it was put, he thought, ought to be dictated by market forces. It might be tilled, or used for grazing, or left fallow, or given over to the preservation of game—whichever was the most profitable. And on the assumption that the economics of agriculture were analogous to those of industry, this might appear to be a tenable hypothesis. But they were not analogous. The landowners held, in effect, a monopoly; and the institution of private property in land relieved them from the necessity of behaving like entrepreneurs. If a businessman did not maintain the profitability of his firm, it would go out of business. A landowner who did not maintain his land's profitability might be poorer than his neighbour, but he would not, except through disastrous mismanagement, be forced to sell out. It was consequently foolish to assume, as Harriet Martineau clearly did in her *Illustrations*, that landowners would behave like economic men. The landowner was just as likely to be a Sir Simon Steeltrap, M.P., J.P., lord of the manor of Springgun-cum-Treadmill—as described by the Lady Clarinda in *Crotchet Castle*:

> . . . a great preserver of game and public morals. By administering the laws which he insists on making, he disposes, at his pleasure, of the land and its livestock, including all the two-legged varieties, with and without feathers, in a circumference of several miles around Steeltrap Lodge. He has enclosed commons and woodlands; abolished cottage gardens; taken the village cricket ground into his own park, out of pure regard to the sanctity of Sunday; shut up foot paths and ale houses (all but those which belong to his electioneering friend, Mr Quassia, the brewer); put down fairs and fiddlers; committed many poachers; shot a few; convicted one third of the peasantry; suspected the rest; and passed nearly the whole of them through a wholesome course of prison discipline, which has finished their education at the expense of the country.

The 1830s: (*top*) plague pit near a London gasworks.
(*below*) London tenements.

Oh, Oh, young Gentleman, so I understands as how
you are going to join the Union!

Nº 17.

Two cartoonists are amused by the presumption of the trade union movement.

Mᶜ LEAN'S MONTHLY SHEET OF CARICATURES. Nº 53.

*Yes Gentlemen, these is my principles, — no K—g, — no L—ds, —no Parsons, —no Police, —no Taxes,—
no Transportation, —no Nothing.*

A MEETING OF THE TRADES' UNIONS.

Unlike Harriet Martineau, Ricardo and Mill were under no illusions about landowners. Mill, in particular, held views not far removed from those of Spence, arguing that a substantial proportion of the rent paid to them was unearned increment, which could legitimately be taxed. But the economists could not work out how to decide *what* proportion of rent was unearned. The capital which he had sunk in the land had to be allowed for; and that might be difficult to compute. In any case, what was to be done about land which had just been sold? It would be hard on a new buyer, who had just paid the full market rate for it, to find himself being taxed, while the former landowner was not taxed on the income from the price he had been paid. So although the new radicals could be, and were, accused of wanting to deprive landowners of some of their property rights, it was in fact the right of private property which prevented them from taking up a Spencean position.

The economists, too, in their endless discussions on the theory of rent, allowed themselves to fall into another misconception. They tended to assume that land from which no rent was derived was not profitable to farm; and this gave them an additional reason, on economic grounds, to oppose State intervention to secure plots of uncultivated land for labourers.

The investigations of the Society for Bettering the Condition of the Poor, though, and of the Labourer's Friend Society had demonstrated that, contrary to a common impression, smallholdings cultivated without the assistance of a plough, let alone of agricultural machinery, could actually be more productive than the same land farmed with the help of the most up-to-date devices. Various explanations were suggested; the farmer watched over, and worked on, his smallholding with greater care and effort than he would work for an employer; his family helped; he could keep a flock of hens and a pig on farmyard scraps, without having to buy food for them— and so on. There was consequently no reason, it was urged, to withhold land from labourers on the excuse that spade husbandry was inefficient; and there was very good reason to provide them with land, to keep them off the rates.

The economists, however, mocked such research as empirical—a word still used pejoratively. Investigations of the kind that the Society had conducted were all very well; but why bother, when rent provided the answer automatically? If the capital and labour involved in spade husbandry yielded more than the same capital and labour involved in plough or machine husbandry, James Mill pointed out, landowners would at once

N

stop consolidating farms, and split them up again, because they would get more rent that way—a proposition which Ricardo echoed approvingly. But as consolidation had continued, it followed that the empirical observations must have been incorrect.

Bacon eventually explained why the economists were wrong. Suppose, for argument's sake, twenty 5-acre farms, cultivated by spade husbandry, together were more productive than a single 100-acre farm using agricultural machinery. This did not mean that the landowner would get more rent from them—far from it. As each 5-acre farm might support a farmer and his family, the amount that tenants could afford to pay in rent would be small. The single tenant farmer, hiring labourers when he needed them, might have a lower yield from his hundred acres, but he would have a larger net profit—and it was from net profit that rent was derived. That was why landowners preferred consolidation.

On the same reasoning, it would have been possible for thousands of labourers to make a living from land which was not being cultivated. But because they would not have produced a sufficient surplus out of which to pay rent, they were denied access to that land. Admittedly, to farm land which did not provide such a surplus would mean a hard and unrewarding life, such as many wretched peasants on the continent had to lead. But it would have been less hard and unrewarding than the alternative—the life of day labourers, supported on the rates; it would have kept them independent; and the ratepayer would have been relieved of the need to provide for them. And the fact that land which could not produce rent could still be used to support families, also disposed of the Malthusian objection that any extension of the land under cultivation must necessarily bring diminishing returns. On the evidence of the investigations by the Societies, this simply was not true; land which had remained uncultivated, because it did not produce rent, could actually be used to produce more food per acre than land in cultivation.

The course which events had taken were not the responsibility of the economists; it might have made no difference even if they had repudiated their early ideas on rent, as they repudiated the theory of population. But they could reasonably be charged with confusing the right of a man to own possessions, such as money and furniture, and to use them how he wished; and the right to own land, and to use it how he wished. To McCulloch, the right overrode any economic or political considerations; 'the property of a landlord is violated whenever he is compelled to adopt any system of cultivation, even supposing it to be really preferable to that which he was previously following'. It followed that even if it could be proved—as the experiments suggested—that a different system of land tenure would greatly reduce the labour surplus, by settling labourers on the land, this was not permissible, except by voluntary action on the part of individual landlords.

But why—Samuel Read argued in his *Inquiry*, in 1829—should political economy accept this view, that property was sacred, without enquiring into the title deeds by which the owners held it? Surely society had the prior claim; no individual, simply by ownership of land, should have the unfettered right to throw men off it, depriving them of work when it could be made available for them. It followed that to leave land idle, when there were men who could make a living farming it, was not to be tolerated.

Scrope agreed: 'the right to landed property is justly made to give way before the paramount right of every individual, born into the world in civilised society, to be saved from starving in the midst of abundance'. Should that right be denied, the destitute individual 'would be restored to a state of nature, and would reacquire all these rights which that state implies; amongst them, the right to derive his subsistence from the earth, and to acquire it how he may'. It was necessary for the land-owner, in other words, to accept that the poor had a right to maintenance; not necessarily on the historical grounds Coleridge put forward—let alone on Spence's argument—but simply for security.

But a parliament dominated by landowners was unlikely to pay any attention to this point of view; and in any case, by the 1830s the social damage had been done. The yeomen, smallholders and cottagers had almost disappeared, not because they made inefficient use of their land, but because it was more profitable, in terms of rent, to get rid of them, and consolidate their farms. Profitable for the landowner—but, as Cobbett never tired of arguing, not necessarily for the community. In society's interests, it might well have been desirable to preserve a balance between large and small farms; and to preserve the old yeoman stock. But because rent had been accepted as the arbiter, the whole pattern of rural life in England had been changed—and, for the great majority of those con-cerned, for the worse. To salve their consciences, and to protect their property, the landowners had introduced the family allowance system. But because it had not been backed by a minimum wage, it had done no more than keep the labouring poor from starving; and the cost had been largely borne by the shopkeepers and small business men—a system, Scrope felt, to which he could 'hardly apply a less harsh term than *swindling*'. Owing to the retention of the Act of Settlement, only the most energetic and resourceful young labourers were in a position to escape, if they chose to take the risk, to look for work in or around the cities; for the rest, the agricultural labourer was to all intents a slave. His only birthright was pauperism, 'the condition from which he cannot, by any exertion of prudence, escape'.

'As mischievous as it is, I conceive, unfounded'

But it was the initial acceptance by the political economists of Malthus's law of population that was to have the most serious consequences for the poor; in spite of the fact that by the 1830s they had come to reject both the principle itself and the propositions derived from it.

Ironically, the final blow to its prestige was delivered in 1831 by Thomas Whately, who had been instrumental in dissuading Senior from open conflict with Malthus on the fundamental principle—whether there really was a 'tendency' for population to grow more rapidly than the means of subsistence. In the introductory lectures which he gave after he succeeded Senior in the Chair of Political Economy at Oxford, Whately politely refrained from referring to Malthus by name; but he took the opportunity to denounce the theory—'as mischievous as it is, I conceive, unfounded'. Everything hinged, Whately explained, on a foolish misconception. If there were a tendency for population to grow faster than the means of subsistence, he pointed out, the pressure of population could be expected to become greater in each successive generation, producing a progressive diminution of human welfare. How could such a doctrine be maintained in defiance of the fact that all civilised countries were proportionately wealthier than they had formerly been? Picking up where he had persuaded Senior to leave off, Whately attributed the error to an ambiguity in the term 'tendency':

By a 'tendency' towards a certain result, is sometimes meant 'the existence of a cause which, if *operating unimpeded,* would produce that result'. In this sense it may be said with truth that the earth, or any body moving round a centre, has a *tendency* to fly off at a tangent; i.e. the centrifugal force operates in that direction, though it is controlled by the centripetal; or again, that man has a greater *tendency* to fall prostrate than to stand erect; i.e. the attraction of gravitation and the position of the centre of gravity, are such that the least breath of air would overset him, but for the voluntary exertion of muscular force: and again, that population has a *tendency* to increase beyond subsistence; i.e. there are in man propensities which, if unrestrained, lead to that result.

But sometimes, again, 'a tendency towards a certain result' is understood to mean 'the existence of such a state of things that that result *may be expected to take place*'. Now it is in these two senses that the word is used, in the two premises of the argument in question. But in this latter sense, the earth has a greater tendency to remain in its orbit than to fly off from it; man has a greater tendency to stand erect than to fall prostrate; and (as may be proved by comparing a more barbarous with a more civilised period in the history of any country) in the progress of a society, subsistence has a tendency to increase at a greater rate than population. In this country, for instance, much as our population has increased within the last five centuries, it yet bears a far less ratio to subsistence (though still a much greater than could be wished) than it did five hundred years ago.

It was errors of this kind, Whately concluded, which had led to 'those discrepancies, and occasional absurdities, from which some persons infer that political economy is throughout a chimera'—in the same way that past errors and bitter contests between theologians led some people to decry and deride religion.

Even before Whately had finally repudiated Malthus, though, the changing attitude of the economists, particularly of McCulloch, had attracted attention, and some derision. 'We cannot quit this branch of our subject', Samuel Read remarked, after surveying the theory of population in his treatise,

without adverting to the late sudden and ample recantation from Mr Malthus' disciples on the subject of the poor laws; very coolly given by them, after having been engaged all the previous part of their lives in dogmatising on the contrary side. After having for years cried down this institution as a great sore in England's side, urging repeatedly on Parliament its entire abolition, as the only means of saving this country from over-pauperism; after treating with ineffable contempt the opinions of those who, from a practical knowledge of these laws, ventured to support them, these writers quietly turn round and, with equal effrontery, trumpet forth their tardily-acquired convictions of the blessings of the poor laws, as a novel and important discovery of their own.

—criticism which Scrope echoed. But what neither the economists nor their critics were prepared for was the reluctance of the public to discard the theory. By 1830, it suffused the thinking of the educated classes in England—and particularly of the clergy, who happened to be in a position to exercise some influence on lay attitudes, because they did much of the work in connection with the national censuses. In his preface to the report of the 1830 census, John Rickman remarked that comments by local clergymen, attributing the increase of the population to the poor laws, were too numerous to quote: 'they suppose persons to marry with a direct view of thereby obtaining a weekly allowance, or at least in reliance on that kind of recourse in time of need'. The 1834 poor law report, too—for all Senior's reservations about the theory of population—could only be read as a Malthusian document. 'Can we wonder', it said at one point about the agricultural labourer, 'if, to increase his income, and to revenge himself on the parish, he marries, and thus helps to increase the local over-population which is gradually eating away the fund out of which he and all the other labourers of the parish are to be maintained?' The *Essay on Population*, Bishop Otter could claim, and the new poor law, would 'stand or fall together. They have the same friends and the same enemies.' And for many years, that was to be the popular assumption.

Of all the influences exerted by political economy, this acceptance of Malthus was the most decisive. In the early part of the nineteenth century the population of England was increasing sufficiently rapidly to put pressure on the country's resources. But the increase in England was not too rapid to have been absorbed if the economic system had been geared to expansion; and in that case, paradoxically, the increase might have slowed down. Malthus's critics could not prove they were right in their belief that it was poverty which had been mainly responsible for the population rise, and that the way to slow it down was to improve the condition of the poor, to give them the kind of prospects which would encourage them to exercise self-restraint; but they happened to be much closer to the truth than Malthus. The fact that Malthus was listened to, and continued to be taken seriously by governments long after his main ideas had been rejected by those who had been responsible for popularising them, meant that social policy took a course which it would be difficult to alter.

3. EMIGRATION: EDUCATION: ECONOMY

Although these three supposedly basic principles of political economy operated on balance against State intervention on behalf of the poor, the economists could claim that it was unfair to say that theirs had been an entirely negative attitude. They were not in the same habit of defending themselves from outside criticism; but in their writings they quite often set up what clearly were defences, without reference, or with only an oblique reference, to their critics. And on some issues, they could point to a reasonably consistent advocacy of State intervention to help the poor; through assistance to emigrants; by the establishment of schools; and by the encouragement of savings schemes.

To Senior, State-aided emigration promised to be the simplest and cheapest way to make lives which had been useless and miserable, productive and happy. Not merely was it a remedy; it was 'a remedy preparatory to the adoption and safety of every other'. The project ought to have been embarked on long before: 'if it had been thought that the removal of a fellow creature from misery to happiness was worth twelve million pounds they might now have founded a flourishing settlement in British America' — and the total cost would have been no more than that of a three months war.

Against emigration, admittedly, there were Cobbett's arguments that exile was a hardship in itself; and that if the economic system was altered, there should be no need for it. On the assumption that the economic system was not going to be altered, though, the economists would have had a strong case — but for one unpalatable fact. State-aided emigration, on a scale large enough to make any impact, was never remotely likely to be accepted by Parliament. To propose it was to be as visionary as Robert Owen.

There were two reasons, both economic. One was provided in the report of the emigration committee of 1826/7: so long as there was freedom of movement of workers from Ireland, it explained, the population surplus there would simply move in to take the place of the emigrants leaving England for the colonies. The other, even more definitive, appeared in the report of a further committee of enquiry in 1832. The report actually turned a favourite argument of the economists against them: it would be impolitic, the committee suggested, for the State 'to undertake the entire charge of large bodies of people, and thus to destroy in them the habit of reliance upon their own personal exertions.' But in any case, it went on, the idea was too expensive to be contemplated. The cost of assisted emigration to the colonies — fourteen pounds a head was the lowest estimate — would be an effective bar to the removal of any considerable numbers; so both the colonies and the mother country 'must relinquish the hopes they have hitherto indulged, of great material benefits from increased emigration'. The Government might reasonably take it upon itself to ensure that emigrants were given appropriate warnings about the hardships which earlier voyagers had all too frequently suffered—but even then, it should restrict itself to advice; 'their comfort during the voyage must continue to depend chiefly on their own prudence.'

State-aided emigration, therefore, was wishful-thinking; and the same was true of the economists' advocacy of state-aided schools for the poor. At the time, England was one of the most backward, in terms of the provision of free education, of all civilised countries. Most of the economists favoured remedying this through the introduction of a national education scheme—'of all the means of providing for the permanent improvement of the poor', McCulloch thought, 'there does not seem to be any that promises to be so effectual'. But, again, there was not the least chance, in the period, of persuading Parliament to accept any such scheme. Apart from the expense, there were irreconcilable differences between the Established Church and the dissenters, as Brougham found whenever he brought the subject up.

The only hope of extending education to the children of the poor lay through the method which Owen had pioneered; factory schools. To these, the Government had no objection; in 1833 it actually offered a small grant in aid. But it was highly questionable whether these schools would benefit the children. Was it right that a child who had just finished a long working day be compelled to go on to school? Thackrah thought not: giving evidence before the Sadler Committee, he had expressed his uneasiness about the project of reducing hours of work to permit education: 'if the present term of labour were reduced I would, as a medical man, rather than the two or three hours a day taken from labour were devoted to sports and pastimes, which are necessary to the preservation of their health'.

Southey agreed—particularly about the proposal to extend Sunday schools. The manufacturers, he complained to Ashley, knew 'that a cry would be raised against them if their little white slaves received no instruction; and so they have converted Sunday into a school-day!' He did not object to Sunday school, but used in this way it was simply an additional cruelty: 'a compromise between covetousness and hypocrisy'.

Nor were the economists as disinterested in their advocacy of education as they liked to appear. When they came to discuss what children should be taught, they were hardly less narrow-minded than Hannah More. Children, McCulloch suggested, 'ought to be made acquainted with the duties enjoined by religion and morality, and with the circumstances which occasion that gradation of ranks and inequality of fortunes which usually exist'; and he quoted approvingly from an author who had urged that if their level of intelligence could be raised, the poor would become 'more likely to listen to any reasonable suggestion'. Whately, too, when he asserted that the remedy for destitution was to be found 'in judicious education, and habits of provident frugality', meant, as he went on to explain, *religious* education; and by religious education, he meant instructions in the precepts of the Church of England. The only concession to secular instruction which he was prepared to make lay in 'some very simple but important truths belonging to the science (political economy) we are now engaged in, which might with the utmost facility be brought down to the capacity of a child, and which, it is not too much to say, the lower orders cannot even safely be left ignorant of'—because in their ignorance, they might listen to demagogues preaching egalitarianism.

The economists, in fact, did not advocate education for its value to the child, but to fit the child to serve society. And much the same applied to their advocacy of savings as a preventive remedy for destitution—a recurring theme in political economy. 'No institution could be more beneficial to the morals of the lower orders' Senior observed in his *Introductory Lecture on Economics* '—that is, to at least nine-tenths of the whole body of any people—than one which should increase their power and their wish to accumulate; none more mischievous than one which should diminish the motives and the means to save'. For when does a labourer 'become sober and industrious, attentive to his health and character? As soon as he begins to save!'

The fatuity of calling on the poor to save, though, had excited the derision of Arthur Young; and it had also been effectively exposed by John Barton. For some years Barton had been a trustee of a savings bank; and he had never known of labourers saving, with a view to rendering themselves independent of parish relief. Why should they? 'After seven years of unremitting self-denial, a young peasant might say to himself, "I shall be able to marry without being beholden to anyone for the maintenance of my children—a great happiness, no doubt. But I shall not enjoy more of the ordinary comforts and gratifications of life than my next-door neighbour who married yesterday without a penny. As much as I derive

from my fund of savings, he will get from the parish . . . and after all, I
cannot be certain that seven years delay will secure me. An unlucky
accident, or a long course of illness, may exhaust my store, and I may die
in a workhouse at last." ' Who, Barton asked, was proof against such an
argument as that? In any case, the great majority of labourers who were
likely to become dependent on the rates were in no position to save, even if
they had wanted to. Labourers were asked 'make provision in the season of
health and vigour for the wants of sickness and old age'; how could they,
when 'their utmost industry and economy only just is sufficient to supply
them with the necessaries of life?'

In the last resort, then, all the economists had to offer the poor was
advice. They had offered it freely—but it had almost invariably been
based on the Malthusian assumption. 'It cannot be too often stated',
Ricardo had urged, 'that the most effectual remedy for the inadequacy of
their wages lies in their own hands'. They could not hope to add to the
nation's capital, McCulloch had told them, but they alone could diminish
the supply of labour. If they had the good sense to avail themselves of this
power, they might, by understocking the market 'render their wages high,
notwithstanding the demand for their services should happen to be
diminished; while if they do not avail themselves of this power, but allow
the principle of population to exert its natural tendency to overstock
the market with labour, wages will be low, to whatever extent the
demand for labour may be increased. It appears, therefore, that the
lower classes are in a very great degree the arbiters of their own
fortune.'

That Ricardo and McCulloch, with all their amused contempt for
visionary dreamers like Owen, should have been capable of such fantasies
themselves on the capacity of the poor to become the arbiters of their own
fortunes, was the measure of the inability of the political economists to
grasp the realities of their time. If they had been theologians, it would not
have mattered; future writers could have corrected their errors. But as
things were, they helped to convince their own generation—and many
generations to come—that the poor could rescue themselves from destitution; and consequently, if they failed to do so, it was their own
fault.

But how were the labourers to decide—assuming that the solemn
warnings had impressed them—at what point they might marry and begin
a family? Malthus told them that 'more children ought not to be born
than the country can support', but how were they to know what the state

of the economy was going to be when their children were born—let alone when those children were old enough to enter the labour market? And what hypocrisy it was—an M.P. told the Commons in 1833—to lecture a handloom weaver on the value of self-restraint as a way to secure a shortage of labour, and thereby put up wages; in view of the fact that the moment that there appeared likely to be a shortage of labour, the employers in the north hurriedly travelled south, and arranged to recruit all the able-bodied paupers they could find?

The political economists were not ogres. They all deplored a social system in which wages were at, or below, the subsistence level. 'I really cannot conceive anything much more detestable', Malthus asserted, 'than the idea of knowingly condemning the labourers of this country to the rags and wretched cabins of Ireland, for the sake of selling a few more broadcloths and calicoes'—a view which Ricardo would have echoed. They also all disliked the way in which child labour was being exploited. Except Ricardo, they were prepared to concede the case for State intervention to control hours and conditions of work for the young. But the Factory Act of 1833 had been their only significant contribution to improving the condition of the labouring poor. Otherwise, the logic of their principles, or what they conceived to be their principles, had prevented any effective intervention. By continuing to cling to the belief that the economy was self-regulating, they had in fact helped to push the standards of the English labourers down towards the Irish level—the opposite of their intentions.

But could they have recommended any different courses, without betraying their principles by encouraging State intervention? Scrope thought that they could. It was ridiculous, he pointed out, for governments to use political economy as an excuse for not interfering to protect the labouring poor from the impact of machinery, when in practice it was intervening to subsidise machinery, by taxing the labouring poor. There was no need, he argued, to interfere with wage bargaining: all that would be required was a shift in the incidence of taxation. Every manufacturer should contribute a small weekly sum, based on the number of workers he employed, into a fund providing for the workers in case of unemployment or redundancy. This device, with the minimum of State interference, would 'throw the expense of maintaining the aged, impotent and destitute poor precisely upon those persons who have profited by their labour'. The employer's contribution, he suggested, could be estimated on an actuarial basis, being enough to ensure that his workers would receive six shillings a week if sick, three shillings a week old age pension, and ten pounds on death. This would not only make provision for the labouring poor, it would also relieve them from the humiliation of having to ask for poor relief; the sums due to them would come to them as of right, not of charity, so 'they would feel that in applying, in sickness or old age, to the appropriate fund, they were only claiming a portion of their fair earnings which had been withheld from them for their own benefit—or rather that they were receiving, at the time they most needed it, *an addition* to the wages they formerly earned, reserved, with all the accumulated interest, for this special purpose, by the paternal foresight and benevolence of the State'.

Up to this time, when compulsory insurance had been put forward, the assumption had been that the premiums must be paid for by the wage-earner. The idea that the employer should have to pay, as Scrope realised, was revolutionary. But it was not, he insisted, impracticable. The sum involved would be very small—perhaps fourpence a week; and precedents for such State intervention existed. Certain producers had demanded, for example—and obtained—bounties on goods they exported. What was that but State intervention to help them, at the rest of the community's expense? Why should not others benefit in the same way? And, as a matter of fact, insurance of this nature was already in force, in one form of employment. The employers of merchant seamen had to pay sixpence a week for each of their workers. Admittedly, it was not, as it ought to be, put into a fund to assist the seamen in their old age: it was unjustly appropriated for the benefit of naval pensioners in the Greenwich hospital. Nevertheless the precedent was there.

The project aroused no interest. Scrope might feel that as against the 'narrow, disheartening and, as he is convinced, utterly false doctrine of a modern school of economists', he had vindicated his position that human happiness could be made continually to increase beyond the proportion of any possible increase of population. But to introduce his scheme would not only have enraged employers; it would have left the government open to the charge of interfering in, and thereby probably disrupting, the national economy.

4. ON THE RECORD

Examination of the record of the political economists in the early nineteenth century had brought three very different writers, in the early 1830s, to a virtually identical conclusion. To Scrope, they had a very indistinct notion of their limitations: their writings showed:

> . . . that they have habitually employed the same terms in contradictory senses, and so rendered their writings, in a great measure, unintelligible, not only to their readers, but to themselves; that there is scarcely one of the numerous topics handled by them, such as the laws regulating value, labour, wages, profits, rent and free trade, which they have not left in a worse condition than they found it; and, finally, that the whole science, as hitherto understood and carried on, has been founded on an entirely false assumption, which must infallibly vitiate the whole superstructure, or render it, in its present condition, anything but the trusty and unerring guide in legislation, for which it has ostentatiously been put forward by its cultivators.

This was an opinion Coleridge had held for years. 'What solemn humbug this political economy is,' he wrote in 1833.

> What they state, they do not truly understand, in its ultimate grounds and causes; hence they have sometimes done more mischief by their half-founded and half-sophisticated reasonings about, and deductions from, well-founded positions, than they could have done by the promulgation of positive error. This particularly applies to their famous ratios of increase between man and the means of his subsistence. Political economy at the highest can never be a pure science. You may demonstrate that certain properties inhere in the arch, which yet no bridge builder can ever reduce into brick and mortar; but an abstract conclusion in a matter of political economy, the premises of which neither exist now nor ever will exist within the range of the wildest imagination, is not a truth, but a chimera – a practical falsehood. For there are no theorems in political economy – but problems only. Certain things being actually so and so; the question is *how* to *do* so and so with them . . . you talk about making this article cheaper by reducing its price in the market from eightpence to sixpence. But suppose, in doing so, you have rendered your country weaker against a foreign foe; suppose you have demoralised thousands of your fellow countrymen, and have sown discontent between one class of society and another, your article is tolerably dear, I take it, after all. Is not its real price enhanced to every Christian and patriot a hundred-fold?

Peacock, too, derided the economists through the mouth of his Dr. Folliot, in *Crotchet Castle*, for conducting their education in public. 'You have given the name of a science to what is yet an imperfect inquiry,' he complained, 'and the upshot of your so-called science is this: that you increase the wealth of a nation by increasing in it the quantity of things which are produced by labour: no matter what they are, no matter how produced, no matter how distributed.' But this kind of wealth was not what a community should be aiming for; 'I say, the nation is best off, in relation to other nations, which has the greatest quantity of the common necessities of life distributed among the greatest number of persons; which has the greatest number of honest hearts and stout arms united in a common interest.' If this was accepted, though—if it were admitted that some things were better worth having than others *without* reference to their cost of production, and 'that a smaller commercial value, with one mode of distribution, is better than a great commercial value with another mode of distribution'—then, 'the whole of the curious fabric of postulates and dogmas, which you call the science of political economy, and which I call *politicae economiae inscientia*, tumbles to pieces'.

And it was clearly tumbling to pieces even so far as the political economists themselves were concerned. The closing of the ranks after the death of Ricardo had been short lived. By 1829, Samuel Read observed, 'the very men who had been chiefly instrumental in those dogmas which have produced all this mischief and misery, come forward and declare them to be wholly unsound'. Deeper fissures quickly began to appear, both among the living economists, and between them and the dead. In 1831 Torrens told the Political Economy Club that all the great principles of Ricardo's work had had to be successively abandoned; that his theories of value, rent and profit were generally acknowledged to have been erroneous. Although not all members went so far, Torrens' admission aroused none of the resentment that might have been expected. And soon, McCulloch and Senior were to be in open conflict over the new poor law. But these differences had no more effect on the informed public than the demolition of the Malthusian theory. From 1830 to 1845, Dicey was to recall, political economy was accepted by that public 'as a science containing very definite and certain principles, from which were logically deduced conclusions of indisputable and universal truth'.

'The taylors of Laputa'

Why? Dicey himself gave the clue in his words 'indisputable and universal truth'. The political economists and their followers had presented their theory as a revelation; and in their reverence for it, they tended to behave like members of a religious sect, with their creed, their theologians, and their lay brethren. Their writings showed little intellectual humility even about their own science; about the ideas of others, who did not accept it, they wrote with that withering contempt which was to be so characteristic of communist authors a century later—and is still not uncommon among scientists. They could not propound some doubtful hypothesis without lending it the sanction of 'no reasonable man would deny that', or some equivalent phrase; they were forever, as Scrope observed, writing *ex cathedra*.

The symptoms had become apparent early, in Burke's *Thoughts and Details on Scarcity*. Burke was an embarrassingly fervent disciple of Adam Smith; 'it is not by breaking the laws of commerce,' he maintained, 'which are the laws of nature, and consequently the laws of God, that we are to place our hope of softening the divine displeasure to remove any calamity under which we suffer'. Even Ricardo, though a rationalist in his attitude to religion, often wrote like a theologian on economics. He would refer, as Adam Smith had done, to his belief that there could not be a redundancy of capital and labour at the same time as 'the true faith'— though he self-consciously added, 'I mean only to express my strong conviction that I am right.' 'Ricardo', an acquaintance noted in his diary in 1820, 'meets you upon every subject that he has studied with *a mind made up*, and opinions in the nature of mathematical truths'—on political as well as economic questions; 'it is the very quality of the man's mind, his entire disregard of experience and practice, which makes me doubtful of his opinions on political economy'.

When, later, the correspondence between Ricardo, Malthus, Trower and others was published, it was to be suggested that the determination, and at times relish, with which they demolished each other's theories proved that they did not behave like a religious sect. But to Scrope, at the time, it was precisely their disputations which heightened the resemblance. Mill and McCulloch, he noted, had 'entangled themselves so completely' over Ricardo's doctrine that labour was the only source of wealth that they had been 'driven at length into a confusion of ideas only to be equalled by those of the Catholic arguments on the Invisible Presence'. As an example, Scrope cited the contortions which McCulloch had gone into to prove that the increase of value acquired by a cask of wine kept in a cellar was occasioned by the increased quantity of labour employed in it. For McCulloch to claim that he was not altering the ordinary meaning of the term 'labour', by applying it to the natural process of fermentation—Scrope felt —was comparable to the way that 'the doctors of the Catholic faith maintain the substance which to the senses appears as water, to be in reality flesh and blood'.

Where the early political economists differed from most religious sects was not in their disputation, but in the remarkably cordial manner in which they conducted it. They showed a most un-Christian tolerance of each other's opinions. But the consequences were unfortunate; their refusal to quarrel helped to preserve the illusion that they were in basic agreement, though in reality they were often hopelessly divided. This was not as difficult for them as it might sound, because of the form their faith took. They believed in the existence of scientific laws, originally revealed in the *Wealth of Nations* in much the same way as the laws of God had been revealed in the Bible; but this did not mean that Adam Smith was necessarily the last word on the subject any more than, say, St Luke had been; and it was their function to elucidate the remaining mysteries. They continued, however, to work from the premise that there were economic laws, just as a Catholic theologian worked from the premise that there were divine laws; and if their interpretation proved incorrect, well, that was simply due to human fallibility; they must try again.

The economists were ready to admit that serious errors had been made in the past—even by Adam Smith. As McCulloch explained, when he first expounded political economy in his *Discourse*, this was not surprising, as no science had ever been 'instantaneously carried to perfection'. This lesson of the past, though, had not then led him, as it was later to do, to caution about the present; 'the errors with which political economy was formerly infected', he continued, 'have now nearly disappeared, and a very few observations will suffice to show that it really admits of as much certainty as any science, founded on *fact and experiment*, can possibly do'— and he went on to lash out against the empirics 'whose vanity or interest prompts them to set up conclusions drawn from their own limited and imperfect range of observations, in opposition to those that are sanctioned by the general experience of mankind'—a phrase that with no alteration at all could have been heard from a pulpit, in a sermon denouncing un-believers.

Malthus was an exception. The principles to which he was devoted, though he would not have admitted it, were essentially mundane; a dislike of egalitarianism and a devotion to the class structure as it stood; but if his theoretical reasoning did not bring him up against one or other of those two preconceptions, he could be more clearsighted than his friends. Quite early on in their acquaintance, Ricardo taxed him with having always in mind 'the immediate and temporary effects of particular changes'; it was the permanent condition which resulted from them, Ricardo maintained, that was important. 'I certainly am disposed', Malthus agreed:

to refer frequently to things as they are, as the only way of making one's writing practically useful to society; and I think also, the only way of being secure from the errors of the taylors of Laputa, and by a slight mistake at the outset, arrive at conclusions the most distant from the truth. . . . A writer may, to be sure, make any hypothesis he pleases; but if he supposes what is not at all true practically, he precludes himself from drawing any practical inference from his hypothesis.

But as Malthus was not taken seriously by the others as a political economist, Ricardo, McCulloch, and Senior could continue to believe that there really was a science, whose principles could be applied in all circumstances. And because they believed this, and believed themselves to be its interpreters, they deluded themselves that their interpretation must also be—or at least, must soon become—scientific. 'I hope', Senior wrote in his *Introductory Lecture on Political Economy*, 'in the course of these lectures to prove the truth of my statement, that the theoretic branch of the science, that which treats of the nature, production and distribution of wealth, is capable of all the certainty that can belong to any science, not founded exclusively on definitions; and I hope also to show that many conclusions, and those of the highest importance, in the practical branch, rest so immediately on the conclusions of the theoretic branch, as to possess equal certainty and universality.'

'Such an essential lie . . .'
To ministers, this aura of sanctity emanating from political economy was just what was wanted. As Sismondi sadly admitted, 'writing makes little impression when it attacks a dominant system'; so long as Ricardian political economy retained dominance, there was no need to worry about its critics—no need even to attempt to refute them. Nor were ministers disturbed by doubts expressed at any given time in the Political Economy Club; what mattered was the residue of ideas which had shaken down into general acceptance. A century later Maynard Keynes was to observe that the ideas of economists and political philosophers,

both when they are right and when they are wrong, are more powerful than is commonly understood. Indeed the world is ruled by little else. Practical men, who believe themselves quite exempt from intellectual influences, are usually the slaves of some defunct economist. Madmen in authority, who hear voices in the air, are distilling their frenzy from some academic scribbler of a few years back. I am sure that the power of vested interest is vastly exaggerated compared with the gradual encroachment of ideas.

When vested interests are actually consolidated by ideas, the ideas become very powerful indeed; particularly when they are presented as ultimate truths. Such truths, admittedly, are not necessarily calculated to impress ministers—let alone individual Prime Ministers as sceptical, in their different ways, as Pitt, Liverpool, Canning, Melbourne and Peel. But the supreme value of political economy to them was that though, like Christianity, it could be cited as a universal truth, it was—also like Christianity—flexible. Had the economists been as united in the interpretation of their science as they were in their belief that it *was* a science, they might have proved an embarrassment. As things were, ministers could put it to whatever purpose they needed.

The sanctity of private property, for example, was not merely valuable as a precept in its own right, to use against Jacobinism; it could be invoked against the introduction of a property tax, to relieve the burden on the poor. This meant that the poor were condemned to pay excise duties; but excise, after all, was paid on goods purchased; and nobody was compelled to purchase the goods on which excise or customs duties were charged. If the corn laws made bread too expensive, the poor could switch to potatoes. In the same way, successive governments might insist on retaining the corn laws, which were certainly contrary to the principles of political economy; yet they used political economy to justify themselves for not interfering to raise wages, or to relieve unemployment. Ministers could take whatever suited them from political economy, and reject whatever did not.

What the economists and the utilitarians had done, unwittingly, was to cater for the owners of property. They had taken for granted, John Stuart Mill was later to recall, that the policies they were advocating were in the interest of the community as a whole. But they had really been in the interest of a class; not because they had intended it but because 'any set of persons who mix much together, and have a common interest, are apt to make that common interest their standard of virtue; and the social feelings of the members of the class are made to play into the hands of their selfish ones; whence the union so often exemplified in history between the most heroic personal disinterestedness, and the most odious class selfishness'.

For this reason, much as he detested the economists, Southey felt that they were not responsible for what had happened; the blame, 'Sir Thomas More' insisted in the *Colloquies*, should be put on the 'miserable politicians who mistake wealth for welfare.' And, when 'Montesinos' ventured to defend them—pointing out that industrialisation was the growth of circumstances, not a system deliberately chosen and planned—More rejected the excuse; 'the facts will not warrant you in saying that it has come upon this country, unsought and unseen. You have prided yourselves upon this system, and have used every means of extending it; you have made it the measure of your national prosperity.' Samuel Read preferred to indict the economists. They might not have been responsible for holding the pass—his argument in effect ran—but they had sold it. Had they shown more humility, they would have been entitled to some sympathy, even though they had been proved wrong. But they had preferred to be dogmatic; and in the circumstances, that was unforgivable:

> Their nostrums had well-nigh seared up the heart, and closed the hand of charity in these kingdoms, and had caused, perhaps, thousands of unfortunate people to perish, from want of that proper nourishment and maintenance which every civilised community is bound, in justice, to administer to all who may be in want within its well stored precincts. For it was nothing else but the prevalence of these nostrums which perverted men's minds, and steeled their hearts, and prevented timely and adequate public relief from being given to numerous bodies of men who were thrown out of employment on several occasions, and at different places, since the conclusion of the late war. And now the very men, who were chiefly instrumental in propagating those dogmas, which have produced all this mischief and misery, come forward and declare them to be wholly visionary and unsound. To acknowledge an error when a person discovers he has fallen into one, is to be but barely honest; but to take up opinions involving such inhuman consequences, and thus to set them down as portions of *eternal truth and science*, is to incur a responsibility which is but ill excused by an unceremonious and disingenuous recantation.

8

THE LEGACY

ISRAELI WAS SOON to describe the most striking consequence of the period in *Sybil*: the split into the Two Nations, rich and poor; haves, and have-nots. On the surface, admittedly, the 'haves' seemed disunited. The landowning aristocracy continued to look down on anybody who was 'in trade'; the industrialist continued to resent their snobbishness, and to feel that they were taking it out on him, for his presumptuousness, by deliberate wrecking tactics in Parliament. The humanitarianism of men like Sadler and Ashley, a *Westminster Review* writer alleged in 1833, was really designed to distract attention from the corn laws—a belief which Richard Cobden was soon to begin to exploit. But the jealousies which set the industrialist apart from the landowner were like those which divide the supporters of two local sports clubs, whenever members of both are playing together against a traditional rival; their common interests were far stronger than their rivalry, for all its asperities. And the concession by the landowners of a greater share of political power to the industrialists turned out to be a small price to pay for the relief of finding that in the reformed Parliament, governments—whether Whig or Tory—were hardly less aristocratic in composition and in temper than they had been before 1832.

The only institution which had the potential wealth and strength to have been a powerful ally of the poor—the Established Church—was siding against them; compelled to do so precisely because it was established. Individual clergy, like Bull, had campaigned actively on behalf of the factory workers; but the Church as an institution was deeply committed to the haves. Giving evidence to a committee set up in 1832 to promote the better observation of the Sabbath, Bishop Blomfield explained that the Ecclesiastical Commissioners were anxious to have churches which would attract the poor, as well as the rich: but it was proving difficult, 'on account of the objections which were made by the richer classes to too great an intermixture of the poor among them; objections which it was absolutely necessary to attend to because the whole income of the minister depends on the pew rent, accruing exclusively from the richer classes'. It was impossible to save the Church, Sadler remarked to Oastler, on seeing that the two bishops on the poor law commission had signed the report: 'she is her own executioner'; and Charles Kingsley was later to describe the despair that he and his contemporaries had felt about her at this time.

There was not even—as there was to be in Kingsley's time—a movement within the Church, trying to recall it to its traditional Christian duty to the poor. Admittedly the Evangelicals had believed that this was what they were doing; but their chief aim was to keep the poor content with their lot. The blessed effects of Christianity, Wilberforce wrote in his *Practical View*, published in 1798, gave the poor certain advantages:

> that if their superiors enjoy more abundant comforts, they are also exposed to many temptations from which the inferior classes are happily exempted; that 'having food and raiment, they should be therewith content', for that their situation in life, with all its evils, is better than they deserved at the hand of God; and finally, that all human distinctions will soon be done away, and the true followers of Christ will all, as children of the same Father, be alike admitted to the possession of the same heavenly inheritance.

It was only with the emergence of the Tory Evangelicalism of Sadler, Oastler and Ashley that a new kind of social conscience about the poor began to manifest itself within the Church; and even then, it was the way that the poor were treated, rather than poverty as such, that was their concern.

Although a few lawyers, too, had given their services to the poor, particularly in connection with trade union cases, the law, as an institution, was as biased as the Church in favour of the rich—and for the same reason; only from the rich could solicitors and barristers earn their living, and judges were drawn exclusively from the bar. One of the achievements of English society that foreign visitors were expected to admire was:

> How the same laws the same protection yield
> Who ploughs the furrow, and who owns the field.

But this, as Brougham showed the Commons in a long and devastating indictment of the English legal system in the spring of 1818, was a myth. Trial by jury had continued to afford some protection to the poor against the grosser forms of injustice: it saved Hardy and his colleagues in 1794; and it saved William Hone in 1817. But in ordinary circumstances, the law afforded little protection—in civil cases it could not ordinarily be invoked by the poor, as they lacked the means. And where laws were passed which were inconvenient to the employer, like the Factory Acts, he rarely had any difficulty in evading them. The reason why the 1833 factory commissioners recommended inspection, they explained, was that the law as it stood had been almost entirely inoperative, 'and has only had the semblance of efficiency under circumstances in which it conformed to the state of things already in existence, or in which that part of its provisions which are adopted in some places would equally have been adopted without legislative interference'. As a result, the workers involved had been 'familiarised with contempt of the law, and with the practice of fraud, evasion and perjury'.

'A stench in the nose of piety'

With the Government, the Church and the Law all ranged against them, discrimination against the poor became easy. It manifested itself in a great variety of ways, ranging from the use of indirect taxation, of a kind which the poor could not avoid paying, but the rich could, to the Sunday observance regulations. The rich could use their carriages and their servants —as Dickens noted on his first visit to the industrial north—to get out into the country, or visit friends, on Sunday; but all recreation grounds, parks and gardens were closed, and there was no public transport for the workers, even if they had been able to afford to use it, to take them out to the country to enjoy the fresh air that they were deprived of the other six days of the week. And of course, the shops were closed—except for the sale of gin. As Peacock put it:

> The poor man's sins are glaring
> In the face of ghostly warning
> He is caught in the fact
> Of an overt act –
> Buying greens on Sunday morning
>
> The rich man's sins are hidden
> In the pomp of wealth and station
> And escape the sight
> Of the children of light
> Who are wise in their generation
>
> . . . The rich man is invisible
> In the crowd of his gay society
> But the poor man's delight
> Is a sore in the sight
> And a stench in the nose of piety.

The economists could hardly be blamed for the activities of the Sunday Observance fanatics; but in other ways, they encouraged the development of the dual standard. One of the points Accum had stressed in his book was that the division of labour, which industrialisation was encouraging, militated against the preservation of quality. The publican who brewed his own beer, or the baker who made his own bread, was clearly responsible for what he sold; but where there were a number of manufacturers, an assembler, a distributor, and a retailer, the opportunity for adulteration increased. The rich were little troubled; they made their own bread and beer, and if they thought they had been cheated in some transaction they could go to law. The poor could not afford to take legal action, however strong their suspicion that their food had been adulterated. Yet to the last, Ricardo clung to *caveat emptor*; shortly before his death, he opposed a bill which would have made it an offence to pass weak beer off as strong.

The way in which the dual standard had begun to lodge itself was very clear in the report of the Poor Law Commission, which was redolent of a zealous, sometimes subservient, respect for wealth and standing, and a disposition wherever possible to disparage the poor. Senior was well aware of the circumstances in which the allowance system had been introduced, and of its disastrous consequences for farm workers. Yet anybody reading the report, knowing nothing of the background, could have formed the impression that the system existed for the labourer's benefit;

> The labourer feels that the existing system, though it generally gives him low wages, always gives him easy work. It gives him also, strange as it may appear, what he values more; a sort of independence. He need not bestir himself to seek work; he need not study to please his master; he need not put any restraint upon his temper; he need not ask relief as a favour. He has all a slave's security for subsistence, without his liability to punishment.

A very different tone was adopted in the report towards the magistrates. One of Senior's chief objectives was to strip them of their powers, blaming them as he did for the deficiencies in the administration of the old poor law. But again, the casual reader would not have been aware of this from the report. It praised the magistrates for their 'integrity and intelligence', and defended them against their critics; if mischief had been done, it was 'not the result of self-interest or partiality, but was, in part, the necessary consequence of their social position, and of the jurisdiction which was confided to them; and in part arose from the errors respecting the nature of pauperism and relief which prevailed among all classes'. There were a few protests against these attitudes in the poor law report, and the Act based on it; Wordsworth objected to the thesis that 'it is a labouring man's own fault if he be not, as the phrase is, beforehand with the world' because it implied that it was the labourer's own fault if from sickness or some other such cause, he could not work—'and who but has observed how distress creeps up upon multitudes without misconduct of their own?' But in general, its bias passed unnoticed, so well did the report's tone blend with popular preconceptions.

The development of the dual standard also provided the excuse for treating the poor as if they were a different species—or, rather, for continuing to treat them as such, without the earlier justification. So long as equality of income would merely have meant that everybody was poor, there had been a good excuse for perpetuating inequality, as the only way to obtain the benefits of civilisation; better that they should be enjoyed by the few, than by nobody. But this did not necessarily carry the implication that the rich were innately superior. Many members of the aristocracy, admittedly, considered that they *were* superior, through breeding as well as training; but this was not the Christian view. Even when it was widely believed that the poor were often responsible for their poverty, as in the seventeenth century, it had always been recognised that there were deserving cases, who were not to blame. There were vagabonds and tramps, who were regarded more as criminals than as paupers—there were the ne'er-do-wells and spongers, who ought to be given the same treatment as vagabonds. But there were also able-bodied men and women who could not find work, as well as the sick, the maimed, the old, and the infirm. All of them should be relieved. But with Ricardo insisting that it was futile to provide work for the able-bodied poor, because it would simply do some other worker out of a job; and with Malthus insisting that the provision of relief would simply encourage the poor to breed, the case gained ground that the destitute were expendable, whether or not they were to blame for their condition. Had there been any way simply to get rid of them, without risk to society, Ricardo and Malthus would certainly have recommended it, and governments would equally certainly have given it their favourable attention, provided that it did not entail any increase in taxation. No such simple solution had presented itself. The next best thing, therefore, had been to find a way to make the distinction Colquhoun had recommended between poverty and destitution—and when that was found, in 'less eligibility', to apply it. The destitute could not be starved, for fear of revolution; nor could they be exiled, because it cost too much. But they could be swept into the workhouse; under the carpet.

So it was that the poor came to be regarded, by the 1830s, almost as the natives were later to be regarded in South Africa; as a labour force, to be regulated in size according to their employers' needs. One of the few serious criticisms which the *Edinburgh* reviewer of Harriet Martineau's *Illustrations* permitted himself was that she concerned herself too much with the condition of the poor; that, the reviewer implied, was really an irrelevance. And Harriet Martineau might have accepted the criticism as just—at the time; though not after her visit to America. What she saw there made her consider the possibility there might be further social changes, 'which will probably work out in time a totally new social state'. And if they did, due credit, she had come to believe, should be given to the man who had unsuccessfully striven for them: Robert Owen.

'For a glittering fiction'

There was one further serious consequence from the period; the development of a new morality, based on what Thomas Carlyle was shortly to term the cash nexus. This, too, was derived from the proposition that private property was sacred; what a man did with that property was, therefore, his own affair, so long as he kept within the law. But what had previously been an excuse for anti-social actions, now became their standard justification. By equating wealth with welfare, the political economists elevated the pursuit of material gain into a philosophy of life, with ethical sanction.

So far as the community was concerned, the most unfortunate results arose out of the abandonment, as a consequence, of an old social precept—enshrined for later generations in many a boarding-house bathroom, 'please leave this room as you find it'.

One of the justifications which had been put forward for the institution of private ownership of land, when it had been questioned, was that an owner, and only an owner, would have an interest in keeping it in good heart. If allowed to, a tenant might be tempted to crop the heart out of it, for short term gain; an owner would see that he was not allowed to. To Southey, as to Sir Walter Scott, the ownership of land was a trust based on this assumption. But industrialists were put under no corresponding obligation. It was not merely that they were allowed to extract coal and iron ore for profit; this, it could reasonably be claimed, was the price that had to be paid for making use of natural resources which, unlike the soil, could not be replaced when dug up. But their claim was also allowed that such damage as they did to the environment was part of the price. They could scar the countryside, fill the air with smoke, encrust buildings with grime, and pollute rivers with industrial waste, or even poisons. Except where influential landowners demanded compensation for salmon killed on their way to the sea, or from the sea, hardly a thought was given to the proposition that the industrialists were making their profits at the community's expense; and that on economic and social as well as aesthetic grounds, there was a case for compelling them either to restore the environment to the condition in which they found it, where that was possible; or to pay compensation sufficient, say, to provide for the cleaning of public buildings and the provision of compensatory amenities.

Also serious was the failure to insist that the workers should be left no worse off, other things being equal, than they had been before industrialisation. The industrialist, Sir Walter Scott complained, had no sense of responsibility; 'a man may assemble five hundred workmen one week, and dismiss them the next, without having any further solicitude about their future fate than if they were so many old shuttles'. But the employers' disregard extended even to the men who were actually working for them—as the report of the factory commission showed. One of the accusations made to the Sadler committee had been that many employers made no effort to protect their workers from dangerous machinery, because, the implication was, safety devices were expensive, and replacement labour cheap; and the factory commission's investigators found that this allegation was justified. A few manufacturers were punctilious about safety; but there were other factories 'by no means few in number, not confined to the smaller mills, in which serious accidents are continually occurring and in which, notwithstanding, dangerous parts of the machinery are allowed to remain unfenced'. The greater the carelessness of owners in this respect, too—the commission noted—'the less their sympathy with the sufferers'. The report accordingly recommended that employers should be compelled to provide protection for their workers from dangerous machinery. Yet the proposal enraged Hume; it was in the interests of masters to protect their workers, he insisted, and it was 'a libel upon human nature to suppose they will allow persons in their employment to be injured for the want of due caution'. Besides, he was perfectly satisfied that 'all legislation of this kind is pernicious, and injurious to those it is intended to protect'—his attitude showing just how far it was possible for a radical to travel in the direction of *laissez nous faire*.

Laissez nous faire did not concern itself with human happiness; and it was *laissez nous faire* which had installed itself. The consequences went far beyond the hardship involved for men, women and children, through their being compelled to work such long hours for such meagre wages, and being compelled to live in such wretched conditions. The life they led left them degraded, and unhealthy; Gaskell felt it actually left its mark on their features. He had often watched them streaming out for their brief dinner break; and 'any man who has stood at twelve o'clock in the single narrow doorway which serves as a place of exit for the hands employed in the great cotton mills must acknowledge that an uglier set of men and women, of boys and girls, it would be impossible to congregate, in a small compass'. How absurd it was, in the circumstances, for McCulloch to claim that because statistics showed that people were living longer, they must be benefiting from industrialisation! And how ironical, Gaskell added, that in the past, the test of a civilisation was the extent to which it helped to elevate men; yet here, the boasted civilisation was degrading him into a species of savage.

The apologists for industrialisation sometimes argued that this did not represent any decline of standards; it was rather that the industrial revolution came upon the English unprepared—still conditioned by the old attitude that life for the masses was nasty, brutish and short, and that nothing could be done about it. But this version was not supported by the evidence; for example, by the history of the attempts to rescue the climbing boys from exploitation.

When the climbing boys were first investigated in the 1780s, the horrified reaction had led promptly to an Act of Parliament, which, if it had proved to be enforceable, would have made it impossible for sweeps to use young children at all; and there was no evidence that the Lords, when they extracted the clause which would have made it enforceable, by providing that sweeps must be licensed, intended to emasculate the bill—they were simply anxious not to give more power to the State. When the subject came up again thirty years later, the general feeling in the Commons was still that protection ought to be given; but the opposition was already powerful, based mainly on two principles sanctioned by the political economists: the sacred right of the property owner to do what he liked with his own, and the right of the employer and the worker to bargain without State interference. As a result, in spite of the fact that the new machines for sweeping chimneys, at trivial expense, could have done away with the need for climbing boys, Parliament had allowed the rejection of the bill to protect them—and by so doing, had also allowed builders to continue to insert ever more tortuous and dangerous flues, like the one in the drying-room of Buckingham Palace. In 1834, a social conscience about the exploitation of children had again been aroused, sufficient to induce Parliament to pass a bill designed to provide the protection promised half a century earlier; but by this time the sanctity of private property and of wage-bargaining was so firmly established that the measure could not be made any less ineffective than its pre-decessor. Where machinery could be exploited for private gain, in other words, it was welcomed. Where it was designed for the public benefit, at some private sacrifice, it was resisted—as Jonas Hanway had warned, in his *Sentimental History*: 'as an opulent *commercial* nation, eager in the pursuit of gain, and the gratifications which attend it, we are more subject to fall into inhuman and impolitic practices than one less affluent, depending more upon strict order and discipline'.

Political economy had been designed by Adam Smith as a way of securing the maximum benefit to the community from whatever material wealth could be provided. It had gradually been perverted, Sismondi argued in his essay on the factory workers, into an instrument for the exploitation by the rich of the labour of the poor. He was no egalitarian: the gifts of a just and beneficent community, he felt, could be unequal; but a community became iniquitous and oppressive 'if it demands from the poorest, labour which the savage is not acquainted with, and does not secure him in return that comfort, content and security as to the future, which he could not find in the woods'. The poor man, in exchange for the labour with which he produced wealth for society, ought to be assured of a reasonable share of it.

> On whatever side we look, the same lesson meets us everywhere, *protect the poor*; and it ought to be the most important study of the legislator and of the government. Protect the poor, for, in consequence of their precarious condition, they cannot contend with the rich without losing every day some of their advantages; protect the poor, that they may keep by law, by custom, by a per-petual contract, rather than by competition – the source of rivalry and hatred – that share of the income of the community which their labour ought to secure to them; protect the poor, for they want support, that they may have some leisure, some intellectual development, in order to advance in virtue; protect the poor, for the greatest danger to law, public peace and stability is the belief of the poor that they are oppressed, and their hatred of government; protect the poor, if you wish industry to flourish, for the poor are the most important con-sumers; protect the poor, if your revenue requires to be increased, for after you

have carefully guarded the enjoyment of the poor, you will find them the most important of contributors.

By the 1830s, the utilitarians were just beginning to realise the force of Sismondi's arguments; to see that they had been deflected from their original purpose, by the worship of false gods. 'Private rights', Kay wrote in the *Westminster* in 1833,

> ought not to be exercised so as to produce a public injury. The law, which describes and punishes offences against the person and property of the subject, should extend its authority by establishing a social code, in which the rights of communities should be protected from the assaults of partial interests. By exercising its function in the former case, it does not wantonly interfere with the liberty of the subject, nor in the latter, would it violate the reverence due to the sacred security of property.

His words could be taken as the utilitarians' new manifesto. But they had left it late. Instead of helping to create a society dedicated to the aim of the greatest good of the greatest number, they had been seduced into helping to create one designed to operate for the greatest good of the property-owning minority. And they were going to have to face a protracted, bitter struggle, for the rest of the century, to try to remedy that mistake.

POSTSCRIPT

Most of the works from which *Poverty and the Industrial Revolution* is derived are to be found in that friendliest of institutions, the London Library, from whose staff I have had every possible assistance. I have had much help, too, from the staff of the British Museum, in pursuit of some of the more obscure writers from the period.

Having some years ago had the good fortune to find that Bernard Levin enjoys that rare endowment, proof-reader's eye, I was lucky enough to be able to waylay him for that purpose. He made some shrewd, not to say caustic, suggestions for improvement of the text, too, of which I was glad to avail myself. Professor Donald Winch, Dean of the School of Social Studies at the University of Sussex, also read the proofs, and made some valuable criticisms; as did Professor Mark Blaug, of London University. But my chief debt has been to Ann Froshaug. Her knowledge of the history of the poor law during the period, and her uncanny talent not merely for exposing the flaws in a chain of argument, but also for warning where others are likely to find them, compelled me to rethink, as well as largely to rewrite, the book. Miss Froshaug also found the illustrations.

Bibliography

As *Poverty and the Industrial Revolution* is based on printed material, much of it available in libraries and virtually all of it in the British Museum, I have not hung it about with source reference footnotes. Instead, I have ordinarily named the author of any quotation in the text, and where relevant, the book or article from which it is taken.

I have been less rigorous than is currently fashionable, academically, in the exact reproduction of quotations. Spelling and punctuation have been modernised, and familiar rather than archaic terminology adopted – for example, 'the poor rate' instead of the then common 'the poor's rate'. For clarity I have occasionally slightly altered the construction of sentences, or silently put in the appropriate proper name, instead of 'he'. And I have kept the original italics only when they were clearly used, as today, for emphasis and not for convention (when they appear, they are the author's, not mine). In statistics, where precision is not required, I have used round numbers.

A catalogue of all the works on and around the subject would fill several volumes (in a recent biography of Robert Owen, the bibliography filled a third of the book). I have included only those contemporary books, articles and reports which are referred to in the text, either by name or, in a few cases, by implication. I have not included biographies and memoirs, or newspapers and magazines; and I have omitted some of the works of the more prolific writers on the subject, from Hanway to the present day.

If, in the text, I quote only from contemporary sources, it is because my intention has been to show the development of attitudes and policies at the time, without the intrusion of hindsight. During the past half-century a controversy has been continuing between the Pessimists, as they have come to be known, who share the view propounded by the Webbs and the Hammonds that the poor in the 1830s were actually worse off than they had been fifty years earlier; and the Optimists, who dispute this contention with the help of what they describe as methodological studies. Although the dispute has led to some distinctly unhistorical wrangling, it has greatly increased our knowledge of the period; and Part II of the bibliography, though far from comprehensive, reflects my indebtedness to writers in both camps – as well as to some who are uncommitted.

I (a)

Acland, John, *A plan for rendering the poor independent*, Exeter, 1786

Accum, Frederick, *A treatise on the adulteration of food*, London, 1820

Aikin, J., *A description of the country around Manchester*, London, 1795

'Alfred' (Samuel Kydd), *The history of the factory movement*, London, 1857

Anon., 'Condition of the working classes', *Westminster Review*, April, 1833

Babbage, Charles, *On the economy of machinery*, London, 1832

Bacon, Richard M., *A letter to Lord Suffield upon the distress of the labourers*, London, 1831

—— *A memoir of Lord Suffield*, Norwich, 1838

Bailey, Samuel, *Dissertation on Value*, London, 1825

Baines, Edward (Sr.), *History of Lancashire*, Manchester, 1836

Baines, Edward (Jr.), *An address to the unemployed*, London, 1826

—— *History of the cotton manufacture in Great Britain*, London, 1835

Barton, John, *Observations on the circumstances which influence the condition of the labouring classes of society*, London, 1817

—— *An inquiry into the causes of the progressive depreciation of agricultural labour in modern times*, London, 1820

Bentham, Jeremy, *Pauper management improved*, London, 1812

—— *Economic Writings*. Edited by W. Stark (three volumes), London, 1952–9

Bernard, Sir Thomas (and others), *Reports of the Society for Bettering the Condition of the Poor*, London, 1801 ff.

Brougham, Henry, 'Lord Lauderdale on public wealth', *Edinburgh Review*, July, 1804

—— 'Inquiry into the state of the poor', *Edinburgh Review*, Oct., 1807

—— 'On Cobbett's *Cottage Economy*', *Edinburgh Review*, Feb., 1823

Brown, John, *A memoir of Robert Blincoe*, Manchester, 1832

Burke, Edmund, *Thoughts on Scarcity*, London, 1795

Burn, Richard, *History of the poor laws*, London, 1764

Chalmers, Thomas, *Tracts on Pauperism*, Glasgow, 1833

—— *The sufficiency of a parochial system without a poor rate for the right management of the poor*, Glasgow, 1841

Cobbett, William, *Rural Rides*, London, 1820 ff.

—— *Cottage Economy*, London, 1823

—— *Poor Man's Friend*, London, 1826

—— *Legacy to Labourers*, London, 1834

Coleridge, Samuel Taylor, *Two addresses on Sir Robert Peel's Bill*, London, 1818

—— *Church and State*, London, 1830

—— *Table Talk*, London, 1835

Colquhoun, Patrick, *An account of a meat and soup charity*, London, 1797

—— *Treatise on Indigence*, London, 1806

[Croker, J. W. and Lockhart, J. G.], 'On Harriet Martineau's *Illustrations of Political Economy*', *Quarterly Review*, April, 1833

Crumpe, Samuel, *Essay on Unemployment*, Dublin, 1793

Davies, David, *The case of labourers in husbandry*, London, 1795

Dawson, E., *Pauperism and Distress*, London, 1831

Defoe, Daniel, *Giving alms no charity*, London, 1704

Demainbray, S., *The poor man's best friend*, London, 1831

De Quincey, Thomas, *Works*. Edited by D. Masson, Edinburgh, 1890

Eden, Sir Frederick Morton, *The State of the Poor* (three volumes), London, 1797

Empson, William, 'Life, writings and character of Mr Malthus', *Blackwood's Edinburgh Magazine*, Jan., 1937

Engels, Friedrich, *The condition of the working class in England in 1844*, London, 1892

Fielding, Henry, *A proposal for making an effectual provision for the poor*, London, 1753

Gaskell, Mrs., *Letters*. Edited by J. A. Chapple, London, 1966

Gaskell, Peter, *The manufacturing population of England*, London, 1833

Gilbert, Thomas, *Observations . . . with respect to the Poor*, London, 1875.

Godwin, William, *Political Justice*, London, 1793

—— *Caleb Williams*, London, 1794

—— *Of Population*, London, 1820

Gray, John, *A lecture on human happiness*, London, 1825

—— *The Social System*, Edinburgh, 1831

[Greg, W. R.], *An inquiry into the state of the manufacturing population*, London, 1831

Hall, Charles, *The effect of civilisation on the people*, London, 1805

Hanway, Jonas, *An earnest appeal for mercy to the children of the poor*, London, 1766

—— *A sentimental history of chimney sweepers*, London, 1785

Hazlitt, William, *A reply to the Essay on Population*, London, 1807

—— *Collected works*. Edited by A. R. Waller and Arnold Glover, London, 1902

Hodgskin, Thomas, *Labour defended against the claims of capital*, London, 1825

—— *Popular Political Economy*, London, 1827

Hone, William, *The three trials of William Hone*, London, 1818

Hopkins, Thomas, *Great Britain for the last forty years*, London, 1834

Howlett, J., *An examination of Dr Price's essay*, Maidstone, 1781

—— *An inquiry into the influence of enclosures*, London, 1786

—— *Examination of Mr Pitt's speech relative to the condition of the poor*, London, 1796

Jarrold, Thomas, *Dissertations on Man*, London, 1806

—— *A letter to Samuel Whitbread*, London, 1807

Kay, James, *The moral and physical condition of the working classes employed in the cotton manufacture in Manchester*, Manchester, 1832

Labourers' Friend, The, London, 1834 ff.

o

Lamb, Charles, *Essays of Elia*, London, 1859

Lauderdale, Earl of, *An inquiry into the nature and origin of public wealth*, Edinburgh, 1804

Lloyd, W. F., *Four lectures on the poor laws*, London, 1835

Lockhart, J. G., *Memoirs of Sir Walter Scott*, Edinburgh, 1837

Macaulay, Thomas Babington, *Essays*, London, 1843

McCulloch, J. R., *A discourse on the rise of political economy*, Edinburgh, 1824

—— *The principles of political economy*, London, 1825

—— 'On the poor laws', *Edinburgh Review*, May, 1828

—— 'On the state of manufactures', *Edinburgh Review*, Oct. 1833

—— *The literature of political economy*, London, 1845

Mallalieu, Alfred, 'The whigs – the radicals – the middle classes – and the people', *Blackwood's Edinburgh Magazine*, April, 1937

Malthus, Thomas, *An Essay on the principle of population*, London, 1798 (and later editions)

—— *A letter to Samuel Whitbread, Esq., on his proposed bill for the amendment of the poor laws*, London, 1807

—— *Principles of political economy*, London, 1820

Mandeville, Bernard, *Fable of the bees*, London, 1714

Marcet, Mrs. Jane, *Conversations of Political Economy*, London, 1816

Martineau, Harriet, *Poor laws and paupers*, London, 1833–4

—— *Illustrations of Political Economy*, London, 1834

—— *Autobiography* (2 volumes), London, 1877

Maxwell, J., *Manual labour versus machinery*, London, 1834

Mill, James, *Elements of political economy*, London, 1821

—— *Selected writings*. Edited by D. Winch, Edinburgh, 1966

Mill, John Stuart, *Autobiography*, London, 1873

Nicholls, Sir George, *History of the English Poor Law* (two volumes), London, 1854

Owen, Robert, *A new view of society*, London, 1814–16

—— *Observations on the effect of the manufacturing system*, London, 1818

—— *Autobiography*, London, 1857

Paine, Thomas, *The Rights of Man*, London, 1792

Paley, W., *The principles of moral and political philosophy*, London, 1785

Peacock, T. L., *Crotchet Castle*, London, 1831

Place, Francis, *Illustrations and proofs of the principle of population*, London, 1821

—— *Essay on the state of the country*, London, 1831

Political Economy Club, *Minutes and questions discussed*, London, 1921

Porter, G. R., *The Progress of the Nation* (three volumes), London, 1836–8

Preston, R., *The poor rates gradually reduced, and pauperism converted into profitable industry*, London, 1818

Proceedings of the Society for superseding the necessity of climbing boys, London, 1916

Radcliffe, William, *Origins of the new system of manufacturing commonly called 'power loom weaving'*, London, 1828

Ravenstone, Piercy, *A few doubts . . . on the subjects of population and political economy*, London, 1821

Read, Samuel, *Political Economy*, London, 1817

Ricardo, David, *Works and Correspondence*. Edited by P. Sraffa and M. H. Dobb (ten volumes), Cambridge, 1951–5

Robinson, David, 'On Political Economy', *Blackwood's Edinburgh Magazine*, 1829–30.

Rose, George, *Observations on the Poor Laws*, London, 1805

Sadler, Michael, *The law of population*, London, 1830

Scrope, George Poulett, *Plea for the abolition of slavery in England, as produced by an illegal absue of the poor law*, London, 1829

—— 'Causes and remedies of pauperism', *Quarterly Review*, May, 1830*

—— 'On the political economists', *Quarterly Review*, Jan., 1831

—— *Principles of political economy*, London, 1833

Senior, Nassau, *Introductory Lecture on Political Economy*, London, 1826

—— *Two lectures on population*, London, 1829

—— *Three lectures on wages*, London, 1830

—— *A letter to Lord Howick*, London, 1831

Shelley, Percy Bysshe, *Essays, Letters from abroad*. Edited by Mrs. Shelley (2 volumes), London, 1840

de Sismondi, J. L., *Political Economy and the Philosophy of government*. Edited by M. Mignot, London, 1847

Smith, Adam, *The Wealth of Nations*, London, 1776

Smith, Southwood, 'Contagion and the sanitary laws'. In January, April issues of the *Westminster Review*, 1825

Smith, Sydney, 'On climbing boys', *Edinburgh Review*, Oct., 1819

—— 'On the poor laws', *Edinburgh Review*, Jan., 1820

Southey, Robert, *Letters from England*, London, 1807

—— *Colloquies*, London, 1829

Spence, Thomas, *The constitution of a perfect Commonwealth*, London, 1798

Thackrah, C. Turner, *The effects of the principal arts, trades and professions . . . on health*, London, 1831

Thompson, Ben (Count Rumford), *Essays*, London, 1796 ff.

Thompson, William, *The distribution of wealth*, London, 1824

Torrens, Robert, 'On Mr Owen's plans for relieving the national distress', *Edinburgh Review*, Oct., 1819

—— *An essay on the production of wealth*, London, 1821

—— *On the wages of labour and on the means of improving the condition of the labouring classes*, London, 1832

* This article has been attributed to Southey, but both style and content suggest that Scrope was the writer.

[Townsend, Joseph], *Dissertation on the poor laws*, London, 1786
Ure, Andrew, *The Philosophy of Manufactures*, London, 1835
Voght, Baron von, *Account of the management of the poor in Hamburg*, London, 1796
Wade, John, *The black book; or corruption unmasked*, London, 1820
Whately, Richard, *Introductory Lectures on Political Economy*, London, 1831
Wilson, John, 'The factory system'. In *Blackwood's Edinburgh Magazine*, April, 1833
Wing, Charles, *Evils of the factory system*, London, 1837
Young, Arthur, *Tours of England and Wales*, London, 1785 ff.
—— *The question of Scarcity plainly stated*, London, 1800
—— *An inquiry into the propriety of applying wastes to the maintenance and support of the poor*, Bury, 1801
—— *Autobiography*, 1816

I (b)

Parliamentary Reports and Minutes of Evidence

On the state of the parish poor infants 1766
On the laws which concern the relief and settlement of the poor 1775
On cotton manufacture 1804, 1808, 1810, 1812
On woollen manufacture 1803, 1804, 1806
On parish apprentices 1815
On the poor laws 1816–19
On the employment of children in factories 1816, 1818, 1819
On the employment of boys in sweeping chimneys 1817, 1818
On labourers' wages 1824
On combinations 1824
On emigration 1826–7
On the poor laws 1828
On the state of the poor in Ireland 1830
On the poor laws 1830–1
On emigration 1832
On the employment of children in factories 1832
On manufacturers, commerce and shipping 1833
On the employment of children in factories (Royal Commission) 1833
On handloom weavers 1834, 1835
On the poor laws (Royal Commission) 1834
On chimney sweepers and their apprentices 1834

II

Ashton, T. S., *The Industrial Revolution, 1760–1830*, Oxford, 1948
—— 'The standard of life of the workers in England, 1790–1830', *Jnl. Econ. Hist.*, 1949 (supp. IX)
—— *An Economic History of England: the Eighteenth Century*, Oxford, 1955
Bagley, J. J., and Bagley, A. J., *The English Poor Law*, London, 1966
Beer, Max, *A History of British Socialism*, London, 1919
Blaug, Mark, 'The myth of the old Poor Law and the making of the new', *Jnl. Econ. Hist.*, June, 1963
—— 'The Poor Law Report re-examined', *Jnl. Econ. Hist.*, June, 1964
—— 'The Classical Economists and the Factory Acts', *Q. J. Econ.*, May, 1958
Bowden, W., *Industrial Society in England towards the end of the 18th Century*, New York, 1925
Bowley, A. L., *Wages in the U.K. in the 19th Century*, Cambridge, 1900
Briggs, Asa, *The age of improvement*, London, 1959
Brinton, Crane, *The political ideas of the English romanticists*, Oxford, 1926
Bruce, Maurice, *The coming of the Welfare State*, London, 1961
Burnett, John, *Plenty and Want*, London, 1966
—— *A history of the cost of living*, London, 1969
Bythell, Duncan, *The handloom weavers*, Cambridge, 1969
Carnall, Geoffrey, *Robert Southey and his age*, Oxford, 1960
Chadwick, W. Edward, *The Church, the State, and the Poor*, London, 1914
Chambers, J. D., 'Enclosure and the small landowners', *Econ. H. R.* Nov., 1940
—— 'Enclosure and labour supply in the Industrial Revolution', *Econ. H. R.* Dec., 1952
Checkland, S. G., *The Rise of Industrial Society in England 1815–85*, London, 1964
Clapham, J. H., *An Economical History of Modern Britain*, Cambridge, 1926
—— 'The Spitalfields Acts 1773–1824', *Econ. J.* Dec., 1916
Clifford, James, *Aspects of Economic Development 1760–1960*, London, 1967
—— *Man versus Society in Eighteenth Century Britain*, Cambridge, 1968
Clokie, H. and Robinson, J. W., *Royal Commissions of Inquiry*, Stanford, Cal., 1937
Coats, A. W., 'Economic thought and poor law policy in the eighteenth century', *Econ. H. R.* 1960
Cole, G. D. H., *Socialist Thought: the forerunners*, London, 1953
Cole, G. D. H., and Postgate, Raymond, *The Common People, 1746–1946*, London, 1938
Derry, John W., *The Radical Tradition*, London, 1967
Dicey, A. V., *Law and Opinion in England*, London, 1905
Eversley, D. E. C., *Social theories of fertility and the Malthusian debate*, Oxford, 1959
Fay, C. R., *Life and Labour in the 19th Century*, London, 1920

Flinn, Michael, *The Origins of the Industrial Revolution*, London, 1966

Galbraith, J. K., *The Affluent Society*, London, 1965

George, M. D., *London Life in the Eighteenth Century*, London, 1925

Glass, D. V., *Introduction to Malthus*, London, 1953

Graupp, William, 'On the politics of the Political Economists', *Q. J. Econ.* Nov., 1948

Gray, B. Kirkman, *Philanthropy and the State*, London, 1908

Griffith, G. T., *Population Problems in the Age of Malthus*, Cambridge, 1926

Gross, John, *The Rise and Fall of the Man of Letters*, London, 1969

Halévy, Élie, *The Growth of Philosophic Radicalism*, London, 1928

Hammond, J. L. and Hammond, Barbara, *The Town Labourer 1760–1832*, London, 1912

—— *The Village Labourer, 1760–1832*, London, 1920

—— *The Bleak Age*, London, 1934

Hammond, J. L., 'The Industrial Revolution and Discontent', *Econ. H. R.* 1936

Hartwell, R. M., 'Interpretation of the Industrial Revolution in England: a methodological inquiry', *Jnl. Econ. Hist.* June, 1959

—— 'The rising standard of living in England 1800–50', *Econ. H. R.* 1961

—— 'The causes of the Industrial Revolution', *Econ. H. R.* Aug., 1965

Hayek, F. A. (editor), *Capitalism and the Historians*, London, 1954

Hilton, G. H., 'The Truck Act of 1831', *Econ. H. R.* April, 1957

Hobsbawm, E. J., 'The British standard of living, 1790–1850', *Econ. H. R.* Aug., 1957

—— *Labouring Men*, London, 1964

—— *Industry and Empire*, London, 1968

Hobsbawm, E. J. and Hartwell, R. M., 'The British standard of living, 1790–1850', *Econ. H. R.* Aug., 1963

Hobsbawm, E. J. and Rudé, George, *Captain Swing*, London, 1969

Hobson, J. A., *Work and Wealth*, London, 1914

Holyoake, G. J., *Self-help 100 years ago*, London, 1888

Hutchins, B. L. and Harrison, A., *A History of Factory Legislation*, London, 1903

Hutt, W. H., 'The Factory System of the Early 19th Century', *Economica*, 1926

Huzell, James P., 'Malthus, the Poor Law, and population in early 19th century England', *Econ. H. R.* Dec., 1969

Jackson, John Archer, *The Irish in Britain*, London, 1963

Jones, E. L. and Mungay, G. E. (editors), *Land, Labour and Population in the Industrial Revolution*, London, 1967

Kent, Graeme, *Poverty*, London, 1968

Krause, J. T., 'Changes in English fertility and mortality, 1781–1851', *Econ. H. R.* Aug., 1958

McCleary, G. F., *The Malthusian Population Theory*, London, 1953

Mantoux, Paul, *The Industrial Revolution in the 18th Century*, London, 1928
Marshall, Dorothy, *The English Poor in the Eighteenth Century*, London, 1926
—— 'The Old Poor Law', *Econ. H. R.* Nov., 1937
Martin, E. W., *The Secret People*, London, 1954
Neale, R. S., 'The standard of living 1780–1844', *Econ. H. R.* Dec., 1966
Opie, Redvers, 'A neglected English economist: George Poulett Scrope', *Q. J. Econ.* Nov., 1929
Perkin, Harold, *The Origins of Modern English Society*, London, 1969
Pinchbeck, I., *Women workers in the Industrial Revolution*, London, 1930
Polanyi, Karl, *Origins of our time*, London, 1945
Pollard, Sidney, 'Factory discipline in the Industrial Revolution', *Econ. H. R.* Dec., 1963
Poynter, J. R., *Society and Pauperism*, London, 1969
Robbins, Lionel, *The theory of Economic Policy in English Classical Economy*, London, 1953
Rodgers, Brian, *The Battle Against Poverty*, London, 1968
Roll, Eric, *A History of Economic Thought*, London, 1938
Salter, F. R., *Some early tracts on Poor Relief*, London, 1926
Seligman, E. R. A., 'Some neglected English economists', *Econ. J.*, 1903
Schumpeter, J. A., *History of Economic Analysis*, London, 1954
Silberling, N. J., 'British Prices and Business Cycles, 1779–1850', *Review of Economic Studies*, 1923
Smelser, Neil J., *Social Change in the Industrial Revolution*, London, 1959
Smith, Kenneth, *The Malthusian Controversy*, London, 1951
Sorensen, R., 'Some classical economists, *laissez faire*, and the Factory Acts', *Jnl. Econ. Hist.* summer, 1952
Sotiroff, O., 'John Barton', *Econ. J.*, March, 1952
Stark, W., 'Bentham as an Economist', *Econ. J.*, Dec., 1946
Stephen, Leslie, *The English Utilitarians*, London, 1900
Tawney, R. H., *Religion and the rise of capitalism*, London, 1926
Taylor, A. J., 'Progress and Poverty in Britain, 1780–1850', *History*, February, 1960
Taylor, Philip (editor), *The Industrial Revolution in Britain: triumph or disaster?*, Boston, 1958
Thompson, E. P., *The making of the English working class*, London, 1963
Tierney, Brian, *Medieval Poor Law*, Los Angeles, 1959
Times, The, History of, London, 1935
Trevelyan, G. M., *English Social History*, London, 1944
Turner, E. S., *Roads to Ruin*, London, 1950
Viner, Jacob, *The long view and the short*, Illinois, 1958
Ward, J. P., *The Factory Movement*, London, 1962
Webb, Sidney and Webb, Beatrice, *English Poor Law Policy*, London, 1910

Webb, Sidney and Webb, Beatrice, *English Poor Law History; the Old Poor Law*, London, 1927

—— *English Local Government*, London, 1927

—— *English Poor Law History: the last 100 years*, London, 1929

White, R. J., *Political Tracts of Wordsworth, Coleridge and Shelley*, Cambridge, 1953

—— *Life in Regency England*, London, 1963

Williams, J. E., 'The British Standard of Living 1750–1850', *Econ. H. R.* Dec., 1966

Williams, Raymond, *Culture and Society*, London, 1958

Woodruff, W., 'Capitalism and the Historians; a contribution to the discussion of the Industrial Revolution in England', *Jnl. Econ. Hist.* 1956

Index